Python for Marketing Research and Analytics

Jason S. Schwarz • Chris Chapman • Elea McDonnell Feit

Python for Marketing Research and Analytics

 Springer

Jason S. Schwarz
Google
Nashville, TN, USA

Chris Chapman
Google
Seattle, WA, USA

Elea McDonnell Feit
Drexel University
Philadelphia, PA, USA

ISBN 978-3-030-49722-4   ISBN 978-3-030-49720-0   (eBook)
https://doi.org/10.1007/978-3-030-49720-0

This Springer imprint is published by the registered company Springer Nature Switzerland AG
The registered company address is: Gewerbestrasse 11, 6330 Cham, Switzerland

Preface

We are here to help you learn Python for marketing research and analytics.

Python is a great choice for marketing analysts. It offers advanced capabilities for fitting statistical models. It is extensible and is able to process data from many different systems, in a variety of forms, for both small and large datasets. The Python ecosystem includes a vast range of established and emerging statistical methods as well as visualization techniques. Yet its use in marketing lags other fields such as econometrics, bioinformatics, and computer science. With your help, we hope to change that!

This book is designed for two audiences: practicing marketing researchers and analysts who want to learn Python and students or researchers from other fields who want to review selected marketing topics in a Python context.

What are the prerequisites? Simply that you are interested in Python for marketing, are conceptually familiar with basic statistical models such as linear regression, and are willing to engage in hands-on learning. This book will be particularly helpful to analysts who have some degree of programming experience and wish to learn Python. In Chap. 1, we describe additional reasons to use Python (and a few reasons perhaps *not* to use Python).

The *hands-on* part is important. We teach concepts gradually in a sequence across the first seven chapters and ask you to *type* our examples as you work; this book is *not* a cookbook style reference. We spend some time (as little as possible) in Part I on the basics of the Python language and then turn in Part II to applied, real-world marketing analytics problems. Part III presents a few advanced marketing topics. Every chapter shows off the power of Python, and we hope each one will teach you something new and interesting.

Specific features of this book are:

- It is organized around marketing research tasks. Instead of generic examples, we put methods into the context of marketing questions.
- We presume only basic statistics knowledge and use a minimum of mathematics. This book is designed to be approachable for practitioners and does not dwell on equations or mathematical details of statistical models (although we give references to those texts).
- This is a didactic book that explains statistical concepts and the Python code. We want you to understand what we are doing and learn how to avoid common problems in both statistics and Python. We intend the book to be *readable* and to fulfill a different need than references and cookbooks available elsewhere.
- The applied chapters demonstrate progressive model building. We do not present "the answer" but instead show how an analyst might realistically conduct analyses in successive steps where multiple models are compared for statistical strength and practical utility.
- The chapters include visualization as a part of core analyses. We do not regard visualization as a standalone topic; rather, we believe it is an integral part of data exploration and model building.
- Most of the analyses use simulated data, which provides practice in the Python language along with additional insight into the structure of marketing data. If you are inclined, you can change the data simulation and see how the statistical models are affected.
- Where appropriate, we call out more advanced material on programming or models so that you may either skip it or read it, as you find appropriate. These sections are indicated by * in their titles (such as *This is an advanced section**).

What do we *not* cover? For one, this book teaches *Python* for marketing and does not teach marketing research in itself. We discuss many marketing topics but omit others that would simply repeat the analytic methods in Python. As noted above, we approach statistical models from a conceptual point of view and skip the mathematics. A few specialized topics have been omitted due to complexity and space; these include customer lifetime value models and econometric time series models.

Overall, we believe the analyses here represent a great sample of marketing research and analytics practice. If you learn to perform these, you will be well equipped to apply Python in many areas of marketing.

For another, this book teaches Python for *marketing* and not all of the complexity or subtlety of the Python programming language or of programming generally. We present the basics of Python programming that are needed to successfully analyze marketing data, but there is much more to Python than we present here.

Companion Book: *R for Marketing Research and Analytics*

This book is closely related to *R for Marketing Research and Analytics* (Chapman and Feit 2019) and shares many datasets and sections of didactic explanation of methods with that R text. In some ways, this Python book and the R text are mutual "translations" of one another from R and Python, respectively.

This was a deliberate choice that we hope will make it easy for readers to move between Python and R. If you understand a method in one language, the companion book will demonstrate how to perform a similar or identical analysis in the other language. For example, if you learned to program R from that text, you will be able to learn Python rapidly using this book. And if you master analyses in Python here, you will be able easily to perform most of the same analyses in R using that text. You will already be familiar with most of the theoretical sections and datasets and can focus on the language.

At the same time, each book has a few topics that are unique to its language and not covered in the other. This Python text has somewhat more emphasis on programming and writing custom functions. The R text includes methods for choice-based conjoint analysis (discrete choice models), market basket analysis with association rules, and methods to model behavior sequences such as weblogs. Those differences reflect the general situation in Python to have somewhat fewer yet often more stable and higher performance tools, contrasting an emphasis in R on a vast ecosystem of tools. In short, there are great reasons to learn both Python and R! The paired texts have been designed to make that easier.

Acknowledgements

We want to give special thanks here to people who made this book possible. First are all the students from our tutorials and classes over the years. They provided valuable feedback, and we hope their experiences will benefit you.

Jason's and Chris's colleagues in the research community at Google provided extensive feedback on portions of the book. We thank the following Googlers: Javier Bargas, Mario Callegaro, Xu Gao, Rohan Gifford, Michael Gilbert, Xiaoyu He, Tim Hesterberg, Shankar Kumar, Kishan Panchal, Katrina Panovich, Michael Quinn, David Remus, Marta Rey-Babarro, Dan Russell, Rory Sayres, Angela Schörgendorfer, Micha Segeritz, Bob Silverstein, Matt Small, Gill Ward, John Webb, Rui Zhong, and Yori Zwols. Their encouragement and reviews have greatly improved the book.

In the broader community, we had valuable feedback from Lynd Bacon, Marianna Dizik, Dennis Fok, Norman Lemke, Paul Litvak, Kerry Rodden, Steven Scott, and Randy Zwitch.

The staff and editors at Springer helped us smooth the process, especially Senior Editor Lorraine Klimowich.

Much of this book was written in public and university libraries, and we thank them for their hospitality alongside their unsurpassed literary resources. Portions of the book were written during pleasant days at the New Orleans Public Library, New York Public Library, Christoph Keller, Jr. Library at the General Theological Seminary in New York, University of California San Diego Giesel Library, University of Washington Suzzallo and Allen Libraries, Sunnyvale Public Library, and the Tokyo Metropolitan Central Library.

Most importantly, we thank *you*, the reader. We are glad you have decided to investigate Python, and we hope to repay your effort. Let us start!

Nashville, TN, USA   Jason S. Schwarz
Seattle, WA, USA   Chris Chapman
Philadelphia, PA, USA   Elea McDonnell Feit
August 2020

Contents

Part I
Basics of Python

Chapter 1
Welcome to Python

1.1 What is Python?

Python is a general-purpose programming language. It has increasingly become the language of choice not only for teaching programming, given its simple syntax and great readability, but for programming applications of all kinds, ranging from data analysis and data science to full stack web development.

If you are a marketing analyst, you have no doubt heard of Python. You may have tried Python or another language like R and become frustrated and confused, after which you returned to other tools that are "good enough." You may know that Python uses a command line and dislike that. Or you may be convinced of Python's advantages for experts but worry that you don't have time to learn or use it.

Or if you come from a programming rather than market analyst background and have little experience with formal analysis, you might have tried to explore complex datasets but gotten frustrated by data transformations, statistics, or visualization.

We are here to help! Our goal is to present *just the essentials*, in the *minimal necessary time*, with *hands-on learning* so you will come up to speed as quickly as possible to be productive analyzing data in Python. In addition, we'll cover a few advanced topics that demonstrate the power of Python and might teach advanced users some new skills.

A key thing to realize is that *Python is a programming language*. It is *not* a "statistics program" like SPSS, SAS, JMP, or Minitab, and doesn't wish to be one. It is extremely flexible; in Python you can write code to fill nearly any requirement, from data ingestions and transformation to statistical analysis and visualization. Python enjoys a thriving open source community. Scientists and statisticians have added a huge amount of statistical and scientific computing functionality to Python through new libraries. These libraries add functionality seen in specialized languages like R or Matlab, turning Python into a powerful tool for data science.

1.2 Why Python?

Python was designed with a priority of *code readability*. Readability is about the ease of quickly understanding what code is doing when reading it. In Python, the functionality of code should be obvious. Why is that important? It's important because code can easily get complicated. Approaching coding with a goal of simplicity and straightforwardness makes for better, less buggy, and more shareable code.

This is the reason why Python is often the first language taught in schools. Programmers sometimes joke that Python is "just pseudocode," meaning that it looks almost exactly like what you would write while you were *designing* your code, not actually implementing it. There is no complicated syntax, no memory management, and it is not strictly typed (See Sect. 2.4.1). And systematic whitespace requirements ensure that code is formatted consistently.

Python balances this simplicity with flexibility, power, and speed. There's a reason that Python recently has been the fastest growing programming language in absolute terms (Robinson 2017). Python is useful not only for scripting and web frameworks, but also for data pipelines, machine learning, and data analysis.

A great thing about Python is that it integrates well into production environments. So if you want to automate a process, such as generating a report, scoring a data stream based on a model, or sending an email based on events, those tasks can

© Springer Nature Switzerland AG 2020

J. S. Schwarz et al., *Python for Marketing Research and Analytics*, https://doi.org/10.1007/978-3-030-49720-0_1

usually be prototyped in Python and then put directly into production in Python, streamlining the development process. (Although, this depends somewhat on the tech stack you use in production).

For analysts, Python offers a large and diverse set of analytic tools and statistical methods. It allows you to write analyses that can be reused and that extend the Python functionality itself. It runs on most operating systems and interfaces well with data systems such as online data and SQL databases. Python offers beautiful and powerful plotting functions that are able to produce graphics vastly more tailored and informative than typical spreadsheet charts. Putting all of those together, Python can vastly improve an analyst's overall productivity.

Then there is the community. Many Python users are enthusiasts who love to help others and are rewarded in turn by the simple joy of solving problems and the fact that they often learn something new. Python is a dynamic system created by its users, and there is always something new to learn. Knowledge of Python is a valuable skill in demand for analytics jobs at a growing number of top companies.

The code for functions you use in Python is also inspectable; you may choose to trust it, yet you are also free to verify. All of its core code and most packages that people contribute are open source. You can examine the code to see exactly how analyses work and what is happening under the hood.

Finally, Python is free. It is a labor of love and professional pride for the Python Core Developers. As with all masterpieces, the quality of their devotion is evident in the final work.

1.2.1   Python vs. R, Julia, and Others

If you are new to programming, you might wonder whether to learn Python or R . . . or Julia, Matlab, Ruby, Go, Java, C++, Fortran, or others. Each of those languages is a great choice, depending on a few differentiating factors.

If your work involves large data transformation, exploration, visualization, and statistical analysis, then Python is a great choice. If machine learning is relevant for you, several of the most powerful machine learning libraries are Python-native, such as Theano, Keras, PyTorch, and Tensorflow. If you want your analytic work to go into production and integrate with a larger system (such as a product or a web site), then, again, Python is a great choice.

Another factor is whether you wish to program more generally beyond analytics, such as writing apps. Python is an excellent general purpose language. It is more approachable than C++, while it also has broader support for statistics and analytics than Go, Java, or Ruby.

If you want to leverage advanced statistics, such as Bayesian analyses or structural equation modeling, then R is unmatched (Chapman and Feit 2019). If high performance is essential to you, such as working with massive datasets or models with high mathematical complexity, then Julia is an excellent choice (Lauwens and Downey 2019). Go is also designed for massive scalability.

If you often do a lot of directly mathematical work, such as writing equations for models, then Python is a fine choice, although Julia, R, Matlab, Mathematica, or even Fortran might be more comfortable for you.

Finally, there is the question of your environment. If you work with others who program, it will be advantageous to use a language they prefer, so you can get expert help. At the same time, most languages interact well with others. For example, it is quite easy to write analytic code in R and to access it from Python (and vice versa). C++ code can be embedded in Python, and in many other languages, when needed (Foundation 2020). In other words, if you learn Python, it will be usable elsewhere. Many programmers end up using several languages and find that transitioning among them is not difficult.

In short, for analyses with high flexibility and a straightforward programming environment, Python is a great choice.

1.3   Why Not Python?

It's hard for us to imagine NOT using Python for analysis, but of course many people don't, so what are the reasons not to use it?

One reason not to use Python is this: until you've mastered the basics of the language, many simple analyses are cumbersome to do in Python. If you're new to Python and want a table of means, cross-tabs, or a t-test, it may be frustrating to figure out how to get them. Python is about power, flexibility, control, iterative analyses, and cutting-edge methods, not point-and-click deliverables.

Another reason is if you do not like programming. If you're new to programming, Python is a great place to start. But if you've tried programming before and didn't enjoy it, Python may be a challenge as well. Our job is to help you as much as we can, and we will try hard to teach basic Python to you. However, not everyone enjoys programming. On the other hand, if you're an experienced coder Python will seem simple (perhaps deceptively so), and we will help you avoid a few pitfalls.

One other concern about Python is the unpredictability of its ecosystem. With packages contributed by thousands of developers, there are priceless contributions along with others that are mediocre or flawed, although that is rare with the major packages (e.g. NumPy, pandas, scikit-learn, statsmodels, etc.). One thing that does happen is occasional version incompatibility between the various packages, which can be frustrating. If you trust your judgment, this situation is no different than with any software. *Caveat emptor.*

We hope to convince you that for many purposes, the benefits of Python greatly outweigh the difficulties.

1.4   When to Use Python?

There are a few common use cases for Python:

- You want access to methods that are newer or more powerful than available elsewhere. Many Python users start for exactly that reason; they see a method in a journal article, conference paper, or presentation, and discover that the method is available in Python.
- You need to run an analysis many, many times. This is how one author (Chris) started his statistical programming journey; for his dissertation, he needed to bootstrap existing methods in order to compare their typical results to those of a new machine learning model.
- You need to apply an analysis to multiple datasets. Because everything is scripted, Python is great for analyses that are repeated across datasets. It even has tools available for automated reporting.
- You need to develop a new analytic technique or wish to have perfect control and insight into an existing method. For many statistical procedures, Python is easier to code than other programming languages.
- Your manager, professor, or coworker is encouraging you to use Python. We've influenced students and colleagues in this way and are happy to report that a large number of them are enthusiastic Python users today.

By showing you the power of Python, we hope to convince you that your current tools are *not* perfectly satisfactory. Even more deviously, we hope to rewrite your expectations about what *is* satisfactory.

1.5   Using This Book

This book is intended to be *didactic* and *hands-on*, meaning that we want to teach you about Python and the models we use in plain English, and we expect you to engage with the code interactively in Python. It is designed for you to type the commands as you read. (We also provide code files for download from the book's web site; see Sect. 1.5.3 below.)

1.5.1   About the Text

Python commands for you to run are presented in code blocks representing samples, like this:

```
In [1]: print('Hello World')

Hello World
```

The code is formatted as found in `Notebooks`, which we introduce in Chap. 2. Briefly, notebooks are interactive coding environments that are commonly used by Python programmers, particularly for data analysis, but for many other applications as well. Notebooks are our recommended interface for learning data analysis in Python (See Sect. 2.1 for more info).

We describe these code blocks and interacting with Python in Chap. 2. The code generally follows the PEP 8 Style Guide for Python (available at https://www.python.org/dev/peps/pep-0008/) except when we thought a deviation might make the code or text clearer. (As you learn Python, you will wish to make your code readable; the guide is very useful for code formatting.)

When we refer to Python commands or data in the text outside of code blocks, we set the names in monospace type like this: `print()`. We include parentheses on function names to indicate that they are functions (i.e. commands that reference a set of code), such as the `open()` function (Sect. 2.4.8), as opposed to a variable such as the `store_df` dataset (Sect. 2.4).

When we introduce or define significant new concepts, we set them in italic, such as *vectors*. Italic is also used simply for *emphasis*.

We teach the Python language progressively throughout the book, and much of our coverage of the language is blended into chapters that cover marketing topics and statistical models. In those cases, we present crucial language topics in *Language Brief* sections (such as Sect. 3.2.1). To learn as much Python as possible, you'll need to read the Language Brief sections even if you only skim the surrounding material on statistical models.

Some sections cover deeper details or more advanced topics, and may be skipped. We note those with an asterisk in the section title, such as *Learning More**.

1.5.2   About the Data

Most of the datasets that we analyze in this book are *simulated* datasets. They are created with Python code to have a specific structure. This has several advantages:

- It allows us to illustrate analyses where there is no publicly available marketing data. This is valuable because few firms share their proprietary data for analyses such as segmentation.
- It allows the book to be more self-contained and less dependent on data downloads.
- It makes it possible to alter the data and rerun analyses to see how the results change.
- It lets us teach important Python skills for handling data, generating random numbers, and looping in code.
- It demonstrates how one can write analysis code while waiting for real data. When the final data arrive, you can run your code on the new data.

We recommend working through the data simulation sections where they appear; they are designed to teach Python and to illustrate points that are typical of marketing data. However, when you need data quickly to continue with a chapter, it is available for download as noted in the next section and again in each chapter.

Whenever possible you should also try to perform the analyses here with your own datasets. We work with data in every chapter, but the best way to learn is to adapt the analyses to other data and work through the issues that arise. Because this is an educational text, not a cookbook, and because Python can be slow going at first, we recommend to conduct such parallel analyses on tasks where you are not facing urgent deadlines.

At the beginning, it may seem overly simple to repeat analyses with your own data, but when you try to apply an advanced model to another dataset, you'll be much better prepared if you've practiced with multiple datasets all along. The sooner you apply Python to your own data, the sooner you will be productive in Python.

1.5.3   Online Material

This book has an online component. In fact, we recommend using Colab (see Sect. 2.1.1) for its ease of setup, in which case your code will live and run online.

There are three main online resources:

- An information website: https://python-marketing-research.github.io
- A Github repository: https://github.com/python-marketing-research/python-marketing-research-1ed
- The Colab Github browser: https://colab.sandbox.google.com/github/python-marketing-research/python-marketing-research-1ed

The website includes links to those other sources, as well as any updates or news.

The Github repository contains all the data files, notebooks, and function code.

The data files can be downloaded directly into Python using the `pandas.read_csv()` command (you'll see that command in Sect. 2.6.2, and will find code for an example download in Sect. 3.1). Links to online data are provided in the form of shortened `bit.ly` links to save typing. The data files can be downloaded individually or as a zip file from the repository (https://bit.ly/PMR-all-data).

The notebooks can be downloaded to be run locally using Jupyter (see Sect. 2.1.3). The notebooks can be browsed directly from Colab and easily run using the Colab Github browser (https://colab.sandbox.google.com/github/python-marketing-research). See Chap. 2 for more information.

Note that while we make the notebooks available, we recommend that you use them sparingly; you will learn more if you type the code and create the datasets by simulation as we describe.

In many chapters we create functions that we will then use in later chapters. Those code files are in the Github repository, in the python_marketing_research_ functions directory, and can be download from there to run. However, a far simpler way to access that code is to install the code using pip. See Sect. 2.4.9 for details.

1.5.4   When Things Go Wrong

When you learn something as complex as Python or new statistical models, you will encounter many large and small warnings and errors. Also, the Python ecosystem is dynamic and things will change after this book is published. We don't wish to scare you with a list of concerns, but we do want you to feel reassured about small discrepancies and to know what to do when larger bugs arise. Here are a few things to know and to try if one of your results doesn't match this book:

- **With Python**. The basic error correction process when working with Python is to check everything very carefully, especially parentheses, brackets, and upper- or lowercase letters. If a command is lengthy, deconstruct it into pieces and build it up again (we show examples of this along the way).
- **With packages** (add-on libraries). Packages are regularly updated. Sometimes they change how they work, or may not work at all for a while. Some are very stable while others change often. If you have trouble installing one, do a web search for the error message. If output or details are slightly different than we show, don't worry about it. The error `"ImportError: No module named ..."` indicates that you need to install the package (Sect. 2.4.9). For other problems, see the remaining items here or check the package's help file (Sect. 2.4.11).
- **With Python warnings and errors**. A Python "warning" is often informational and does not necessarily require correction. We call these out as they occur with our code, although sometimes they come and go as packages are updated. If Python gives you an "error," that means something went wrong and needs to be corrected. In that case, try the code again, or search online for the error message. Another very useful tool is adding `print()` statements to print the values of variables referenced in the error or warning; oftentimes a variable having an unexpected value offers a clue to the source of the problem.
- **With data**. Our datasets are simulated and are affected by random number sequences. If you generate data and it is slightly different, try it again from the beginning; or load the data from the book's website (Sect. 1.5.3).
- **With models**. There are three things that might cause statistical estimates to vary: slight differences in the data (see the preceding item), changes in a package that lead to slightly different estimates, and statistical models that employ random sampling. If you run a model and the results are very similar but slightly different, you can assume that one of these situations occurred. Just proceed.
- **With output**. Packages sometimes change the information they report. The output in this book was current at the time of writing, but you can expect some packages will report things slightly differently over time.
- **With names that can't be located**. Sometimes packages change the function names they use or the structure of results. If you get a code error when trying to extract something from a statistical model, check the model's help file (Sect. 2.4.11); it may be that something has changed names.

Our overall recommendation is this. If the difference is small—such as the difference between a mean of 2.08 and 2.076, or a p-value of 0.726 vs. 0.758—don't worry too much about it; you can usually safely ignore these. If you find a large difference—such as a statistical estimate of 0.56 instead of 31.92—try the code block again in the book's code file (Sect. 1.5.3).

1.6   Key Points

At the end of each chapter we summarize crucial lessons. For this chapter, there is only one key point: if you're ready to learn Python, let's get started with Chap. 2!

Chapter 2
An Overview of Python

2.1 Getting Started

In this chapter, we cover just enough of Python to get you going. If you're new to programming, this chapter will get you started well enough to be productive and we'll call out ways to learn more at the end. Python is a great place to learn to program because its syntax is simpler and it has less overhead (e.g. memory management) than traditional programming languages such as Java or C++. If you're an experienced programmer in another language, you should skim this chapter to learn the essentials.

We recommend you work through this chapter *hands-on* and be patient; it will prepare you for marketing analytics applications in later chapters.

There are a few options for how to interact with and run Python, which we introduce in the next few sections.

2.1.1 Notebooks

Notebooks are the standard interface used by data scientists in Python. The notebook itself is a document that contains a mix of code, descriptions, and code output. The document is created and managed using a Notebook app, which is an application that includes a browser app that renders notebook documents, along with a "computational engine" which is a server that inspects and runs code (also called a "kernel"). You use a browser to connect to that server and run Python code in *cells* of the notebook, with output, when present, being printed from each cell. These notebooks allow figures to be embedded, enabling interleaved code, tables, and figures in a single document.

A common workflow is to use a notebook to explore a new dataset and prototype an analysis pipeline. A clean, streamlined version of that pipeline can then be put in another notebook and shared or into a script to be run regularly, or even moved into production code.

Google Colaboratory

The easiest way to get started in Python, and the way that we used in writing the book, is to use Google Colaboratory ("Colab") notebooks. These are free hosted Python notebooks. The notebooks themselves are saved by default in a Google Drive (a cloud storage drive), but can also be saved to Github or downloaded as .ipynb files.

The Python installation running in Colab includes most of the scientific Python libraries that we will use throughout the book. Additional libraries can be installed using the *pip* or *apt* package management systems (see Sect. 2.4.9).

To get started using Colab, go to https://colab.research.google.com/. The initial landing page will be a "Getting started" notebook. To create a new notebook, if you are already viewing an existing notebook, go to the menu bar, open the *File* menu and select *New Notebook*. On subsequent visits, a "Recent notebooks" panel will be displayed when the site is visited, and clicking "New Notebook" will allow you to do so.

If you prefer to run Colab locally, it can also run locally using Jupyter (see Sect. 2.1.3). Visit https://research.google.com/colaboratory/local-runtimes.html for more information.

© Springer Nature Switzerland AG 2020

J. S. Schwarz et al., *Python for Marketing Research and Analytics*, https://doi.org/10.1007/978-3-030-49720-0_2

2.1.2   Installing Python Locally

If you would rather not use a cloud-based system, you can install Python locally.

If you use Linux or Mac OS X, it is likely that Python is already installed. You can check this using the Terminal application to access the command line. Terminal can found in the Applications folder on Mac OS X. On graphical Linux, it is usually prevalent in the Applications explorer, but will sometimes be under "Administration" or "Utilities." Open a Terminal window and type `which python` to check. The command `python --version` will return the version.

All of the code in this book was written and tested using Python version 3.6.7. We recommend using Python 3 rather than Python 2. For the purposes of this book the differences are minor, but there is code that will not run properly in Python 2. Python 2 lost official support on January 1, 2020 (Peterson 2008–2019) and many important libraries dropped Python 2 support long ago (e.g. the `pandas` package stopped support Python 2 on December 31, 2018).

If you don't already have Python 3 installed, the most straightforward way to install Python and all the necessary libraries is using (Anaconda, Inc. 2019) https://www.anaconda.com/. The benefit of using Anaconda rather than a manual install is that it includes all of the libraries that are commonly used in data science applications of Python (see Sect. 2.4.9). Anaconda has a straightforward installation process for Windows, Mac, and Linux.

If you already have Python 3 installed, you can use that, but unless you already have all of the scientific Python libraries, we still recommend installing Anaconda since it includes all of the necessary libraries and tools. Alternatively, you could manually install those libraries (see Sect. 2.4.9).

2.1.3   Running Python Locally

Command Line

If you open a Terminal (Linux/Mac) or Command window (Windows) and type `python`, you will start running Python on the command line in interactive mode. From there, you can run any Python commands that you like. You could perform analyses directly in the command line. However, such a process would be frustrating and not reusable (the command history may not persist across sessions). Better is to save your work so it can be easily modified and repeated.

Scripts

Python code can be written to a file, which is customarily given a `.py` file extension. That file can be run from the command line with the syntax `python <path/to/file>`. For example, we might write code that analyzes monthly sales numbers and call it `monthly_sales.py`, we could run it with the command `python monthly_sales.py`. This file is generally referred to as a *script*.

Scripts are often used when you want to repeatedly run an analysis and generate the same output each time, such as running a monthly or daily analysis. However, they are not necessarily the best development environment for data science applications, as they do not enable interactive exploration. Additionally, any data will need to be loaded into memory each time the script is run, which can slow down development especially if the dataset is large and takes time to load into memory.

Local Notebooks

We have already introduced Google Colaboratory notebooks, which can be run on a free cloud virtual machine instance. But notebooks can also be run locally using Jupyter (Kluyver et al. 2016). Jupyter is included in Anaconda. A Jupyter notebook server can be started by running `jupyter notebook` in the terminal. This will start the server and also launch a browser window to the server overview page, from which you can see any existing notebooks in the current directory or create a new directory. Jupyter supports not only Python but many other programming languages. A local Jupyter runtime can also run Google Colab notebooks. Visit https://jupyter.org for more information.

A Note About Notebooks

As may be clear already, we really like notebooks as tools for analyzing data. Why do we like them so much? The main reason is that they function as *self-contained end-to-end analysis documents*.

When first examining a new dataset, the first step is a series of exploratory analyses, which help to understand the nature of the data. When you perform those exploratory analyses in a notebook, you can always come back to the exact set of steps you performed and see the output at each step. You can annotate each of those steps as well, to make your logic explicit.

Oftentimes, an exploratory analysis like this is not saved, especially in environments where it is tedious to do so (e.g. having to write out the steps in a document or copy over to a script). But in a notebook this exploratory analysis is saved *de facto* and we find ourselves regularly returning to our initial exploratory analysis notebooks even when we have a finalized analysis notebook, to remember the directions we did not yet fully explore.

When an analysis is complete, its associated notebook documents the entire analysis, including data import, data transformation, data summarization, statistical testing or model building, table generation, figure production, and data export. You could write a script that performs the same functions, without the compiled output that a notebook shows. But how useful would that script be to a non-technical stakeholder? Most likely, it would not be very helpful because they would have to read and interpret the code directly. Yet a notebook contains the relevant output along with its context. Now consider a technical colleague. If you share only the output files with them, they will be interested to see how they were generated. You might share a script along with data files, that would require the colleague to rerun all the steps, which may be complex and time-consuming. A notebook solves that problem by combining the code with its results for immediate reference.

Also a notebook is easy to read. We return to past analyses regularly, and having them in notebook form makes it much simpler to find particular results and understand exactly what we did.

Integrated Development Environments

Integrated development environments, generally referred to as IDEs, are applications that simplify development by bringing multiple functions into a single application, such as an interactive command prompt, a file browser, an error console, figure windows, etc. RStudio (2019) is a very popular IDE among R users, and it also supports Python and is available in Anaconda. Some companies may have questions about RStudio's Affero General Public License (AGPL) terms because it poses questions for those who create proprietary code. If relevant, ask your technology support group if they allow AGPL open source software.

A Python-specific IDE is the Spyder IDE, also included with Anaconda (under the less contentious MIT License). The Pycharm IDE is another option. Many general purpose IDEs also work well for Python, including Vim, Emacs, Visual Studio Code, and others. If you are an experienced programmer and already have a development pipeline, chances are it can be easily modified to work with Python in a data science application.

In this book, we assume usage of notebooks, and we encourage everyone to try notebooks out as we feel like they are extremely powerful tools not only for analysis but also for sharing. However, if you are already comfortable with an IDE of your own choice, it is likely to work with Python and this book.

2.2 A Quick Tour of Python Data Analysis Capabilities

Before we dive into the details of programming, we'd like to start with a tour of a relatively powerful analysis in Python. This is a partial preview of other parts of this book, so don't worry if you don't understand the commands. We explain them briefly here to give you a sense of how a Python analysis might be conducted. In this and later chapters, we explain all of these steps in more detail and many more analyses.

If you are not running in Colab or an Anaconda install, you would first need to install a few libraries, which can be done using `pip` on the command line:

```
pip install pandas seaborn statsmodels
```

or in a Colab or Jupyter notebook using the `!` command, which instructs the notebook to run that as a shell command:

```
In [4]: !pip install pandas

Requirement already satisfied: pandas in /usr/local/lib/python3.6/
  dist-packages
```

Colab has pandas installed by default, so no action was necessary.

A quick note about this format. Throughout the book, we format the code so it matches how it will appear in a notebook. The "In" indicates that this is an input cell: we entered code there and ran it. Output cells will be indicated by "Out" and will be present following an output-generating input cell. The number, "4" in this case, indicates the order in which that cell was run, in this case it was the fourth cell to be run in the notebook (there are some earlier demonstration cells in the notebook).

To run a cell, hit "control-Enter" or "command-Enter" (on PC or Mac, respectively). To add a new cell, you can hit the "+ Code" button or hit "control/command + m" and then "a". You can view all Colab keyboard shortcuts by selecting *Keyboard Shortcuts...* from the *Tools* menu.

Most analyses require one or more libraries in addition to the built-in standard Python libraries. After you install a package once, you don't have to install it again unless there is an update, although in Colab it would need to be reinstalled whenever the runtime is "factory reset," which can be done manually (via the "Runtime" menu) or will happen automatically after a few days.

The `import` command is one we'll see often; it loads a package or module with additional functionality, in this case pandas, a data manipulation and analysis package that we will use extensively throughout the book (McKinney 2010).

Now we load a dataset from this book's website and examine it:

```
In [5]: import pandas as pd
        sat_df = pd.read_csv('http://bit.ly/PMR-ch2')
        sat_df.Segment = sat_df.Segment.astype(pd.api.types.
                                            CategoricalDtype())
        sat_df.head()
```

```
Out[5]:    iProdSAT  iSalesSAT  Segment  iProdREC  iSalesREC
       0          6          2        1         4          3
       1          4          5        3         4          4
       2          5          3        4         5          4
       ...
```

```
In [6]: sat_df.describe()
```

```
Out[6]:           iProdSAT    iSalesSAT     iProdREC    iSalesREC
       count    500.000000   500.000000   500.000000   500.000000
       mean       4.130000     3.802000     4.044000     3.444000
       std        1.091551     1.159951     1.299786     1.205724
       ...
       max        7.000000     7.000000     7.000000     7.000000
```

This dataset represents observations from a simple sales and product satisfaction survey. It has 500 (simulated) consumers' answers to a survey with 4 items asking about satisfaction with a product (`iProdSAT`), sales experience (`iSalesSAT`), and likelihood to recommend the product and salesperson (`iProdREC` and `iSalesREC` respectively). Each respondent is also assigned to a numerically coded segment (`Segment`). In the third line of code above, we set `Segment` to be a categorical type variable.

Next we chart the correlation matrix, which automatically omits the categorical `Segment` variable in column 3:

```
In [7]: import seaborn as sns
        sns.heatmap(sat_df.corr())
```

The resulting chart is shown in Fig. 2.1 as a heatmap. The satisfaction items are highly correlated with one another, as are the likelihood-to-recommend items.

Does product satisfaction differ by segment? We compute the mean satisfaction for each segment using the `groupby()` method:

```
In [8]: sat_df.groupby('Segment').iProdSAT.mean()
```

```
Out[8]: Segment
        1    3.462963
        2    3.725191
        3    4.103896
        4    4.708075
        Name: iProdSAT, dtype: float64
```

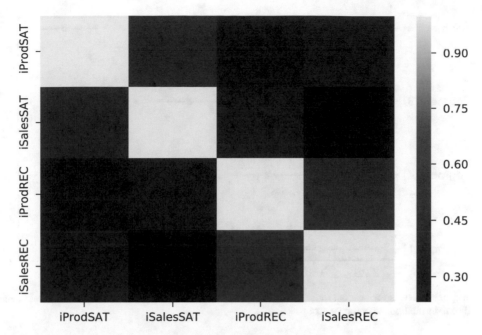

Fig. 2.1 A plot visualizing correlation between satisfaction and likelihood to recommend variables in a simulated consumer dataset, $N = 500$. All items are positively correlated with one another, and the two satisfaction items are especially strongly correlated with one another, as are the two recommendation items. Chapter 4 discusses correlation analysis in detail

Segment 4 has the highest level of satisfaction, but are the differences statistically significant? We perform a oneway analysis of variance (ANOVA) and see in the PR column that satisfaction differs significantly by segment:

```
In [9]: import statsmodels.formula.api as smf
        from statsmodels.stats import anova as sms_anova
        segment_psat_lm = smf.ols('iProdSAT ~ -1 + Segment',
                                  data=sat_df).fit()
        sms_anova.anova_lm(segment_psat_lm)
```

	df	sum_sq	mean_sq	F	PR(>F)
Out[9]:					
Segment	4.0	8627.850038	2156.962510	2160.66543	3.569726e-312
Residual	496.0	495.149962	0.998286	NaN	NaN

We plot the coefficients and confidence intervals from the ANOVA model to visualize confidence intervals for mean product satisfaction by segment:

```
In [10]: import matplotlib.pyplot as plt
         plt.errorbar(y=segment_psat_lm.params.index,
                      x=segment_psat_lm.params.values,
                      xerr=segment_psat_lm.conf_int()[1].T
                         - segment_psat_lm.params,
                      fmt='ko')
```

The resulting chart is shown in Fig. 2.2. It is easy to see that Segments 1, 2, and 3 differ modestly while Segment 4 is much more satisfied than the others. We will learn more about comparing groups and doing ANOVA analyses in Chap. 5.

In just a few lines of code, we have:

- Imported a dataset
- Done a preliminary inspection of the data
- Checked the correlation between variables
- Compared the mean values by segment
- Run an ANOVA to see if those means vary significantly
- Visualized the confidence intervals of the means to understand the basis of the difference

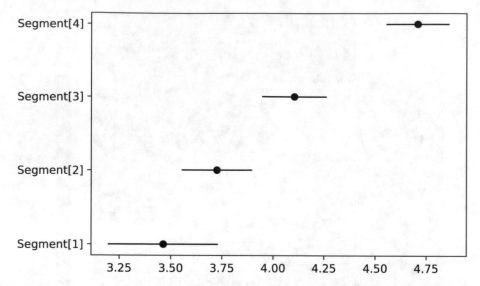

Fig. 2.2 Mean and confidence intervals for product satisfaction by segment. The x-axis represents a Likert rating scale ranging 1–7 for product satisfaction. Chapter 5 discusses methods to compare groups

We ran through this very quickly and did not explain each step; in future chapters we explain all of this (and much more) in detail. Next, we introduce Python as a programming language.

2.3 Basics of Working with Python Commands

Python provides a powerful suite of analytical tools, but fundamentally it is a programming language. The remainder of this chapter serves as an introduction to Python as a programming language. It introduces types and control flow, and then goes onto the data science-focused packages that we will use throughout the book. If you are already familiar with programming in another language, much of this will be very familiar, perhaps except for the data science packages, but if not, it will be helpful to go through these following sections carefully to be sure you understand the fundamentals.

Like most programming languages, Python is *case sensitive*. Thus, x and X are different:

```
In [11]: x = [1, 23, 6]
         print(x)

[1, 23, 6]
```

```
In [12]: print(X)

         NameError: name 'X' is not defined
```

It is helpful to add comments to your code, whether it is in a script or a notebook. These document your thought process and explain what the code is doing. They are essential when sharing code with others, and you will be thankful for them even when reading your own code in the future. The "#" symbol signifies a *comment* in Python, and everything on a line after it is ignored. For example:

```
In [13]: x = [1, 23, 6] # Initialize a list
```

In this book, you don't need to type any comments; they just make the code more understandable.

The command above defines x and ends with a comment. One might instead prefer to comment a whole line:

```
In [14]: # Initialize a list
         x = [1, 23, 6]
```

Our code includes comments wherever we think it might help. As a politician might say about voting, we say *comment early and comment often*. It is much easier to document your code while writing it rather than later.

2.3.1 Python Style

Python is a very flexible language, but Python programmers take "style" very seriously. There are heated discussions on what the most "Pythonic" way to solve a problem is! Throughout this book, we aim to conform to style as outlined in the PEP 8 Style Guide for Python Code (https://www.python.org/dev/peps/pep-0008/). The following naming conventions are rules that most Python programmers follow. If you don't follow these rules, your code will run, but other Python programmers may have trouble reading it.

Naming Conventions

Variables are objects that represent a value, such as a number or a string. By convention, all variables in Python are lower cased. If multiple words occur in the variable name, they are separated by an underscore (e.g. `variable_one`), and not camel-cased (e.g. `variableOne`). All variable names must start with an alphabetical character, but can contain any alphanumeric character. Besides underscores, other special characters are excluded.

Class names are upper cased, with each new word being upper cased as well, for example `MyAdder`. See Sect. 2.4.8 for an introduction to Classes.

Single-letter variable names should be avoided unless it is obvious what a name means or it is used as a temporary variable in a single statement (e.g. in a list comprehension, see Sect. 2.4.8). We sometimes skirt that rule in this book with toy example that use `x` or `y` as variables, but for any substantial amount of code you should avoid single-letter variable names.

Line Width

The maximum line width in Python code files should be 79 characters. In this book, we do not exceed 70 characters (due to the margin width). The reason for this rule is that many code editors wrap lines that are longer than 79 characters, which makes it extremely hard to read.

This rule sometimes requires breaking up statements across multiple lines. This is preferably done using parentheses or other brackets, because once they are opened they will extend across lines or, if necessary, using the '\' character. We will see examples of this throughout the book.

White Space

White space is **very** important in Python. Unlike many other language, white space is meaningful. We go into depth on this topic in Sect. 2.4.8.

2.4 Basic Types

Python has several built-in data types that are important to understand. You can check the Python documentation at https://docs.python.org/3/library/stdtypes.html for more detailed information on each type.

2.4.1 Objects and Type

Nearly all of the entities in Python are *objects*. From numbers and strings to functions and classes, these are all objects. Python is a *weakly typed* or *dynamically typed* language, which means a few things.

One, that after declaring an object, not only can its value be changed, but its type as well. In some languages the following would lead to a `TypeError`:

```
a = 3   # Declare a as an int (integer number)
a = 'b' # Reassign a with a string value (text)
```

In Python, such a type change is allowed. Another feature of Python is that many functions don't check the type of their inputs, which can lead to unexpected behavior. Additionally, many basic operators (e.g. the + operator) are *overloaded*, meaning that they function differently depending on the type of their inputs. These two facts combined can lead to some very tricky bugs.

Overall, Python's weak typing makes the language more flexible and easier to code in than a strongly typed language like Java, but it is worth being aware of the potential pitfalls of dynamic typing.

Now to introduce some of the basic types in Python.

2.4.2   Booleans

A boolean (or 'bool') can have only one of two values `True` or `False`.

Bools are often produced from comparisons:

```
In [15]: 1 == 1

Out[15]: True

In [16]: 1 < 2

Out[16]: True

In [17]: 1 == 2

Out[17]: False
```

Bools can also be compared using the `and`, `or`, and `not` operators:

```
In [18]: x = True
         y = False
         x or y

Out[18]: True

In [19]: x and y

Out[19]: False

In [20]: x and not y

Out[20]: True
```

Bools are extremely important for procedural control (see Sect. 2.4.10) and also for indexing dataframes.

2.4.3   Numeric Types

Python has three built-in numeric types: *int*, *float*, and *complex*. Given that this book is focused on data analysis, numeric types are of paramount importance.

A *float* is the Python type for floating-point numbers, which can represent all real numbers (although there are caveats with binary representation of floating point numbers, see https://docs.python.org/3/tutorial/floatingpoint.html and Bush 1996).

Floats can represent decimal values, unlike *ints*, which only represent integers. ints are more memory efficient, so it is best practice to use int types when possible (i.e. whenever representing integer, non-decimal values).

Complex objects represents complex numbers, those that include an imaginary component. We won't make use of them in this book.

Simple arithmetic operations are supported for numeric types, such as addition using the + operator:

```
In [21]: x = 2
         y = 4
         x + y

Out[21]: 6
```

Division using the / operator:

```
In [22]: w = x/y
         w
```

```
Out[22]: 0.5
```

```
In [23]: type(w)
```

```
Out[23]: float
```

Exponentiation using the ** operator:

```
In [24]: x ** y
```

```
Out[24]: 16
```

And other operations as well. Note that in the division operation, despite the fact that both numerator and denominator are ints, the output is of type float. This behavior differs between Python 3 and Python 2 (Python 2 would return an `int` with the decimal component truncated; that was a source of many bugs!)

Similarly, if the inputs to an operation include both ints and floats, the output will be a float:

```
In [25]: z = 3.2
         type(x * z)
```

```
Out[25]: float
```

2.4.4 Sequence Types

Python contains three *sequence* types, each of which is an ordered array of objects.

Lists

Lists are ordered, mutable sequences of objects. They are defined with square brackets, []:

```
In [26]: x = [0, 1, 2, 3, 4, 5]
         y = ['a', 'b', 'c']
```

Lists can be added together, which concatenates them:

```
In [27]: x + y
```

```
Out[27]: [0, 1, 2, 3, 4, 5, 'a', 'b', 'c']
```

Objects can be added to the end of a list using the append() method:

```
In [28]: x.append('r')
         x
```

```
Out[28]: [0, 1, 2, 3, 4, 5, 'r']
```

Unlike many other languages, appending to a list in Python is memory efficient, so there is no need to preallocate the list if you are generating it by iterating through some other object.

Note that lists can contain a mix of types, e.g. ints and strings in the past two examples.

The built-in len() function returns the length of lists (as well as other objects):

```
In [29]: len(x)
```

```
Out[29]: 7
```

Indexing

Indexing in Python is extremely powerful. Note that lists and other sequence objects in Python are *zero-indexed*, which means that the index starts at 0, not 1. So the *first* item has index *0* and the *last* item has index *length minus 1*.

In the list x that we already defined, the second value is 1, which we access with the index 1:

```
In [30]: x[1]
```

```
Out[30]: 1
```

A range of values can be indexed using the : operator:

```
In [31]: x[2:4]
```

```
Out[31]: [2, 3]
```

Note that in Python, the lower bound is *inclusive* whereas the upper bound is *exclusive*. The command x[2:4] grabs the items with indices 2 and 3 (which, in this case also corresponds to the values).

If you want to start indexing from the beginning of the list, a starting number does not need to be specified. For example, to retrieve the first two elements of x:

```
In [32]: x[:2]
```

```
Out[32]: [0, 1]
```

Similarly, if you want to index all the way to the end of the list, the final index does not need to be specified:

```
In [33]: x[1:]
```

```
Out[33]: [1, 2, 3, 4, 5, 'r']
```

Negative indices are relative to the end of the list. So, for example, to retrieve the last two elements of x you can grab everything from the $-2th$ element:

```
In [34]: x[-2:]
```

```
Out[34]: [5, 'r']
```

This makes for somewhat cleaner, more readable code than in many other languages, where the length of the list would need to be calculated to get the same functionality.

As mentioned before, lists are mutable. This means that they can be appended to, but also that the value at any index can be changed:

```
In [35]: x[2] = 'freeze'
         x
```

```
Out[35]: [0, 1, 'freeze', 3, 4, 5, 'r']
```

Tuples

Tuples are similar to lists with one major caveat: they are immutable.

Tuples are defined with parenthetical brackets, (,):

```
In [36]: z = (7, 8, 9)
```

Tuples are indexed just like lists:

```
In [37]: z[1]
```

```
Out[37]: 8
```

Attempting to modify a tuple leads to a TypeError:

```
In [38]: z[1] = 'boil'
```

```
TypeError: 'tuple' object does not support
    item assignment
```

We will not make extensive use of tuples in this book, but it is good to be aware of them. Since tuples are immutable, they can be *hashed*, which enables them to be used in sets and dictionaries, which we introduce later in the chapter.

Ranges

Ranges are *immutable* sequences of *numbers*, most commonly used for looping via `for` loops.

A range is defined by positional arguments `start`, `stop`, and `step`. Only `stop` is required. If only `stop` is provided, the range will start at 0 and increment by 1 up to that value:

```
In [39]: range(10)

Out[39]: range(0, 10)

In [40]: list(range(10))

Out[40]: [0, 1, 2, 3, 4, 5, 6, 7, 8, 9]
```

A few things to note. One, that a `range` must be cast to a list in order to view its contents (note: in Python 2 this is not true, but rather the output of `range()` is a `list` rather than a `range` object).

Secondly, that much like indexing, the upper limit is *exclusive*, that is, the sequence stops at the last value prior to the `stop` argument value. This makes sense, as given that lists are zero-indexed, it means that the list will have length equal to `stop`.

And again, the `start` argument is *inclusive*:

```
In [41]: list(range(2,12))

Out[41]: [2, 3, 4, 5, 6, 7, 8, 9, 10, 11]
```

If `step` is specified, the range will start at `start`, increment by `step` while the value remains less than `stop`:

```
In [42]: list(range(2, 12, 2))

Out[42]: [2, 4, 6, 8, 10]
```

2.4.5 Text Type: String

Python has a single type for specifying text: `str` or *strings*. Strings can be specified by `'single'`, `''double''`, or `'''triple'''` quotes. Single and double quotes behave identically; triple quotes act across lines.

Strings share some characteristics with lists, such as concatenation through +:

```
In [43]: x = 'Hello'
         y = "World"
         x+y

Out[43]: 'HelloWorld'
```

And indexing using []:

```
In [44]: x[3:]

Out[44]: 'lo'
```

Strings also have many string-specific methods as well such as case modification:

```
In [45]: x.upper()

Out[45]: 'HELLO'
```

Value replacement:

```
In [46]: x.replace('lo', 'p')

Out[46]: 'Help'
```

A list of strings can be joined on another string:

```
In [47]: ', '.join([x,y, 'what a day!'])

Out[47]: 'Hello, World, what a day!'
```

Or split on a delimiter:

```
In [48]: 'Hello, World, what a day!'.split(',')

Out[48]: ['Hello', ' World', ' what a day!']
```

This functionality can be extremely valuable for importing data from a text file.

Format

A useful tool that can be used with strings is the `format()` method. This offers an elegant way to insert values from variables into a string. The substitution locations are specified using `{}` and the values to be substituted in are passed as arguments to the `format()` method:

```
In [49]: temperature = 21.34
         'The temperature today is {} degrees'.format(temperature)

Out[49]: 'The temperature today is 21.34 degrees'
```

Multiple values can be included:

```
In [50]: x = 18.93
         y = 345.234
         '{} divided by {} equals {}        '.format(x, y, x/y)

Out[50]: '18.93 divided by 345.234 equals 0.05483237456333965'
```

We can also specify names for each substitution. That can make the code more reusable and, if even we're referencing a value more than once, it only needs to be specified once:

```
In [51]: '{x} plus {x} plus {y} equals {r}'.format(x=x, y=y, r=x + x + y)

Out[51]: '18.93 plus 18.93 plus 345.234 equals 383.094'
```

We will use this throughout the book to create more readable outputs.

2.4.6 Set Type

Sets are unordered collections of *distinct* objects. Those objects must be *hashable*, which is true for immutable built-in types, such as ints, strs, floats, tuples, but not lists or dictionaries.

Sets can be used to grab all unique values from a collection of objects, such as a list:

```
In [52]: x = [1, 1, 3, 8, 12, 12]
         set(x)

Out[52]: {1, 3, 8, 12}
```

Sets also allow for rapid membership checking. The `in` operator checks whether an objects is included in a collection, such as a set:

```
In [53]: 3 in x

Out[53]: True

In [54]: 5 in x

Out[54]: False
```

in also works on lists and tuples, but for lists and tuples, Python will iterate through the entire collection until it finds (or doesn't find) the matching object. This means that the larger the list, the more time this will take. For a set, however, a search for one item takes *fixed time*. No matter how large a collection is, any item can be found quickly, in the same amount of time as any other item.

Sets also can be used for set-theory mathematical operations, such as *union*, *intersection*, *difference* and others.

```
In [55]: x = set([1, 1, 3, 8, 12, 12])
         y = set([2, 2, 8, 9])
         x.intersection(y)

Out[55]: {8}

In [56]: y.difference(x)

Out[56]: {2, 9}

In [57]: x.union(y)

Out[57]: {1, 2, 3, 8, 9, 12}
```

2.4.7 Mapping Type

Hashmaps, called *dictionaries* or *dicts* in Python, are data structures that use one object to index another object. Lists or tuples can store any object, but their indices are strictly integers.

That difference may not seem very profound, but it is incredibly valuable.

Imagine that we wanted to count the occurrences of every word within a long text file. How might we approach that problem using a list? We need to store each word that we have observed and its count. We could do this with a list of lists of the form [[word_0, count_0], [word_1, count_1], ..., [word_n, count_n]]. For each word observed, we would need to iterate through the entire list until we saw that word, at which point we would increment the count on that list. Or if we didn't see that word, we would append a new list with that word and a count of one.

How might a dictionary help here? A dictionary has two types of objects: *keys* and *values*, each of which forms a pair. The keys are hashed, so limited to hashable types, i.e. no lists, but strings, tuples, floats, and integers all work. Just like for a set, the lookup time to see if a key is present is fixed, so we can immediately determine whether a key is present. The values can be of any type.

If we store our counts in the form { word_0: count_0, word_1: count_1, ..., word_n: count_n}, for each word we observe, we can check if it is present in the dictionary in fixed time. If it's present, we increment its value. If it's not present, we add a new key-value pair to the word count dictionary.

The distinction here is subtle, but important. Imagine we were counting all the words in Wikipedia, which has approximately 1.5 billion (1.5B) total words and approximately 2 million (2M) unique words in English.

We will need to look at every single word; that is unavoidable and would require a minimum of 1.5 billion operations. But for each word observed, how many operations will we need to perform to count them? If we search a list-based structure that comprises 2M unique words, then an average word would be found in about 1M operations. If we repeated that for each of 1.5B words, then the total would be roughly 1.5B * 2M == *1.5 quadrillion* total operations! In contrast, a dictionary-based data structure requires only two operations per observed word (to find it and then update it), so that would take a total of 3B operations. That is still a lot of computing, but is much more efficient than the list-based alternative (which would require 500,000 times as many operations).

Dictionaries can be created using the dict() function:

```
In [58]: x = dict(a=1, b=2, c=3)
         x
```

```
Out[58]: {'a': 1, 'b': 2, 'c': 3}
```

Or using curly brackets, {key: value}:

```
In [59]: x = {'a': 1, 'b': 2, 'c': 3}
         x
```

```
Out[59]: {'a': 1, 'b': 2, 'c': 3}
```

```
In [60]: y = {1: 'a', 2: 'b', 3: 'c'}
         y
```

```
Out[60]: {1: 'a', 2: 'b', 3: 'c'}
```

As for lists and tuples, indices are passed using square brackets:

```
In [61]: x['a']
```

```
Out[61]: 1
```

The key-value pairs can be accessed directly as tuples using the items() method:

```
In [62]: y.items()
```

```
Out[62]: dict_items([(1, 'a'), (2, 'b'), (3, 'c')])
```

Note that, as of Python 3.6, dictionaries are *insertion ordered*, so output from the items() method will be consistently ordered. In previous versions of Python, dictionaries are *unordered*, so the output from the items() will not be consistent in those earlier versions.

Similarly for the keys() and values() methods, which return the keys or values of the dictionary, respectively:

```
In [63]: y.keys()
```

```
Out[63]: dict_keys([1, 2, 3])
```

```
In [64]: y.values()
```

```
Out[64]: dict_values(['a', 'b', 'c'])
```

Dictionaries are used extensively in Python for data analysis. Throughout the book we will use them, largely as *constructors* for creating pandas Series and dataframe objects, which act as specialized HashMap structures. What is a *constructor*? In this context, it means that we assemble the dataset using a dictionary and then cast the dictionary into a Series or dataframe. Constructing the dataset in a dictionary is generally simpler than doing so directly as a Series or Dataframe, but we will see examples of both approaches throughout the book. We will introduce Series and Dataframe structures in Sect. 2.5.3.

2.4.8   Functions, Classes, and Methods

Functions

A very important class of objects are *functional* objects which, rather than representing a discrete unit of information, such as a word or number, represent *processes* or *collections of processes and attributes* that perform operations.

The simplest of these are *functions*, which are nothing more than snippets of code. Functions often take inputs, referred to as *arguments* or *parameters*, and often produce output, referred to as *return values*. Functions serve a few purposes.

Imagine that you have a complex metric that you need to calculate, which requires 6 lines of code, and that you need to make that calculation on a few dozen datasets. Rather than copying and pasting the code each time, you can write a function, and just call it each time.

This has several advantages.

First, it can dramatically improves code *readability*. The importance of this is not to be understated. Especially if you are sharing code with others, but also if you return to your code weeks, months, or years later, it can take considerable time to understand exactly what the code is doing.

Functions improve readability in a few ways. They reduce the overall lines of code required to perform the same action. Fewer lines of code means fewer lines to read when returning to the code.

Functions also make the logic of your code more explicit. Rather than having a long script that does everything, you break that into functions, each of which performs one task. Then, when trying to understand the code, you can break it down more easily. This can help not only in reading code, but also in writing it. You can compartmentalize the overall analysis into a sequence of larger steps. For example:

- Import and clean the data
- Transform the data and calculate metrics
- Fit a model
- Create figures
- Export the analysis

Each of those could be its own function, perhaps with finer-scale functions within it.

In addition to improving readability, functions also improve code *reliability* in at least two important ways. The first is that they avoid any copy-paste-edit errors. Imagine you are calculating your metric twelve times and in each instance you need to make a small change on three of the lines. There's a high risk of missing one of those 36 changes, which would likely be a difficult bug to detect. With a function, you would just need to change the arguments to the function in each instance, which is fewer edits but, more importantly, is easier to debug if you run into an issue.

The second way that functions improve reliability is through improved maintainability. Imagine that you want to change the way you calculate your metric. If you are using a function, you would change the code within the function and be done. Without a function, you would need to do a find-replace operation, which can be quite error prone.

In Python, functions are defined using the `def` keyword, the `:` operator, and *indentation*:

```
In [65]: def add(a, b):
             return a + b
```

Arguments are passed to that function using parentheses:

```
In [66]: add(3, 4)

Out[66]: 7
```

Arguments can be passed *positionally* as above, or via keywords:

```
In [67]: add(a=3, b=4)

Out[67]: 7
```

In the function definition, a default value can be set for each argument. This makes that argument *optional*:

```
In [68]: def add(a, b=0):
             return a + b

In [69]: add(3)

Out[69]: 3

In [70]: add(3, 4)

Out[70]: 7
```

Throughout this book, we will make use of functions to leverage code we have already written.

Whitespace

It is worthwhile to have a brief digression on whitespace. Whitespace in Python is critical. Code blocks are identified by the indentation level. Unlike many programming language that use brackets to indicate the scope of functions, loops, and conditionals, Python strictly uses whitespace. That means that we must be very careful with how we use whitespace.

A common pitfall is mixing tabs and spaces. The Python interpreter does not treat these equally. Intermixed tabs and spaces can be something of a nightmare for the beginning Python programmer. Most Python-focused coding environments, including notebooks, will not insert the tab character when the tab key is pressed, but instead insert a set number of spaces, usually two or four. In some environments that setting must be enabled.

Standard indentations are two or four spaces. In this book we use two spaces.

The fact that whitespace has meaning can be a bit jarring to new Python programmers. But the benefit of it is improved code readability. And aside from the possible issue of mixed tab and space characters, it doesn't generally lead to a lot of problems. But if you are new to Python, it is worth being mindful about the importance of whitespace.

Classes and Methods

Classes are objects that bundle *data* and *functionality* together. All of the basic types that we introduced in this chapter are actually built-in classes. But we can also define our own classes. Custom classes with complex functionality are a hallmark of object-oriented programming. Detailing the usage of classes is beyond the scope of this book, but we want to introduce them as a concept.

Classes contain other objects, notably *attributes* and *methods*, which correspond to the data and the functionality, respectively.

Attributes can be of any type and are attached to a particular instance of that class.

Methods are functions attached to that class which can act upon those attributes as well as other arguments.

We can create a new class `Adder`, which has two attributes, a and b, and one method `add()` which returns the sum of a and b:

```
In [71]: class Adder:
            '''A class that adds its parameters'''
            def __init__(self, a, b):
              self.x = a
              self.y = b

            def add(self):
              return self.x + self.y
```

Note that, by convention, class names are capitalized in Python (See Sect. 2.3.1).

There are a variety of reserved methods that get called by internal Python operations when they interact with instances of the class. `__init__` is an important method which gets called whenever a new instance of that class is created. In this case, a new instance of the class must specify two values: a and b.

The class definition also includes a method, `add`, which simply returns a + b. A method is just a function attached to a particular class object. Our primary objective in introducing classes is to introduce the concept of a method, as throughout the book we will use both functions and methods. The key distinction is that methods are attached to an object and generally use that object's attributes as arguments whereas functions stand alone and must have all arguments explicitly passed.

Let's take a look at how we can use our `Adder` class:

```
In [72]: adder = Adder(3, 4)
         adder

Out[72]: <__main__.Adder at 0x7f3887065e48>
```

We've created a `Adder` object, adder, which we can see is an `Adder` object attached to `__main__`, which is the top-level script environment, and with a particular memory address.

We can check the value of the attribute x using dot notation:

```
In [73]: adder.x

Out[73]: 3
```

And similarly can run the `add()` method:

```
In [74]: adder.add()

Out[74]: 7
```

Note that we did not constrain our class or method in any way, and the + operator is *overloaded*, with different functionalities on different types. So if we initialize an `Adder` object with arguments of other types we get different behavior:

```
In [75]: adder2 = Adder('frog', 'coyote')
         adder2.add()

Out[75]: 'frogcoyote'
```

We don't use custom classes in this book, but we leverage attributes and methods from many built-in and third party classes.

2.4.9 Modules and Packages

We've learned about some of the built-in types and function in Python so far, but what if we need expanded functionality, either through our own code or third party code? The solution come in the form of Python modules and packages.

Modules

A module is simply a file containing Python definitions and statements. The file name is the module name with a `.py` suffix. Modules offer a simple way to make your own code reusable. You can save your functions and classes into a file and import them as a module. For this book we a have a module file for each chapter in which we have written a function, allowing us to call those functions should they be useful in later chapters.

To import a local module, the path to that module first needs to be added to the Python path. That can be done using the `sys` service and adding the path. That path can be *relative* to the path from which Python is being run or *absolute* from the root of the filesystem:

```
In [76]: import sys
         sys.path.append('/absolute/path/to/module.py')
```

As you write your own modules, that is how you would import them. However, for the modules that are part of the book, the most straightforward way is to use pip to install them:

```
In [77]: !pip install python_marketing_research
```

Once the package has been installed, the module can be imported and its definitions accessed:

```
In [78]: from python_marketing_research_functions import chapter2

chapter2.add(3, 4)

Out[78]: 7

In [79]: adder = chapter2.Adder(3, 4)
         adder.add()

Out[79]: 7
```

Packages

Much of the functionality in Python lives in *packages*. There are a multitude of first-party, built-in packages, such as `math` (which includes mathematical functions), `re` (which includes regular expression functionality), `os` (which gives access to OS-related functions), and many others.

There is also a great deal of third party code written by others, often in large open source projects. Python's power in data analysis and machine learning stems from the huge community of contributors that generate powerful and easy to use code.

We describe in detail those packages that are most important for data analysis in Sect. 2.5.

As mentioned in Sect. 2.2, most new packages can be installed using pip.

List of Packages Used in This Book

If you are running Python locally in a non-Anaconda install, here are the packages that you will need for this book:

- matplotlib v3.2.1 (Hunter 2007)
- numpy v1.18.2 (Oliphant 2006–2020)
- pandas v1.0.3 (McKinney 2010)
- statsmodels v0.10.2 (Seabold and Perktold 2010)
- scikit-learn v0.0 (Pedregosa et al. 2011)
- seaborn v0.10.0 (Waskom et al. 2018).

Installing those packages will also install a host of dependencies.

If you are having a compatibility issue (if, for example, a newer version of a library no longer works with the code in the book), you can set all packages versions to match the versions used to create the book using the `requirements.txt` downloaded from the book repository: https://raw.githubusercontent.com/python-marketing-research/python-marketing-research-1ed/master/requirements.txt. You can also use that to see all the packages used in this book (although it will also include packages *not* used in the book, as many are installed by default in Colab).

To align your versions, you can download that file and then pip install from it, for example, in Colab the commands would be:

```
In[80]:  !wget https://raw.githubusercontent.com/python-marketing-research/\
         python-marketing-research-1ed/master/requirements.txt
         !pip install -r requirements.txt
```

Importing

In order to be used, packages must be imported. There are a few different ways that packages can be imported.

First, the entire package can be imported, for example:

```
import numpy
```

By convention, packages are often given an alias when the root of the package is imported like this:

```
import numpy as np
```

Several other packages the we use a lot and their conventional alias are as follows:

```
import matplotlib.pyplot as plt
import numpy as np
import pandas as pd
import seaborn as sns
```

Rather than importing the entire package, you can also import a subset of it using the `from <package> import <module>` syntax:

```
from scipy import stats
```

You will see these pattern of importing packages throughout the book; importing packages is very important, so it is worth familiarizing yourself with the syntax.

2.4.10   Control Flow Statements

Control flow is the order in which the statements in a program are evaluated. There are two main classes of control flow expressions that are important for us: *conditionals* and *loops*.

Conditional statements leverage boolean conditions to create branch points in the code, evaluating particular statements conditional on specific sets of conditions.

Loops allow us to run the same set of code statements multiple times while systematically varying one or more parameters. `while` and `for` loops are the most common forms of loops.

`if` Statements

`if` statements are essential tools across imperative programming languages. We will use them throughout this book for data generation and processing. `if` statements are very simple: if they evaluate to `True`, then the following code block is executed, otherwise that block is skipped:

```
In [81]: x = 5
         if x > 2:
             print('x = {}, which is greater than 2'.format(x))
         print('Done!')

x = 5, which is greater than 2
Done!

In [82]: x = 0
         if x > 2:
             print('x = {}, which is greater than 2'.format(x))
         print('Done!')

Done!
```

When x was 5, the print statement in the `if` block was evaluated, but when it was 0, it was not evaluated. Conditionals and Booleans are closely linked: the conditional statement *must* evaluate to a boolean `True` or `False`. Note that Python will *coerce* many values into Booleans. For example, an empty `list` will evaluate to `False` whereas a non-empty `list` will evaluate to `True`. This behavior can be useful, although it may lead to bugs or other problems if used carelessly.

`if` statements often include a paired `else` statement, which gates a block of code that is evaluated *only when the `if` evaluates to `False`*:

```
In [83]: x = 0
         if x > 2:
             print('x = {}, which is greater than 2'.format(x))
         else:
             print('x = {}, which is less than or equal to 2'.format(x))

x = 0, which is less than or equal to 2
```

In this case, since x is not greater than two, the block under the `else` statement was evaluated. There is also an *else if* statement, `elif` in Python, which only evaluates if the previous `if` (or `elif`) statement evaluated to `False`:

```
In [84]: x = 2
         if x > 2:
             print('x = {}, which is greater than 2'.format(x))
         elif x == 2:
             print('x = {}, which equals 2!'.format(x))
         else:
             print('x = {}, which is less than 2'.format(x))

x = 2, which equals 2!
```

`if...elif...else` statement is a very common construction. Only the `if` is required. Any number of `elif` statements can follow and an `else` statement is optional.

One way in which we might use an `if` statement in practice is to process data differently based on its properties, such as containing a particular value or type of value. For example, we can check to see if a particular value is present in a list of values, which might lead to different processing of the set of values in a real data processing problem:

```
In [85]: def check_present(value, values):
             if value in values:
                 print('{} was found in the values'.format(value))
             else:
                 print('{} was NOT found in the values'.format(value))
```

```
In [86]: a = set([4, 2, 5, 1, 12, 33])
         check_present(38, a)
         check_present(12, a)

38 was NOT found in the values
12 was found in the values
```

while Loops

Loops allow one to run the same code repeatedly while systematically changing specific variables.

while loops will iteratively run the associated code block so long as the while statement evaluates to True.

This means that while statements are very similar to if statements, with the crucial difference that whereas the code block gated by an if statement will only be run once, the code block gated by a while statement will run *indefinitely* until either the condition changes (i.e. the while clause no longer is True) or the loop is broken (using the break command). while loops can easily become *infinite* loops, a loop that will never stop running unless the program is forced to quit, so be careful when writing while statements.

We can use a while statement to count to an arbitrary value:

```
In [87]: x = 0
         while x < 5:
           print(x)
           x += 1

0
1
2
3
4
```

The loop ran until i was no longer less than 5.

We can also iterate through an array and operate on each element:

```
In [88]: a = [4, 2, 5, 1, 12, 33]
         a_squared = []
         i = 0
         while i < len(a):
           a_squared.append(a[i]**2)
           i += 1
         print('a_squared generated: {}'.format(a_squared))

a_squared generated: [16, 4, 25, 1, 144, 1089]
```

Here we incremented an index, i from 0 and used it to step through the list a, storing the square of each value in the a_squared list. Note that i += 1 is a shorthand for i = i + 1. In each iteration, we made sure that our index stayed within a by comparing i to len(a). Once the index i was the equal to the length of a (i.e. was no longer less than len(a)), the loop broke.

In both of these examples, we would actually be better served by a for loop.

for Loops

In Python, for loops iterate through a *collection* or *iterator*. This is a bit different from many other languages, where for loops act much like a while loop but with a built in index start and end. For example, when looping through a list, it means that rather than working with an index to reference into the list, we iterate through the list *directly*:

```
In [89]: a = [4, 2, 5, 1, 12, 33]
         a_squared = []
         for x in a:
```

```
            a_squared.append(x**2)
        print('a_squared generated: {}'.format(a_squared))
```

```
a_squared generated: [16, 4, 25, 1, 144, 1089]
```

Here we iterated through a, with x taking on each sequential value in a. There was no need to worry about an index or the length of a, we can just use the values directly. This makes working with collections, such as lists, dictionaries, etc., very straightforward.

But what if we do want to iterate through a set of numbers? That is easy using the range objects that we introduced in Sect. 2.4.4:

```
In [90]: for i in range(5):
            print(i)
```

```
0
1
2
3
4
```

We can use those numbers as indices to index into a list if we don't want to iterate through the elements of the list directly:

```
In [91]: a_squared = []
        for i in range(len(a)):
          a_squared.append(a[i]**2)
        print('a_squared generated: {}'.format(a_squared))
```

```
a_squared generated: [16, 4, 25, 1, 144, 1089]
```

Remember that range() can take multiple arguments to create different kinds of sequences, for example, starting at 21 and going to 100 with a step size of 12:

```
In [92]: for i in range(21, 100, 12):
            print(i)
```

```
21
33
45
57
69
81
93
```

zip() is a function that "zips" together two collections and iterates through a pair of values:

```
In [93]: for x, y in zip(range(6), range(6, 18, 2)):
            print(x,y)
```

```
0 6
1 8
2 10
3 12
4 14
5 16
```

Note that if one of the collections is shorter than the other, the iteration will only proceed for the length of the shorter collection:

```
In [94]: for j, k in zip(range(6), range(6, 12, 2)):
            print(j, k)
```

```
0 6
1 8
2 10
```

Another useful iteration function is enumerate, which returns not only the value from a collection, but also its index:

```
In [95]: for i, x in enumerate(a):
             print(i, x)

0 4
1 2
2 5
3 1
4 12
5 33
```

This can be useful when you need to modify another array at a matched index as you iterate.

So, when would we actually want to use a while loop rather than a for loop? while loops are best used *when the number of iterations is hard to predict in advance*. As a toy example, let's imagine we wanted to find the largest factor of 34, and rather than iterating up from 2, we want to iterate down from 34. We can use a while loop and break as soon as we find the first factor, using *modulo (%)*, which returns the remainder when the first number is divided by the second:

```
In [96]: x = 34
         y = x-1
         while True:
           if x % y == 0:
             break
           y -= 1
         print('{y} is the largest factor of {x},\n{f2} times {y} equals {x}'
               .format(y=y, x=x, f2=x/y))

17 is the largest factor of 34,
2.0 times 17 equals 34
```

List Comprehension

List comprehension is a concise syntax for generating a list from another list. Rather than instantiating an empty list, creating a for statement to iterate through the source list, and writing the statements to append to the new list, all of those operations can be done in a single line:

```
In [97]: a = [4, 2, 5, 1, 12, 33]

In [98]: a_plus_one = [x + 1 for x in a]
         a_plus_one

Out[98]: [5, 3, 6, 2, 13, 34]
```

Here, we generated a new list where each element has been incremented by one.

We can also include an if clause in the list comprehension. The relative placement of the if and for operators leads to different behaviors.

If the if follows the for, it acts as a filter, only including values in the final list the satisfy the if condition. In this case an else statement cannot be included:

```
In [99]: a_plus_one_filtered = [x + 1 for x in a if x < 12]
         a_plus_one_filtered

Out[99]: [5, 3, 6, 2]
```

However, if we want differential behavior based on a particular condition, we can place the if before the for, in which case an else statement is required:

```
In [100]: a_modified = [x + 1 if x < 12 else x * 100 for x in a]
          a_modified

Out[100]: [5, 3, 6, 2, 1200, 3300]
```

List comprehension can also be used to generate list of tuples (a reminder: ** is the exponentiation operator):

```
In [101]: a_square_tuples = [(v, v**2) for v in a]
          a_square_tuples

Out[101]: [(4, 16), (2, 4), (5, 25), (1, 1), (12, 144), (33, 1089)]
```

Iterate through lists of tuples:

```
In [102]: a_reconstructed = [w/v for v,w in a_square_tuples]
          a_reconstructed

Out[102]: [4.0, 2.0, 5.0, 1.0, 12.0, 33.0]
```

And to generate dictionaries:

```
In [103]: a_square_dict = {v: v**2 for v in a}
          a_square_dict

Out[103]: {1: 1, 2: 4, 4: 16, 5: 25, 12: 144, 33: 1089}
```

List comprehension can be marginally faster than a `for` loop, but its main value is its concision: in the simplest case, writing in one line what would otherwise require three.

We don't make extensive use of list comprehension in this book. We mostly use it for "prettifying" results from statistical analysis functions, e.g. for our `pca_summary()` function from Chap. 9.

2.4.11 Help! A Brief Detour

If you are running into a problem where code from the book will not run, one possible problem is a package version incompatibility. Packages that we use could have breaking updates, meaning that code written for previous versions will no longer run. If that is the case, you can downgrade the problematic package. See Sect. 2.4.9 for details on how to align the versions of all packages with those we use in the book.

This is a good place to introduce help in Python. Python and its add-on packages form an enormous system and even advanced Python users regularly consult the documentation.

Python has a built-in `help()` function. This function is called with a Python object, such as a function, and it prints the *docstring*, short for "documentation string." The docstring is defined by triple quotes and is the first statement in a function, class, or module.

We can learn more about the `range()` function:

```
In [104]: help(range)

Help on class range in module builtins:

class range(object)
 |  range(stop) -> range object
 |  range(start, stop[, step]) -> range object
 |
 |  Return an object that produces a sequence of integers from start (inclusive)
 |  to stop (exclusive) by step.  range(i, j) produces i, i+1, i+2, ..., j-1.
 |  start defaults to 0, and stop is omitted!  range(4) produces 0, 1, 2, 3.
 |  These are exactly the valid indices for a list of 4 elements.
 |  When step is given, it specifies the increment (or decrement).
 |
```

```
|   Methods defined here:
|
|   __bool__(self, /)
|       self != 0
...
```

Note that Colab displays not only the docstring, but also all the defined methods. Other environments, such as the Python CLI and Jupyter notebooks display only the docstring.

Since we wrote a docstring in our definition of the `Adder` class in Sect. 2.4.8, we can also view that using `help()`:

```
In [105]: help(Adder)

Help on class Adder in module __main__:

class Adder(builtins.object)
 |  A class that adds its parameters
 |
 |  Methods defined here:
 |
 |  __init__(self, a, b)
 |      Initialize self.  See help(type(self)) for accurate signature.
 |
 |  add(self)
 |
 |  ----------------------------------------------------------------
 |  Data descriptors defined here:
 |
 |  __dict__
 |      dictionary for instance variables (if defined)
 |
 |  __weakref__
 |      list of weak references to the object (if defined)
```

If you are working in a notebook or IDE, you likely have an alternative to the `help()` function, the `?` operator. For example, in Colab or Jupyter, entering `?range` will bring up a panel with the docstring. This is generally preferable to using `help()`, as then it doesn't interrupt the flow of the notebook.

Colab notebooks also bring up the docstring when the cursor is within the parentheses of a function (in Jupyter, the behavior is the same, but you must press shift-tab). We find this to be particularly valuable, as you can view the docstring very much in real time.

Most notebooks and IDEs also offer *tab completion*, which will display possible arguments based on the current location of the cursor when tab is pressed.

The tab-based functionality is a bit hard to explain, but we are confident that if you explore its usage, you will find it becoming an invaluable part of your workflow.

But what if you are stuck on a broader question, not on the details of a specific function? In that case, there are a few main routes.

The first would be to look at documentation to better understand the system you are using. Python and its libraries generally have excellent documentation. docs.python.org is the home of the most current Python documentation. A simple web search for the library, along with the keywords "python documentation" will generally yield excellent results.

Another option would be to consult community expert sites, such as Stackoverflow (stackoverflow.com) for general Python questions or Cross Validated (stats.stackexchange.com) for statistics and data analysis question.

A general web search can also yield informative results.

And of course, there are many books that go into much more detail on specific areas than this book does. We suggest resources for learning more at the end of each chapter, but those lists are far from exhaustive.

2.5 Data Science Packages

The Python built-in types are powerful. But one of the key attributes of Python is its flexibility and extensibility.

Python enjoys a large community that actively contributes to open source projects, including many powerful data science packages. In this section we will briefly introduce several of these packages.

2.5.1 NumPy

NumPy is an extremely powerful library for Python which is all-but-essential for scientific computing and data analysis. Python built-in types do not include support for mathematical operations on multi-dimensional arrays and matrices. NumPy was developed to add this functionality.

NumPy operations on arrays are much faster than equivalent Python code. The reason for this is that the operations run in pre-compiled C code rather than Python interpreted code. These operations are called *vectorized* operations, which we introduce below.

NumPy must first be imported. By convention, it is imported as np:

```
In [106]: import numpy as np
```

NumPy Arrays

NumPy arrays superficially are a lot like lists. Both represent a vector of values. There are several differences.

One difference is that NumPy arrays are of uniform type. That is, all values within the array are, by definition, of the same type. We can check the data type of the array on the dtype parameter:

```
In [107]: x = np.array([1, 3, 4])
          print(x)
          print(x.dtype)

[1 3 4]
int64
```

The Python ints were cast to NumPy int64 objects.

Converting a list of mixed types into an array will lead to all values being cast into a single type:

```
In [108]: x = np.array([1, 3, 4, 'a', 'b'])
          print(x)
          print(x.dtype)

['1' '3' '4' 'a' 'b']
<U21
```

In this case the integers were cast to unicode strings (as shown by "U21").

Indexing into NumPy arrays in general is much more flexible and powerful than lists. While in lists we can select a continuous slice, for example the first 3 elements of the list, NumPy arrays can be indexed arbitrarily.

Getting a slice of an array is equivalent to getting a slice from a list:

```
In [109]: a = [7, 4, 2, 22, -12]
          a[:3]

Out[109]: [7, 4, 2]

In [110]: x = np.array(a)
          x[:3]

Out[110]: array([7, 4, 2])
```

However, an array can be indexed with another array or list, such as one that contains indices of interest:

```
In [111]: x[[0, 3]]
```

```
Out[111]: array([ 7, 22])
```

This leads to a `TypeError` if the same operation is attempted on a list:

```
In [112]: a[[0, 3]]

...
TypeError: list indices must be integers or slices, not list
```

Arrays can also be indexed using an array of Booleans matching the shape of the array:

```
In [113]: x[[True, False, False, True, False]]
```

```
Out[113]: array([ 7, 22])
```

We will see the power of this capability in Sect. 2.5.3.

Another difference is that while lists can be nested, representing multiple dimensions, e.g. a matrix, NumPy arrays (or ndarrays, short for n-dimensional array) can represent higher dimensional structures and these can be indexed directly.

A difference to be mindful of is that whereas iteratively appending to a list is efficient, iteratively appending to a NumPy array is not: at each iteration the entire array will need to be copied. For this reason, when constructing arrays, we should either *preallocate* the array or iteratively construct a list and then *cast* the list to an array.

The array can be preallocated using either the `empty()` method, in which the values will be uninitialized, the `zeros()` method, or the `ones()` method, depending on one's goal:

```
In [114]: x = np.empty(shape=5, dtype=np.int32)
          x
```

```
Out[114]: array([       0,        0, 16842752, 16843009, 16843009], dtype=int32)
```

```
In [115]: x = np.zeros(shape=5)
          x
```

```
Out[115]: array([0., 0., 0., 0., 0.])
```

Be warned that the uninitialized values in an empty array can lead to unexpected behavior, so a zeroes or ones array is safer.

Vectorized Operations

NumPy arrays enable vectorized operations, which means that rather than having to operate on each element of a list, we can operate on the entire array as a whole.

For example, if, as before, we want to square each element of a list, we can use a `for` loop:

```
In [116]: a = [7, 4, 2, 22, -12]
          a_squared = []
          for v in a:
            a_squared.append(v**2)
          a_squared
```

```
[49, 16, 4, 484, 144]
```

We can make this much more concise using list comprehension:

```
In [117]: [v**2 for v in a]
```

```
Out[117]: [49, 16, 4, 484, 144]
```

But even more efficient is element-wise operations on an entire array:

```
In [118]: x = np.array(a)
          x**2

Out[118]: array([ 49,  16,   4, 484, 144])
```

This is not only a more compact way to write the same thing, *vectorized operations* are much faster. As mentioned above, this is because vectorized operations run in pre-compiled C code, which is much faster than the equivalent Python code (which has to be "interpreted," i.e. translated into bytecode).

We can also perform comparison operations element-wise on the whole array. For example, if we want to check which values of x are greater than 5:

```
In [119]: x > 5

Out[119]: array([ True, False, False,  True, False])
```

We can also take into the fact that `True` values will count as 1 in mathematical operations to count the number of elements that are greater than 5 using the `sum()` method on the array:

```
In [120]: (x > 5).sum()

Out[120]: 2
```

And if we divide that by the length of x, we get the proportion of values in x that are greater than 5:

```
In [121]: (x > 5).sum()/len(x)

Out[121]: 0.4
```

Another use for the boolean array is to index on it, for example to get all the values of x that are greater than 5:

```
In [122]: x[x > 5]

Out[122]: array([ 7, 22])
```

These types of approaches are very valuable for preliminary analysis of data.

Arrays can also be multiplied together directly, which will perform element-wise operations across vectors, e.g., in this case, it will divide the *zeroeth* element of x by the *zeroeth* element of y, the *fourth* element of x by the *fourth* element of y, etc.

```
In [123]: y = np.array([34, 2, 9, -5, -18])
          x / y

Out[123]: array([ 0.20588235, 2.        , 0.22222222, -4.4       , 0.66666667])
```

NumPy contains much more than just arrays and vectorized operations. Throughout this book we will use many NumPy functions, such as for random number generation.

2.5.2   Using Python for Mathematical Computation

As a programming environment for computational statistics, Python combined with NumPy has powerful capabilities for mathematics. In particular, it is highly optimized for vector and matrix operations, which include everything from indexing and iteration to complex operations such as matrix inversion and decomposition. This makes Python an attractive alternative to software like Matlab for computation, simulation and optimization.

We do not cover such math in detail here for several reasons: it is tedious to read, many operations are obvious or easy to find, and advanced math is not necessarily used in day to day marketing analytics. Instead, we use math commands and operators with minor explanations as needed, trusting that you may use `help()` to learn more.

2.5.3 *pandas*

pandas (McKinney 2010) is another powerful Python library. It introduces several types that simplify data structuring and analysis, Series and Dataframes, as well as associated operations. pandas builds on NumPy types and methods. If you have coded in R, these types will be familiar.

pandas is imported as `pd` by convention:

```
In [124]: import pandas as pd
```

Series

In the last section we introduced NumPy arrays. Series objects in pandas exhibit properties very similar to arrays, but with the addition of an *index*, which is another ordered array that can contain values of any hashable type. Series have the properties of an array, but effectively add the functionality of a dictionary.

We can create a Series from a list:

```
In [125]: a = [7, 4, 2, 22, -12]
          x = pd.Series(a)
          x

Out[125]: 0     7
          1     4
          2     2
          3    22
          4   -12
          dtype: int64
```

In this case, the default index is numerical: identical, in fact, to the *de facto* index of an array. We can access the index on the `index` parameter:

```
In [126]: x.index

Out[126]: RangeIndex(start=0, stop=5, step=1)
```

And we can access the *values* of the Series, which is a NumPy array, using the `values` parameter:

```
In [127]: x.values

Out[127]: array([  7,    4,    2,   22,  -12])
```

But the real power of a Series comes when we give it a non-numeric index, enabling us to access data as if it were in a dictionary:

```
In [128]: x = pd.Series(a, index=['a', 'b', 'c', 'd', 'e'])
          x['a']

Out[128]: 7
```

But unlike a dictionary, we can access whole subsets of the Series at one time, much like an array, but using arbitrary keys (such as strings in this case):

```
In [129]: x[['b', 'd', 'e']]

Out[129]: b     4
          d    22
          e   -12
          dtype: int64
```

And rather than strings, we can use date or times as an index, storing the value of data over time:

```
In [130]:  start_time = pd.datetime.strptime('2019-04-09', '%Y-%m-%d')
           x = pd.Series(a,
                      index=pd.date_range(start=start_time,
                                          normalize=True, periods=5)
                      )
           x

Out[130]:  2019-04-09     7
           2019-04-10     4
           2019-04-11     2
           2019-04-12    22
           2019-04-13   -12
           Freq: D, dtype: int64
```

We will use Series extensively throughout the book, largely in the context of Dataframes

Dataframes

Much of the data that we analyze is multi-dimensional. Dataframes are the workhorse objects in Python data analysis, used to hold datasets and to provide data to statistical functions and models. A dataframe's general structure will be familiar to any analyst: it is a rectangular object comprised of columns of varying data types (often referred to as "variables") and rows that have a values across the columns ("observations").

Each column is actually a Series, with all the columns sharing the same index.

A dataframe can be constructed with the `DataFrame()` function:

```
In [131]:  a = [7, 4, 2, 22, -12]
           b = [34, 2, 9, -5, -18]
           ab_df = pd.DataFrame({'a': a, 'b': b})
           ab_df

Out[131]:       a    b
           0    7   34
           1    4    2
           2    2    9
           3   22   -5
           4  -12  -18
```

Dictionaries serve well as constructors for dataframes, with the keys becoming the column names.

If no index argument is passed, as for a Series, the constructor will create an index of sequential integers. However, an explicit argument can be passed, which will be shared by all columns. In this case we use the same data range index that we used in the series above, again constructing it with the pandas `date_range()` function:

```
In [132]:  a = [7, 4, 2, 22, -12]
           b = [34, 2, 9, -5, -18]
           ab_df = pd.DataFrame({'a': a, 'b': b},
                            index=pd.date_range(start=start_time,
                                          normalize=True, periods=5))
           ab_df

Out[132]:                 a    b
           2019-04-09     7   34
           2019-04-10     4    2
           2019-04-11     2    9
           2019-04-12    22   -5
           2019-04-13   -12  -18
```

Columns can be accessed using square brackets:

```
In [133]: ab_df['a']

Out[133]: 2019-04-09     7
          2019-04-10     4
          2019-04-11     2
          2019-04-12    22
          2019-04-13   -12
          Freq: D, Name: a, dtype: int64
```

Or using dot notation:

```
In [134]: ab_df.a

Out[134]: 2019-04-09     7
          2019-04-10     4
          2019-04-11     2
          2019-04-12    22
          2019-04-13   -12
          Freq: D, Name: a, dtype: int64
```

Rows can be accessed with the row index and the .loc operator:

```
In [135]: ab_df.loc['2019-04-10']

Out[135]: a    4
          b    2
          Name: 2019-04-10 00:00:00, dtype: int64
```

And rows or columns can also be indexed by their position using the .iloc operator:

```
In [136]: ab_df.iloc[3]

Out[136]: a    22
          b    -5
          Name: 2019-04-12 00:00:00, dtype: int64

In [137]: ab_df.iloc[:, 1]

Out[137]: 2019-04-09    34
          2019-04-10     2
          2019-04-11     9
          2019-04-12    -5
          2019-04-13   -18
          Freq: D, Name: b, dtype: int64
```

Note that to get a column, we use the : operator to indicate that we are referencing a column. The : indicates we want all rows. We could have included this when we grabbed the row, but it is optional in that case: ab_df.iloc[3, :].

We can print just the first few rows using head():

```
In [138]: ab_df.head(3)

Out[138]:              a   b
          2019-04-09   7  34
          2019-04-10   4   2
          2019-04-11   2   9
```

By default it displayed the first five rows; in this case we displayed just the first three rows by passing 3 as an argument. In this case head() wasn't very useful, but as you'll see throughout the book, we use this extensively. It is generally the first thing we do to start inspecting a new data source, along with describe(), which we introduce below.

Operations on Dataframes

Some statistical functions, such as `mean()` can be accessed directly as methods on the dataframe object:

```
In [139]: ab_df.mean()

Out[139]: a    4.6
          b    4.4
          dtype: float64
```

Note that by default, such methods act on columns (`axis=0`). If you want a method to act on rows, you must explicitly specify the `axis` parameter as 1:

```
In [140]: ab_df.mean(axis=0)

Out[140]: a    4.6
          b    4.4
          dtype: float64

In [141]: ab_df.mean(axis=1)

Out[141]: 2019-04-09    20.5
          2019-04-10     3.0
          2019-04-11     5.5
          2019-04-12     8.5
          2019-04-13   -15.0
          Freq: D, dtype: float64
```

We can create a dataframe that has more realistic data:

```
In [142]: store_id = pd.Series([3, 14, 21, 32, 54],dtype='category') #store id
          store_rev = [543, 654, 345, 678, 234] # store revenue, $1000
          store_visits = [45, 78, 32, 56, 34] # visits, 1000s
          store_manager = ['Annie', 'Bert', 'Carla', 'Dave', 'Ella']
          store_df = pd.DataFrame({'id': store_id,
                                   'rev': store_rev,
                                   'visits': store_visits,
                                   'manager': store_manager})
          store_df

Out[142]:    id manager  rev  visits
          0   3   Annie  543      45
          1  14    Bert  654      78
          2  21   Carla  345      32
          3  32    Dave  678      56
          4  54    Ella  234      34
```

We specify that `id` is categorical so that it does not get treated as a numeric.

We can get a list of our store managers using dot notation:

```
In [143]: store_df.manager

Out[143]: 0    Annie
          1     Bert
          2    Carla
          3     Dave
          4     Ella
          Name: manager, dtype: object
```

And find our mean revenue across stores:

```
In [144]: store_df.rev.mean()
```

```
Out[144]: 490.8
```

We can also correlate per-store revenue and visits:

```
In [145]: store_df.corr()

Out[145]:              rev     visits
          rev      1.000000  0.829103
          visits   0.829103  1.000000
```

The `describe()` method gives us a numerical summary of the dataframe:

```
In [146]: store_df.describe()

Out[146]:              rev       visits
          count     5.000000   5.000000
          mean    490.800000  49.000000
          std     194.683589  18.841444
          min     234.000000  32.000000
          25%     345.000000  34.000000
          50%     543.000000  45.000000
          75%     654.000000  56.000000
          max     678.000000  78.000000
```

This shows statistics for the numeric columns. If we wanted to see statistics for non-numeric columns, we can pass the `include='all'` argument to the `describe()` method.

2.5.4 Missing Values

In statistics, missing values are important, and NumPy and pandas offer some tools for dealing with missing data. Missing data are usually represented with the `numpy.nan` object. NaN stands for *Not a Number*.

```
In [147]: np.nan

Out[147]: nan
```

`np.nan` is actually a float, so its best to cast datasets with missing data as floats if possible.

```
In [148]: type(np.nan)

Out[148]: float
```

Python also includes a `None` object, but it generally should not be used to used to represent missing data, as it can lead to odd behavior.

Any math performed on a value of NaN will return NaN. For example, if we create an array with a NaN value, and take its mean:

```
In [149]: x = np.array([3., 4., 6., 2., np.nan, 18., np.nan])
          x

Out[149]: array([ 3.,  4.,  6.,  2., nan, 18., nan])

In [150]: np.mean(x)

Out[150]: nan
```

But NumPy has a `nanmean()` function, which will *ignore* NaN values and calculate the mean of the numeric values:

```
In [151]: np.nanmean(x)

Out[151]: 6.6
```

There are "nan" versions of most of the descriptive statistics methods, such as `nanmax()`, `nanstd()`, `nanpercentile()`, etc. But in many cases we will need to explicitly deal with any missing data. The `np.isnan()` function returns a boolean array that is `True` at the indices of NaN values in the input vector:

```
In [152]: np.isnan(x)

Out[152]: array([False, False, False, False,  True, False,  True])
```

This can be used to filter out the NaN values. First we need to *complement* the array, that is convert all `False` to `True` and vice versa, using ~, the *bitwise complement operator*:

```
In [153]: ~np.isnan(x)

Out[153]: array([ True,  True,  True,  True, False,  True, False])
```

We can then index x on that output and take its mean:

```
In [154]: np.mean(x[~np.isnan(x)])

Out[154]: 6.6
```

One thing *never* to do in Python is to use an actual numeric value such as -999 to indicate missing data. That will cause headaches at best and wrong answers at worst. Instead, as soon as you load such data, replace those values with NaN using indices:

```
In [155]: x = np.array([3., 4., 6., 2., -999, 18., -999])
          x.mean()

Out[155]: -280.7142857142857

In [156]: x[x == -999] = np.nan
          np.nanmean(x)

Out[156]: 6.6
```

Infinity values are handled similarly, with a constant `np.inf`. For example, if we take the natural logarithm of positive and negative numbers:

```
In [157]: np.log(np.array([-1, 0, 1]))

/usr/local/lib/python3.6/dist-packages/ipykernel_launcher.py:1:
RuntimeWarning: divide by zero encountered in log

/usr/local/lib/python3.6/dist-packages/ipykernel_launcher.py:1:
RuntimeWarning: invalid value encountered in log

Out[157]: array([ nan, -inf,   0.])
```

We get a warning because `log()` is undefined for negative numbers and `log(0)` gives a value of `-inf`.

You should watch for "`Warning message`" and clean up your data or math when it appears.

2.6 Loading and Saving Data

There many ways to load and save data in Python. In this section, we focus on the methods for storing data that are common in typical projects including how to save and read Python objects and how to read and write CSV formats to move data in and out of other environments like Microsoft Excel.

In addition, we discuss loading and saving data when working with cloud-based notebooks.

2.6.1 Saving Python Objects: Pickle

The standard format for saving Python objects is *pickle*. *Pickling* serializes Python object structure, writing it to disk. *Unpickling* reads a pickle file.

We also need to introduce the open() function, which *opens* a file for reading or writing, and the close() method, which must be run on any file once reading or writing activity is complete.

We can use pickle.dump() and open() to write the store_df variable to disk:

```
In [158]: import pickle

          f = open('store_df.pkl', 'wb')
          pickle.dump(store_df, f)
          f.close()
```

The 'wb' is the *mode* in which the file is being opened. We can see all the modes using the help() function:

```
In [159]: help(open)

Help on built-in function open in module IO:

open(file, mode='r', buffering=-1, encoding=None, errors=None, newline=None,
        closefd=True, opener=None)
Open file and return a stream.  Raise IOError upon failure.

file is either a text or byte string giving the name (and the path
if the file isn't in the current working directory) of the file to
be opened or an integer file descriptor of the file to be
wrapped. (If a file descriptor is given, it is closed when the
returned I/O object is closed, unless closefd is set to False.)

mode is an optional string that specifies the mode in which the file
is opened. It defaults to 'r' which means open for reading in text
mode.  Other common values are 'w' for writing (truncating the file if
it already exists), 'x' for creating and writing to a new file, and
'a' for appending (which on some Unix systems, means that all writes
append to the end of the file regardless of the current seek position).
...
```

w specified that the file is being opened for writing. If a file of that name already exists on that path, it will be overwritten. b specifies that we want to write a binary file rather than a text file, which is the default or can be explicitly specified with t.

The more correct way to open a file is actually using the with operator. with defines a code block, in which all the file interactions should occur, and then automatically closes the file at the end of the code block. This eliminates the risk of failing to close the file, which can cause file corruption.

```
In [160]: with open('store_df.pkl', 'wb') as f:
              pickle.dump(store_df, f)
```

If we want to read the file we just wrote, we again use the open() function, but with pickle.load() and with mode rb:

```
In [161]: with open('store_df.pkl', 'rb') as f:
              store_df_reload = pickle.load(f)
          store_df_reload

Out[161]:     id manager  rev  visits
          0    3   Annie  543      45
          1   14    Bert  654      78
          2   21   Carla  345      32
          3   32    Dave  678      56
          4   54    Ella  234      34
```

pandas has functions that simplify these operations: `to_pickle()` and `read_pickle()`:

```
In [162]: store_df.to_pickle('store_df.pkl')

In [163]: store_df_reload2 = pd.read_pickle('store_df.pkl')
          store_df_reload2

Out[163]:    id manager  rev  visits
          0   3   Annie  543      45
          1  14    Bert  654      78
          2  21   Carla  345      32
          3  32    Dave  678      56
          4  54    Ella  234      34
```

When working with pandas objects, these functions simplify saving and loading objects.

One thing to keep in mind is that unpickling should not be run on any files that you do not trust, as it can be leveraged to run malicious code.

2.6.2 Importing and Exporting Data

Many analysts save data in *delimited* files such as comma-separated value (CSV) files and tab-separated value (TSV) files to move data between tools such as Python, databases, and Microsoft Excel. We focus on CSV files; TSV and other delimited files are handled similarly.

First, let's create a CSV by writing `store_df` to a file. This works similarly to the `to_pickle()` command above. We recommend adding the option `index=False` to eliminate an extra, unnamed column containing labels for each row; those mostly get in the way when interchanging CSV files with other programs.

A handy way to test CSV files is to use the command *without* a file name, which sends the output to the console just as it would be written to a file:

```
In [164]: store_df.to_csv()

Out[164]: ',id,manager,rev,visits\n0,3,Annie,543,45\n1,14,Bert,654,78\n...'
```

Now let's write a real file and then read it using `pd.read_csv()`:

```
In [165]: store_df.to_csv('store_df.csv', index=False)

In [166]: store_df_from_csv = pd.read_csv('store_df.csv')
          store_df_from_csv.id = store_df_from_csv.id.astype('category')
          store_df_from_csv

Out[166]:    id manager  rev  visits
          0   3   Annie  543      45
          1  14    Bert  654      78
          2  21   Carla  345      32
          3  32    Dave  678      56
          4  54    Ella  234      34
```

After reading the CSV file, we recreate `id` as a factor variable. One of the problems with CSV files is that they lose such distinctions because they are written out in plain text.

Now we check that the values are identical to the original dataframe:

```
In [167]: store_df == store_df_from_csv

Out[167]:      id manager   rev  visits
          0  True    True  True    True
          1  True    True  True    True
          2  True    True  True    True
          3  True    True  True    True
          4  True    True  True    True
```

The operator == tests whether the two dataframes are the same, element-by-element.

Python can handle many other file formats that we do not discuss in this book. These include *fixed format* files, *databases*, and *binary* files from other software such as Microsoft Excel, MATLAB, SAS, and SPSS. If you need to work with such data, pandas has an extensive I/O API, which can be found at https://pandas.pydata.org/pandas-docs/stable/user_guide/io.html or by searching for "pandas read hdf5," "pandas read excel," etc.

2.6.3   Using Colab: Importing and Exporting Data

Working in a Colab notebook using a cloud runtime (rather than a local runtime) presents an issue: we don't have direct access to the machine on which the notebook is running! Fortunately, there are tools to enable uploading and downloading files directly from the notebook.

First, let's download our CSV file:

```
In [168]: from google.colab import files

          files.download('store_df.csv')
```

The files.download() command downloads it to our hard drive, to the default browser download directory.

We can then upload the file using files.upload(), which brings up a dialog box to select the file to upload. For this to run, we need to select the file we just downloaded:

```
In [169]: files.upload()
```

```
Saving store_df.csv to store_df (1).csv
```

We can see the files present local to the notebook using !ls:

```
In [170]: !ls
```

```
gdrive    'store_df (1).csv'    store_df.pkl
sample_data       segment_dataframe_Python_intro_Ch5.csv
store_df.csv
```

We can see all the files we have written as well as the uploaded file, which had the same name as the file we just downloaded, unsurprisingly, so it has a (1) modification to the file name. We can now import this file using pd.read_csv() just as we did earlier:

```
In [171]: store_df_uploaded = pd.read_csv('store_df (1).csv')
```

```
In [172]: store_df_uploaded == store_df
```

```
Out[172]:        id  manager   rev  visits
          0    True     True  True    True
          1    True     True  True    True
          2    True     True  True    True
          3    True     True  True    True
          4    True     True  True    True
```

Note that pd.read_csv() accepts not only file paths, but also URLs. So if your are importing data that are hosted publicly, you can import it directly.

Working in a cloud-based runtime does add an extra step or two, but it also offers advantages, such as simplicity of getting started and the convenience of always having access to your notebooks from any device.

2.7   Clean Up!

Python keeps everything in memory by default, and when you exit all variables will be lost. Variables can be saved as pickles, either individually or wrapped in a dictionary, e.g. pickle.dump({'var1': var1, 'var2': var2,...}, f).

Particularly in exploratory analysis, the workspace will become crowded. which can lead to subtle and irreproducible bugs in your analyses, when you believe an object has one value but in reality it has been kept around with some other, forgotten value.

Individual variables can be removed using the `del` command:

```
In [173]: del store_df_uploaded, store_df
```

Or the entire workspace can be cleared by restarting the kernel (if using a notebook) or quitting Python (using `quit()` from the CLI).

If you find yourself struggling with a weird bug, it's often a good idea to restart the environment. And before "finalizing" an analysis, be sure to restart your kernel and run it from end-to-end.

2.8 Learning More*

In this chapter, we have described enough of the Python language to get you started for the applications in this book. Later chapters include additional instruction on the language as needed for their problems, often presented as separate *Language Brief* sections.

If you wish to delve more deeply into the language itself, the book recommendations and interactive courses linked from the python.org Beginner's guide https://wiki.python.org/moin/BeginnersGuide might be very helpful.

For data-science-focused introductions (McKinney 2018), is a great resource written by the creator of pandas.

2.9 Key Points

Most of the present chapter is foundational to Python, yet there are a few especially important points:

- There are multiple environments for running Python: CLI, IDE, scripts, and notebooks. We recommend giving notebooks a try, but the most important thing is to find an environment that works well for you (Sect. 2.1)
- Indexing collections is very powerful in Python, particularly in NumPy. Slices can be indexed using colon notation, e.g. `list[2:5]`, and NumPy arrays and pandas dataframes can be indexed using index arrays and boolean masks as well (Sects. 2.4.4, 2.5.1, and 2.5.3)
- Writing functions to improve reproducibility and reliability of your code is standard practice in Python (Sect. 2.4.9)
- A lot of Python functionality lies in packages, which can be installed using pip (Sect. 2.4.9)
- NumPy and pandas introduce critical data science functionality to Python in the form of NumPy arrays and pandas dataframes, along with methods and functions to manipulate and analyze them (Sects. 2.5.1 and 2.5.3)
- Missing values must be dealt with explicitly. NumPy includes the `np.nan` constant for this purpose (Sect. 2.5.4)
- Helpful docstrings can be accessed using the `help()` function (Sect. 2.4.11)
- Python objects can be saved as pickle files. pandas offers functions to read and write dataframes from and to pickle files (Sect. 2.6.1)
- Data can also be easily imported and exported as CSVs (Sect. 2.6.2)
- Clean up your workspace regularly to avoid clutter and bugs from obsolete variables (Sect. 2.7)

Part II
Fundamentals of Data Analysis

Chapter 3
Describing Data

In this chapter, we tackle our first marketing analytics problem: exploring a new dataset. The goals for this chapter are to learn how to:

- Simulate a dataset
- Summarize and explore a dataset with descriptive statistics (mean, standard deviation, and so forth)
- Explore simple visualization methods

Such investigation is the simplest analysis one can do yet also the most crucial. It is important to describe and explore any dataset before moving on to more complex analysis. This chapter will build your Python skills and provide a set of tools for exploring your own data.

3.1 Simulating Data

We start by creating data to be analyzed in later parts of the chapter. Why simulate data and not work entirely with real datasets? There are several reasons. The process of creating data lets us practice and deepen Python skills from Chap. 2. It makes the book less dependent on vagaries of finding and downloading online datasets. And it lets you manipulate the synthetic data, run analyses again, and examine how the results change.

Perhaps most importantly, data simulation highlights a strength of Python: because it is easy to simulate data, Python analysts often use simulated data to prove that their methods are working as expected. When we know what the data *should* say (because we created it), we can test our analyses to make sure they are working correctly before applying them to real data. If you have real datasets that you work with regularly, we encourage you to use those for the same analyses alongside our simulated data examples. (See Sect. 2.6.2 for more information on how to load data files.)

We encourage you to create data in this section step by step because we teach Python along the way. However, if you are in a hurry to learn how to compute means, standard deviations and other summary statistics, you could quickly run the commands in this section to generate the simulated data. Alternatively, the following command will load the data from the book's web site, and you can then go to Sect. 3.2:

```
In [0]: import pandas as pd
        store_sales = pd.read_csv('http://bit.ly/PMR-ch3')
```

But if you're new to Python data analysis, don't do that! Instead, work through the following section to create the data from scratch. If you accidentally ran the command above, you can use `del store_sales` to remove the data before proceeding.

3.1.1 Store Data: Setting the Structure

Our first dataset represents observations of total sales by week for two competing products at a chain of stores. We begin by creating a data structure that will hold the data, a simulation of sales for the two products in 20 stores over 2 years, with price

© Springer Nature Switzerland AG 2020

J. S. Schwarz et al., *Python for Marketing Research and Analytics*, https://doi.org/10.1007/978-3-030-49720-0_3

and promotion status. We remove most of the Python output here to focus on the input commands. Type the following lines, but feel free to omit the comments (following "#"):

```
In [0]:  # import numpy and pandas
         import pandas as pd
         import numpy as np

         # Constants
         N_STORES = 20
         N_WEEKS = 104

         # create a dataframe of initially missing values to hold the data
         columns = ('store_num', 'year', 'week', 'p1_sales', 'p2_sales',
                    'p1_price', 'p2_price', 'p1_promo', 'p2_promo', 'country')
         n_rows = N_STORES * N_WEEKS
         store_sales = pd.DataFrame(np.empty(shape=(n_rows, 10)),
                                    columns=columns)
```

Here we first set a few constants, the number of stores and the number of weeks of data for each store. We then import the NumPy and pandas libraries, which we will use extensively throughout this book, and create the empty dataframe. We could also have generated all the columns first and then put them together into a dataframe at the end, as we did in 2.5.3.

We see the simplest summary of the dataframe by looking at the shape parameter:

```
In [1]: store_sales.shape

Out[1]: (2080, 10)
```

As expected, store_sales has 2080 rows and 10 columns.

We can use head() to inspect store_sales:

```
In [2]: store_sales.head()

Out[2]:    store_num  year  week  p1_sales  p2_sales  p1_price  p2_price  \
        0        0.0   0.0   0.0       0.0       0.0       0.0       0.0
        1        0.0   0.0   0.0       0.0       0.0       0.0       0.0
        2        0.0   0.0   0.0       0.0       0.0       0.0       0.0
        3        0.0   0.0   0.0       0.0       0.0       0.0       0.0
        4        0.0   0.0   0.0       0.0       0.0       0.0       0.0

           p1_promo  p2_promo  country
        0       0.0       0.0      0.0
        1       0.0       0.0      0.0
        2       0.0       0.0      0.0
        3       0.0       0.0      0.0
        4       0.0       0.0      0.0
```

As expected, it is empty; all values are set to zero.

First, we will create a set of store "numbers" or "ids," which will serve to identify each store:

```
In [3]: store_numbers = range(101, 101 + N_STORES)
        list(store_numbers)

Out[3]: [101,
         102,
         103,
         104,
         105,
         106,
         107,
         108,
```

```
        109,
        110,
        111,
        112,
        113,
        114,
        115,
        116,
        117,
        118,
        119,
        120]
```

We used `range` to create store numbers ranging from 101 to 120. Note that we cast the `Range` object to a `list` in order to print it out. See Sect. 2.4.4 for an overview of Range objects.

Next, we assign each store a country:

```
In [4]: store_country = dict(zip(store_numbers,
                          ['USA', 'USA', 'USA', 'DEU', 'DEU', 'DEU',
                           'DEU', 'DEU', 'GBR', 'GBR', 'GBR', 'BRA',
                           'BRA', 'JPN', 'JPN', 'JPN', 'JPN', 'AUS',
                           'CHN', 'CHN']))
        store_country

Out[4]: {101: 'USA',
         102: 'USA',
         103: 'USA',
         104: 'DEU',
         105: 'DEU',
         106: 'DEU',
         107: 'DEU',
         108: 'DEU',
         109: 'GBR',
         110: 'GBR',
         111: 'GBR',
         112: 'BRA',
         113: 'BRA',
         114: 'JPN',
         115: 'JPN',
         116: 'JPN',
         117: 'JPN',
         118: 'AUS',
         119: 'CHN',
         120: 'CHN'}
```

Here we created a dictionary that maps from store number to the country of that store. We used `zip()`, introduced in Sect. 2.4.10 to combine the store number with a list of countries. We passed that zip object to `dict` to create the `store_country` mapping.

Now we will start filling in the `store_sales` dataframe:

```
In [5]: i = 0
        for store_num in store_numbers:
          for year in [1, 2]:
            for week in range(1, 53):
              store_sales.loc[i, 'store_num'] = store_num
              store_sales.loc[i, 'year'] = year
              store_sales.loc[i, 'week'] = week
```

```
        store_sales.loc[i, 'country'] = store_country[store_num]
        i += 1
```

What did we do here? For every store, we went through both years and every week and set the store number, year, week, and country. We used a set of nested `for` loops to do this. We used `i` to track the row count, incrementing it each time we set the values for a single row. The operator `+=` may be new to you. It *increments* a variable by the amount given; in this case it adds 1 to `i` and stores the result back into `i`. This is a shorter, more readable way to write `i = i + 1`.

We can check the overall data structure with `head()`:

```
In [6]: store_sales.head()

Out[6]:      store_num   year   week   p1_sales   p2_sales   p1_price   p2_price  \
          0      101.0    1.0    1.0        0.0        0.0        0.0        0.0
          1      101.0    1.0    2.0        0.0        0.0        0.0        0.0
          2      101.0    1.0    3.0        0.0        0.0        0.0        0.0
          3      101.0    1.0    4.0        0.0        0.0        0.0        0.0
          4      101.0    1.0    5.0        0.0        0.0        0.0        0.0

             p1_promo   p2_promo  country
          0       0.0        0.0      USA
          1       0.0        0.0      USA
          2       0.0        0.0      USA
          3       0.0        0.0      USA
          4       0.0        0.0      USA
```

All of the specific measures (sales, price, promotion) are shown as missing values (indicated by zeros) because we haven't assigned other values to them yet, while the store numbers, year counters, week counters and country assignments look good.

We can check the `type` of each column in the `dtypes` attribute:

```
In [7]: store_sales.dtypes

Out[7]: store_num    float64
        year         float64
        week         float64
        p1_sales     float64
        p2_sales     float64
        p1_price     float64
        p2_price     float64
        p1_promo     float64
        p2_promo     float64
        country       object
        dtype: object
```

The types for all of the variables in our dataframe were dictated by the input data. For example, the values assigned to `store_sales.country` were of type `str` and pandas by default stores strings as `object` type:

```
In [8]: type(store_sales.country[0])

Out[8]: str
```

However, country labels are actually discrete values and not just arbitrary text. So it is better to represent country explicitly as a categorical variable. Similarly, `store_num` is a label, not a number as such. By converting those variables to categorical types, they will be treated as a categorical in subsequent analyses such as regression models. It is good practice to set variable types correctly as they are created; this will help you to avoid errors later.

We redefine `store_sales.store_num` and `store_sales.country` as categorical using the `astype()` method:

```
In [9]: store_sales.country = store_sales.country.astype(
            pd.CategoricalDtype())
        store_sales.store_num = store_sales.store_num.astype(
```

```
            pd.CategoricalDtype())
        print(store_sales.store_num.head())
        print(store_sales.country.head())
```

```
0    101.0
1    101.0
2    101.0
3    101.0
4    101.0
Name: store_num, dtype: category
Categories (20, float64): [101.0, 102.0, 103.0, ..., 118.0, 119.0, 120.0]
0    USA
1    USA
2    USA
3    USA
4    USA
Name: country, dtype: category
Categories (7, object): [AUS, BRA, CHN, DEU, GBR, JPN, USA]
```

```
In [10]: store_sales.dtypes
```

```
Out[10]: store_num    category
         year         float64
         week         float64
         p1_sales     float64
         p2_sales     float64
         p1_price     float64
         p2_price     float64
         p1_promo     float64
         p2_promo     float64
         country      category
         dtype: object
```

store_num and country are now defined as categories with 20 and 7 levels, respectively.

It is a good idea to inspect dataframes in the first and last rows because mistakes often surface there. You can use head() and tail() commands to inspect the beginning and end of the dataframe and sample() to inspect a random sample (we omit long output from the these commands):

```
In [11]: # Not shown
        store_sales.head(60) # 60 rows can be displayed without truncation;
        store_sales.tail(60) # make sure end looks OK too;
        store_sales.sample(60) # inspecting a random sample is also helpful;
```

It's always useful to debug small steps like this as you go.

3.1.2 Store Data: Simulating Data Points

We complete store_sales with random data for *store-by-week* observations of the sales, price, and promotional status (e.g. advertisement, endcap display, etc.) of these two competing products.

Before simulating random data, it is important to set the random number generation *seed* to make the process replicable. After setting a seed, when you draw random samples in the same sequence again, you get exactly the same (*pseudo-*)random numbers. Pseudorandom number generators (PRNGs) are a complex topic whose issues are out of scope here. If you are using PRNGs for something important you should review the literature; it has been said that whole shelves of journals could be thrown away due to poor usage of random numbers. A starting point to learn more about PRNGs is Knuth (1997).

If you don't set a PRNG seed, numpy.random will select one for you, but you will get different random numbers each time you repeat the process. If you set the seed and execute commands in the order shown in this book, you will get the results that we show.

```
In [12]: np.random.seed(37204)
```

Now we can draw the random data. For each store in each week, we want to randomly determine whether each product was promoted or not. We can do this by drawing from the *binomial distribution*: this counts the number of "heads" in a collection of coin tosses. The coin can be "weighted", meaning it can have any proportion of heads, not just 50%.

To detail that process: we use the `np.random.binomial(n, p, size)` function to draw from the binomial distribution. For every row of the store data, as noted by `size=n_rows`, we draw from a distribution representing the number of heads in a single coin toss (`n=1`) with a coin that has probability `p=0.1` for product 1 and `p=0.15` for product 2.

We will use this distribution to represent promotional status. In other words, we randomly assign 10% likelihood of promotion for product 1, and 15% likelihood for product 2.

```
In [13]: # 10% promoted
         store_sales.p1_promo = np.random.binomial(n=1, p=0.1, size=n_rows)
         # 15% promoted
         store_sales.p2_promo = np.random.binomial(n=1, p=0.15, size=n_rows)
         store_sales.head(10) # how does it look so far? (not shown)
```

We can look at the count of promotions for product 1 to confirm that the values are realistic:

```
In [14]: store_sales.p1_promo.value_counts()

Out[14]: 0    1871
         1     209
         Name: p1_prom, dtype: int64
```

Next we set a price for each product in each row of the data. We suppose that each product is sold at one of five distinct price points ranging from $2.19 to $3.19 overall. We randomly draw a price for each week by defining a vector with the five price points and using `np.random.choice(a, size, replace)` to draw from it as many times as we have rows of data (`size=n_rows`). The five prices are sampled many times, so we sample with replacement (`replace=True`, which is the default so we don't write it):

```
In [15]: store_sales.p1_price = np.random.choice([2.19, 2.29, 2.49, 2.79,
                                                   2.99],
                                                  size=n_rows)
         store_sales.p2_price = np.random.choice([2.29, 2.49, 2.59, 2.99,
                                                   3.19],
                                                  size=n_rows)
         store_sales.sample(5) # now how does it look?
```

```
Out[15]:       store_num  year  week     p1_sales        p2_sales  p1_price  \
         61         101.0   2.0  10.0  0.000000e+00    0.000000e+00      2.49
         1259       113.0   1.0  12.0  0.000000e+00    0.000000e+00      2.79
         1784       118.0   1.0  17.0  3.326077e-316   3.326077e-316     2.79
         20         101.0   1.0  21.0  0.000000e+00    0.000000e+00      2.49
         1815       118.0   1.0  48.0  3.326128e-316   3.326128e-316     2.79

               p2_price  p1_promo  p2_promo  country
         61         2.49         0         0      USA
         1259       2.29         0         0      BRA
         1784       2.49         0         0      AUS
         20         3.19         1         0      USA
         1815       2.99         0         0      AUS
```

We can see that all columns appear correct, except for the sales columns, which we have yet to set. Note that depending on your environment, some of the unset values may not be zero, but rather very small numbers such as 3.326128e–316 (which is $3.32 * 10^{-316}$, or effectively zero). That is because these values are uninitialized and may show *floating point error* (tiny variations due to how the infinite range of real numbers is stored in the finite space allocated to a variable in memory). If you are running this in Colab, these values will display as zeroes.

Question: if *price* occurs at five discrete levels, does that make it a categorical variable? That depends on the analytic question, but in general probably not. We often perform math on price, such as subtracting cost in order to find gross margin, multiplying by units to find total sales, and so forth. Thus, even though it may have only a few unique values, price is a number, not a factor.

Our last step is to simulate the sales figures for each week. We calculate sales as a function of the relative prices of the two products along with the promotional status of each.

Item sales are in unit counts, so we use the Poisson distribution to generate count data: `np.random.poisson(lam, size)`, where `size` is the number of draws and `lam` represents *lambda*, the defining parameter of the Poisson distribution. Lambda represents the *expected*, or mean, value of units per week.

We draw a random Poisson count for each row (`size=n_rows`), and set the mean sales (`lam`) of Product 1 to be higher than that of Product 2:

```
In [16]:  # sales data, using poisson (counts) distribution, np.random.poisson()
          # first, the default sales in the absence of promotion
          sales_p1 = np.random.poisson(lam=120, size=n_rows)
          sales_p2 = np.random.poisson(lam=100, size=n_rows)
```

Now we scale those counts up or down according to the relative prices. Price effects often follow a logarithmic function rather than a linear function (Rao 2009), so we use `np.log(price)` here:

```
In [17]:  # scale sales according to the ratio of log(price)
          log_p1_price = np.log(store_sales.p1_price)
          log_p2_price = np.log(store_sales.p2_price)


          sales_p1 = sales_p1 * log_p2_price/log_p1_price
          sales_p2 = sales_p2 * log_p1_price/log_p2_price
```

We have assumed that sales vary as the *inverse* ratio of prices. That is, sales of Product 1 go up to the degree that the `log(price)` of Product 1 is lower than the `log(price)` of Product 2.

Finally, we assume that sales get a 30 or 40% lift when each product is promoted in store. We simply multiply the promotional status vector (which comprises all {0, 1} values) by 0.3 or 0.4 respectively, and then multiply the sales vector by that. We use the `floor()` function to drop fractional values and ensure integer counts for weekly unit sales, and put those values into the dataframe:

```
In [18]:  # final sales get a 30% or 40% lift when promoted
          store_sales.p1_sales = np.floor(sales_p1 *
                                          (1 + store_sales.p1_promo * 0.3))
          store_sales.p2_sales = np.floor(sales_p2 *
                                          (1 + store_sales.p2_promo * 0.4))
          store_sales.sample(10)
```

Out [18]:		store_num	year	week	p1_sales	p2_sales	p1_price	p2_price	\
	2001	120.0	1.0	26.0	187.0	79.0	2.29	3.19	
	1076	111.0	1.0	37.0	114.0	111.0	2.79	2.49	
	...								
	233	103.0	1.0	26.0	195.0	66.0	2.19	2.99	
	1990	120.0	1.0	15.0	146.0	98.0	2.79	2.99	

		p1_promo	p2_promo	country
	2001	0	0	CHN
	1076	0	0	GBR
	...			
	233	0	0	USA
	1990	0	0	CHN

Inspecting the dataframe, we see that the data look plausible on the surface. Note that we truncated the response, as indicated by the "...."

Thanks to the power of Python, we have created a simulated dataset with 20800 values (2080 rows × 10 columns) using a total of 29 assignment commands. In the next section we explore the data that we created.

3.2 Functions to Summarize a Variable

Observations may comprise either *discrete* data that occurs at specific levels or *continuous* data with many possible values. We look at each type in turn. But first, let's consider an important tool for aggregation: the `groupby()` method.

3.2.1 Language Brief: groupby()

What should we do if we want to break out data by factors and summarize it, a process you might know as "cross-tabs" or "pivot tables"? For example, how can we compute the mean sales by store? We have voluminous data (every store by every week by each product) but many marketing purposes only need an aggregate figure such as a total or mean. We will see how to summarize by a factor within the data itself using the `groupby()` command.

`groupby()` is a method on pandas dataframes. The by argument specifies the column by which to group, for example `store_num`:

```
In [19]: store_sales.groupby('store_num')

Out[19]: <pandas.core.groupby.SeriesGroupBy object at 0x7f98df746668>
```

That function returns a `SeriesGroupBy` object, which can be saved to a variable or acted upon directly. That object contains each other column within the dataframe, which can be accessed via dot notation. Pandas analytical methods can then be applied to that group, such as `mean()`, `sum()`, etc. Also, `apply()` can be used, allowing any function to be used on the grouping. We can easily calculate the per-store mean:

```
In [20]: store_sales.groupby('store_num').p1_sales.mean()

Out[20]: store_num
         101.0    133.500000
         102.0    138.807692
         103.0    132.682692
         ...
         Name: p1_sales, dtype: float64
```

To group it by more than one factor, use a list of factors. For instance, we can obtain the mean of `p1_sales` by store and by year:

```
In [21]: store_sales.groupby(['store_num', 'year']).p1_sales.mean()

Out[21]: store_num    year
         101.0        1.0        132.538462
                      2.0        134.461538
         102.0        1.0        139.692308
                      2.0        137.923077
         103.0        1.0        130.557692
                      2.0        134.807692
         ...
         Name: p1_sales, dtype: float64
```

A limitation of `groupby()` is that the result is not always easy to read and not structured for reuse. How can we save the results as data to use for other purposes such as plotting?

For a single-level grouping, the output can be cast into a dataframe with the `pandas.DataFrame()` function. But for multi-level groupings, one option is to use the `unstack()` method which pivots the indices and returns a nicely formatted dataframe. "Pivoting" means what had been a set of outputs that look like rows become columns in the new dataframe:

```
In [22]: store_sales.groupby(['store_num', 'year']).p1_sales.mean().unstack()
```

```
Out[22]: year                  1.0          2.0
         store_num
         101.0           132.538462   134.461538
         102.0           139.692308   137.923077
         103.0           130.557692   134.807692
         ...
```

Another example is computing the total (`sum()`) sales of P1 by country:

```
In [23]: p1_sales_by_country = store_sales.groupby(['country']).p1_sales.sum()
         p1_sales_by_country
```

```
Out[23]: country
         AUS     13980.0
         BRA     27857.0
         CHN     27642.0
         DEU     70323.0
         GBR     41915.0
         JPN     54817.0
         USA     42119.0
         Name: p1_sales, dtype: float64
```

We saved the result to `p1_sales_by_country` because we will use it in Sect. 3.4.5 to make a map. `groupby()` is the primary tool for aggregation of data that we will use throughout the book.

3.2.2 Discrete Variables

A basic way to describe discrete data is with frequency counts. The `value_counts()` method will count the observed prevalence of each value that occurs in a variable (i.e., a vector or a column in a dataframe). In `store_sales`, we may count how many times product 1 was observed to be on sale at each price point:

```
In [25]: store_sales.p1_price.value_counts()
```

```
Out[25]: 2.29     420
         2.19     417
         2.49     416
         2.99     415
         2.79     412
         Name: p1_price, dtype: int64
```

Note, `value_counts()` by default sorts by the descending count. If `sort=False` is passed as an argument, it will not be sorted. Another useful argument is `normalize=True`, which will return proportions rather than counts.

If your counts vary, that may be due to running commands in a different order or setting a different random number seed. The counts shown here assume that the commands have been run in the exact sequence shown in this chapter. There is no problem if your data are modestly different; just remember that it won't match the output here, or try Sect. 3.1.1 again.

One of the most useful features of Python is that most functions produce an object that you can store and use for further commands. So, for example, if you want to store the table that was created by `value_counts()`, you can just assign the same command to a named object:

```
In [26]: p1_table_0 = store_sales.p1_price.value_counts()
         p1_table_0
```

```
Out[26]:  2.29      420
          2.19      417
          2.49      416
          2.99      415
          2.79      412
          Name: p1_price, dtype: int64

In [27]: type(p1_table_0)

Out[27]: pandas.core.series.Series
```

The `type()` command shows us that the object produced by `value_counts()` is a pandas series, as introduced in 2.5.3, which is the pandas *vector* type. A pandas dataframe is composed of an indexed set of series.

We can use the `plot()` method on `p1_table0` to produce a quick plot:

```
In [28]: p1_table_0.plot.bar()
```

You can see from the resulting bar plot in Fig. 3.1 that the product was on sale at each price point roughly the same number of times. However, it is fairly ugly and the labels could be clearer. Later in this chapter we show how to modify a plot to get better results.

An analyst might want to know how often each product was promoted at each price point. The `pandas.crosstab()` function produces counts of observations at each level for two variables, i.e. a two-way *cross tab*:

```
In [29]: pd.crosstab(store_sales.p1_promo, store_sales.p1_price)

Out[29]: p1_price    2.19    2.29    2.49    2.79    2.99
         p1_promo
         0           371     380     378     371     371
         1            46      40      38      41      44
```

However, as discussed in Sect. 3.2.1 a more general approach is using the `groupby()` method:

```
In [30]: store_sales.groupby('p1_promo').p1_price.value_counts().unstack()

Out[30]: p1_price    2.19    2.29    2.49    2.79    2.99
         p1_promo
         0           371     380     378     371     371
         1            46      40      38      41      44
```

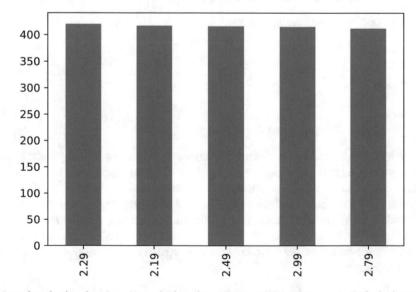

Fig. 3.1 A simple bar plot produced using the `plot()` method on the series containing sales counts. Default charts are sometimes unattractive, but there are many options to make them more attractive and useful

Again, the `unstack()` command is not crucial, but pivots the multi-index series returned by the `groupby()` into a dataframe, which offers a more intuitive display of the data and simplifies downstream analysis.

`groupby()` allows calculation of not just counts, but other functions as well, such as the arithmetic mean. Additionally, the data can be grouped by an arbitrary set of columns. For example, we can calculate the mean price by product, promotion status, and country:

```
In [31]: store_sales.groupby(['p1_promo', 'country']).p1_price.mean().unstack()
Out[31]: country        AUS        BRA        CHN        DEU        GBR        \
         p1_promo
         0          2.515843   2.554398   2.543093   2.553956   2.570212
         1          2.550000   2.454706   2.647143   2.530000   2.586552


         country        JPN        USA
         p1_promo
         0          2.544521   2.533463
         1          2.570000   2.538276
```

Returning to the initial cross tab, at each price level Product 1 is observed to have been promoted approximately 10% of the time (as expected, given how we created the data in Sect. 3.1.1). In fact, we can compute the exact fraction of times product 1 is on promotion at each price point if we assign the result to a variable and then divide it by the total sales by price in `p1_table_0`:

```
In [32]: p1_table_1 = store_sales.groupby('p1_promo').p1_price.value_counts()
         p1_table_1 = p1_table_1.unstack()
         p1_table_1.div(p1_table_0)
Out[32]:               2.19       2.29       2.49       2.79       2.99
         p1_promo
         0          0.889688   0.904762   0.908654   0.900485   0.893976
         1          0.110312   0.095238   0.091346   0.099515   0.106024
```

The `div()` method applies element-wise division between the series of counts in `p1_table_0` and each row of `p1_table_1` (each of which is a series). Pandas uses the series indices, in this case the price, to match the division.

By combining operating results in this way, you can produce exactly the results you want along with code that can repeat the analysis on demand. This is very helpful to marketing analysts who produce weekly or monthly reports for sales, web traffic, and similar data.

3.2.3 Continuous Variables

Counts are useful when we have a small number of categories, but with continuous data it is more helpful to summarize the data in terms of its distribution. The most common way to do that is with mathematical functions that describe the range of the data, its center, the degree to which it is concentrated or dispersed, and specific points that may be of interest (such as the 90th percentile). Table 3.1 lists some pandas functions to calculate statistics for numeric vector data, such as numeric columns in a dataframe.

Table 3.1 Distribution functions that operate on a numeric vector

Describe	Function	Value
Extremes	`min(x)`	Minimum value
	`max(x)`	Maximum value
Central tendency	`mean(x)`	Arithmetic mean
	`median(x)`	Median
Dispersion	`var(x)`	Variance around the mean
	`std(x)`	Standard deviation (`sqrt(var(x))`)
	`mad(x)`	Median absolute deviation (a robust variance estimator)
Points	`quantile(x, q=[...])`	Percentiles

Following are examples of those common functions:

```
In [33]: store_sales.p2_sales.min()

Out[33]: 51.0

In [34]: store_sales.p1_sales.max()

Out[34]: 265.0

In [35]: store_sales.p1_promo.mean()

Out[35]: 0.10048076923076923

In [36]: store_sales.p2_sales.median()

Out[36]: 96.0

In [37]: store_sales.p1_sales.var()

Out[37]: 861.7204626392133

In [38]: store_sales.p1_sales.std()

Out[38]: 29.355075585649807

In [39]: store_sales.p1_sales.mad()

Out[39]: 23.253990384615314

In [40]: store_sales.p1_sales.quantile(q=[0.25, 0.5, 0.75])

Out[40]: 0.25     113.0
         0.50     130.0
         0.75     151.0
         Name: p1_sales, dtype: float64
```

In the case of quantile() we have asked for the 25th, 50th, and 75th percentiles using the argument q=[0.25, 0.5, 0.75], which are also known as the *median* (50th percentile, same as the median() function) and the edges of the *interquartile range*, the 25th and 75th percentiles.

Change the q= argument in quantile() to find other quantiles:

```
In [41]: store_sales.p1_sales.quantile(q=[0.05, 0.95])

Out[41]: 0.05      93.0
         0.95     187.0
         Name: p1_sales, dtype: float64

In [42]: store_sales.p1_sales.quantile(q=np.arange(0, 1.1, 0.1))

Out[42]: 0.0       68.0
         0.1      100.0
         0.2      109.0
         0.3      116.0
         0.4      123.0
         0.5      130.0
         0.6      138.0
         0.7      146.0
         0.8      158.0
         0.9      174.0
         1.0      265.0
         Name: p1_sales, dtype: float64
```

The second example here shows that we may use sequences in many places in Python; in this case, we find every 10th percentile by creating a sequence using `numpy.arange(start, stop, step)` to yield the vector `0, 0.1, 0.2 ... 1.0`. Note that `numpy.arange()` is used here rather than the built-in `range()` function since we want decimal values; `range()` only supports integer values. Note also that `numpy.arange()` follows the Python iteration convention (see 2.4.4 that the `start` argument is *inclusive* whereas the `stop` argument is *exclusive*, so to include `1.0` in the vector, we must set the `stop` argument to be equal to the maximum value we desire plus the step (`1.1` in this case).

For skewed and asymmetric distributions that are common in marketing, such as unit sales or household income, the arithmetic `mean()` and standard deviation `std()` may be misleading; in those cases, the `median()` and interquartile range (IQR, the range of the middle 50% of data) are often more useful to summarize a distribution. Pandas does not have a built-in IQR function, but we can create one and apply it to our data:

```
In [43]: def iqr(x):
             return x.quantile(0.75) - x.quantile(0.25)
         iqr(store_sales.p1_sales)
```

```
Out[43]: 38.0
```

Notice that when we use the `iqr()` function that we wrote, the syntax is `iqr(store_sales.p1_sales)`. For a built-in method associated with the `DataFrame` class like `mean()`, the syntax is `store_sales.p1_sales.mean()`.

Suppose we wanted a summary of the sales for product 1 and product 2 based on their median and interquartile range. We might assemble these summary statistics into a dataframe that is easier to read than the one-line-at-a-time output above. We create a dataframe to hold our summary statistics and then populate it using functions from 3.1. We name the columns and rows, and fill in the cells with function values:

```
In [44]: pd.DataFrame([[store_sales.p1_sales.median(),
                  store_sales.p2_sales.median()],
                 [iqr(store_sales.p1_sales),
                  iqr(store_sales.p2_sales)]],
                index=['Median sales', 'IQR'],
                columns=['p1_sales', 'p2_sales'])
```

```
Out[44]:               p1_sales  p2_sales
         Median sales    130.0      96.0
         IQR              38.0      33.0
```

With this custom summary we see that median sales are higher for product 1 (130 versus 96) and that the variation in sales of product 1 (the IQR across observations by week) is also higher. Once we have this code, we can run it again the next time we have new sales data to produce a revised version of our table of summary statistics. Such code might be a good candidate for a custom function you can reuse (see Sects. 2.4.8 and 10.3.1). We'll see a shorter way to create this summary in Sect. 3.3.3.

3.3 Summarizing Dataframes

As useful as functions such as `mean()` and `quantile()` are, it is tedious to apply them one at a time to columns of a large dataframe, as we did with the summary table above. Pandas provides a variety of ways to summarize dataframes without writing extensive code. We describe two approaches: the basic `describe()` command and the Pandas approach to iterating over variables with `apply()`.

3.3.1 *describe()*

As we saw in Sect. 2.5.3, `describe()` is a good way to do a preliminary inspection of a dataframe or other object. When you use `describe()` on a dataframe, it reports a few descriptive statistics for every variable:

```
In [45]: store_sales.describe()
Out[45]:             year        week     p1_sales      p2_sales  \
         count  2080.00000  2080.00000  2080.000000   2080.000000
         mean      1.50000    26.50000   133.967788     99.911058
         std       0.50012    15.01194    29.355076     24.453788
         min       1.00000     1.00000    68.000000     51.000000
         25%       1.00000    13.75000   113.000000     82.000000
         50%       1.50000    26.50000   130.000000     96.000000
         75%       2.00000    39.25000   151.000000    115.000000
         max       2.00000    52.00000   265.000000    210.000000

                   p1_price      p2_price      p1_promo      p2_promo
         count  2080.000000   2080.000000   2080.000000   2080.000000
         mean      2.548654      2.716106      0.100481      0.145673
         std       0.300716      0.333559      0.300712      0.352863
         min       2.190000      2.290000      0.000000      0.000000
         25%       2.290000      2.490000      0.000000      0.000000
         50%       2.490000      2.590000      0.000000      0.000000
         75%       2.790000      2.990000      0.000000      0.000000
         max       2.990000      3.190000      1.000000      1.000000
```

describe() works similarly for single vectors:

```
In [46]: store_sales.p1_price.describe()
Out[46]: count    2080.000000
         mean        2.548654
         std         0.300716
         min         2.190000
         25%         2.290000
         50%         2.490000
         75%         2.790000
         max         2.990000
         Name: p1_price, dtype: float64
```

Perhaps the most important use for describe() is this: *after importing data, use* describe() *to do a quick quality check.* Check the min and max for outliers or miskeyed data, and check to see that the mean and 50% (median) are reasonable and similar to one another (if you expect them to be similar, of course). This simple inspection often turns up errors in the data!

3.3.2 Recommended Approach to Inspecting Data

We can now recommend a general approach to inspecting a dataset after compiling or importing it; replace "my_data" and "DATA" with the names of your objects:

1. Import your data with pandas.read_csv() or another appropriate function and check that the importation process gives no errors.
2. Convert it to a dataframe if needed (my_data=pd.DataFrame(DATA)) and set column names (my_data.columns = [...]) if needed.
3. Examine shape to check that the dataframe has the expected number of rows and columns.
4. Use head() and tail() to check the first few and last few rows; make sure that header rows at the beginning and blank rows at the end were not included accidentally. Also check that no good rows were skipped at the beginning.
5. Use sample() to examine a few sets of random rows.
6. Check the dataframe structure with dtypes to ensure that variable types are appropriate. Change the type of variables— especially to categorical types—as necessary.
7. Run describe() and look for unexpected values, especially min, max, count that are unexpected.

3.3.3 `apply()` *

As we've seen, it is very useful to employ operations on each column of a dataframe, such as finding the mean on all numeric columns (columns 3–8):

```
In [47]: store_sales.iloc[:, 3:9].mean()

Out[47]: p1_sales    133.967788
         p2_sales     99.911058
         p1_price      2.548654
         p2_price      2.716106
         p1_promo      0.100481
         p2_promo      0.145673
         dtype: float64
```

We can also use the `axis` argument to run the function across rows rather than columns (the default is columns: `axis=0`):

```
In [48]: store_sales.iloc[:, 3:9].mean(axis=1).head()

Out[48]: 0    39.830000
         1    40.780000
         2    42.363333
         3    37.663333
         4    43.846667
         dtype: float64
```

That isn't very useful in this dataset, but can certainly be invaluable.

But what if we want to make a calculation that isn't a default pandas dataframe method, like our `iqr()` function? Let's try the syntax we've been using:

```
In [49]: store_sales.iloc[:, 3:9].iqr()


         ----------------------------------------------------------------

         AttributeError                          Traceback (most recent call last)

         <ipython-input-46-1ff1629f4f16> in <module>()
    ----> 1 store_sales.iloc[:, 3:9].iqr()
         ...
         AttributeError: 'DataFrame' object has no attribute 'iqr'
```

We get an AttributeError because we were trying to use `iqr()` as a method, which is effectively an attribute on the dataframe object that acts as a function on itself (see 2.4.8 for more information). But `iqr()` is a function that we defined. How do we apply that to the dataframe columns?

An advanced and powerful tool in pandas is the `apply()` method. `apply(function, axis, ...)` runs any function that you specify on each of the rows (when `axis=1`) and/or columns (the default, or when `axis=0`) of a dataframe. This allows any function to be applied to all columns or rows of the dataframe:

```
In [50]: store_sales.iloc[:, 3:9].apply(iqr)

Out[50]: p1_sales    38.0
         p2_sales    33.0
         p1_price     0.5
         p2_price     0.5
         p1_promo     0.0
         p2_promo     0.0
         dtype: float64
```

```
In [51]: store_sales.iloc[:, 3:9].apply(iqr, axis=1).head()

Out[51]: 0       81.750
         1       59.425
         2       60.200
         3       76.500
         4       84.775
         dtype: float64
```

What if we want to know something more complex? We can define an ad hoc *anonymous function*, known in Python as a *lambda* function. Imagine that we are checking data and wish to know the difference between the mean and median of each variable, perhaps to flag skew in the data. Lambda function to the rescue! We can `apply()` that calculation to multiple columns using an lambda function:

```
In [52]: store_sales.iloc[:, 3:9].apply(lambda x: x.mean() - x.median())

Out[52]: p1_sales    3.967788
         p2_sales    3.911058
         p1_price    0.058654
         p2_price    0.126106
         p1_promo    0.100481
         p2_promo    0.145673
         dtype: float64
```

This analysis shows that the mean of `p1_sales` and the mean of `p2_sales` are larger than the median by about three sales per week, which suggests there is a right-hand tail to the distribution. That is, there are some weeks with very high sales that pull the mean up. (Note that we only use this to illustrate an anonymous function; there are better, more specialized tests of skew, such as the `skew()` method.)

Experienced programmers: your first instinct, based on experience with procedural programming languages, might be to solve the preceding problem with a `for()` loop that iterates the calculation across columns. That is possible in Python, of course, but less efficient and less Pythonic in this case. Instead, try to think in terms of functions that are applied across data as we do here.

`apply()` also works on series objects, where the function is applied element-wise rather than to the series as a whole:

```
In [53]: store_sales.p1_sales.apply(lambda x: 'high' if x > 130 else 'low')[:5]

Out[53]: 0       low
         1       high
         2       high
         3       low
         4       low
         Name: p1_sales, dtype: object
```

All of these functions, including `apply()` and `describe()` return values that can be assigned to an object. For example, using `apply`, we can produce our customized summary dataframe from Sect. 3.2.3 more efficiently:

```
In [54]: pd.DataFrame([store_sales[['p1_sales', 'p2_sales']].median(),
                       store_sales[['p1_sales', 'p2_sales']].apply(iqr)],
                      index=['Median sales', 'IQR'])

Out[54]:                 p1_sales  p2_sales
         Median sales      130.0      96.0
         IQR                38.0      33.0
```

If there were many products instead of just two, the code would still work if we changed the number of allocated rows, and `apply()` would run automatically across all of them.

Now that we know how to summarize data with statistics, it is time to visualize it.

3.4 Single Variable Visualization

The standard plotting library in Python is matplotlib. In concert with NumPy (Sect. 2.5.1), it produces a MATLAB-like plotting interface and is a dependency of most other plotting libraries (such as seaborn). There are many other plotting libraries to explore beyond matplotlib, such as seaborn, ggplot, Bokeh, Altair, and many other.

Pandas dataframes and series can be plotted using matplotlib-based methods. Here we examine histograms, density plots, and box plots, and take an initial look at more complex graphics including maps. Later chapters build on these foundational plots and introduce more that are available in other packages.

A quick note about plotting in Python. If you are using a Colab or Jupyter notebook, the plot will be shown inline (for Jupyter, the magic `%matplotlib inline` is required; for Colab this is default behavior). If you are using the Python command line interface (CLI) or running it as a script, the command `matplotlib.pyplot.show()` must follow the plot for it to appear (by convention, matplotlib.pyplot is imported as plt, in which case the command is `plt.show()`). Throughout this book, we omit `plt.show()`, but be sure to add it if you are not using a notebook interface.

3.4.1 Histograms

A fundamental plot for a single continuous variable is the *histogram*. Such a plot can be produced using the `hist()` method on a series (i.e. a column):

```
In [55]: store_sales.p1_sales.hist()
```

The result is shown in Fig. 3.2. It is not a bad start. We see that the weekly sales for product 1 range from a little less than 100 to a bit more than 250. But there are no axis labels present!

That plot was easy to make but the visual elements are less than pleasing, so we will improve it. For future charts, we will show either the basic chart or the final one, and will not demonstrate the successive steps to build one up. However, we go through the intermediate steps here so you can see the process of how to evolve a graphic in Python.

As you work through these steps, there are four things you should understand about graphics in Python:

- Python graphics are produced through commands that often seem tedious and require trial and iteration.
- Notebooks with inline plotting enabled are very convenient for developing figures, as they allow for rapid iteration.
- Despite the difficulties, Python graphics can be very high quality, portable in format, and even beautiful.
- Once you have code for a useful graphic, you can reuse it with new data. It is often helpful to tinker with previous plotting code when building a new plot, rather than recreating it.

Our first improvement to Fig. 3.2 is to change the title and axis labels. We do that by importing matplotlib.pyplot and using several functions:

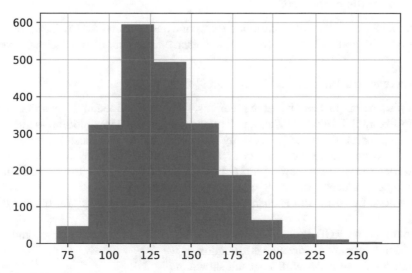

Fig. 3.2 A basic histogram using `hist()`

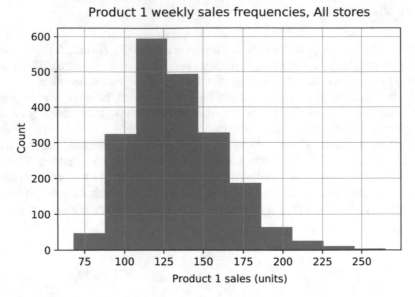

Fig. 3.3 The same histogram, with improved labels

```
plt.title('...')    : sets the main title
plt.xlabel('...')   : sets the x-axis label
plt.ylabel('...')   : sets the y-axis label
```

We add the title and axis labels to our plot command:

```
In [56]: import matplotlib.pyplot as plt
         store_sales.p1_sales.hist()
         plt.title('Product 1 weekly sales frequencies, All stores')
         plt.xlabel('Product 1 sales (units)')
         plt.ylabel('Count')
```

The result is shown in Fig. 3.3 and is improved but not perfect; it would be nice to have more granularity (more bars) in the histogram. While we're at it, let's tweak the appearance by removing the background as well as coloring and adding borders to the bars. Here are a few additional arguments we can use with the `hist()` method:

```
bins=NUM    : call for NUM bars in the result
facecolor="..."    : color the bars
edgecolor="..."    : color the bar borders
```

And the function `plt.box(False)` removes the plot background and `plt.grid(False)` removes the grid.

Additionally, the font is a bit small. We can set the font in the `rcParams` module, which will persist throughout the rest of the notebook:

```
In [57]: plt.rcParams.update({'font.size': 12})
```

There are many different parameters that can be set in rcParams, which are defined in the matplotlibrc file. A sample file can be found at https://matplotlib.org/3.1.1/tutorials/introductory/customizing.html#matplotlibrc-sample.

When specifying colors, matplotlib knows many by name, including the most common ones in English ("red", "blue", "green", etc.) and less common (such as "coral" and "papayawhip"). Many of these can be modified by adding the prefix "light" or "dark" (thus "lightgray", "darkred", and so forth). For a list of built-in color names, run the `matplotlib.colors.get_named_colors_mapping()` command.

For a set of common colors, there are single character representations, such as "k" for black, "r" for red, "g" for green, etc.

Colors can also be specified as RGB tuples, RGBA tuples, hex RGB or RGBA strings, and other ways. See https://matplotlib.org/tutorials/colors/colors.html for more information.

We add these modifications to our code, with the result shown in Fig. 3.4:

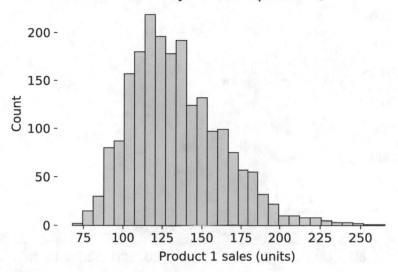

Fig. 3.4 The histogram after adjusting color and dividing the counts into a larger number of bins

```
In [58]: store_sales.p1_sales.hist(bins=30,
                                    edgecolor='k',
                                    facecolor='lightblue')
         plt.title('Product 1 weekly sales frequencies, All stores')
         plt.xlabel('Product 1 sales (units)')
         plt.ylabel('Count')
         plt.grid(False)
         plt.box(False)
```

Comparing Fig. 3.4 with 3.3 we notice a new problem: the y-axis value for the height of the bars changes according to count. The count depends on the number of bins and on the sample size. We can make it absolute by using *relative frequencies* (technically, the *density* estimate) instead of counts for each point. This makes the y-axis comparable across different sized samples.

Figure 3.4 has reasonable x-axis tick marks, but imagine we want more or fewer. Instead of using the default *tick marks* (axis numbers) for hist(), we can specify the x-axis number explicitly. The argument for relative frequency is density=True and the x-axis numbers are specified using the plt.xticks() function:

```
In [59]: store_sales.p1_sales.hist(bins=30,
                                    edgecolor='k',
                                    facecolor='lightblue',
                                    density=True)
         plt.title('Product 1 weekly sales frequencies, All stores')
         plt.xlabel('Product 1 sales (units)')
         plt.ylabel('Relative frequency')
         plt.xticks(range(60, 300, 20))
         plt.grid(False)
         plt.box(False)
```

With plt.xticks(), we have to tell it where to put the labels, which may be made with the range() function to generate a sequence of numbers. We could also specify a label to appear at each of those points rather than a number (see Fig. 3.9). The updated histogram is shown in Fig. 3.5. It is looking good now!

Finally, we add a smoothed estimation line. To do this, we use the density() plotting method on the p1_sales series. The density plot disrupted the axis autoscaling, so we also use plt.xlim() to specify the x-axis range.

```
In [60]: store_sales.p1_sales.hist(bins=30,
                                    edgecolor='k',
                                    facecolor='lightblue',
```

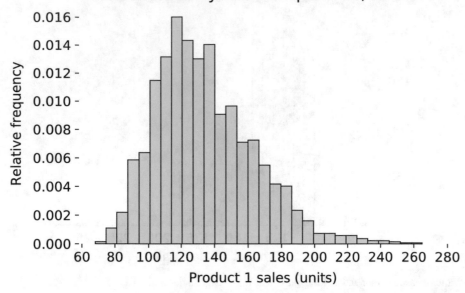

Fig. 3.5 Histogram with relative frequencies (density estimates) and improved axis tick mark labels

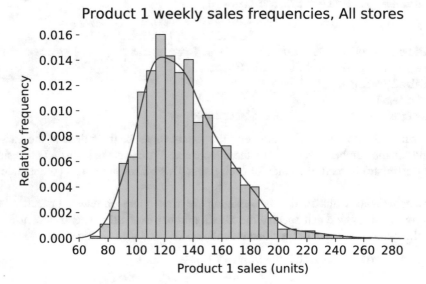

Fig. 3.6 Final histogram with density curve

```
                         density=True)
store_sales.p1_sales.plot.density(color='red')
plt.title('Product 1 weekly sales frequencies, All stores')
plt.xlabel('Product 1 sales (units)')
plt.ylabel('Relative frequency')
plt.xticks(range(60, 300, 20))
plt.xlim((60, 290))
plt.box(False)
```

Figure 3.6 is now very informative. Even someone who is unfamiliar with the data can see that this plot describes weekly sales for product 1 and that the typical sales range from about 80 to 200.

The process we have shown to produce this graphic is representative of how analysts use Python for visualization. You start with a default plot, change some of the options, and use functions like `plt.title()` and `density()` to alter features of the plot with complete control. Although at first this will seem cumbersome compared to the drag-and-drop methods of other visualization tools, it really isn't much more time consuming if you use a code editor and become familiar with the plotting functions' examples and help files. It has the great advantage that once you've written the code, you can reuse it with different data.

Exercise Modify the code to create the same histogram for product 2. It requires only minor change to the code whereas with a drag-and-drop tool, you would start all over. If you produce a plot often, you could even write it as a custom function.

3.4.2 Boxplots

Boxplots are a compact way to represent a distribution. The pandas `box()` method is straightforward; we add labels, use the argument `vert=False` to rotate the plot 90° to look better, and use `sym='k.'` to specify the outlier marker:

```
In [61]: p = store_sales.p2_sales.plot.box(vert=False, sym='k.')
         plt.title('Weekly sales of P2, All stores')
         plt.xlabel('Weekly sales')
         p.set_facecolor('w')
```

Figure 3.7 shows the resulting graphic. The boxplot presents the distribution more compactly than a histogram. The median is the center line while the 25th and 75th percentiles define the *box*. The outer lines are *whiskers* at the points of the most extreme values that are no more than 1.5 times the width of the box away from the box. Points beyond the whiskers are outliers drawn as individual points. This is also known as a *Tukey boxplot* (after the statistician, Tukey) or as a *box-and-whiskers* plot.

Boxplots are even more useful when you compare distributions by some other factor. How do different stores compare on sales of product 2? The `boxplot()` method makes it easy to compare these with the `by` argument, which specifies the column by which to group. The `column` argument indicates the column represented by the boxplot distribution, `p2_sales` in this case. These correspond to the response variable `p2_sales` which we plot with regards to the explanatory variable `store_num`:

```
In [62]: store_sales.boxplot(column='p2_sales', by='store_num', vert=False,
                             sym='k.')
         plt.suptitle('')
         plt.title('Weekly sales of p2 by store')
         plt.xlabel('Weekly unit sales')
         plt.ylabel('Store')
         plt.box(False)
```

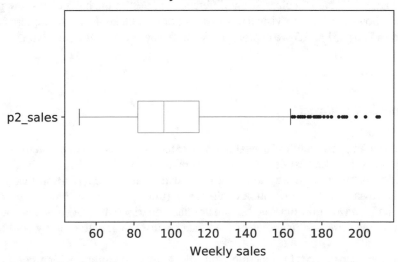

Fig. 3.7 A simple example of `boxplot()`

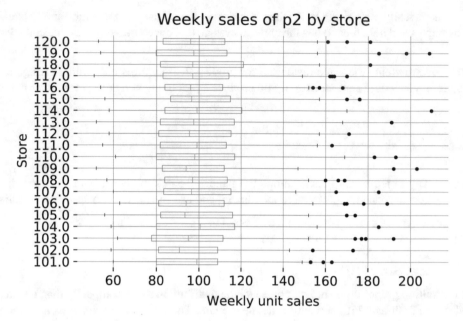

Fig. 3.8 boxplot() of sales by store

The result is Fig. 3.8, where stores are roughly similar in sales of product 2 (this is not a statistical test of difference, just a visualization). Note that plt.suptitle() removes the default title that the boxplot() method adds, as we'd prefer to specify a more informative title.

We see in Fig. 3.8 that the stores are similar in unit sales of P2, but do P2 sales differ in relation to in-store *promotion*? In this case, our explanatory variable would be the promotion variable for P2, so we use boxplot() now replacing store_num with the promotion variable p2_promo.

```
In [63]: store_sales.boxplot(column='p2_sales', by='p2_promo', vert=False,
                             sym='k.')
         plt.suptitle('')
         plt.title('Weekly sales of p2 with and without promotion')
         plt.xlabel('Weekly unit sales')
         plt.ylabel('P2 promo in store?')
         plt.yticks([1, 2], ['No', 'Yes'])
         plt.box(False)
```

The result is shown in Fig. 3.9. There is a clear visual difference in sales on the basis of in-store promotion!

To wrap up: boxplots are powerful tools to visualize a distribution and make it easy to explore how an outcome variable is related to another factor. In Chaps. 4 and 5 we explore many more ways to examine data association and statistical tests of relationships.

3.4.3 QQ Plot to Check Normality*

This is an optional section on a graphical method to evaluate a distribution more formally. You may wish to skip to Sect. 3.4.4 on cumulative distributions or Sect. 3.4.5 that describes how to create maps in Python.

Quantile-quantile (QQ) plots are a good way to check one's data against a distribution that you think it should come from. Some common statistics such as the correlation coefficient r (to be precise, the *Pearson product-moment correlation coefficient*) are interpreted under an assumption that data are normally distributed. A QQ plot can confirm that the distribution is, in fact, normal by plotting the *observed* quantiles of your data against the quantiles that would be *expected* for a normal distribution.

To do this, we can use the probplot() function from the scipy.stats library, which compares data vs. a specified distribution, for example the normal distribution. We check p1_sales to see whether it is normally distributed:

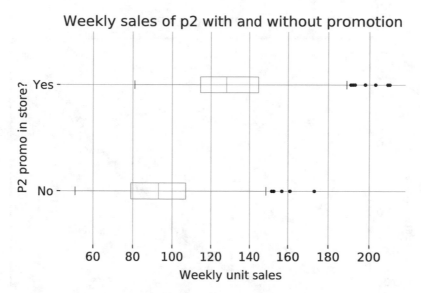

Fig. 3.9 Boxplot of product sales by promotion status

```
In [64]: from scipy import stats
         plt.figure(figsize=(7,7))
         stats.probplot(store_sales.p1_sales, dist='norm', plot=plt)
```

The QQ plot is shown in Fig. 3.10. The distribution of p1_sales is far from the line at the ends, suggesting that the data are not normally distributed. The upward curving shape is typical of data with high positive skew.

What should you do in this case? If you are using models or statistical functions that assume normally distributed data, you might wish to transform your data. As we've already noted, a common pattern in marketing data is a logarithmic distribution. We examine whether p1_sales is more approximately normal after a log() transform:

```
In [65]: plt.figure(figsize=(7,7))
         stats.probplot(np.log(store_sales.p1_sales), dist='norm', plot=plt)
```

The QQ plot for log(p1_sales) is shown in Fig. 3.11. The points are much closer to the solid line, indicating that the distribution of log(store_sales.p1_sales) is more approximately normal than the untransformed variable.

We recommend that you use scipy.stats.probplot() regularly to test assumptions about your data distribution. Web search will reveal further examples of common patterns that appear in QQ plots and how to interpret them.

3.4.4 Cumulative Distribution*

This is another optional section, but one that can be quite useful. If you wish to skip ahead to cover just the fundamentals, you should continue with Sect. 3.4.5.

Another useful univariate plot involves the impressively named *empirical cumulative distribution function* (ECDF). It is less complex than it sounds and is simply a plot that shows the cumulative proportion of data values in your sample. This is an easy way to inspect a distribution and to read off percentile values.

We plot the ECDF of p1_sales by combining a few steps. We can use the ECDF() function from the statsmodels library to find the ECDF of the data. Then we put the results into plot(), adding options such as titles.

Suppose we also want to know the value for which 90% of weekly sales of P1 will be lower than that value, i.e., the 90th percentile for weekly sales of P1. We can use plot() to add vertical and horizontal lines at the 90th percentile. We do not have to specify the exact value at which to draw a line for the 90th percentile; instead we use quantile(, pr=0.9) to find it. The 'k-' positional argument indicates that we want the lines to be black and dashed and the alpha=0.5 sets the transparency level of the lines to 50%:

```
In [66]: from statsmodels.distributions.empirical_distribution import ECDF
         e = ECDF(store_sales.p1_sales)
```

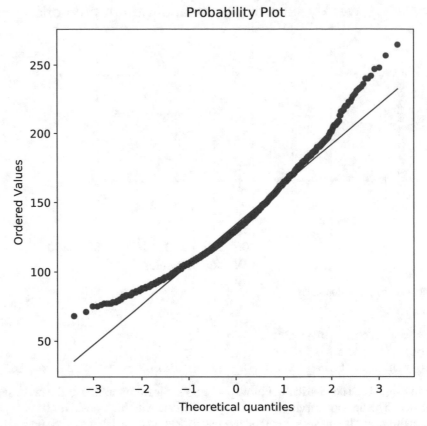

Fig. 3.10 QQ plot to check distribution. The tails of the distribution bow away from the line that represents an exact normal distribution, showing that the distribution of `p1_sales` is skewed

```
plt.subplot(2,1,1)
plt.plot(e.x, e.y)
plt.title('Cumulative distribution of p1 weekly sales')
plt.ylabel('Cumulative proportion')
plt.plot([60, 270], [0.9, 0.9], 'k--', alpha=0.5)
plt.plot([store_sales.p1_sales.quantile(.9),
         store_sales.p1_sales.quantile(.9)],
        [0, 1], 'k--', alpha=0.5)
plt.box(False)
```

We can see the resulting plot in Fig. 3.12.

ECDF() calculation is fairly simple. We can replicate the plot through a manual calculation (figure not shown):

```
In [67]: ecdf_x = store_sales.p1_sales.sort_values()
         ecdf_y = np.arange(0, 1, 1/len(store_sales.p1_sales))
         plt.subplot(2,1,2)
         plt.plot(ecdf_x, ecdf_y)
         plt.xlabel('P1 weekly sales, all stores')
         plt.ylabel('Cumulative proportion')
         plt.plot([60, 270], [0.9, 0.9], 'k--', alpha=0.5)
         plt.plot([store_sales.p1_sales.quantile(.9),
                  store_sales.p1_sales.quantile(.9)],
                 [0, 1], 'k--', alpha=0.5)
         plt.box(False)
```

If you run the code block above, you will get a plot just like that Fig. 3.12.

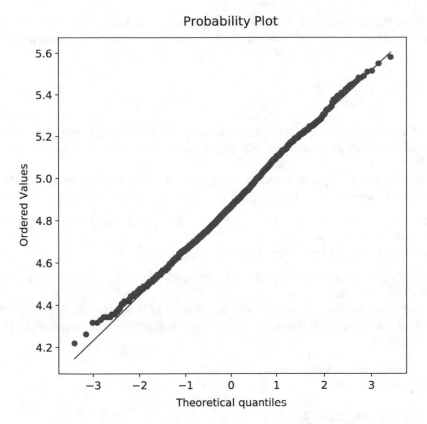

Fig. 3.11 QQ plot for the data after `log()` transformation. The sales figures are now much better aligned with the solid line that represents an exact normal distribution

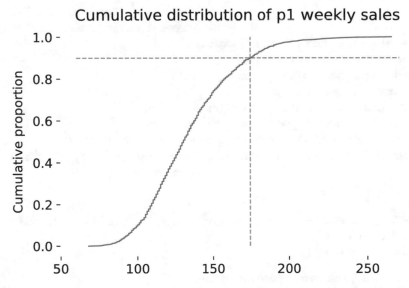

Fig. 3.12 Cumulative distribution plot with lines to emphasize the 90th percentile. The chart identifies that 90% of weekly sales are lower than or equal to 171 units. Other values are easy to read off the chart. For instance, in roughly 10% of weeks fewer than 100 units are sold, and in the upper 5% more than 200 units are sold

We often use cumulative distribution plots both for data exploration and for presenting data to others. They are a good way to highlight data features such as discontinuities in the data, long tails, and specific points of interest.

3.4.5 Maps

We often need to plot marketing data on a map. A common variety is a *choropleth* map, which uses graphics or color to indicate values of a variable such as income or sales. We consider how to do this for a world map using the `cartopy` library (Met Office 2010–2015).

`cartopy` is not a standard numerical Python library, so we may need to install it (see Sect. 2.4.9. In Colab, we can do this using the `!` operator to access the shell, allowing installation of the package with `pip` (output not shown):

```
In [68]: !apt-get -qq install python-cartopy python3-cartopy
         !pip uninstall -y shapely
         !pip install shapely --no-binary shapely
```

Here is a routine example. Suppose that we want to chart the total sales by country. We use `aggregate()` as in Sect. 3.2.1 to find the total sales of P1 by country:

We can then use cartopy functions to overlay sales data on a map. Note that this requires code more advanced than we've seen up to this point. We're not going to go through it in detail, but include it as a demonstration of the power of Python to analyze and visualize complex data.

```
In [69]: from cartopy.io import shapereader
         from cartopy import crs

         plt.figure(figsize=(16,6))
         ax = plt.axes(projection=crs.PlateCarree())

         shpfile = shapereader.natural_earth(resolution='110m',
                                             category='cultural',
                                             name='admin_0_countries')
         reader = shapereader.Reader(shpfile)
         countries = reader.records()
         max_sales = p1_sales_by_country.max()
         for country in countries:
           country_name = country.attributes['ADM0_A3']
           if country_name in p1_sales_by_country:
             ax.add_geometries(country.geometry, crs.PlateCarree(),
               facecolor=plt.cm.Greens(p1_sales_by_country[country_name]
                                       /max_sales),
               edgecolor='k')
           else:
             ax.add_geometries(country.geometry, crs.PlateCarree(),
               facecolor='w',
               edgecolor='k')
```

The result is shown in Fig. 3.13, known as a *choropleth* chart.

Although such maps are popular, they can be misleading. In *The Wall Street Journal Guide to Information Graphics*, Wong explains that choropleth charts are problematic because they confuse geographic area with scaled quantities (Wong (2013), p. 90). For instance, in Fig. 3.13, China is more prominent than Japan not because it has a higher value but because it is larger in size. We acknowledge the need for caution despite the popularity of such maps.

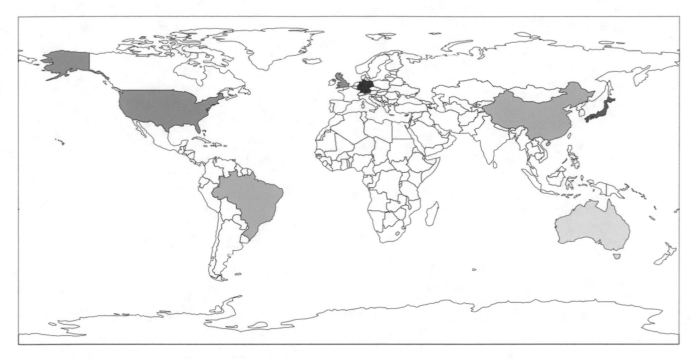

Fig. 3.13 World map for P1 sales by country, using `cartopy`

3.5 Learning More*

Plotting We demonstrate plotting in Python throughout this book. Python has multiple, often disjoint solutions for plotting and in this text we use plots as appropriate without going deeply into their details. The *base* plotting system is `matplotlib.pyplot`, which is leveraged by most other plotting libraries and is integrated into pandas.

Wong's *The Wall Street Journal Guide to Information Graphics* (Wong 2013) presents fundamentals of good style for effective graphics in any business context (not specific to Python).

Maps Producing maps in Python is an especially complex topic. Maps require three essential components: *shape files* that define the borders of areas (such as country or city boundaries); *spatial translation* of one's data (for instance, a database to match Zip codes in your data to the relevant areas on a map); and *plotting software* to perform the actual plotting. Python libraries such as `cartopy` usually provide access to all three of those elements.

3.6 Key Points

The following guidelines and pointers will help you to describe data accurately and quickly:

- Consider simulating data before collecting it, in order to test your assumptions and develop initial analysis code (Sect. 3.1).
- Always check your data for proper structure and data quality using `dtypes`, `head()`, `describe()`, and other basic inspection commands (Sect. 3.3.2).
- Describe discrete (categorical) data with `value_counts()` (Sect. 3.2.2) and inspect continuous data with `describe()` (Sect. 3.3).
- Histograms (Sect. 3.4.1) and boxplots (Sect. 3.4.2) are good for initial data visualization.
- Use `groupby()` to break out your data by grouping variables (Sect. 3.2.1).
- Advanced visualization methods include cumulative distribution (Sect. 3.4.4), normality checks (Sect. 3.4.3), and mapping (Sect. 3.4.5).

Chapter 4
Relationships Between Continuous Variables

Experienced analysts understand that the most important insights in marketing analysis often come from understanding relationships between variables. While it is helpful to understand single variables, such as how many products are sold at a store, more valuable insight emerges when we understand relationships such as "Customers who live closer to our store visit more often than those who live farther away," or "Customers of our online shop buy as much in person at the retail shop as do customers who do not purchase online."

Identifying these kinds of relationships helps marketers understand how to reach customers more effectively. For example, if people who live closer to a store visit more frequently and buy more, then an obvious strategy would be to send advertisements to people who live in the area.

In this chapter we focus on understanding the relationships between pairs of variables in multivariate data, and examine how to visualize the relationships and compute statistics that describe their associations (correlation coefficients). These are the most important ways to assess relationships between continuous variables. While it might seem appealing to go straight into building regression models (see Chap. 7), we caution against that. The first step in any analysis is to explore the data and their basic properties. This chapter continues the data exploration and visualization process that we reviewed for single variables in Chap. 3. It often saves time and heartache to begin by examining the relationships among pairs of variables before building more complex models.

4.1 Retailer Data

We simulate a dataset that describes customers of a multi-channel retailer and their transactions for 1 year. These data include a subset of customers for whom we have survey data on product satisfaction.

As in Chap. 3, we present the code that generates these data as a way to teach more about Python syntax. However, if you prefer to jump right into the analysis, you could quickly run all the commands in Sect. 4.1.1 and then continue with Sect. 4.2 where we begin plotting the data.

Alternatively, the following will load the data from this book's website, after which you may continue with Sect. 4.2:

```
In [2]: import pandas as pd
        cust_df = pd.read_csv('http://bit.ly/PMR-ch4')
```

However, you will learn more about Python if you work through the simulation code instead of downloading the data.

4.1.1 Simulating the Data

In this section, we create a dataset for 1000 customers of a multi-channel retailer that sells products in stores and online. These data are typical of what one might sample from a company's customer relationship management (CRM) system. We begin by setting a random number seed to make the process repeatable (as described in Sect. 3.1.2) and creating a dataframe to store the data:

© Springer Nature Switzerland AG 2020

J. S. Schwarz et al., *Python for Marketing Research and Analytics*, https://doi.org/10.1007/978-3-030-49720-0_4

```
In [3]:  # Import numpy and pandas
         import pandas as pd
         import numpy as np

         n_cust = 1000

         np.random.seed(21821)

         cust_df = pd.DataFrame({'cust_id': pd.Categorical(range(n_cust))})
```

We declare a variable n_cust for the number of customers in the synthetic dataset and use that variable wherever we need to refer to the number of customers. This is a good practice, as it allows you to change n_cust in just one place in your code and then re-run the code to generate a new dataset with a different number of customers.

Next we create a number of variables describing the customers, add those variables to the cust_df dataframe, and inspect them with describe():

```
In [4]:  cust_df['age'] = np.random.normal(loc=35, scale=5, size=n_cust)
         cust_df['credit_score'] = np.random.normal(loc=3 * cust_df.age + 620,
                                                     scale=50,
                                                     size=n_cust)
         cust_df['email'] = pd.Categorical(np.random.choice(a=['yes', 'no'],
                                                            p=[0.8, 0.2],
                                                            size=n_cust))
         cust_df['distance_to_store'] = np.exp(np.random.normal(loc=2,
                                                                scale=1.2,
                                                                size=n_cust))
```

```
In [5]:  cust_df.describe(include='all')
```

```
Out[5]:           cust_id          age   credit_score  email  distance_to_store
         count      1000.0  1000.000000    1000.000000   1000        1000.000000
         unique     1000.0          NaN            NaN      2                NaN
         top         999.0          NaN            NaN    yes                NaN
         freq          1.0          NaN            NaN    807                NaN
         mean          NaN    34.933972     725.224636    NaN          15.765725
         ...
         max           NaN    50.523265     872.288340    NaN         352.723643
```

We add new variables to cust_df dataframe using simple assignment (=) to a name with ['COLUMN_NAME'] notation. Columns in dataframes can be easily created or replaced in this way, as long as the vector you assign to the new column has the appropriate length. Note that this is slightly different from how we simulate our data in Sect. 3.1.1: there is often more than one way to do the same thing in Python. As you become more experienced you will settle on your preferred approach.

The customers' ages in years (age) are drawn from a normal distribution with mean 35 and standard deviation 5 using numpy.random.normal(loc, scale, size). Credit scores (credit_score) are also simulated with a normal distribution, but in that case we specify that the mean of the distribution is related to the customer's age, with older customers having higher credit scores on average. We create a variable (email) indicating whether the customer has an email on file, using the numpy.random.choice() function that was covered in Chap. 3.

Our final variable for the basic CRM data is distance_to_store, in miles, which we assume follows the exponential of the normal distribution. That gives distances that are all positive, with many distances that are relatively close to the nearest store and fewer that are far from a store. To see the distribution for yourself, try cust_df.distance_to_store.hist(). Formally, we say that distance_to_store follows a *lognormal* distribution. (This is sufficiently common that there is a built-in function called numpy.random.lognormal(mean, sigma, size) that does the same thing as taking the exponential of numpy.random.normal().)

4.1.2 Simulating Online and In-store Sales Data

Our next step is to create data for the online store: 1 year totals for each customer for online visits and transactions, plus total spending. We simulate the number of visits with a *negative binomial* distribution, a discrete distribution often used to model counts of events over time. Like the lognormal distribution, the negative binomial distribution generates positive values and has a long right-hand tail, meaning that in our data most customers make relatively few visits and a few customers make many visits. Data from the negative binomial distribution can be generated using `numpy.random.negative_binomial(n, p, size)`:

```
In [6]: mu = 15 + ((cust_df.email == 'yes') * 15 -
                    0.7 * (cust_df.age - cust_df.age.median()))
        n = 0.3
        prob = n / (n + mu)
        cust_df['online_visits'] = np.random.negative_binomial(n=0.3,
                                                               p=prob,
                                                               size=n_cust)
```

The negative binomial takes *n* and *p* as shape parameters, where *n* is the target number of successes, sometimes referred to as the *dispersion parameter* as it sets the degree of dispersion in the samples, and *p* is the probability of a single success. An alternative parameterization using the mean is more intuitive: `p = n / (n + mean)`. We model the mean (`mu`) of the negative binomial with a baseline value of 15. We add an average 15 online visits for customers who have an email on file (`(cust_df.email == 'yes') * 15`). Finally, we add or subtract visits from the target mean based on the customer's age relative to the sample median; customers who are younger are simulated to make more online visits. We then calculate `prob` using `mu` and `n`. To see exactly how this works, try running pieces of the code above in Python.

For each online visit that a customer makes, we assume there is a 30% chance of placing an order and use `numpy.random.binomial()` to create the variable `online_trans`. We assume that amounts spent in those orders (the variable `online_spend`) are lognormally distributed:

```
In [7]: cust_df['online_trans'] = np.random.binomial(n=cust_df.online_visits,
                                                      p=0.3,
                                                      size=n_cust)
        cust_df['online_spend'] = (np.exp(np.random.normal(loc=3,
                                                           scale=0.1,
                                                           size=n_cust))
                                   * cust_df.online_trans)
```

The random value for amount spent per transaction—sampled with `numpy.exp(numpy.random.normal())` is multiplied by the variable for number of transactions to get the total amount spent. Note the use of parentheses outside of the entire expression; this allows the partial expression "`* cust_df.online_trans`" to appear on the successive line while staying within our per-line character limit (Sect. 2.3.1).

Next we generate in-store sales data similarly, except that we don't generate a count of store visits; most customers who visit a physical store make a purchase and even if customers did visit without buying, the company probably couldn't track the visit. We assume that transactions follow a negative binomial distribution, with lower average numbers of visits for customers who live farther away. We model in-store spending as a lognormally distributed variable simply multiplied by the number of transactions:

```
In [8]: mu = 3 / np.sqrt(cust_df.distance_to_store)
        n = 5
        prob = n / (n + mu)
        cust_df['store_trans'] = np.random.negative_binomial(n=n,
                                                             p=prob,
                                                             size=n_cust)
        cust_df['store_spend'] = (np.exp(np.random.normal(loc=3.5,
                                                         scale=0.4,
                                                         size=n_cust))
                                  * cust_df.store_trans)
```

As always, we check the data along the way:

```
In [9]: cust_df.describe()

Out[9]:                    age   credit_score   distance_to_store   online_visits  \
        count   1000.000000   1000.000000          1000.000000      1000.000000
        mean      34.933972    725.224636            15.765725        29.693000
        std        5.070098     50.152653            26.808774        58.749198
        min       16.413932    561.349990             0.082841         0.000000
        ...


                online_trans   online_spend   store_trans   store_spend
        count    1000.000000    1000.000000   1000.000000   1000.000000
        mean        8.906000     179.999631      1.274000     44.729630
        std        17.693451     363.217007      1.694637     62.723694
        min         0.000000       0.000000      0.000000      0.000000
        ...
```

4.1.3   Simulating Satisfaction Survey Responses

It is common to for retailers to survey their customers and record responses in the CRM system. Our last simulation step is to create survey data for a subset of the customers.

To simulate survey responses, we assume that each customer has an unobserved overall satisfaction with the brand. We generate this overall satisfaction from a normal distribution:

```
In [10]: sat_overall = pd.Series(np.random.normal(loc=3.1,
                                                   scale=0.7,
                                                   size=n_cust))

         sat_overall.describe()

Out[10]: count    1000.000000
         mean        3.119406
         std         0.775489
         min         1.079336
         25%         2.589930
         50%         3.138375
         75%         3.638397
         max         5.098524
         dtype: float64
```

We assume that overall satisfaction is a psychological construct that is not directly observable. Instead, the survey collects information on two items: satisfaction with service, and satisfaction with the selection of products. We assume that customers' responses to the survey items are based on unobserved levels of satisfaction *overall* (sometimes called the "halo" in survey response) plus the specific levels of satisfaction with the service and product selection.

To create such a score from a halo variable, we add `sat_overall` (the halo) to a random value specific to the item, drawn using `numpy.random.normal()`. Because survey responses are typically given on a discrete, ordinal scale (i.e., "very unsatisfied", "unsatisfied", etc.), we convert our continuous random values to discrete integers using the `numpy.floor()` function.

```
In [11]: sat_service = np.floor(sat_overall + np.random.normal(loc=0.5,
                                                               scale=0.4,
                                                               size=n_cust))

         sat_selection = np.floor(sat_overall + np.random.normal(loc=-0.2,
                                                                 scale=0.6,
                                                                 size=n_cust))

         sat_service.describe()
```

```
Out[11]:  count     1000.000000
          mean         3.113000
          std          1.113315
          min          0.000000
          ...
          max          6.000000
          dtype: float64
```

The summary shows that our data now range from 0 to 6. However, a typical satisfaction item might be given on a 5-point scale. To fit that, we replace values that are greater than 5 with 5, and values that are less than 1 with 1. This enforces the *floor* and *ceiling* effects often noted in survey response literature.

We set the ceiling by indexing with a vector that tests whether each element of sat_service is greater than 5: sat_service[sat_service > 5]. This might be read as "sat_service, where sat_service is greater than 5." For the elements that are selected—which means that the expression evaluates as True—we replace the current values with the ceiling value of 5. We do the same for the floor effects (< 1, replacing with 1) and likewise for the ceiling and floor of sat_selection. While this sounds quite complicated, the code is simple:

```
In [12]:  sat_service[sat_service > 5] = 5
          sat_service[sat_service < 1] = 1
          sat_selection[sat_selection > 5] = 5
          sat_selection[sat_selection < 1] = 1
          sat_service.describe()
```

```
Out[12]:  count     1000.000000
          mean         3.106000
          std          1.065786
          min          1.000000
          ...
          max          5.000000
          dtype: float64
```

Using this type of syntax to replace values in a vector or matrix is common in pandas, and we recommend that you try out some variations (being careful not to overwrite the cust_df data, of course). Note that we could also use numpy.clip() to achieve the same ends.

4.1.4 Simulating Non-response Data

Because some customers do not respond to surveys, we eliminate the simulated answers for a subset of respondents who are modeled as not answering. We do this by creating a series of True and False values called no_response and then assigning a value of numpy.nan for the survey response for customers whose no_response is True. As we have discussed, numpy.nan is the numpy constant for missing data.

We model non-response as a function of age, with higher likelihood of not responding to the survey for older customers:

```
In [13]:  no_response = np.random.binomial(n=1,
                                           p=cust_df.age/100,
                                           size=n_cust).astype(bool)
          sat_service[no_response] = np.nan
          sat_selection[no_response] = np.nan
          sat_service.describe()
```

```
Out[13]:  count      612.000000
          mean         3.068627
          std          1.065082
          min          1.000000
          25%          2.000000
          50%          3.000000
```

```
         75%       4.000000
         max       5.000000
         dtype: float64
```

In `describe()`, now counts only 612 responses, recognizing the 388 customers with NaN values and excludes them from the statistics.

Finally, we add the survey responses to `cust_df`:

```
In [14]: cust_df['sat_service']   = sat_service
         cust_df['sat_selection'] = sat_selection
         cust_df.describe()
```

```
Out[14]:                age    credit_score   distance_to_store   online_visits  \
         count   1000.000000    1000.000000         1000.000000     1000.000000
         mean      34.933972     725.224636           15.765725       29.693000
         ...
         max       50.523265     872.288340          352.723643      626.000000

                online_trans   online_spend   store_trans   store_spend   sat_service  \
         count   1000.000000    1000.000000   1000.000000   1000.000000    612.000000
         mean       8.906000     179.999631      1.274000     44.729630      3.068627
         ...
         max      187.000000    3646.052599     19.000000    547.976139      5.000000

                sat_selection
         count     612.000000
         mean        2.442810
         ...
         max         5.000000
```

The dataset is now complete and ready for analysis.

4.2 Exploring Associations between Variables with Scatterplots

Our analysis begins by checking the dataframe with `head()` and `dtypes` to review its structure, as described in Sect. 3.3:

```
In [15]: cust_df.head()
```

```
Out[15]:   cust_id         age    credit_score  email   distance_to_store   online_visits  \
         0        0   46.719825      735.837331    yes            9.186310               0
         1        1   39.283359      656.599440    yes            0.781894              46
         2        2   33.574168      665.934422    yes            1.204119              64
         3        3   43.564256      718.456166    yes            9.736359              29
         4        4   31.358552      626.323897    yes           33.782715               0

            online_trans   online_spend   store_trans   store_spend   sat_service  \
         0             0       0.000000             1     33.603505           NaN
         1            18     352.735573             0      0.000000           2.0
         2            21     355.833505             6    162.685187           4.0
         3            11     186.594784             1     51.327653           2.0
         4             0       0.000000             0      0.000000           NaN

            sat_selection
         0            NaN
         1            2.0
         2            4.0
         3            3.0
         4            NaN
```

```
In [16]: cust_df.dtypes

Out[16]: cust_id              category
         age                   float64
         credit_score          float64
         email                category
         distance_to_store     float64
         online_visits           int64
         online_trans            int64
         online_spend          float64
         store_trans             int64
         store_spend           float64
         sat_service           float64
         sat_selection         float64
         dtype: object
```

As we noted above, in this dataframe each row represents a different customer. For each, there is a flag indicating whether the customer has an email address on file (`email`), along with the customer's `age`, `credit_score`, and distance to the nearest physical store (`distance_to_store`).

Additional variables report 1-year total visits to the online site (`online_visits`) as well as online and in-store transaction counts (`online_trans` and `store_trans`) plus 1-year total spending online and in store (`online_spend` and `store.spend`). Finally, the data contain survey ratings of satisfaction with the service and product selection at the retail stores (`sat_service` and `sat_selection`). Some of the survey values are NaN for customers without survey responses. All values are numeric, except that `cust_df.cust_id` and `cust_df.email` are factors (categorical). We'll say more shortly about why the details of the data structure are so important.

4.2.1 Creating a Basic Scatterplot with `plot()`

We begin by exploring the relationship between each customer's age and credit score using the `plot()` dataframe method, which is a wrapper function for a variety of plot types using matplotlib (Hunter 2007). In this case, we specify `kind='scatter'` and the *x* values to represent age and the *y* values `credit_score`:

```
In [17]: cust_df.plot(kind='scatter', x='age', y='credit_score')
```

The code above produces the graphic shown in the left panel of Fig. 4.1, a fairly typical scatterplot. There is a large mass of customers in the center of the plot with age around 35 and credit score around 725, and fewer customers at the margins. There are not many younger customers with very high credit scores, nor older customers with very low scores, which suggests an association between age and credit score.

The default settings in `plot()` produce a quick plot that is useful when you are exploring the data for yourself; `plot()` adjusts the *x*- and *y*-axes to accommodate the range of the data and labels the axes using variable names.

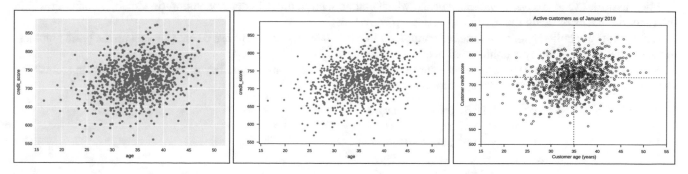

Fig. 4.1 Basic scatterplot of customer age versus credit score using default settings in `plot()` function (left), and a properly labeled version of the same plot (right)

Matplotlib allows changing of default setting, and there are pre-configured styles that can be selected, which can adjust the figure to your taste:

```
In [18]: import matplotlib.pyplot as plt


         plt.style.use('seaborn-notebook')
         plt.style.use('seaborn-white')
         plt.style.use('seaborn-ticks')


         cust_df.plot(kind='scatter', x='age', y='credit_score')
```

The result is seen in the center panel of Fig. 4.1. Note that styles, particularly those from seaborn, can be combined as we have done here. Note also that over the period of time that we were writing this book, the default matplotlib settings in Colab changed, so your default settings may produce a plot more similar to the center panel than the left panel of Fig. 4.1.

But if we present the plot to others, we ought to provide more informative labels for the axes and chart title, as can be seen in the right panel of Fig. 4.1:

```
In [19]: cust_df.plot(kind='scatter',
                       x='age',
                       y='credit_score',
                       c='none',
                       edgecolor='darkblue',
                       xlim=[15, 55],
                       ylim=[500, 900])
         plt.plot([15, 55], [cust_df.credit_score.mean(),
                             cust_df.credit_score.mean()], 'k:')
         plt.plot([cust_df.age.mean(), cust_df.age.mean()],
                  [500, 900],
                  'k:')
         plt.title('Active customers as of January 2019')
         plt.xlabel('Customer age (years)')
         plt.ylabel('Customer credit score')
```

Much as we did in Sect. 3.4.1, we have modified the figure to make it more interpretable. Given the high density of points at the center of the figure, we've removed the fill, using c='none', and specified a color for the edge using edgecolor='darkblue'. xlim and ylim set a range for each axis. plt.title(), plt.xlabel() and plt.ylabel() provide a descriptive title and axis labels for the chart. The result in the right panel of Fig. 4.1 is labeled well enough that someone viewing the chart can easily understand what it depicts.

We've also added lines to the plot, to indicate the average age and average credit score in the data using the basic plt.plot() function. We add a horizontal line at cust_df.credit_score.mean() by specifying the x values to match the x-limits we set, and the y values to be equal to the mean credit score. For a vertical line at the mean age we do the same, but with the mean age as the x values and the y values set to match the y-limits. 'k:' specifies that we want this to be a black dotted line. Note that we didn't specify x= and y= here; when names of arguments are omitted, the function assumes they are *positional* arguments, which can be seen in the help documentation (in Colab, by tabbing within the function braces or using the ? command, e.g. ?plt.plot).

Often, plots are built-up using a series of commands like this. The first step is to use plot() to set up the basic graphics; then add features with other graphics commands.

We next turn to an important marketing question: in our data, do customers who buy more online buy less in stores? We start by plotting online sales against in-store sales:

```
In [20]: cust_df.plot(kind='scatter',
                       x='store_spend',
                       y='online_spend',
                       c='none',
                       edgecolor='darkblue',
                       s=8)
         plt.title('Customers as of January 2019')
```

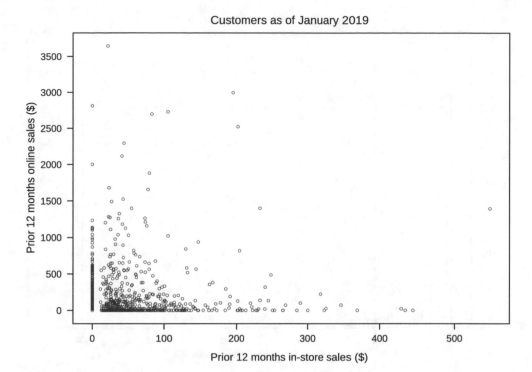

Fig. 4.2 Scatterplot of online sales versus in-store sales for the customers in our dataset

```
plt.xlabel('Prior 12 months in-store sales ($)')
plt.ylabel('Prior 12 months online sales ($)')
```

The resulting plot in Fig. 4.2 is typical of the skewed distributions that are common in behavioral data such as sales or transaction counts; most customers rarely make a purchase so the data are dense near zero. The resulting plot has a lot of points along the axes; we use the s=8 argument, which scales down the plotted points so that we can see the points a bit more clearly (the argument specifies the size in points squared). The plot shows that there are a large number of customers who didn't buy anything on one of the two channels (the points along the axes), along with a smaller number of customers who purchase fairly large amounts on one of the channels.

Because of the skewed data, Fig. 4.2 does not yet give a good answer to our question about the relationship between online and in-store sales. We investigate further with a histogram of just the in-store sales (see Sect. 3.4 for hist()):

```
In [21]: cust_df.store_spend.hist(bins=100,
                                   edgecolor='k',
                                   facecolor='none',
                                   linewidth=1.2)
         plt.title('Customers as of January 2019')
         plt.xlabel('Prior 12 months online sales ($)')
         plt.ylabel('Count of customers')
```

The histogram in Fig. 4.3 shows clearly that a large number of customers bought nothing in the online store (about 400 out of 1000). The distribution of sales among those who do buy has a mode around $20 and a long right-hand tail with a few customers whose 12 month spending was high. Such distributions are typical of spending and transaction counts in customer data. Note that we are using a histogram despite this being a section on scatter plots; in practice, these two visualizations are complementary. Scatterplots reveal relationships between two variables, but do not perform well when many values are very similar and overlay each other, as in this case. We can use a histogram to better visualize the actual density of points in those regions.

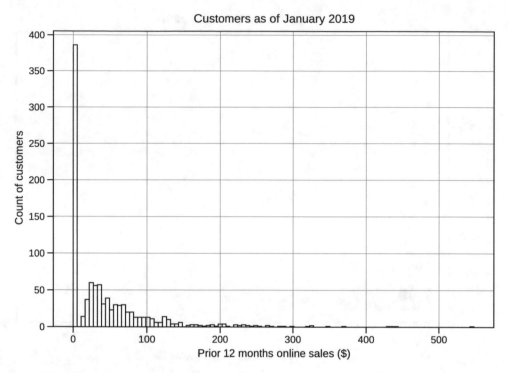

Fig. 4.3 A histogram of prior 12 months online sales reveals more clearly a large number of customers who purchase nothing along with a left-skewed distribution of sales among those who purchase something

4.2.2 Color-Coding Points on a Scatterplot

Another question is whether the propensity to buy online versus in store is related to our email efforts (as reflected by whether or not a customer has an email address on file). We can add the `email` dimension to the plot in Fig. 4.2 by coloring in the points for customers whose email address is known to us. To do this, we use `groupby()` (introduced in 3.2.1) along with mapping dictionaries specifying the color for each email category (e.g., where `email == 'yes'` the edge will be `'g'` (green) and the fill `'none'` (empty). We iterate through the groups and use the `scatter()` function to plot each subset. We also include a legend using `plt.legend()` and specify the title as `email`:

```
In [22]: edge_mapper = {'yes': 'g',
                        'no': 'k'}
         fill_mapper = {'yes': 'none',
                        'no': 'k' }

         fig, ax = plt.subplots()
         for name, group in cust_df.groupby('email'):
           ax.scatter(x=group.store_spend,
                      y=group.online_spend,
                      edgecolor=edge_mapper[name],
                      c=fill_mapper[name],
                      s=8,
                      label=name)
         plt.legend(title='email')
         plt.title('Customers as of January 2019')
         plt.xlabel('Prior 12 months in-store sales ($)')
         plt.ylabel('Prior 12 months online sales ($)')
```

The resulting plot appears in the left panel of Fig. 4.4.

The function plt.subplots() creates a blank figure (think of this as a blank canvas), which is made up of subplots. The command `fig, ax = plot.subplot()` creates a figure called `fig` which has a single subplot called `ax`. (Try running

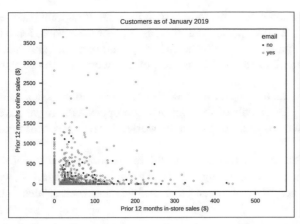
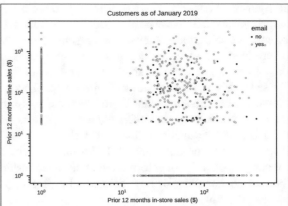

Fig. 4.4 Scatterplots of online sales vs. in-store sales by customer. On the left, we see a typical extremely skewed plot using raw sales values; data are grouped along the x and y axes because many customers purchase nothing. On the right, plotting the logarithm of sales separates zero and non-zero values more clearly, and reveals the association among those who purchase in the two channels (see Sect. 4.2.3)

the code chunk up to that line to see the blank figure that is created). We can then use the `ax.scatter()` method to add points to the blank plot. We do this within a for loop so that we can change colors for the two groups using the dictionaries we created. Here we loop over the pairs of numbers created by `cust.df.groupby('email')` (see Sect. 2.4.10 for a refresher on for loops).

Note that rather than using the `plot()` method on the `cust_df` dataframe, we are using the `scatter()` method on the `ax` axis object. We can create an identical figure in either manner, but using this approach simplifies operations on the dataframe (see the next section).

4.2.3 Plotting on a Log Scale

With raw values as plotted in the left panel of Fig. 4.4, it is still difficult to see whether there is a different relationship between in-store and online purchases for those with and without emails on file, because of the heavy skew in sales figures. A common solution for such scatterplots with skewed data is to plot the data on a *logarithmic* scale. This is easy to do with the `plt.xscale('log')` and `plt.yscale()` functions to plot the x-axis or y-axis on the log scale, respectively.

For `cust_df`, because both online and in-store sales are skewed, we use a log scale for both axes:

```
In [23]: fig, ax = plt.subplots()
         for name, group in cust_df.groupby('email'):
           ax.scatter(x=group.store_spend+1,
                   y=group.online_spend+1,
                   edgecolor=edge_mapper[name],
                   c=fill_mapper[name],
                   s=8,
                   label=name)
         plt.legend(title='email')
         plt.title('Customers as of January 2019')
         plt.xlabel('Prior 12 months in-store sales ($)')
         plt.ylabel('Prior 12 months online sales ($)')
         plt.xscale('log')
         plt.yscale('log')
```

In this code, we plot ...*spend* + 1 to avoid an error due to the fact that $\log(0)$ is not defined. This transformation is a bit harder to accomplish with the `plot()` method on the `cust_df` dataframe; this is why we used the matplotlib `scatter()` method on the axis object. In the right hand side of Fig. 4.4, the axes are now logarithmic; for instance, the distance from 1–10 is the same as 10–100.

On the right-hand panel of Fig. 4.4, it is easy to see a large number of customers with no sales (the points at $x = 1$ or $y = 1$, which correspond to zero sales because we added 1). It now appears that there is little or no association between online and in-store sales; the scatterplot among customers who purchase in both channels shows no pattern. Thus, there is no evidence here to suggest that online sales have cannabalized in-store sales (a formal test of that would be complex, but the present data do not argue for such an effect in any obvious way).

We also see in Fig. 4.4 that customers with no email address on file appear to show slightly lower online sales than those with addresses; there are somewhat more black circles in the lower half of the plot than the upper half. If we have been sending email promotions to customers, then this suggests that the promotions might be working. An experiment to confirm that hypothesis could be an appropriate next step.

Did it take work to produce the final plot on the right side of Fig. 4.4? Yes, but the result shows how a well-crafted scatterplot can present a lot of information about relationships in data. Looking at the right-hand panel of Fig. 4.4, we have a much better understanding of how online and offline sales are related to each other, and whether each relates to having customers' email status.

4.3   Combining Plots in a Single Graphics Object

Sometimes we want to visualize several relationships at once. For instance, suppose we wish to examine whether customers who live closer to stores spend more in store, and whether those who live further away spend more online. Those involve different spending variables and thus need separate plots. If we plot several such things individually, we end up with many individual charts. Luckily, in Python it is easy to produce a single graphic that consists of multiple plots. You do this using the subplot() function to specify that you want multiple plots in a single graphical object then simply plot each one with plot() as usual.

It is easiest to see how this works with an example:

```
In [24]: plt.subplot(221)
         plt.scatter(x=cust_df.distance_to_store,
                     y=cust_df.store_spend,
                     c='none',
                     edgecolor='darkblue',
                     s=8)
         plt.title('store')
         plt.ylabel('Prior 12 months in-store sales ($)')

         plt.subplot(223)
         plt.scatter(x=cust_df.distance_to_store,
                     y=cust_df.online_spend,
                     c='none',
                     edgecolor='darkblue',
                     s=8)
         plt.title('online')
         plt.xlabel('Distance to store')
         plt.ylabel('Prior 12 months online sales ($)')

         plt.subplot(222)
         plt.scatter(x=cust_df.distance_to_store,
                     y=cust_df.store_spend+1,
                     c='none',
                     edgecolor='darkblue',
                     s=8)
         plt.title('store, log')
         plt.xscale('log')
         plt.yscale('log')

         plt.subplot(224)
```

```
    plt.scatter(x=cust_df.distance_to_store,
                y=cust_df.online_spend+1,
                c='none',
                edgecolor='darkblue',
                s=8)
plt.title('online, log')
plt.xlabel('Distance to store')
plt.xscale('log')
plt.yscale('log')

plt.tight_layout()
```

Instead of four separate plots from the individual plot() or scatter() commands, this code produces a single graphic with four panels as shown in Fig. 4.5. Prior to each plotting command, we specify the subplot in which we want that plot to appear. The argument to subplot is of the form rows, columns, index (the commas are optional for single-digit numbers of rows or columns). The index is numbered from left to right and top to bottom. In this case we wanted two rows and two columns. We can select the upper left panel in such an arrangement using plt.subplot(221) or, equivalently, plt.subplot(2, 2, 1). The upper right has the index 2, the lower left 3, and lower right 4. plt.tight_layout() adjusts the spacing so that all labels are visible.

Although the plots in Fig. 4.5 are not completely labelled, we see in the upper right panel that there may be a negative relationship between customers' distances to the nearest store and *in-store* spending. Customers who live further from their nearest store spend less in store. However, on the lower right, we don't see an obvious relationship between distance and *online* spending.

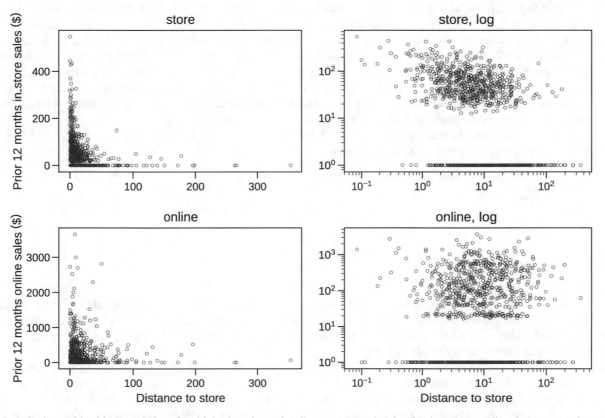

Fig. 4.5 A single graphic object consisting of multiple plots shows that distance to store is related to in-store spending, but seems to be unrelated to online spending. The relationships are easier to see when spending and distance are plotted on a log scale in the two right panels

4.4   Scatterplot Matrices

4.4.1   scatter_matrix()

In our customer data, we have a number of variables that might be associated with each other; age, distance_to_store, and email all might be related to online and offline transactions and to spending. When you have several variables such as these, it is good practice to examine scatterplots between all pairs of variables before moving on to more complex analyses.

To do this, Pandas provides the convenient function pandas.plotting.scatter_matrix(dataframe), which makes a separate scatterplot for every combination of variables:

```
In [25]:  _ = pd.plotting.scatter_matrix(cust_df, figsize=(12,12),
                                     c='none', edgecolor='darkblue')
```

scatter_matrix() will produce output given just a dataframe of numeric data, but there are a variety of optional arguments, such as figsize, which we use here to set the size of the figure.

Additionally, it will accept any arguments that the matplotlib scatter() function does. In this case, we specified the c and edgecolor parameters to create unfilled, dark blue markers.

We have set the call equal to '_', which is used as a placeholder in Python when we know we will not use the output or, in this case, to suppress the automatic printing of the returned object. This is used often when a function will return multiple objects, but we only care about a subset of those.

Use the help function to view all the customization available (see Sect. 2.4.11).

The resulting plot is shown in Fig. 4.6 and is called a *scatterplot matrix*. Each position in this matrix shows a scatterplot between two variables, except along the diagonal which has a histogram for each variable. For example, the plot in the first row and third column is a scatterplot of cust_df.age on the *y*-axis versus cust_df.distance_to_store on the *x*-axis. And the plot in the first row and first column is a histogram of cust_df.age while that in the third row and third column is a histogram of cust_df.distance_to_store. The diagonal argument allows selection of either 'hist', for a histogram as we have here, or 'kde' for a kernel density estimation plot in panels along the diagonal.

We can see relationships between variables quickly in a scatterplot matrix. In the fourth row and fifth column we see a strong linear association between online_visits and online_trans; customers who visit the website more frequently make more online transactions. Looking quickly over the plot, we also see that customers with a higher number of online transactions have higher total online spending (not a surprise), and similarly, customers with more in-store transactions also spend more in-store. This simple command produced a lot of information to consider.

A subset of columns can be selected using normal pandas column indexing, for example, to plot just the age, distance_to_store, and store_spend columns:

```
In [26]:  _ = pd.plotting.scatter_matrix(cust_df[['age', 'distance_to_store',
                                     'store_spend']],
                              c='none', edgecolor='darkblue')
```

4.4.2   PairGrid()

Scatterplot matrices are so useful for data exploration that several add-on packages offer additional versions of them. The excellent plotting package seaborn (Waskom et al. 2018) provides a very powerful function, PairGrid(), which enables highly customized matrices of plots. Additionally, it offers a simple way to color code the markers by a categorical variable, such as whether a customer has an email on file.

Creating a plot using PairGrid() is a multistep process. First, we create a PairGrid() object, passing it our dataframe (here we look at just age, distance_to_store, and store_spend, along with email for setting the colors), We specify the size of each panel using the size argument and set the hue of plotted elements to reflect values of the email column. We add a few arguments that customize how different email values will be represented by setting a color palette and passing a list of markers (shapes) to be plotted in the hue_kws argument. When specifying markers, there must be a marker defined for each category. In this case we have two categories, so we pass two markers: 'o' which indicates a circle and 's' which indicates a square.

To define how the data will be plotted, we also need to define a *map*. PairGrid() has a variety of functions that allow setting the same plotting function for all panels (map(func)), for the panels along the diagonal (map_diag(func)),

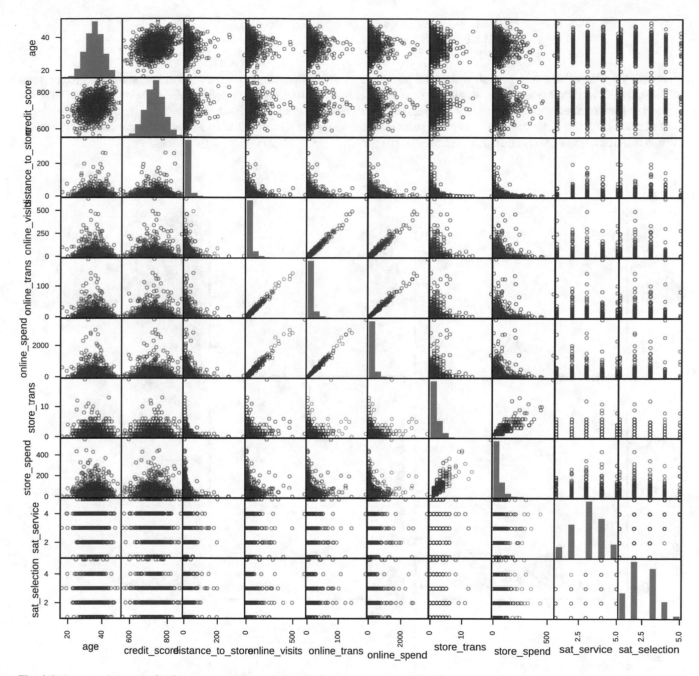

Fig. 4.6 A scatterplot matrix for the customer dataset produced using `scatter_matrix()`

for the panels *off* the diagonal (`map_offdiag(func)`), for the upper triangle (`map_upper(func)`), and for the lower triangle (`map_lower(func)`). The `func` argument is a plotting function, such as `plt.hist` or `plt.scatter`. Any additional arguments are passed to that plotting function.

Here's an example:

```
In [55]: import seaborn as sns

         g = sns.PairGrid(cust_df[['age', 'distance_to_store',
                          'store_spend', 'email']],
                      size=2.5,
                      hue='email', palette='Set2',
                      hue_kws={"marker": ['o', 's']})
```

```
    _ = g.map_offdiag(plt.scatter, s=20, alpha=0.5)
    _ = g.map_diag(plt.hist, bins=20)
    _ = g.add_legend()
```

Figure 4.7 shows the result. In each scatterplot panel, the values from customers without an email on file are green circles whereas those from customers with email are orange squares. The histograms are color-coded as well, although they are somewhat hard to interpret due to the fact that we have many fewer customers without email.

`PairGrid()` is a powerful tool to explore pairwise relationships in data and it allows substantial customization beyond the options in `pandas.plotting.scatter_matrix()`.

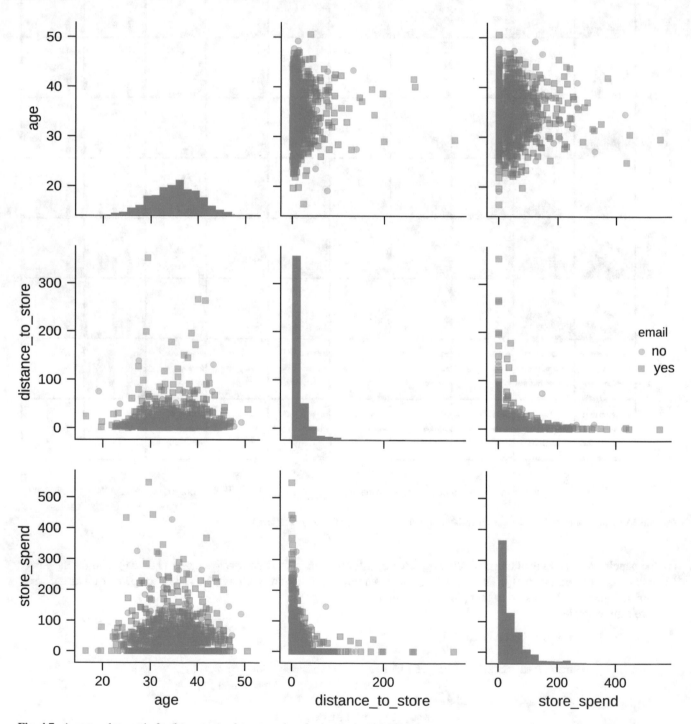

Fig. 4.7 A scatterplot matrix for the customer dataset produced using `PairGrid()`

93

4.5   Correlation Coefficients

Although scatterplots provide a lot of visual information, when there are more than a few variables, it can be helpful to assess the relationship between each pair with a single number. One measure of the relationship between two variables is the *covariance*. As implied by its name, covariance measures the degree that two variables vary together. For example, imagine that we have two variables and twenty observations of each. We can find the mean value for each variable and then, for each observation, measure whether each variable is higher or lower than its mean value. Covariance measures the degree to which both variables are higher or lower than the mean at the same time. A positive covariance indicates that their patterns match, and a negative covariance indicate that their patterns are offset, i.e. when one is higher than its mean the other is lower its mean.

Covariance can be computed for any two variables using the `numpy.cov()` function:

```
In [28]: np.cov(cust_df.age, cust_df.credit_score)

Out[28]: array([[  25.70589016,    74.54758431],
                [  74.54758431, 2515.28862282]])
```

If values x_i and y_i tend to go in the same direction—to be both higher or both lower than their respective means—across observations, then they have a positive covariance. If $cov(x, y)$ is zero, then there is no (linear) association between x_i and y_i. As mentioned above, negative covariance means that the variables go in opposite directions relative to their means: when x_i is lower, y_i tends to be higher.

Note that this is a variance-covariance matrix, with the variance of each variable on the diagonal. The covariance between age and credit score is in the off-diagonal: 74.55.

It is difficult to interpret the magnitude of covariance because the scale depends on the variables involved. Covariance will be different if the variables are measured in cents versus dollars or in inches versus centimeters. This is clear in the output of our covariance function: the covariance of age with itself is 25.71 and the covariance of credit score with itself is 2515.29! That makes the covariance between age and credit score, 74.55, very hard to interpret!

So, it is helpful to scale the covariance by the standard deviation for each variable, which results in a standardized, rescaled *correlation coefficient* known as the *Pearson product-moment correlation coefficient*, often abbreviated as the symbol r.

Pearson's r is a continuous metric that falls in the range $[-1, +1]$. It is $+1$ in the case of a perfect positive linear association between the two variables, and -1 for perfect negative linear association. If there is little or no linear association, r will be near 0. On a scatterplot, data with $r = 1$ or $r = -1$ would have all points along a straight line (angled up or down, respectively). This makes r an easily interpreted metric to assess whether two variables have a close linear association or not.

In Python, we can compute the matrix of correlation coefficients r with the `numpy.corrcoef()` function:

```
In [29]: np.corrcoef(cust_df.age, cust_df.credit_score)

Out[29]: array([[1.        , 0.29317257],
                [0.29317257, 1.        ]])
```

`corrcoef` is identical to rescaling the covariance by the joint standard deviations (but more convenient):

```
In [30]: np.cov(cust_df.age,
                cust_df.credit_score)[0,1]/(cust_df.age.std() *
                                            cust_df.credit_score.std())

Out[30]: 0.29317257253555756
```

What value of r signifies an *important* correlation between two variables in marketing? In engineering and physical sciences, physical measurements may demonstrate extremely high correlations; for instance, r between the lengths and weights of pieces of steel rod might be 0.9, 0.95, or even 0.999, depending on the uniformity of the rods and the precision of measurement. However, in social sciences such as marketing, we are concerned with human behavior, which is less consistent and more difficult to measure. This results in lower correlations, but they are still important.

To determine whether a correlation is important, we often use *Cohen's Rules of Thumb*, which come out of the psychology tradition (Cohen 1988). Cohen proposed that for correlations between variables describing people, $r = 0.1$ should be considered a *small* or *weak* association, $r = 0.3$ might be considered to be *medium* in strength, and $r = 0.5$ or higher could be considered to be *large* or *strong*. Cohen's interpretation of a *large* effect was that such an association would be easily noticed by casual observers. A *small* effect would require careful measurement to detect yet might be important to our understanding and to statistical models.

Importantly, interpretation of r according to Cohen's rules of thumb depends on the assumption that the variables are *normally distributed* (also known as *Gaussian*) or are approximately so. If the variables are not normal, but instead follow a logarithmic or other distribution that is skewed or strongly non-normal in shape, then these thresholds do not apply. In those cases, it can be helpful to transform your variables to normal distributions before interpreting, as we discuss in Sect. 4.5.3 below.

4.5.1 Correlation Tests

In the code above, np.corrcoef(age, credit_score) shows $r = 0.29$, a medium-sized effect by Cohen's standard. Is this also statistically significant? We can use a function from the scipy stats module, scipy.stats.pearsonr() to find out:

```
In [31]: from scipy import stats

         stats.pearsonr(cust_df.age, cust_df.credit_score)
Out[31]: (0.29317257253555756, 2.848458409183363e-21)
```

This tells us that $r = 0.29$ and the two-tailed p-value at the 95% level is very close to zero. This value is the probability that r would be greater than or equal to the reported r value under the null hypothesis that $r = 0$. In this case we can reject that null hypothesis with reasonable confidence. Such a correlation, showing a medium-sized effect and statistical significance, probably should not be ignored in subsequent analyses.

Note, again, that this test assumes that the inputs are bivariate normal data. Note also, that the p-values are approximate, but reasonable for datasets larger than 500 or so.

4.5.2 Correlation Matrices

For more than two variables, it is more convenient to use the pandas corr() method to compute the correlations between all pairs x, y at once as a *correlation matrix*. As with the numpy function, such a matrix shows $r = 1.0$ on the diagonal because $cor(x, x) = 1$. It is also symmetric; $cor(x, y) = cor(y, x)$. But unlike numpy.corrcoef() it returns its output as a dataframe and ignores any non-numeric data:

```
In [32]: cust_df.corr()
Out[32]:                        age    credit_score    distance_to_store    online_visits  \
         age               1.000000        0.293173             0.018909        -0.050954
         credit_score      0.293173        1.000000             0.053541        -0.015363
         distance_to_store 0.018909        0.053541             1.000000        -0.008321
         online_visits    -0.050954       -0.015363            -0.008321         1.000000
         online_trans     -0.050772       -0.013135            -0.008004         0.992050
         online_spend     -0.050662       -0.008845            -0.010778         0.985861
         store_trans      -0.045477       -0.041787            -0.247095         0.058719
         store_spend      -0.024672       -0.024324            -0.229249         0.024198
         sat_service      -0.026356       -0.018062             0.011372        -0.055680
         sat_selection    -0.063342       -0.013233            -0.002108         0.043876

                            online_trans    online_spend    store_trans    store_spend  \
         age                   -0.050772       -0.050662      -0.045477      -0.024672
         credit_score          -0.013135       -0.008845      -0.041787      -0.024324
         distance_to_store     -0.008004       -0.010778      -0.247095      -0.229249
         online_visits          0.992050        0.985861       0.058719       0.024198
         online_trans           1.000000        0.994954       0.058749       0.025554
         online_spend           0.994954        1.000000       0.060693       0.026421
         store_trans            0.058749        0.060693       1.000000       0.896367
         store_spend            0.025554        0.026421       0.896367       1.000000
```

sat_service	-0.049443	-0.051517	0.000464	-0.013511
sat_selection	0.056386	0.056939	0.065107	0.059270

	sat_service	sat_selection
age	-0.026356	-0.063342
credit_score	-0.018062	-0.013233
distance_to_store	0.011372	-0.002108
online_visits	-0.055680	0.043876
online_trans	-0.049443	0.056386
online_spend	-0.051517	0.056939
store_trans	0.000464	0.065107
store_spend	-0.013511	0.059270
sat_service	1.000000	0.535021
sat_selection	0.535021	1.000000

In the second column of the first row, we see that cor(age, credit.store) = 0.29 as above. We can easily scan to find other large correlations; for instance, the correlation between store_trans, distance_to_store = -0.25, showing that people who live further from a store tend to have fewer in-store transactions. For sat_selection and sat_service, the corr() function drops any NaN values.

Rather than requiring one to scan a matrix of numbers, we can pass the correlation matrix to plt.imshow() to visualize the correlations:

```
In [33]: plt.imshow(cust_df.corr())
         plt.colorbar()
```

The resulting graphic is shown in the left panel of Fig. 4.8. A nicer plot with proper axis labels can be generated with the seaborn heatmap() function, visualized in the right panel of Fig. 4.8:

```
In [34]: sns.heatmap(cust_df.corr(), center=0)
```

We can also customize the output of heatmap() to make it even easier to interpret:

```
In [35]: sns.heatmap(cust_df.corr(),
                     vmin=-0.3,
                     vmax=0.6,
                     center=0,
                     annot=True,
                     fmt='.2f',
                     mask=~np.tri(cust_df.corr().shape[1], k=-1, dtype=bool),
                     cbar=False)
```

This chart, in the bottom panel of Fig. 4.8, has a number of optimizations to make it easier to interpret. We have set vmin and vmax to improve the dynamic range, added an annotation and set that annotation to be rounded to two decimal places (annot=True, fmpt='2f'). Since the upper and lower triangles are identical, the diagonal is all 1.0, we can also add a mask to only include the lower triangle using the numpy.tri() function to simplify the visualization. We also disable the color bar, as we've added an annotation directly on the figure (cbar=False).

In the bottom panel of Fig. 4.8, the colored and numeric values of r are shown in the lower triangle of the matrix. This makes it easy to find the larger correlations in the data: age is positively correlated with credit_score; distance_to_store is negatively correlated with store_trans and store_spend; online_visits, online_trans, and online_spend are all strongly correlated with one another, as are store_trans and store_spend. In the survey items, sat_service is positively correlated with sat_selection.

While it is impossible to draw strong conclusions based on associations such as in Fig. 4.8, finding large correlations should inform subsequent analysis or suggest hypotheses.

4.5.3 Transforming Variables before Computing Correlations

Correlation coefficient r measures the *linear* association between two variables. If the relationship between two variables is not linear, it would be misleading to interpret r. For example, if we create a random variable that ranges from -10 to

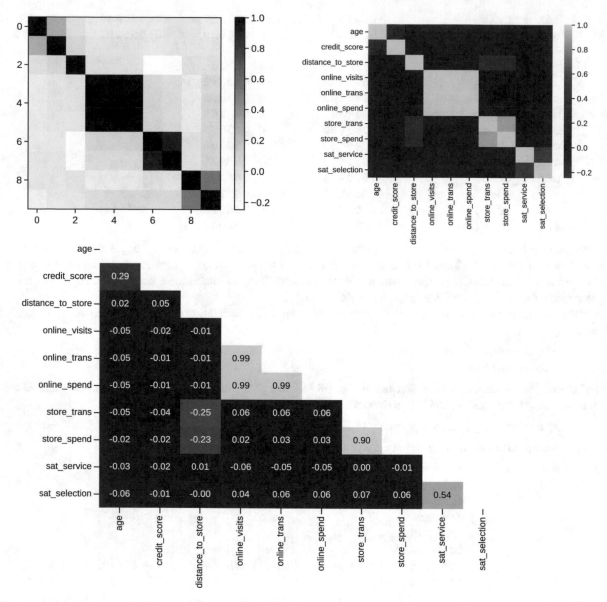

Fig. 4.8 Correlation plots produced using several methods, including `plt.imshow()` (left), `seaborn.heatmap()` with default settings (right), and `seaborn.heatmap()` with modified settings (lower). Such plots highlight correlated variables

10—using `numpy.random.uniform()` to sample random uniform values—and then compute the correlation between that variable and its square (which is a nonlinear relationship by definition), we get a correlation close to zero:

```
In [36]: x = np.random.uniform(low=-10, high=10, size=1000)
         np.corrcoef(x, x**2)

Out[36]: array([[1.        , 0.0333763],
                [0.0333763, 1.        ]])
```

r is near zero despite the fact that there is a perfect *nonlinear* relationship between x and x^2. So, it is important that we consider transformations before assessing the correlation between two variables. (It might be helpful to plot x and x^2 by typing `plt.scatter(x, x**2)`, so that you can see the relationship.)

Many relationships in marketing data are nonlinear. For example, as we see in the `cust_df` data, the number of trips a customer makes to a store may be *inversely* related to distance from the store. When we compute the correlation between the raw values of `distance_to_store` and `store_spend`, we get a modest negative correlation:

```
In [37]: np.corrcoef(cust_df.distance_to_store, cust_df.store_spend)

Out[37]: array([[ 1.        , -0.22924927],
                [-0.22924927,  1.        ]])
```

However, if we transform `distance_to_store` to its *inverse* (1/*distance*), we find a much stronger linear association:

```
In [38]: np.corrcoef(1/cust_df.distance_to_store, cust_df.store_spend)

Out[38]: array([[1.        ,  0.43516955],
                [0.43516955,  1.        ]])
```

In fact, the inverse square root of distance shows an even greater linear association:

```
In [39]: np.corrcoef(1/np.sqrt(cust_df.distance_to_store),
                     cust_df.store_spend)

Out[39]: array([[1.        ,  0.50263393],
                [0.50263393,  1.        ]])
```

How do we interpret this? Because of the inverse *square root* relationship, there is a smaller effect per mile as you get further away. Someone who lives 1 mile from the nearest store will spend quite a bit more than someone who lives 5 miles away, yet someone who lives 20 miles away will only buy a little bit more than someone who lives 30 miles away.

These transformations are important when creating scatterplots between variables as well. For example, examine the scatterplots in Fig. 4.9 for raw `distance_to_store` versus `store_spend`, as compared to the inverse square root of `distance.to.store` versus `store.spend`. We create those two charts as follows:

```
In [40]: plt.scatter(cust_df.distance_to_store, cust_df.store_spend)
         plt.xlabel('Distance to store')
In [41]: plt.scatter(1/np.sqrt(cust_df.distance_to_store), cust_df.store_spend)
         plt.xlabel('1/sqrt(distance_to_store)')
```

The association between distance and spending is much clearer with the transformed data as shown in the right-hand panel of Fig. 4.9, with distances becoming shorter toward the right.

To review, it is important to consider transforming variables to approximate normality before computing correlations or creating scatterplots; the appropriate transformation may help you to see associations more clearly. As we noted in Sect. 4.5, interpretation of *r* with rules of thumb requires data to be approximately normal.

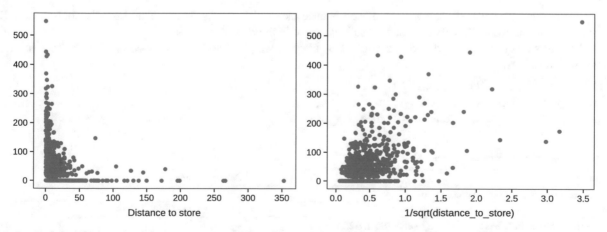

Fig. 4.9 A transformation of `distance_to_store` to its inverse square root makes the association with `store_trans` more apparent in the right-hand chart, as compared to the original values on the left

4.5.4 Typical Marketing Data Transformations

Considering all the possible transforms may seem impossible, but because marketing data often concern the same kinds of data in different datasets—counts, sales, revenue, and so forth—there are a few common transformations that often apply. For example, as we discussed when simulating the data for Chap. 3, unit sales are often related to the logarithm of price.

In Table 4.1, we list common transformations that are often helpful with different types of marketing variables.

For most purposes, these standard transformations are appropriate and theoretically sound. However, when these transformations don't work or you want to determine the very best transformation, there is a general-purpose transformation function that can be used instead, and we describe that next.

4.5.5 Box-Cox Transformations*

The remaining sections in the chapter are optional, although important. If you're new to this material, you might skip to the Key Points at the end of this chapter (Sect. 4.8). Remember to return to these sections later and learn more about correlation analysis!

Many of the transformations in Table 4.1 involve taking a power of x: x^2, $1/x = x^{-1}$, and $\sqrt{x} = x^{-0.5}$. The *Box-Cox transformation* generalizes this use of power functions and is defined as:

$$y_i^{(lambda)} \begin{cases} = \frac{y_i^{lambda} - 1}{lambda} & \text{if } lambda \neq 0 \\ = log(y_i) & \text{if } lambda = 0 \end{cases} \tag{4.1}$$

where *lambda* can take any value and *log* is the natural logarithm. One could try different values of *lambda* to see which transformation makes the distribution best fit the normal distribution. (We will see in Chap. 7 that it is also common to use transformed data that make a linear regression have normally distributed residuals.) Because transformed data can be more approximately normal, it is more suitable to assess the strength of association using the rules of thumb for r (Sect. 4.5).

Instead of trying values of *lambda* by hand, the `scipy.stats.boxcox()` function calculates the optimal *lambda* for the input data and then transforms the data using that lambda. We find the best Box-Cox transformation for `distance_to_store` using `boxcox()` as follows:

```
In [42]: dts_bc, lmda = stats.boxcox(cust_df.distance_to_store)
         lmda

Out[42]: 0.018447910668186362
```

This tells us that the value of *lambda* to make distance as similar as possible to a normal distribution is 0.01844. `boxcox()` also returned the transformed data, which we saved in the `dts_bc` variable.

To see how this changes `cust_df.distance_to_store`, we plot two histograms comparing the transformed and untransformed variables:

```
In [43]: plt.figure(figsize=(8,4))
         plt.subplot(1,2,1)
         plt.hist(cust_df.distance_to_store,
```

Table 4.1 Common transformations of variables in marketing

Variable	Common transform
Unit sales, revenue, household income, price	$log(x)$
Distance	$1/x$, $1/x^2$, $log(x)$
Market or preference share based on a utility value (Sect. 8.2.1)	$\frac{e^x}{1+e^x}$
Right-tailed or positively skewed distributions (generally)	$\sqrt{x}$ or $log(x)$ (watch out for $log(x \leq 0)$)
Left-tailed or negatively skewed distributions (generally)	x^2

```
                   bins=20,
                   edgecolor='k',
                   facecolor='none',
                   linewidth=1.2)
         plt.xlabel('Distance to nearest store')
         plt.ylabel('Count of customers')
         plt.box(False)
         plt.subplot(1,2,2)
         plt.hist(dts_bc,
                   bins=20,
                   edgecolor='k',
                   facecolor='none',
                   linewidth=1.2)
         plt.xlabel('Box-Cox transform of distance')
         plt.ylabel('Count of customers')
         plt.box(False)
```

The resulting graphs in Fig. 4.10 shows the highly skewed original distribution on the left and the transformed distribution on the right, which is more approximately normally distributed.

If you attempt to transform a variable that is already close to normally distributed, boxcox() will report a value of lambda that is close to 1. For example, if we find the Box-Cox transform for age, we get lambda close to 1, suggesting that a transformation is not required:

```
In [44]: sspend_bc, lmda_age = stats.boxcox(cust_df.age)
         lmda_age
```

```
Out[44]: 1.2309735168227953
```

Finally, we can compute correlations for the transformed variable. These correlations will often be larger in magnitude than correlations among raw, untransformed data points. We check r between distance and in-store spending. We already transformed distance_to_store and stored it in dts_bc. Now we will transform store_spend and look at the correlations of both the transformed and untransformed values:

```
In [45]: sspend_bc, lmda_sspend = stats.boxcox(cust_df.store_spend+.001)
         lmda_sspend
```

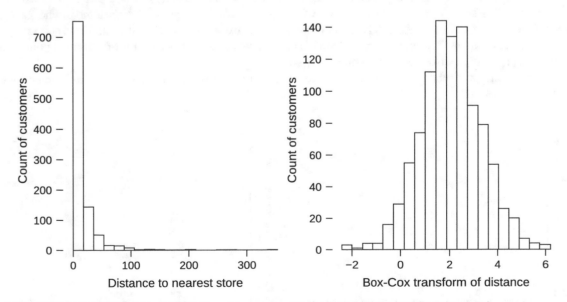

Fig. 4.10 A Box-Cox transformation of distance_to_store makes the distribution more approximately normal

```
Out[45]:  0.10663101100109183

In  [46]:  np.corrcoef(cust_df.distance_to_store, cust_df.store_spend)

Out[46]:  array([[ 1.          ,  -0.22924927],
                  [-0.22924927,   1.          ]])

In  [47]:  np.corrcoef(dts_bc, sspend_bc)

Out[47]:  array([[ 1.          ,  -0.42182049],
                  [-0.42182049,   1.          ]])
```

The relationship between distance to the store and spending can be interpreted as strong and negative.

In practice, you could consider Box-Cox transformations on all variables with skewed distributions before computing correlations or creating scatterplots. This will increase the chances that you will find and interpret important associations between variables.

4.6   Exploring Associations in Survey Responses*

Many marketing datasets include variables where customers provide ratings on a discrete scale, such as a 5- or 7-point rating scale. These are *ordinal* (ranked) variables and it can be a bit tricky to assess associations among them. For instance, in the cust_df data, we have response on a 5-point scale for two satisfaction items, satisfaction with the retailer's service and with the retailer's product selection.

What is the problem? Consider a simple plot() of the two 5-point items:

```
In  [48]:  plt.scatter(x=cust_df.sat_service,
                        y=cust_df.sat_selection,
                        c='none',
                        edgecolor='darkblue')
           plt.xlabel('Customer satisfaction with service')
           plt.ylabel('Customer satisfaction with selection')
```

The resulting plot shown in the left-hand panel of Fig. 4.11 is not very informative. Because cust_df.sat_service and cust_df.sat_selection only take integer values from 1 to 5, the points for customers who gave the same responses are drawn on top of each other. The main thing we learn from this plot is that customers reported most of the possible pairs of values, except that ratings rarely showed a difference between the two items of 3 or more points (there were no pairs for (1, 4), (1, 5), (5, 1), or a few other combinations).

This poses a problem for visualization, as well as for assessing strength of association. In the next section we look at how to improve the visualization.

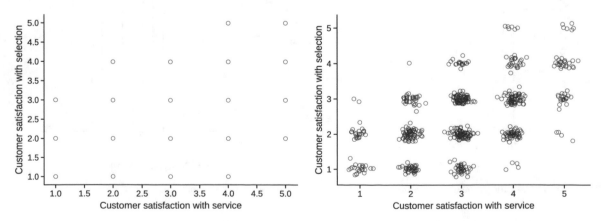

Fig. 4.11 A scatter plot of responses on a survey scale (left) is not very informative. Adding a random jitter (right) makes the plot more informative and reveals the number of observations for each pair of response values

*4.6.1 Jitter: Make Ordinal Plots More Informative**

One way to make a plot of ordinal values more informative is to *jitter* each variable, adding a small amount of random noise to each response. This moves the points away from each other and reveals how many responses occur at each combination of (x, y) values.

We can use `np.random.normal()` to do this:

```
In [49]: plt.scatter(x=cust_df.sat_service + np.random.normal(scale=0.1,
                                                              size=n_cust),
                      y=cust_df.sat_selection + np.random.normal(scale=0.1,
                                                                 size=n_cust),
                      c='none',
                      edgecolor='darkblue')
         plt.xlabel('Customer satisfaction with service')
         plt.ylabel('Customer satisfaction with selection')
```

The result is shown in the right-hand panel of Fig. 4.11, where it is easier to see that the ratings (3, 2) and (3, 3) were the most common responses. It is now clear that there is a positive relationship between the two satisfaction variables. People who are more satisfied with selection tend to be more satisfied with service.

4.7 Learning More*

Plotting As we mentioned at the end of Chap. 3, plotting in Python is a complex topic. We've demonstrated fundamental plotting methods that work for many analyses. Those who do a great deal of plotting or need to produce high-quality graphics for presentation might consider exploring `matplotlib`, `seaborn` (Waskom et al. 2018) more deeply, as well as other Python visualization libraries, such as `bokeh`, `plotly`, and others.

Correlation Analysis The analysis of variable associations is important for several reasons: it often reveals interesting patterns, it is relatively straightforward to interpret, and it is the simplest case of multivariate analysis. Despite the apparent simplicity there are numerous issues to consider, some of which we have considered here. A classic text for learning about correlation analysis in depth and how to perform it well while avoiding pitfalls, is Cohen, Cohen, and West (2003), *Applied Multiple Regression/Correlation Analysis for the Behavioral Sciences* (Cohen et al. 2003), although it is not specific to Python.

4.8 Key Points

Following are some of the important points to consider when analyzing relationships between variables.

Visualization
- `dataframe.plot(kind='scatter', x, y)` creates scatterplots where x and y are column names to be plotted. An identical plot can be produced with `plt.scatter(x, y)`, where x is a vector of *x*-values to be plotted and y is a vector of the same length with *y*-values (Sect. 4.2.1.)
- When preparing a plot for others, the plot should be labeled carefully using arguments such as `xlabel`, `ylabel` and `title`, so that the reader can easily understand the graphic (Sect. 4.2.1.)
- You can color-code a plot by using `groupby` and a color map (Sect. 4.2.2).
- Use the `legend()` command to add a legend so that readers will know what your color coding means (Sect. 4.2.2).
- The `s=` argument is helpful to adjust point sizes on a scatterplot (Sect. 4.2.1)
- A scatterplot matrix is a good way to visualize associations among several variables at once; options include `pandas.plotting.scatter_matrix()` (Sect. 4.4.2) and `seaborn.PairGrid()` (Sect. 4.4.1).
- When variables are highly skewed, it is often helpful to draw the axes on a logarithmic scale using the by setting the axes to a log scale using `plt.xscale()` and `plt.yscale()` functions, e.g. `plt.xscale('log')` (Sect. 4.2.3). Alternatively, the variables might be transformed to a more interpretable distribution (Sect. 4.5.3).

Statistics

- `np.corrcoef(x, y)`, `scipy.stats.pearsonr(x, y)` and `dataframe.corr()` each computes the Pearson correlation coefficient r between variables x and y (or all columns in the case of the dataframe method). This measures the strength of the linear relationship between the variables (Sect. 4.5).
- `dataframe.corr()` will produce a correlation matrix. A handy way to visualize these is with the `seaborn.heatmap()` function (Sect. 4.5.2).
- `scipy.stats.pearsonr()` returns statistical significance in addition to r (Sect. 4.5.1).
- For many kinds of marketing data, the magnitude of r may be interpreted by Cohen's rules of thumb ($r = 0.1$ is a weak association, $r = 0.3$ is medium, and $r = 0.5$ is strong), although this assumes that the data are approximately normal in distribution (Sect. 4.5).
- When the relationship between two variables is nonlinear, r does not give an accurate assessment of the association. Computing r between transformed variables may make associations more apparent (Sect. 4.5.3.)
- There are common distributions that often occur in marketing, such as unit sales being related to $log(price)$. Before modeling associations, plot histograms of your variables and assess potential transformations of them (Sect. 4.5.4).
- An automated way to select an optimal transformation is to use a Box-Cox transform (Sect. 4.5.5).

Chapter 5
Comparing Groups: Tables and Visualizations

Marketing analysts often investigate differences between groups of people. Do men or women subscribe to our service at a higher rate? Which demographic segment can best afford our product? Does the product appeal more to homeowners or renters? The answers help us to understand the market, to target customers effectively, and to evaluate the outcome of marketing activities such as promotions.

Such questions are not confined to differences among people; similar questions are asked of many other kinds of groups. One might be interested in grouping data geographically: does Region A perform better than Region B? Or by time period: did same-store sales increase after a promotion such as a mailer or a sale? In all such cases, we are comparing one group of data to another to identify an effect.

In this chapter, we examine the kinds of comparisons between groups that often arise in marketing, with data that illustrate a consumer segmentation project. We review Python procedures to find descriptive summaries by groups, and then visualize the data in several ways.

5.1 Simulating Consumer Segment Data

We begin by creating a dataset that exemplifies a consumer segmentation project. For this example, we are offering a subscription-based service (such as cable television or membership in a warehouse club) and have collected data from $N = 300$ respondents on *age*, *gender*, *income*, *number of children*, whether they *own or rent* their homes, and whether they currently *subscribe* to the offered service or not. We use these data in later chapters as well.

Questions around customer segments are common in marketing research. These segments might be produced via a clustering algorithm (which we look at in Chap. 10) or could be created by some other heuristic, such as geographic location combined with age. In these data, we have assigned each respondent to one of four consumer segments: "Suburb mix," "Urban hip," "Travelers," or "Moving up." In this chapter we do not address *how* such segments might be identified; we just presume to know them. We will then look at how we might determine how to form these groups based on other factors, such as age, gender, or subscription status. If you know the group assignments, as we presume here, the segments themselves may be viewed as arbitrary; the same methods may be used to compare groups based on region or any another factor instead.

Segmentation data are moderately complex and we separate our code into three parts:

1. Definition of the data structure: the demographic variables (age, gender, and so forth) plus the segment names and sizes.
2. Parameters for the distributions of demographic variables, such as the mean and variance of each.
3. Code that iterates over the segments and variables to draw random values according to those definitions and parameters.

By organizing the code this way, it becomes easy to change some aspect of the simulation to draw data again. For instance, if we wanted to add a segment or change the mean of one of the demographic variables, only minor change to the code would be required. We also use this structure to teach new Python commands that appear in the third step to generate the data.

If you wish to load the data directly, it is available from the book's web site:

```
In [1]: import pandas as pd
        segment_data = pd.read_csv('http://bit.ly/PMR-ch5')
        segment_data.head()
```

© Springer Nature Switzerland AG 2020

J. S. Schwarz et al., *Python for Marketing Research and Analytics*, https://doi.org/10.1007/978-3-030-49720-0_5

```
Out [1]:
            Segment        age  gender          income  kids  own_home  \
         0  travelers  60.794945    male    57014.537526     0      True
         1  travelers  61.764535  female    43796.941252     0     False
         ...
         4  travelers  60.594199  female   103020.070798     0      True

            subscribe
         0      False
         1      False
         ...
         4      False
In [2]: segment_data.describe()
Out [2]:
                age         income          kids
         count  300.000000     300.000000   300.000000
         mean    40.923350   50669.454237     1.273333
         ...
         max     79.650722  108830.388732     7.000000
```

However, we recommend that you at least read the data generation sections. We demonstrate important Python language skills on simulating a dataset given a few basic statistics we want the dataset to represent.

5.1.1 Segment Data Definition

Our first step is to define general characteristics of the dataset: the variable names and the type of distribution from which they are drawn:

```
In [3]: segment_variables = ['age', 'gender', 'income', 'kids', 'own_home',
                             'subscribe']
        segment_variables_distribution = dict(zip(segment_variables,
                                             ['normal', 'binomial',
                                              'normal','poisson',
                                              'binomial', 'binomial']))

        segment_variables_distribution['age']
Out [3]: 'normal'
```

We have defined six variables: age, gender, income, kids, own_home, and subscribe, defined in `segment_variables`. `segment_variables_distribution` defines what kind of data will be present in each of those variables: normal data (continuous),   binomial   (yes/no),   or   Poisson   (counts).   `segment_variables_` `distribution` is a dictionary keyed by the variable name. For example, we see that when we pass `'age'` into `segment_variables_distribution` we get `'normal'`, indicating that we want age drawn from a normal distribution.

Next we start defining the statistics for each variable in each segment:

```
In [4]: segment_means = {'suburb_mix': [40, 0.5, 55000, 2, 0.5, 0.1],
                         'urban_hip':  [24, 0.7, 21000, 1, 0.2, 0.2],
                         'travelers':  [58, 0.5, 64000, 0, 0.7, 0.05],
                         'moving_up':  [36, 0.3, 52000, 2, 0.3, 0.2]}
```

`segment_means` is a dictionary keyed by the segment names. Each segment name has the means associated with it in a list. The list is ordered based on the `segment_variables` list we defined before. So the first value is the mean age for that segment, the second values is the mean `gender` (i.e. the gender ratio), the third value is the mean `income`, and so forth. We used lists here because it makes it easy to compare the means to each other. We can quickly see that the mean age of 'suburb_mix' is 40 whereas for travelers it is 58. When we draw the random data later in this section, our routine will look up values in this matrix and sample data from distributions with those parameters.

In the case of binomial and Poisson variables, we only need to specify the mean. In these data, `gender`, `own_home`, and `subscribe` will be simulated as binomial (yes/no) variables, which requires specifying the probability for each draw. `kids` is represented as a Poisson (count) variable, whose distribution is specified by its mean. Note that we use these distributions for simplicity and do not mean to imply that they are necessarily the *best* distributions to fit real observations of these variables. For example, real observations of income are better represented with a skewed distribution.

However, for normal variables—in this case, `age` and `income`, the first and third variables—we additionally need to specify the *variance* of the distribution, the degree of dispersion around the mean. So we create another dictionary that defines the standard deviation for the variables that require it:

```
In [5]:  # standard deviations for each segment
         # None = not applicable for the variable)
         segment_stddev = {'suburb_mix': [5, None, 12000, None, None, None],
                           'urban_hip':  [2, None, 5000, None, None, None],
                           'travelers':  [8, None, 21000, None, None, None],
                           'moving_up':  [4, None, 10000, None, None, None]}
```

Our next step is somewhat optional, but is good practice. We now have nearly all we need to generate a simulated dataset. But we can make our process cleaner by getting all values keyed by exactly what they are. What do we mean by that? We used set the mean and standard deviation values in lists above, but those are keyed numerically, so if we changed the order of our variables, we would use the wrong value. Instead, it's best practice to key them by the variable name. So we will now create a dictionary that contains all the statistics for each segment in a resilient structure from which we could create the entire dataset without referencing any other variables.

There is one more statistic left to set, which is the segment sizes. Here, we set those, and then we iterate through all the segments and all the variables and create a dictionary to hold everything:

```
In [6]:  segment_names = ['suburb_mix', 'urban_hip', 'travelers', 'moving_up']
         segment_sizes = dict(zip(segment_names,[100, 50, 80, 70]))

         segment_statistics = {}
         for name in segment_names:
           segment_statistics[name] = {'size': segment_sizes[name]}
           for i, variable in enumerate(segment_variables):
             segment_statistics[name][variable] = {
                 'mean': segment_means[name][i],
                 'stddev': segment_stddev[name][i]
             }
```

What does this give us? We can check the values we get for the moving_up segment:

```
In [7]:  segment_statistics['moving_up']
```

```
Out[7]:  {'age': {'mean': 36, 'stddev': 4},
          'gender': {'mean': 0.3, 'stddev': None},
          'income': {'mean': 52000, 'stddev': 10000},
          'kids': {'mean': 2, 'stddev': None},
          'own_home': {'mean': 0.3, 'stddev': None},
          'size': 70,
          'subscribe': {'mean': 0.2, 'stddev': None}}
```

We see all the statistics for each variable defined explicitly. We can see that the mean income for moving_up is $52,000 with a standard deviation of $10,000. And that the mean age is 36 and the segment will be 30% male. There is a similar dictionary for each segment. With this dictionary (called a *lookup table*), we can create our simulated dataset.

5.1.2   Final Segment Data Generation

To generate the segment data, the logic we follow is to use nested `for` loops, one for the segments and another within that for the set of variables.

    To outline how this will work, consider the following *pseudocode* (sentences organized like code):

```
Set up dictionary "segment_constructor" and pseudorandom number sequence
For each SEGMENT i in "segment_names" {
  Set up a temporary dictionary "segment_data_subset" for this SEGMENT's data
  For each VARIABLE in "seg_variables" {
    Check "segment_variable_distribution[variable]" to find distribution type for VARIABLE

    Look up the segment size and variable mean and standard deviation in segment_statistics for
    that SEGMENT and VARIABLE to
    ... Draw random data for VARIABLE (within SEGMENT) with
    ... "size" observations
  }
  Add this SEGMENT's data ("segment_data_subset") to the overall data ("segment_constructor")

  Create a DataFrame "segment_data" from "segment_constructor"
}
```

Pseudocode is a good way to outline and debug code conceptually before you actually write it. In this case, you can compare the pseudocode to the actual Python code to see how we accomplish each step. Translating the outline into Python, we write:

```
In [8]: import numpy as np

        np.random.seed(seed=2554)
        segment_constructor = {}

        # Iterate over segments to create data for each
        for name in segment_names:
          segment_data_subset = {}
          print('segment: {0}'.format(name))
          # Within each segment, iterate over the variables and generate data
          for variable in segment_variables:
            print('\tvariable: {0}'.format(variable))
            if segment_variables_distribution[variable] == 'normal':
              # Draw random normals
              segment_data_subset[variable] = np.random.normal(
                  loc=segment_statistics[name][variable]['mean'],
                  scale=segment_statistics[name][variable]['stddev'],
                  size=segment_statistics[name]['size']
              )
            elif segment_variables_distribution[variable] == 'poisson':
              # Draw counts
              segment_data_subset[variable] = np.random.poisson(
                  lam=segment_statistics[name][variable]['mean'],
                  size=segment_statistics[name]['size']
              )
            elif segment_variables_distribution[variable] == 'binomial':
              # Draw binomials
              segment_data_subset[variable] = np.random.binomial(
                  n=1,
                  p=segment_statistics[name][variable]['mean'],
                  size=segment_statistics[name]['size']
              )
```

```
        else:
            # Data type unknown
            print('Bad segment data type: {0}'.format(
                segment_variables_distribution[j])
                )
            raise StopIteration
    segment_data_subset['Segment'] = np.repeat(
        name,
        repeats=segment_statistics[name]['size']
    )
    segment_constructor[name] = pd.DataFrame(segment_data_subset)
segment_data = pd.concat(segment_constructor.values())
```

The core commands occur inside the if statements: according to the data type we want ("normal", "poisson", or "binomial"), use the appropriate pseudorandom function to draw data (the function np.random.normal(loc, scale, size), np.random.poisson(lam, size), or np.random.binomial(n, size, p), respectively). We draw all of the values for a given variable within a given segment with a single command (drawing all the observations at once, with length specified by segment_statistics[name]['size']).

We can see an example of how this works by setting name = 'suburb_mix' and variable = 'age' and running one of the commands from the loop. We set size=10 so we don't get too many values:

```
In [9]:name = 'suburb_mix'
    variable = 'age'
    print(segment_statistics[name][variable]['mean'])
    print(segment_statistics[name][variable]['stddev'])
    np.random.normal(
        loc=segment_statistics[name][variable]['mean'],
        scale=segment_statistics[name][variable]['stddev'],
        size=10
    )
40
5
Out[9]: array([37.16950666, 45.23743976, 44.23421807, 41.62070249, 30.66891058,
        44.86711234, 34.48936766, 42.63618686, 45.16799349, 42.61294136])
```

Note that the input code ends with the). The numbers 40 and 5 are the result of the print statement, which will appear in the output block in a Colab notebook or as printed here in a Jupyter notebook.

On the last two lines of output, we see that this output has ten values. Those values are distributed around 40 and a standard deviation of 5 seems believable, although it is hard to really assess that with such a small sample.

For the Segment variable, we merely want a repetition of the segment name. To do this, we can use np.repeat(a, repeats), which will repeat the input a repeats times:

```
In [10]: np.repeat(name, repeats=10)
Out[10]: array(['suburb_mix', 'suburb_mix', 'suburb_mix', 'suburb_mix',
        'suburb_mix', 'suburb_mix', 'suburb_mix', 'suburb_mix',
        'suburb_mix', 'suburb_mix'], dtype='|S10')
```

Back to the main simulation code, there are a few things to note. To see that the code is working and to show progress, we use print() to print out the segment and variable names as the loop iterates. That results in the following output as the code runs:

```
segment: suburb_mix
        variable: age
        variable: gender
        variable: income
        variable: kids
        variable: own_home
        variable: subscribe
```

```
segment: urban_hip
        variable: age
        variable: gender
        variable: income
        variable: kids
        variable: own_home
        variable: subscribe
segment: travelers
        variable: age
        variable: gender
        variable: income
        variable: kids
        variable: own_home
        variable: subscribe
segment: moving_up
        variable: age
        variable: gender
        variable: income
        variable: kids
        variable: own_home
        variable: subscribe
```

Inside the first loop (name loop), we define `segment_data_subset` as a dictionary. In vectorized programming languages, such as R or Matlab, it would be advisable to *preallocate* the data structures as in those languages, whenever an object grows in memory—such as adding a row—a copy is made of the object. This uses twice the memory and slows things down. Preallocating avoids that problem.

Python, however is extremely efficient at growing native iterable types, such as `lists` and `dicts`, in memory. For this reason, we generate the data in a `dict`, and then convert it to a Pandas `DataFrame` for analysis.

Exceptions to this preallocation rule would be when using non-native, vectorized objects such as Numpy `arrays` and Pandas `DataFrames`. Whenever there is a need to iteratively generate data in such types, rather than converting to them from a native type, it is advisable to preallocate the data arrays. Another benefit of preallocating is that it adds a bit of error checking: if a result doesn't fit into the dataframe where it *should* fit, we will get a warning or error.

We finish the `if` blocks in our code with a `StopIteration` error that is raised in the case that a proposed data type doesn't match what we expect. There are three `if` tests for the expected data types, and a final `else` block in case none of the `if`s matches. This protects us in the case that we mistype a data type or if we try to use a distribution that hasn't been defined in the random draw code, such as a gamma distribution. This error condition would cause the code to exit immediately and print an error string.

Notice that we are doing a lot of thinking ahead about how our code might change and potentially break in the future to ensure that we would get a warning when something goes wrong. Our code also has another advantage that you may not notice right away: we call each random data function such as `np.random.normal` in exactly one place. If we discover that there was something wrong with that call—say we wanted to change one of the parameters of the call—we only need to make the correction in one place. This sort of planning is a hallmark of good programming in Python or any other language. While it might seem overly complex at first, many of these ideas will become habitual as you write more programs.

To finish up the dataset, we perform a few housekeeping tasks, converting each binomial variable to clearer values, booleans or strings:

```
In [11]: segment_data['gender'] = segment_data['gender'].apply(
             lambda x: 'male' if x else 'female'
         )
         segment_data['own_home'] = segment_data['own_home'].apply(
             lambda x: True if x else False
         )
         segment_data['subscribe'] = segment_data['subscribe'].apply(
             lambda x: True if x else False
         )
```

We may now inspect the data. As always, we recommend a data inspection plan as noted in Sect. 3.6, although we only show one of those steps here:

```
In [12]: segment_data.describe(include='all')
```

```
Out[12]:           Segment         age gender        income        kids  \
         count         300  300.000000    300    300.000000  300.000000
         unique          4         NaN      2           NaN         NaN
         top    suburb_mix         NaN   male           NaN         NaN
         freq          100         NaN    156           NaN         NaN
         mean          NaN   40.923350    NaN  50669.454237    1.273333
         std           NaN   12.827494    NaN  19336.497748    1.413725
         min           NaN   18.388730    NaN  11297.309231    0.000000
         25%           NaN   32.870035    NaN  41075.804389    0.000000
         50%           NaN   38.896711    NaN  51560.344807    1.000000
         75%           NaN   47.987569    NaN  62172.668698    2.000000
         max           NaN   79.650722    NaN 108830.388732    7.000000

                own_home subscribe
         count       300       300
         unique        2         2
         top       False     False
         freq        167       265
         mean        NaN       NaN
         std         NaN       NaN
         min         NaN       NaN
         25%         NaN       NaN
         50%         NaN       NaN
         75%         NaN       NaN
         max         NaN       NaN
```

The dataframe is now suitable for exploration. And we have reusable code: we could create data with more observations, different segment sizes, or segments with different distributions or means by simply adjusting the matrices that define the segments and running the code again.

As a final step we save the dataframe as a backup and to use again in later chapters (Sects. 10.2 and 11.1.2). Change the destination if you have created a folder for this book or prefer a different location:

```
In [13]: from google.colab import files
         with open('segment_dataframe_Python_intro_Ch5.csv', 'w') as f:
             segment_data.to_csv(f)


         files.download('segment_dataframe_Python_intro_Ch5.csv')
```

Note that if you are running Python locally, the `files.download()` command is unnecessary, as is importing the `files` module (which is Colab-specific).

5.2 Finding Descriptives by Group

For our consumer segmentation data, we are interested in how measures such as household income and gender vary for the different segments. With this insight, a firm might develop tailored offerings for the segments or engage in different ways to reach them.

An ad hoc way to do this is with dataframe indexing: find the rows that match some criterion, and then take the mean (or some other statistic) for the matching observations on a variable of interest. For example, to find the mean income for the "moving_up" segment:

```
In [14]: segment_data.loc[segment_data.Segment == 'moving_up']['income'].mean()
Out[14]: 51763.55266630597
```

This says "from the income observations, take all cases where the Segment column is 'moving_up' and calculate their mean." We could further narrow the cases to "moving_up" respondents who also do not subscribe using Boolean logic:

```
In [15]: segment_data.loc[
             (segment_data['Segment'] == 'moving_up') &
             (segment_data['subscribe'] == False)
         ]['income'].mean()

Out[15]: 52495.6820839035
```

This quickly becomes tedious when you wish to find values for multiple groups.

As we saw briefly in Sect. 3.2.1, a more general way to do this is with `data.groupby(INDICES)[COLUMN].FUNCTION`. The result of `groupby()` is to divide `data` into groups for each of the unique values in `INDICES` and then apply the `FUNCTION` function to the data in `COLUMN` for each group:

```
In [16]: segment_data.groupby('Segment')['income'].mean()

Out[16]: Segment
         moving_up      51763.552666
         suburb_mix     55552.282925
         travelers      62609.655328
         urban_hip      20267.737317
         Name: income, dtype: float64
```

With `groupby()`, keep in mind that it is a method on `data` and the splitting factors `INDICES` are the argument. The `FUNCTION`, `mean()` in this case, is applied to a single `COLUMN`, 'income' in this case. There are a subset of defined methods that can be applied to the columns, such as `mean()` and `sum()`, but any method can be applied using the `apply` method as described in Sect. 3.3.3.

You can break out the results by multiple factors if you supply factors in a `list`. For example, we can break out by segment and subscription status:

```
In [17]: segment_data.groupby(['Segment', 'subscribe'])['income'].mean()

Out[17]: Segment      subscribe
         moving_up    False        52495.682084
                      True         49079.078135
         suburb_mix   False        55332.038973
                      True         58478.381142
         travelers    False        62940.429960
                      True         49709.444658
         urban_hip    False        20496.375001
                      True         19457.112800
         Name: income, dtype: float64
```

Here, we can use the `unstack()` method on the output to get a nicer formatting of the output:

```
In [18]: segment_data.groupby(
             ['Segment', 'subscribe']
         )['income'].mean().unstack()

Out[18]: subscribe           False           True
         Segment
         moving_up     52495.682084   49079.078135
         suburb_mix    55332.038973   58478.381142
         travelers     62940.429960   49709.444658
         urban_hip     20496.375001   19457.112800
```

What does `unstack()` do? Since we grouped by two different columns, we wound up with a hierarchical index. We can "unstack," or pivot, that hierarchy, making one dimension a column and the other a row using `unstack()`. This can make the output easier to read and to work with.

Suppose we wish to add a "segment mean" column to our dataset, a new observation for each respondent that contains the mean income for their respective segment so we can compare respondents' incomes to those typical for their segments. We can do this by using `groupby()` to get the segment means, and then using `join()` to add the mean segment income as a column `income_seg`. We generally do not like adding derived columns to primary data because we like to separate data from subsequent computation, but we do so here for illustration:

```
In [19]: np.random.seed(4532)
         segment_income = segment_data.groupby('Segment')['income'].mean()
         segment_data = segment_data.join(segment_income,
                                          on='Segment',
                                          rsuffix='_segment')
         segment_data.head(5)

Out[19]:       age   gender      income    kids   own_home   subscribe  \
         0  44.057078  female  54312.575694    3     False      False
         1  34.284213  female  67057.192182    1     False      False
         2  45.159484  female  56306.492991    3      True      False
         3  41.032557    male  66329.337521    1     False       True
         4  41.781819  female  56500.410372    2     False      False

               Segment    income_segment
         0    suburb_mix     55552.282925
         1    suburb_mix     55552.282925
         2    suburb_mix     55552.282925
         3    suburb_mix     55552.282925
         4    suburb_mix     55552.282925
```

When we check the data, we see that each row has an observation that matches its segment mean.

It is worth thinking about how this works. In a `join()`, two DataFrames, two Series, or a DataFrame and a Series can be combined using a common column as an index, in this case `Segment`. Even though `segment_income` only had 4 rows, one for each segment, a value was added to every row of `seg` based on the shared value of the `Segment` column. The result is a dataframe in which each row of `segment_mean` occurs many times in the order requested.

Again, we don't want a derived column in our primary data, so we now remove that column by using the `drop()` method:

```
In [20]: segment_data.drop(labels='income_segment', axis=1, inplace=True)
         segment_data.head(5)

Out[20]:       age   gender      income    kids   own_home   subscribe  \
         0  44.057078  female  54312.575694    3     False      False
         ...
         4  41.781819  female  56500.410372    2     False      False

               Segment
         0    suburb_mix
         ...
         4    suburb_mix
```

As an aside, `drop()` removes an entire row or column from a dataframe. We specify whether we want it to be a row or column with the `axis` argument: 0 for row and 1 for column. Which column or row to remove is specified with the `label` argument, which can specify a single label or can be a list of labels to be removed. The `inplace=True` argument specifies that this should be done on the object itself. The default value for `inplace` is `False`, in which case `drop()` will return a copy of the input dataframe rather than modifying it.

Going back to our main point, which was being quickly able to compare an individual response to the segment mean, we see that `groupby()` exemplifies the power of Python and pandas to extract and manipulate data with simple and concise commands.

5.2.1 Descriptives for Two-way Groups

A common task in marketing is cross-tabulating, separating customers into groups according to two (or more) factors. We can use `groupby()` to aggregate across multiple factors. For example:

```
In [21]: segment_data.groupby(['Segment', 'own_home'])['income'].mean()
```

```
Out[21]: Segment     own_home
         moving_up   False       51430.222115
                     True        52363.547659
         suburb_mix  False       56764.508540
                     True        54239.038508
         travelers   False       62923.233941
                     True        62449.907732
         urban_hip   False       20139.092369
                     True        21057.984851
         Name: income, dtype: float64
```

We now have a separate group for each combination of `Segment` and `own_home` and can begin to see how `income` is related to both the `Segment` and the `own_home` variables.

The grouping can be extended to include as many grouping variables as needed:

```
In [22]: segment_data.groupby(
             ['Segment', 'own_home', 'subscribe']
         )['income'].mean()
```

```
Out[22]: Segment     own_home  subscribe
         moving_up   False     False        52380.092911
                               True         47630.738931
                     True      False        52714.693149
                               True         51251.586942
         suburb_mix  False     False        56478.645027
                               True         59451.625569
                     True      False        54160.506701
                               True         56045.270075
         travelers   False     False        62923.233941
                     True      False        62949.533735
                               True         49709.444658
         urban_hip   False     False        20171.798013
                               True         20031.163747
                     True      False        22281.548438
                               True         13716.603325
         Name: income, dtype: float64
```

And, again, we can use `unstack()` to make it more readable:

```
In [23]: segment_data.groupby(
             ['Segment', 'own_home', 'subscribe']
         )['income'].mean().unstack()
```

```
Out[23]: subscribe                  False           True
         Segment     own_home
         moving_up   False       52380.092911   47630.738931
                     True        52714.693149   51251.586942
         suburb_mix  False       56478.645027   59451.625569
                     True        54160.506701   56045.270075
         travelers   False       62923.233941            NaN
                     True        62949.533735   49709.444658
```

```
urban_hip    False        20171.798013    20031.163747
             True         22281.548438    13716.603325
```

The `groupby` method allows us to compute functions of continuous variables, such as the `mean` of `income` or `age`, for any combination of factors (`Segment`, `own_home` and so forth). This is such a common task in marketing research that there used to be entire companies who specialize in producing cross tabs. As we've just seen, these are not difficult to compute in Python.

We might also want to know the *frequency* with which different combinations of `Segment` and `own_home` occur. We can compute frequencies using `groupby()` along with the `count()` method to obtain one-way or multi-way counts:

```
In [24]: segment_data.groupby(
             ['Segment', 'own_home']
         )['subscribe'].count().unstack()
```

```
Out[24]: own_home     False    True
         Segment
         moving_up       45      25
         suburb_mix      52      48
         travelers       27      53
         urban_hip       43       7
```

There are 7 observed customers in the "Urban hip" segment who own their own homes, and 53 in the "Travelers" segment.

Suppose we want a breakdown of the number of kids in each household (`kids`) by segment:

```
In [25]: segment_data.groupby(
             ['kids', 'Segment']
         ).subscribe.count().unstack(level=1)
```

```
Out[25]: Segment   moving_up   suburb_mix   travelers   urban_hip
         kids
         0               13.0         15.0        80.0        14.0
         1               18.0         27.0         NaN        21.0
         2               21.0         21.0         NaN        12.0
         3                9.0         29.0         NaN         1.0
         4                5.0          3.0         NaN         1.0
         5                2.0          3.0         NaN         1.0
         6                1.0          2.0         NaN         NaN
         7                1.0          NaN         NaN         NaN
```

This tells us that we have 14 "Urban hip" respondents with 0 kids, 21 "Suburb mix" respondents with 2 kids, and so forth. It represents purely the count of incidence for each crossing point between the two factors, `kids` and `Segment`. In this case we are treating `kids` as a factor and not a number. Note that `NaN` indicates that there were no values for that combination of factors, i.e., the count is zero.

We can also use the `crosstabs()` function to get the same result:

```
In [26]: pd.crosstab(segment_data['kids'], segment_data['Segment'])
```

```
Out[26]: Segment   moving_up   suburb_mix   travelers   urban_hip
         kids
         0               13           15          80          14
         1               18           27           0          21
         2               21           21           0          12
         3                9           29           0           1
         4                5            3           0           1
         5                2            3           0           1
         6                1            2           0           0
         7                1            0           0           0
```

However, `kids` is actually a count variable; if a respondent reported 3 kids, that is a count of 3 and we could add together the counts to get the total number of children reported in each segment.:

```
In [27]: segment_data.groupby('Segment')['kids'].sum()
Out[27]: Segment
         moving_up       130
         suburb_mix      195
         travelers         0
         urban_hip        57
         Name: kids, dtype: int64
```

Python typically has many ways to arrive at the same result. This may seem overly complex yet it is a good thing. One reason is that there are multiple options to match your style and situation. Each method produces results in a different format, and one format might work better in some situation than another. Another reason is that you can do the same thing in two different ways and compare the answers, thus testing your analyses and uncovering potential errors.

5.2.2 Visualization by Group: Frequencies and Proportions

Tables are very valuable for exploring data and interactions between various factors. However, visualizations can rapidly reveal associations that may be less obvious when observed within a table.

The most commonly used plotting library in Python, and default pandas plotting library is `matplotlib` (Hunter 2007). Its integration with pandas makes plotting DataFrames straightforward.

Suppose we plot the count of subscribers for each segment to understand better which segments use the subscription service, as in Fig. 5.1:

```
In [28]: import matplotlib.pyplot as plt

         segments_groupby_segments = segment_data.groupby(['Segment'])
         segments_groupby_segments['subscribe'].value_counts().unstack().plot(
             kind='barh',
             figsize=(8, 8)
         )
         plt.xlabel('counts')
```

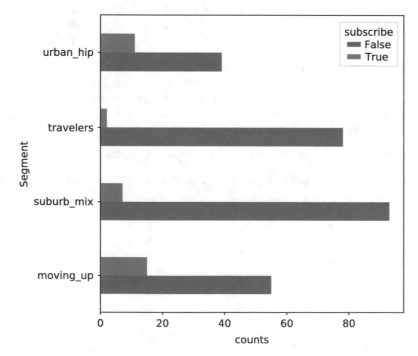

Fig. 5.1 Conditional histogram for count of subscribers within each segment

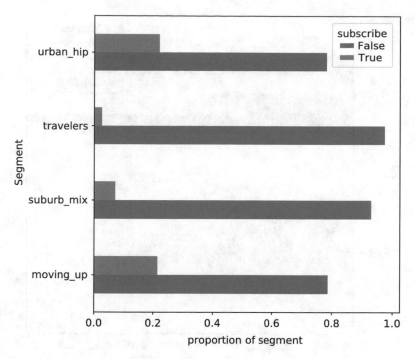

Fig. 5.2 Conditional histogram for proportion of subscribers within each segment

Here, we used the `value_counts()` function introduced in 3.2.2. `unstack()` *unstacks* the indices, turning the series object in to a dataframe that we can easily plot.

By passing `normalize=True` to `value_counts()` we can get proportions within each segment that subscribe, as in Fig. 5.2:

```
In [29]: segments_groupby_segments['subscribe'].value_counts(
             normalize=True
         ).unstack().plot(
             kind='barh',
             figsize=(8, 8)
         )
         plt.xlabel('proportion of segment')
```

And by aggregating by `subscribe` and running `value_count()` on `Segment` we can see breakdown of subscribers and non-subscribers by segment (Fig. 5.3):

```
In [30]: segment_data.groupby(['subscribe'])['Segment'].value_counts(
             normalize=True
         ).unstack().plot(kind='barh', figsize=(8, 8))
         plt.xlabel('proportion of subscribers')
```

Another popular packages is `seaborn`, which simplifies some of the aggregation steps and makes attractive figures with the default options. We can easily create something similar to Fig. 5.2 (not shown):

```
In [31]: import seaborn as sns
         sns.barplot(y='Segment', x='subscribe', data=segment_data,
                     orient='h', ci=None)
```

Seaborn also includes the `facetgrid()` function which allows the creation of multipanel figures, as in Fig. 5.4:

```
In [32]: g = sns.FacetGrid(segment_data, col='Segment')
         g.map(sns.barplot, 'subscribe', orient='v', ci=None)
```

This particular usage is not very interesting, but we can now separate out another factor, such as home ownership and have the respective bars in separate rows (Fig. 5.5):

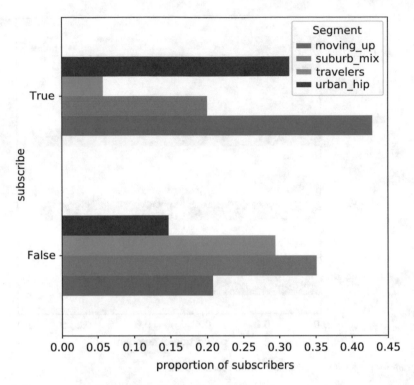

Fig. 5.3 Conditional histogram for proportion of segments within each subscription state

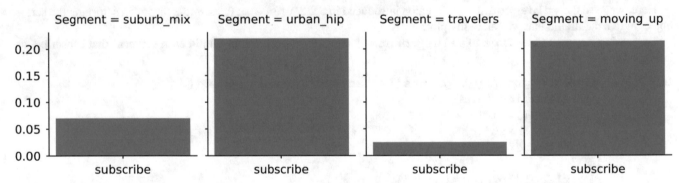

Fig. 5.4 Conditional histogram for proportion of segments within each subscription state generate using Seaborn facetgrid()

```
In [33]: g = sns.FacetGrid(segment_data, col='Segment', row='own_home')
         g.map(sns.barplot, 'subscribe', orient='v', ci=None)
```

5.2.3 Visualization by Group: Continuous Data

In the previous section we saw how to plot counts and proportions. What about continuous data? How would we plot income by segment in our data? A simple way is to use groupby() to find the mean income, and then use the plot(kind='bar') method to plot the computed values:

```
In [34]: segment_data.groupby(['Segment'])['income'].mean().plot.bar()
```

The result is in the left panel of Fig. 5.6. We can also use seaborn barplot() to produce a similar plot, shown in the right panel of Fig. 5.6:

```
In [35]: sns.barplot(x='Segment', y='income', data=segment_data, color='.6',
                      estimator=np.mean, ci=95)
```

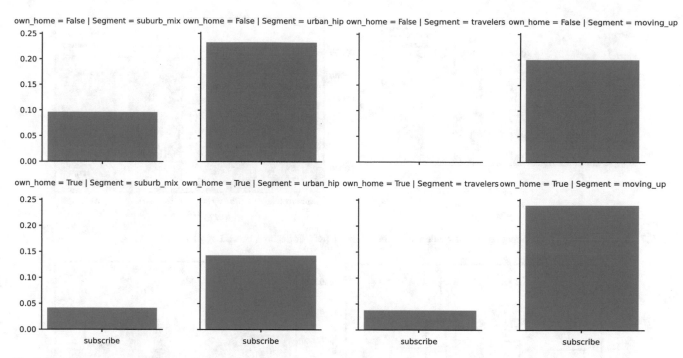

Fig. 5.5 Conditional histogram for proportion of segments within each subscription state generate using Seaborn facetgrid()

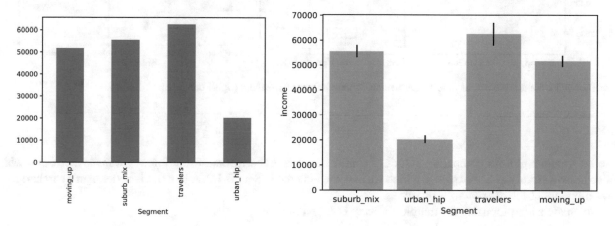

Fig. 5.6 Average income by segment using `groupby()` and `plot()` in the left panel and seaborn `barplot()` in the right panel

Note that the two plotting functions order the segments differently. Seaborn does more processing of the data and does things like sorting the columns. In general, Seaborn figures work better out of the box, but can be more difficult to customize.

Adding Another Factor

How do we split this out further by home ownership? Using matplotlib, we can add another `groupby` factor, `own_home`, shown in Fig. 5.7 left panel:

```
In [36]: segment_data.groupby(
            ['Segment', 'own_home']
        )['income'].mean().unstack().plot.bar()
```

Using Seaborn, an additional factor may be added in the form of a facet grid, as in Fig. 5.6, or by setting the hue parameter, as shown in the right panel of Fig. 5.7:

```
In [37]: sns.barplot(x='Segment', y='income', hue='own_home',
                data=segment_data, estimator=np.mean, ci=95)
```

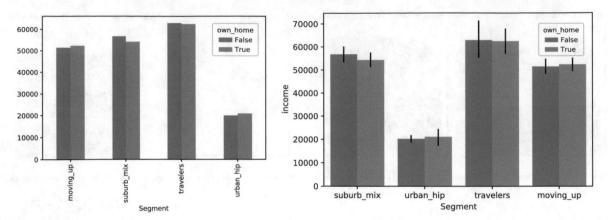

Fig. 5.7 Average income by segment and home ownership using `plot()` (left) or Seaborn `barplot()` (right)

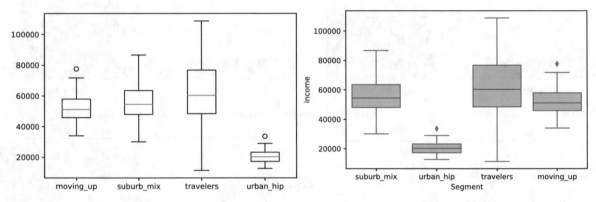

Fig. 5.8 Box-and-whiskers plot for income by segment using matplotlib (left) Seaborn (right) `boxplot()` functions

Box Plot

A more informative plot for comparing values of continuous data, like `income` for different groups is a *box-and-whiskers* plot (also known simply as a "boxplot"), which we first encountered in Sect. 3.4.2. A boxplot is better than a barchart because it shows more about the *distributions* of values.

We can create a boxplot using the matplotib `boxplot()` function:

```
In [38]: x = segment_data.groupby('Segment')['income'].apply(list)
         _ = plt.boxplot(x=x.values, labels=x.index)
```

Seaborn `boxplot()` works with a DataFrame and two factors (at least one of which must be numeric):

```
In [39]: sns.boxplot(x='Segment', y='income', data=segment_data,
                      color='0.7', orient='v')
```

Figure 5.8 shows that the income for "Travelers" is higher and also has a greater range, with a few "Travelers" reporting very low incomes. The range of income for "Urban hip" is much lower and tighter. Although box-and-whisker plots are not common in business reporting, we think they should be. They encode a lot more information than the averages shown in Fig. 5.6.

To break this down by more factors, we may add a `hue` argument. The Seaborn `facetgrid()` method allows us to condition on more factors. However, for two factors, such as comparing income by segment and home ownership, we might use `hue`:

```
In [40]: sns.boxplot(y='Segment', x='income', hue='own_home',
                      data=segment_data, color='0.7', orient='h')
```

In Fig. 5.9, it is clear that within segments there is no consistent relationship between income and home ownership.

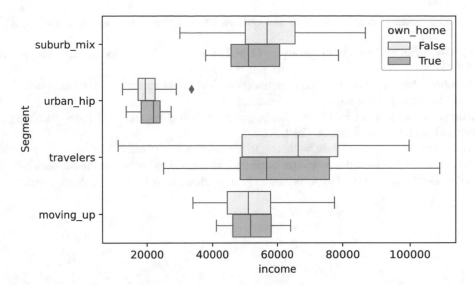

Fig. 5.9 Box-and-whiskers plot for income by segment and home ownership using `boxplot`

5.2.4 Bringing It All Together

We have learned how to approach comparing groups. How might we use this? As analysts, we explore data in order to learn new information that we can share and to inform marketing and product decisions. So how might we interpret what we have seen so far?

We have not yet done any statistical analysis, which we introduce in Chap. 6, so any conclusions must be tempered. But, directionally, we observe that the segments differ in several ways that may affect how we should market our subscription product. If our subscription is an expensive, luxury product, we might want to target only the wealthier segments. Perhaps those without children are more likely to have disposable income, and they may be members of the "travelers segment," which has a very low rate of subscription. On the other hand, if our product is intended for young urbanites (i.e., "urban hip"), who show a high subscription rate, we might take more care with pricing, as the average income is lower in that group.

The exact interpretation depends on what problem we are trying to solve. Are we trying to understand our current customers so we can get more similar customers? Or are we trying to expand our customer base into different groups?

The way we approach an analysis is driven by the questions we want to answer, not by the data we have. Sometimes our ability to answer those questions is hampered by the data we have available. In that case, we might think about new data sources, or apply cautious interpretation.

5.3 Learning More*

The topics in this chapter are foundational both for programming skills in Python and for applied statistics.

For categorical data analysis, the best starting place is—although not specific to Python—is Agresti's *An Introduction to Categorical Data Analysis* (Agresti 2012).

In Chap. 6 we continue our investigation with methods that formalize group comparisons and estimate the statistical strength of differences between groups.

5.4 Key Points

This was a crucial chapter for doing everyday analytics with Python. Here are some of the key points.

- We generated a very complicated dataset; to do so, we defined each segment variable, its distribution type, and the parameters of those distributions. We used those initializations in a set of for loops to generate the dataset (Sect. 5.1)

- The `groupby()` command can split up data and automatically apply functions such as `mean()` and `count()` (Sect. 5.2)
- Frequency of occurrence can be found with `groupby()` and the `count()` function or using the pandas `crosstabs()` function (Sect. 5.2.1)
- matplotlib and Seaborn both offer valuable plotting functions. Seaborn plots tend to look better in default settings, but are more complex to customize than matplotlib plots (Sect. 5.2.2)
- Charts of proportions and occurrence by a factor can be generated using `groupby()` along with the `plot()` method or by using the Seaborn `barplot()` function (Sect. 5.2.2)
- The Seaborn `FacetGrid()` class extends such plots to multiple factors (Sect. 5.2.2)
- Plots for continuous data by factor can also use `groupby()` along with `plot()` or the Seaborn `barplot()` function, or even better, box-and-whiskers plots with `boxplot()`, from either matplotlib or Seaborn. (Sect. 5.2.3)

Chapter 6
Comparing Groups: Statistical Tests

In Chap. 5 we saw how to break out data by groups and inspect them with tables and charts. In this chapter we continue our discussion and address the question, "It looks different, but is it really different?" This involves our first inferential statistical procedures: chi-square, t-tests, and analysis of variance (ANOVA).

6.1 Data for Comparing Groups

In this chapter, we continue with the data from Chap. 5. If you saved it at that time, you could load it again with a command such as:

```
In [0]: from google.colab import files
        import pandas as pd

        uploaded = files.upload()
        seg_df = pd.read_csv('segment_dataframe_Python_intro_Ch5.csv',
                             index_col=0)
        seg_df.head()

Saving segment_data_Ch5.csv to segment_data_Ch5.csv
```

```
Out[0]:      Segment        age  gender         income  kids  own_home  \
        0   travelers  60.794945    male   57014.537526     0      True
        1   travelers  61.764535  female   43796.941252     0     False
        2   travelers  47.493356    male   51095.344683     0      True
        3   travelers  60.963694    male   56457.722237     0      True
        4   travelers  60.594199  female  103020.070798     0      True

            subscribe
        0       False
        1       False
        2       False
        3        True
        4       False
```

The file selector interface is used to select the file to upload and the key passed to `uploaded` (e.g. `segment_dataframe_Python_intro_Ch5.csv`) will need to match the name of the uploaded file.

Alternatively, you could create the data following the procedure in Sect. 5.1. Or download it from this book's web site:

```
In [1]: import pandas as pd
        seg_df = pd.read_csv('http://bit.ly/PMR-ch5')
        seg_df.head()
```

© Springer Nature Switzerland AG 2020

J. S. Schwarz et al., *Python for Marketing Research and Analytics*, https://doi.org/10.1007/978-3-030-49720-0_6

```
Out[1]:          Segment        age  gender          income  kids  own_home  \
         0      travelers  60.794945    male    57014.537526     0      True
         ...
         4      travelers  60.594199  female   103020.070798     0      True

              subscribe
         0        False
         ...
         4        False
```

6.2 Testing Group Frequencies: `scipy.stats.chisquare()`

Much of the work we do in marketing analytics and marketing research involves summarizing the differences between groups using group averages and cross tabs as we described in Sect. 5.2. However, a good analyst is able to use *statistical tests* to determine whether differences are real or might instead be due to minor variation ("noise") in the data. In the rest of the book, we largely focus on statistical tests that help to identify real differences.

One of the simplest statistical tests is the *chi-square* test, which is used with frequency counts. A chi-square test determines whether the frequencies in cells are significantly different from what one would expect on the basis of their total counts.

In our segment data, we might ask whether there are equal numbers of respondents in each segment, given a marginal count of N=300 observations. In Python, we can use the `chisquare()` command from Scipy `stats`. One thing to remember is that in general `chisquare` operates on frequency counts (such as produced by NumPy `unique()` or pandas `value_counts()`). To see how this works, let's look at the process using simple data before we tackle the question for our segments. Experimenting with simple data is always a good idea when trying a new command.

For the first example, we create a table where the data comprises 95 observations of the numbers 0 to 3 and where the counts of each are almost, but not quite identical. We then test this with `scipy.stats.chisquare()`.

First, we generate the data:

```
In [2]: import numpy as np
        tmp = np.repeat(range(4), [25, 25, 25, 20])
        tmp
```

```
Out[2]: array([0, 0, 0, 0, 0, 0, 0, 0, 0, 0, 0, 0, 0, 0, 0, 0, 0, 0, 0, 0, 0,
               0, 0, 0, 1, 1, 1, 1, 1, 1, 1, 1, 1, 1, 1, 1, 1, 1, 1, 1, 1, 1,
               1, 1, 1, 1, 1, 1, 2, 2, 2, 2, 2, 2, 2, 2, 2, 2, 2, 2, 2, 2, 2,
               2, 2, 2, 2, 2, 2, 2, 2, 2, 2, 3, 3, 3, 3, 3, 3, 3, 3, 3, 3, 3, 3,
               3, 3, 3, 3, 3, 3, 3])
```

We then use the `unique()` method from NumPy to get the count of each value:

```
In [3]: tmp_values, tmp_counts = np.unique(tmp, return_counts=True)
        tmp_counts
```

```
Out[3]: array([25, 25, 25, 20])
```

We import `stats` from Scipy and use the `stats.chisquare()` method:

```
In [4]: from scipy import stats
        stats.chisquare(tmp_counts)
```

```
Out[4]: Power_divergenceResult(statistic=0.78947, pvalue=0.85198)
```

In this code, we generate 95 observations of 0 to 3, compile those into a table, and then test that table for chi-square independence. The test evaluates the likelihood of seeing such a result under the *null hypothesis* that the data were randomly sampled from a large population where the values 0, 1, 2, and 3 are *equally distributed*, given a marginal count of N=95 observations. The *p-value* of 0.852 tells us that there is an estimated 85% chance of seeing a dataset with differences similar to or greater than those in our table if the null hypothesis is true. We conclude that under the assumptions of the chi-square test, our table does not suggest real differences in frequency between the four cells. Put another way, these data show no evidence that the groups in the population are of unequal size, under the assumption of random sampling.

Compare that to the following, which differs from the code above by a single character—we change the number of observations of "3" from 20 to 10:

```
In [5]: tmp_values, tmp_counts = np.unique(np.repeat(range(4),
                                           [25, 25, 25, 10]),
                                 return_counts=True)
        print(tmp_counts)
        print(stats.chisquare(tmp_counts))
        print('Expected values: {}'.format(np.ones(4)*tmp_counts.sum()/4))

[25 25 25 10]
Power_divergenceResult(statistic=7.9411764705882355, pvalue=0.04724318343092867)
Expected values: [21.25 21.25 21.25 21.25]
```

In this case, we could conclude from the *p*-value of 0.047 that we can reject the null hypothesis of no difference between the cells with "95% confidence." In other words, the data in this sample suggest that the distribution of the values 0 to 3 is likely to be unequal in the larger population, assuming the data are a random sample of N=85 observations. In general, a *p*-value less than 0.10 or 0.05 suggests that there is a difference between groups.

As an aside, there are disagreements among statisticians about the meaning of null hypotheses and the value of traditional significance testing. We do not advocate classical significance testing in particular, but report the methods here because they are widely used in marketing to gauge the strength of evidence in a dataset. We believe the classical methods are imperfect but nevertheless useful and important to know. For review and discussion of the controversies and alternatives see Cohen 1994, Kruschke 2010, and Hubbard and Armstrong 2006.

In the results above, if we had a smaller sample we would not get the same result for the significance test even if the relative proportion of customers in each group were the same. Significance tests are sensitive to both the observed difference and the sample size. To see this, we can create data with the same proportions but one fifth as many observations by dividing `tmp_counts` by 5.

```
In [6]: tmp_counts_small = tmp_counts/5
        print(tmp_counts_small)
        print(stats.chisquare(tmp_counts_small))
        print('Expected values: {}'.format(np.ones(4)*tmp_counts_small.sum()/4))

[5. 5. 5. 2.]
Power_divergenceResult(statistic=1.5882352941176472, pvalue=0.6620603202525777)
Expected values: [4.25 4.25 4.25 4.25]
```

This shows a non-significant result—no evidence of a real difference in group sizes—even though the proportion of people in the "3" group is the same as in the larger sample above where the result was significant. This highlights one of the cautions about statistical significance testing: it is dependent on sample size as well as on the real effect.

As a general rule, the required sample sizes for a chi-squared test is greater than 20 overall and the expected count for each category should be greater than 5.

It's not only *low* sample sizes that can be problematic, but *high* sample sizes as well. Let's modify our original demonstration, but rather than reduce the sample size fivefold, let's increase it:

```
In [7]: tmp_counts_large = tmp_counts*10 + 1900
        print(tmp_counts_large)
        print(stats.chisquare(tmp_counts_large))
        print('Expected values: {}'.format(np.ones(4)*tmp_counts_large.sum()/4))

[2150 2150 2150 2000]
Power_divergenceResult(statistic=7.988165680473372, pvalue=0.04625691960442831)
Expected values: [2112.5 2112.5 2112.5 2112.5]
```

The *p*-value is again less than 0.05, and very similar to our previous example (`0.047` vs `0.046`). But given the large sample size, this is true even though the proportional differences between the groups are relatively small. In this case, the business context matters. The "3" group has about 100 fewer members than expected. That is statistically significant, but is it meaningful? That depends on what the units are and what decisions might be made based on this analysis.

Oftentimes, with large numbers, the statistical significance itself is not very useful, and it might be more valuable to use the *effect size*, which estimates the magnitude of the difference. In this case, the deviation between the observed and expected value for category "3" is about 5% (2000 vs 2112.5). Whereas, in our earlier example, which had nearly the same *p*-value, the difference is over 200% (10 vs 21.25).

Returning to our simulated segment data, which has N=300 observations, we ask whether the segment sizes are significantly different from one another (assuming that our 300 customers are a random sample of a larger population). We use the same procedure as above:

```
In [7]: segment_values, segment_counts = np.unique(seg_df.Segment,
                                                 return_counts=True)
        print(segment_counts)
        stats.chisquare(segment_counts)

[ 70 100  80  50]


Out[7]: Power_divergenceResult(statistic=17.33333, pvalue=0.00060)
```

The answer to our question is "yes, there are differences in segment size." That is, with $p = 0.0006$, our sample does not support the hypothesis that there is an identical number of customers in each segment.

Here we used the NumPy `unique()` method, as before. But since `seg_df` is a `DataFrame`, we can also use the Pandas `value_counts()` method:

```
In [8]: seg_df.Segment.value_counts()

Out[8]: suburb_mix    100
        travelers      80
        moving_up      70
        urban_hip      50
        Name: Segment, dtype: int64
```

This can be passed directly to the `chisquare()` method:

```
In [9]: stats.chisquare(seg_df.Segment.value_counts())

Out[9]: Power_divergenceResult(statistic=17.33333, pvalue=0.00060)
```

Is subscription status independent from home ownership, as we hypothesized when we plotted the data in Sect. 5.2? That is, in our simulated data, are respondents just as likely to subscribe or not, without regard to home ownership status (and conversely, are they just as likely to own a home or not, independent of subscription status)? We construct a two-way table using the Pandas `crosstab()` method and test it using `chisquare_contingency()`:

```
In [10]: pd.crosstab(seg_df.subscribe, columns=seg_df.own_home)

Out[10]: own_home    False   True
         subscribe
         False         143    122
         True           24     11

In [11]: stats.chi2_contingency(pd.crosstab(seg_df.subscribe,
                                          columns=seg_df.own_home))

Out[11]: (2.114527405072716,
          0.14590708913184341,
          1,
          array([[147.51666667, 117.48333333],
                 [ 19.48333333,  15.51666667]]))
```

The output from `chi2_contingency()` is not labeled. Looking at the docs, we can wrap the function in a `print` statement to make the output easier to understand:

```
In [12]: sub_by_home = pd.crosstab(seg_df.subscribe,
                                    columns=seg_df.own_home)
         print('chisq_stat: {0}\np_value: {1}\ndof: {2}\nexpected_values: {3}'
               .format(*stats.chi2_contingency(sub_by_home)))

chisq_stat: 2.114527405072716
p_value: 0.14590708913184341
dof: 1
expected_values: [[147.51666667 117.48333333]
 [ 19.48333333  15.51666667]]
```

The null hypothesis in this case is that the factors are unrelated, i.e., that the counts in the cells are as one might expect from the marginal proportions. Based on the high *p*-value, we cannot reject the null hypothesis, but instead must conclude that there is no evidence to show that the factors are related, i.e. that there is no evidence that home ownership is *not* independent of subscription status in our data. Although people in general have a low subscription rate—and thus there are many more non-subscribers than subscribers in both groups—there is insufficient evidence to indicate a *relationship* between subscription rate and home ownership.

Note that `chi2_contingency()` defaults to using *Yates' correction*, which adjusts the chi-square statistic in light of the fact that the assumption of continuous data is imperfect when data come from a lumpy binomial distribution. If you want the results to match traditional values such as calculation by hand or spreadsheet, turn that off with `correction=False`:

```
In [13]: print('chisq_stat: {0}\np_value: {1}\ndof: {2}\nexpected_values: {3}'
               .format(*stats.chi2_contingency(sub_by_home,
                                               correction=False)))

chisq_stat: 2.6737316360934784
p_value: 0.10201657409843726
dof: 1
expected_values: [[147.51666667 117.48333333]
 [ 19.48333333  15.51666667]]
```

The test statistics and *p*-values change slightly between these commands, but the overall conclusion is the same, namely that there is no evidence that the factors are related.

6.3 Testing Observed Proportions: `binom_test()`

When we are dealing with observations that have only two values, we can consider them to be a binomial (two-valued) variable. We illustrate this by taking a brief break from marketing data. On the day of Superbowl XLVIII in 2014, played in the New York City area, Chris took a walk in Manhattan and observed 12 groups of Seattle fans and 8 groups of Denver fans.

Suppose we assume the observations are a random sample of a binomial value (either Seattle or Denver fandom). Is the observed value of 60% Seattle fans significantly different from equal representation (which would be 50% each)? To do this, we will introduce a new package: Statsmodels. Statsmodels provides classes and functions for many statistical models and tests.

We use `statsmodels.proportion.binom_test()` to test the likelihood of randomly observing 12 cases out of 20 in one direction, if the true likelihood is 50%:

```
In [14]: from statsmodels.stats import proportion as sms_proportion
In [15]: sms_proportion.binom_test(count=12, nobs=20, prop=0.5)

Out[15]: 0.5034446716308595
```

We could interpret the *p*-value (p=0.5034) as being non-significant, i.e., as failing to support the idea that the results are different from the null hypothesis. It would be helpful to also look at the 95% confidence interval:

```
In [16]: sms_proportion.proportion_confint(count=12, nobs=20, alpha=0.05)
```

```
Out[16]: (0.38529670275394107, 0.8147032972460588)
```

Based on our data, the 95% confidence interval is 36–81%, which includes the null hypothesis value of 50%. Thus, we conclude that observing 60% Seattle fans in a sample of 20 does not conclusively demonstrate that there are more Seattle fans in the larger group of fans roaming New York.

6.3.1 About Confidence Intervals

We have mentioned *confidence intervals* several times, and should take a moment to discuss them because they are widely misunderstood. Our definition of a 95% confidence interval is this: it is the range of possible estimates that we would expect to see 95% of the time if we repeatedly estimate a statistic using *random samples* of the *same sample size* under the assumption that the *true value* in an *infinite* or very large population is the same as our current estimate. In other words, it is the best guess of the range of possible answers we would expect with repeated random samples. When the confidence interval excludes the null hypothesis (such as a probability of 0.5 for equal chances, or a mean difference of 0 for no difference between groups), then the result is said to be *statistically significant*.

There are many misunderstandings of confidence intervals and statistical significance. Confidence intervals (CIs) do *not* express "how confident we are in the answer" because they do not reflect the degree of confidence in the assumptions. For example, true random sampling is rare, so the presumption of random sampling is usually not completely justified; but that additional uncertainty is not reflected in the CI. CIs are often misunderstood to imply that "the true value lies in the CI range," when in fact it is the other way around; *if* the true value is what we obtained, then we would expect additional estimates to fall within this CI 95% of the time under further rounds of random sampling. The CI is about *estimates*, not about the true value. Additionally, statistical significance does not imply practical importance or the meaningfulness of a result; a tiny difference can be statistically significant with a large sample even when it is not actionable or interpretable as a business matter.

In practice, we suggest that before interpreting a result, make sure it is statistically significant for some level of confidence interval (95%, or possibly 90% or 99% depending on how sensitive the matter is). If it is not significant, then your evidence for the result is weak, and you should not interpret it. In that case, either say that, ignore the result, or collect more data. If the result *is* significant, then proceed with your interpretation and reporting (taking care with how you describe "confidence"). Interpret results in light of their importance, not their statistical significance (once it has been established). We recommend to report—and when appropriate, to chart—confidence intervals whenever feasible rather than reporting single point estimates. By reporting CIs, one presents a more complete and accurate description to stakeholders. Note that this discussion applies to the interpretation of significance in classical statistics (which covers most of this book, and is what practitioners mostly use).

There are several methods in Python to determine the confidence intervals for a statistical model (when appropriate): `statsmodel.proportion.proportion_confint()`, is a specific one. Scipy `stats` also has the `interval()` method on most distribution types, e.g. `stats.t.interval()`, which we introduce in Sect. 6.4.

6.3.2 More About `binom_test()` and Binomial Distributions

Now that we understand confidence intervals, let's look at `binom_test()` and `proportion_confint()` again. What if we had observed 120 out of 200 to be Seattle fans, the same proportion as before but in a larger sample?

```
In [17]: sms_proportion.binom_test(count=120, nobs=200, prop=0.5)

Out[17]: 0.0056851559967502265

In [18]: sms_proportion.proportion_confint(count=120, nobs=200, alpha=0.05)

Out[18]: (0.5321048559554297, 0.6678951440445703)
```

With 120/200 cases, the confidence interval no longer includes 50%. If we had observed this, it would be evidence for a preponderance of Seattle fans. Correspondingly, the *p*-value is less than 0.05, indicating a statistically significant difference.

With Python, we can ask much more about the distribution. For example, what are the odds that we would observe 8–12 Seattle fans out of 20, if the true rate is 50%? Using Scipy `stats.binom`, we use the density estimate for a binomial distribution across the range of interest and sum the point probabilities:

```
In [19]: stats.binom.pmf([8, 9, 10, 11, 12], p=0.5, n=20).sum()

Out[19]: 0.7368240356445304

In [20]: stats.binom.pmf(range(8,13), p=0.5, n=20).sum()

Out[20]: 0.7368240356445304
```

If we observe 20 fans, and the true split is 50%, there is a 73.7% chance that we would observe between 8 and 12 fans (and thus a $1 - p$ or 27.3% chance of observing fewer than 8 or more than 12). Note, we used two different approaches here: in the first case we specified each expected number in a `list`. In the second case, we used the `range()` method to generate the `list` programmatically. The result is the same.

An "exact" binomial test (the classical method) may be overly conservative in its estimation of confidence intervals (Agresti and Coull 1998). One alternative method is to use `proportion_confint(count, nobs, method="agresti-coull")`:

```
In [21]: sms_proportion.proportion_confint(12, 20, method='agresti_coull')

Out[21]: (0.3860303790620197, 0.7817445893274164)
```

With the Agresti–Coull method, the confidence interval is slightly smaller but still includes 50%.

Finally, Chris also observed that among the 20 groups, 0 had a mixture of Seattle and Denver fans (as inferred from their team clothing). Based on that observation, what should we conclude is the *most likely* proportion of groups that comprise mixed fans? We use the Agresti–Coull method because exact tests have no confidence interval for 0 or 100% observations:

```
In [22]: sms_proportion.proportion_confint(0, 20, method='agresti_coull')

Out[22]: (0.0, 0.18980956054248888)
```

We conclude that although Chris observed 0 cases, the occurrence of mixed fandom groups is likely to be somewhere between 0 and 19%.

6.4 Testing Group Means: t Test

A t-test compares the mean of one sample against the mean of another sample (or against a specific value such as 0). The important point is that it compares the *mean* for exactly *two* sets of data. For instance, in the segment data we might ask whether household income is different among those who own a home and those who do not.

Before applying any statistical test or model, it is important to examine the data and check for skew, discontinuities, and outliers. Many statistical tests assume that the data follow a normal distribution or some other smooth continuous distribution; skewness or outliers violate those assumptions and might lead to an inaccurate test. For example, a single person with extremely high income may skew the mean value.

One way to check for non-normal distributions is to plot the data with a boxplot, histogram, or QQ plot (see Chap. 3). We have already plotted `income` above (Figs. 5.8 and 5.9) and thus skip that step. Additionally, we can check histograms for income overall as well as by home ownership:

```
In [23]: from scipy import stats
         import matplotlib.pyplot as plt

         income_own_home = seg_df.income[seg_df.own_home]
         income_dont_own_home = seg_df.income[~seg_df.own_home]

         seg_df.income.hist() # Not shown
         income_own_home.own_home.hist(alpha=0.5) # Not shown
         income_dont_own_home.hist(alpha=0.5) # Not shown
         seg_df.boxplot(column='income', by='own_home') # Not shown
         plt.figure()
         _ = stats.probplot(seg_df.income, dist='norm', plot=plt) # Not shown
```

We omit those figures for brevity. Overall, in these histograms and in the boxplots above, income is approximately normally distributed (as it should be, given the data generation procedure, Sect. 5.1).

We want to measure whether income as the response variable can be explained by own_home as the explanatory variable.

First, we can look at the sample means and standard deviations for our data:

```
In [24]: income_dont_own_home.mean(), income_dont_own_home.std()

Out[24]: (46892.35166, 20335.071081)

In [25]: income_own_home.mean(), income_own_home.std()

Out[25]: (55412.13191, 16917.48248)
```

Mean income is $46,892 for the rent (own_home is False) condition, and $55,412 for the ownership condition.

Now we are ready to test whether home ownership overall is related to differences in income, across *all* segments, using the scipy.stats.ttest_ind(a, b, equal_var=False).

```
In [26]: stats.ttest_ind(income_dont_own_home, income_own_home,
                          equal_var=False)

Out[26]: Ttest_indResult(statistic=-3.96032, pvalue=9.37281e-05)
```

There are several important pieces of information in the output of ttest_ind(). First we see that the *t statistic* is -3.96, with a *p*-value of 0.00009. This means that the null hypothesis of *no difference* in income by home ownership is rejected. The data suggest that people who own their homes have higher income.

Additionally, it would be valuable to look at the 95% confidence interval of the difference in mean income between home owners and non-home owners. To do this we can use the stats.t.interval(alpha, df, loc, scale), where alpha specifies the interval width (e.g., 0.95), df is the degrees of freedom (i.e., group *a* sample count plus group *b* sample count minus 2), loc is the difference in means between group *a* and group *b*, and scale is the geometric mean of the standard errors for each group:

```
In [27]: count_dont_own_home = income_dont_own_home.shape[0]
         count_own_home = income_own_home.shape[0]
         dof = count_dont_own_home + count_own_home - 2
         geometric_mean_sem = np.sqrt(((count_dont_own_home - 1)
                              * stats.sem(income_dont_own_home)**2
                              + (count_own_home - 1)
                              * stats.sem(income_own_home)**2)/dof)
         stats.t.interval(alpha=0.95,
                          df=dof,
                          loc=income_dont_own_home.mean()\
                          - income_own_home.mean(),
                          scale=geometric_mean_sem)

Out[27]: (-11525.353750453647, -5514.206739896753)
```

Next we see that the 95% confidence interval for the difference is -11525 to -5514. If these are representative data of a larger population, we can have 95% confidence that the group difference would be between those values on repeated sampling.

What about the difference within the Travelers segment? In Fig. 5.9, we saw that household income appeared to have a wider distribution among members of the Travelers segment who own homes than those who do not. Does that also reflect a difference in the mean income for the two groups?

Rather than rewriting all the code above, we can write a function to simplify repeated analyses:

```
In [28]: def ttest(a, b):
             # This function displays statistics on two groups, runs a t-test,
             # and finds the 95% confidence interval of the mean difference
             # between groups
```

```
# Get means and standard deviation of each group
mean_a = a.mean()
mean_b = b.mean()

std_a = a.std()
std_b = b.std()

print('Group a - mean: {0}  standard deviation: {1}'
      .format(mean_a, std_a))
print('Group b - mean: {0}  standard deviation: {1}\n'
      .format(mean_b, std_b))

# Run a Welch's t-test between the groups
ttest_out = stats.ttest_ind(a, b, equal_var=False)
print("Welch's t-test statistic: {0}\np-value: {1}\n"
      .format(ttest_out.statistic, ttest_out.pvalue))

# Find the 95% confidence interval using scipy.statst.interval
# function. The difference in means is the location of the
# distribution (loc parameter). The geometric mean of the
# standard error of each group is the scale
count_a = a.shape[0]
count_b = b.shape[0]
dof = count_a + count_b - 2

geometric_mean_sem = np.sqrt(((count_a - 1) * stats.sem(a)**2
                      + (count_b -1) * stats.sem(b)**2)/dof)
print('95% confidence interval of the mean difference between a and'
      ' b:\n{0}'
      .format(stats.t.interval(alpha=0.95, df=dof,
                               loc=mean_a - mean_b,
                               scale=geometric_mean_sem)))
```

Writing functions to simplify complex or repeated analysis simplifies subsequence analysis and improves repeatability. Here we can use this function to repeat our earlier analysis:

```
In [29]: ttest(income_dont_own_home, income_own_home)

Group a - mean: 46892.35166  standard deviation: 20335.07108
Group b - mean: 55412.131907  standard deviation: 16917.48248

Welch's t-test statistic: -3.96032
p-value: 9.37281e-05

95% confidence interval of the mean difference between a and b:
(-11525.35375, -5514.20673)
```

We note that this is a lot to type! How can we be confident that we didn't introduce an error? The best way to do that would be with *unit testing*, but that is beyond the scope of the book. In this case, a good test would be, first, that the function runs. But a subtle error could definitely be present without breaking the function. A better test would be passing in a few distributions and seeing if the results make sense. For example, we might compare np.random.normal(100000, 15000, 300) to np.random.normal(101000, 15000, 300, which we would *not* expect to be significantly different, and to np.random.normal(80000, 15000, 300, which we *would* expect to be significantly different.

Returning to our question: within the Travelers segment, is there a difference in income between those who and do not own homes?

We simply filter using `seg_df.Segment == 'travelers'` to select just Travelers and repeat the test:

```
In [30]: traveler_subset = seg_df.loc[seg_df.Segment == 'travelers']
         ttest(traveler_subset.income[~traveler_subset.own_home],
               traveler_subset.income[traveler_subset.own_home])

Group a - mean: 62923.23394   standard deviation: 22233.49398
Group b - mean: 62449.90773   standard deviation: 19580.36094

Welch's t-test statistic: 0.09366
p-value: 0.92578

95% confidence interval of the mean difference between a and b:
(-6107.12069, 7053.77310)
```

The confidence interval of -6107 to 7054 includes 0, and thus we conclude—as suggested by the p-value of 0.93—that there is not a significant difference in mean income among those Travelers in our data who own homes and who don't.

We might be puzzled: we saw in the first t-test that there *is* a significant difference in income based on home ownership, but in the second test that there's *no* significant difference within Travelers. Any difference must lie largely outside the Travelers group.

How can we locate where the difference lies? A t-test across all segments will not work because there are four segments and a t-test only compares two groups. We could test income within each segment, one at a time, but this is not a good idea because multiple tests increase the likelihood of finding a spurious difference (a "Type I error"). To track down the difference, we need a more robust procedure that handles multiple groups; we turn to that next.

6.5 Testing Multiple Group Means: Analysis of Variance (ANOVA)

6.5.1 A Brief Introduction to Formula Syntax

The S programming language (and, subsequently, the R language) (Chambers et al. 1990) provided a common syntax to describe relationships among variables through *formula* specification. A formula uses the tilde ($\sim$) operator to separate *response variables* on the left from *explanatory variables* on the right. The basic form is:

$$y \sim x \qquad \text{(Simple formula)}$$

This is used in many contexts in R. It has proven so valuable, that many Python packages, particularly those related to statistical modeling such as the Statsmodels package, employ a similar syntax. In linear regression, the simple formula above would model y as a linear function of x.

6.5.2 ANOVA

An *analysis of variance* (ANOVA) compares the means of multiple groups. Technically, it does this by comparing the degree to which groups differ as measured by variance in their means (from one another), relative to the variance of observations around each mean (within each group). Hence the importance of *variance* in the name. More casually, you can think of it as testing for difference among multiple means, assuming that the groups have similar variance.

An ANOVA can handle single factors (known as *one-way* ANOVA), two factors (*two-way*), and higher orders including interactions among factors. A complete discussion of ANOVA would take more space than we have here, yet we use it to address our question from the previous section: which factors are related to differences in mean income in the segment data? Specifically, is income related to home ownership, or to segment membership, or both?

Scipy `stats` has a one-way ANOVA method, `f_oneway()`, which given multiple arrays of values will return the F-value and associated p-value:

```
In [31]:  stats.f_oneway(income_dont_own_home, income_own_home)

Out[31]:  F_onewayResult(statistic=15.04833, pvalue=0.00013)
```

A more fully featured set of ANOVA methods are found in the Statsmodels `stats.anova` module, which uses the formula notation introduced above, using `statsmodels.formula.api.smf.ols(formula, data)` to set up the model and `statsmodels.stats.anova.anova_lm(linear_model)` to display a standard ANOVA summary. We look at income by home ownership first, and assign the `ols()` model to an object so we can use it with `anova_lm()`. The `ols()` function uses the standard formula interface to model `income` as a response to `own_home`:

```
In [32]:  import statsmodels.formula.api as smf
          from statsmodels.stats import anova as sms_anova

In [33]:  income_home_lm = smf.ols('income ~ own_home', data=seg_df).fit()
In [34]:  sms_anova.anova_lm(income_home_lm)

Out[34]:               df        sum_sq        mean_sq          F      PR(>F)
          own_home    1.0   5.374074e+09   5.374074e+09   15.048327   0.000129
          Residual  298.0   1.064221e+11   3.571210e+08        NaN         NaN
```

The value of `Pr(>F)` for `own_home` is the *p*-value and reflects that there is significant variation in `income` between those who do and do not own their own homes. (This is a slightly different test but the same conclusion that we obtained from the t-test in Sect. 6.4.)

What about income by segment? We model that and save the `ols` object:

```
In [35]:  income_segment_lm = smf.ols('income ~ Segment', data=seg_df).fit()
          sms_anova.anova_lm(income_segment_lm)

Out[35]:              df        sum_sq        mean_sq          F        PR(>F)
          Segment    3.0   6.008669e+10   2.002890e+10   114.651236   2.794439e-49
          Residual 296.0   5.170946e+10   1.746941e+08        NaN           NaN
```

The value of `Pr(>F)` is very close to zero, confirming that income varies significantly by segment.

If income varies by *both* home ownership and segment, does that mean that a more complete model should include both? We can add both factors into the ANOVA model to test this:

```
In [36]:  income_home_segment_lm = smf.ols('income ~ Segment + own_home',
                                           data=seg_df).fit()
          sms_anova.anova_lm(income_home_segment_lm)

Out[36]:              df        sum_sq        mean_sq          F        PR(>F)
          Segment    3.0   6.008669e+10   2.002890e+10   114.352374   3.858516e-49
          own_home   1.0   4.000708e+07   4.000708e+07     0.228415   6.330554e-01
          Residual 295.0   5.166945e+10   1.751507e+08        NaN           NaN
```

The results indicate that when we try to explain income differences in income by both `Segment` and `own_home`, segment is a significant predictor (p <<.01) but home ownership is *not* a significant predictor. Yet the previous results said that it *was* significant. What's the difference? What is happening is that segment and home ownership are not independent, and the effect is captured sufficiently by segment membership alone. Home ownership accounts for little more over and above what can be explained by `Segment`.

Could it be that home ownership is related to income in some segments but not in others? This would be represented in our model by an *interaction* effect. In a model formula, "+" indicates that variables should be modeled for main effects only. We can instead write ":" for an interaction or "*" for both main effect and interaction. We test main effects and interaction of home ownership and segment:

```
In [37]:  income_home_segment_lm = smf.ols('income ~ Segment * own_home',
                                           data=seg_df).fit()
          sms_anova.anova_lm(income_home_segment_lm)

Out[37]:                    df        sum_sq        mean_sq          F    \
          Segment          3.0   6.008669e+10   2.002890e+10   113.502010
```

```
own_home              1.0   4.000708e+07   4.000708e+07      0.226717
Segment:own_home      3.0   1.422781e+08   4.742603e+07      0.268759
Residual            292.0   5.152717e+10   1.764629e+08           NaN


                               PR(>F)
Segment               9.839888e-49
own_home              6.343252e-01
Segment:own_home      8.479014e-01
Residual                       NaN
```

Again, segment is a significant predictor, while home ownership and the interaction of segment with home ownership are not significant. In other words, segment membership is again the best predictor on its own. We discuss interaction effects further in Chap. 7.

6.5.3 Model Comparison in ANOVA*

Another capability of the anova_lm() command is to compare two or more models, using the syntax anova_lm(model1, model2, ...) We can compare the ols() model with segment alone vs. the model with both segment and income:

```
In [38]: sms_anova.anova_lm(smf.ols('income ~ Segment', data=seg_df).fit(),
                            smf.ols('income ~ Segment + own_home',
                                    data=seg_df).fit(),
                            typ=1)

Out[38]:    df_resid            ssr   df_diff       ss_diff         F     Pr(>F)
        0      296.0   5.170946e+10       0.0           NaN       NaN        NaN
        1      295.0   5.166945e+10       1.0   4.000708e+07  0.228415   0.633055
```

This tells us that Model 1—which includes both segment and home ownership—is not significantly different in overall fit from Model 0. If it were better, the null hypothesis of no difference would be rejected, as shown by a p-value ("Pr(>F)") less than 0.05. You may see some RuntimeWarning displayed; in this case those are inconsequential, but are related to null values in certain comparisons (these warnings are even found in the examples in the statsmodels documentation!).

It is essential to note that model comparison as performed by the anova_lm() command *only* makes sense in the case of nested models. In this context, a model *A* is *nested* within another model *B* when one or more parameters of *B* can be fixed or removed to yield model *A*. In the present case, income ~ Segment is nested within income ~ Segment + own_home because we can remove own_home and arrive at the former model. Because they are nested, the two models may be compared by anova_lm() or other functions that perform likelihood comparisons.

The model income ~ Segment is *not* nested within income ~ subscribe + own_home because no amount of removing or fixing parameters in the latter model will produce the former. Thus, those two models could not be compared by anova_lm() in a meaningful way. If you try to compare them, the method may produce some output but it is not generally interpretable.

The question of how to compare non-nested models is one we do not tackle in depth in this book. If you wish to learn more about the issues and methods for general model comparison, a good place to start is to review the literature on the Akaike information criterion (AIC) and Bayesian information criterion (BIC). We review BIC briefly in Sect. 10.3.5.

6.5.4 Visualizing Group Confidence Intervals

A good way to visualize the results of an ANOVA is to plot confidence intervals for the group means. This will reveal more about whether the differences are substantial in magnitude or not. We can directly inspect a fitted ols() object:

```
In [39]: income_segment_lm = smf.ols('income ~ Segment', data=seg_df).fit()
         income_segment_lm.summary()
```

```
Out[39]: <class 'statsmodels.iolib.summary.Summary'>
                           OLS Regression Results
==============================================================================
Dep. Variable:                 income   R-squared:                       0.537
Model:                            OLS   Adj. R-squared:                  0.533
Method:                 Least Squares   F-statistic:                     114.7
Date:                Wed, 19 Jun 2019   Prob (F-statistic):           2.79e-49
Time:                        16:18:49   Log-Likelihood:                -3270.5
No. Observations:                 300   AIC:                             6549.
Df Residuals:                     296   BIC:                             6564.
Df Model:                           3
Covariance Type:            nonrobust
==============================================================================
                         coef    std err          t      P>|t|      [0.025      0.975]
------------------------------------------------------------------------------
Intercept              5.176e+04   1579.756     32.767      0.000    4.87e+04    5.49e+04
Segment[T.suburb_mix]  3788.7303   2059.750      1.839      0.067    -264.880    7842.341
Segment[T.travelers]   1.085e+04   2163.170      5.014      0.000    6588.960    1.51e+04
Segment[T.urban_hip]   -3.15e+04   2447.348    -12.869      0.000   -3.63e+04   -2.67e+04
==============================================================================
Omnibus:                       14.628   Durbin-Watson:                   2.046
Prob(Omnibus):                  0.001   Jarque-Bera (JB):               35.432
Skew:                           0.089   Prob(JB):                     2.02e-08
Kurtosis:                       4.674   Cond. No.                         5.02
==============================================================================
```

There is a problem: the default `ols()` model has an intercept term (corresponding to the Moving up segment) and all other segments are relative to that. It is clearer looking just at the parameters:

```
In [40]: income_segment_lm.params

Out[40]: Intercept              51763.552666
         Segment[T.suburb_mix]   3788.730259
         Segment[T.travelers]   10846.102661
         Segment[T.urban_hip]  -31495.815349
         dtype: float64
```

And the confidence intervals:

```
In [41]: income_segment_lm.conf_int()

Out[41]:                                 0             1
         Intercept              48654.575215  54872.530118
         Segment[T.suburb_mix]   -264.880397   7842.340915
         Segment[T.travelers]    6588.959959  15103.245364
         Segment[T.urban_hip]  -36312.222507 -26679.408192
```

This may be difficult for decision makers or clients to understand, so we find it preferable to remove the intercept by adding "-1" to the model formula:

```
In [42]: income_segment_lm_adjusted = smf.ols('income ~ -1 + Segment',
                                      data=seg_df).fit()

         income_segment_lm_adjusted.summary()
```

```
Out[42]: <class 'statsmodels.iolib.summary.Summary'>
                           OLS Regression Results
=================================================================================
Dep. Variable:                   income   R-squared:                      0.537
Model:                              OLS   Adj. R-squared:                 0.533
Method:                   Least Squares   F-statistic:                    114.7
Date:                 Thu, 31 May 2018   Prob (F-statistic):          2.79e-49
Time:                         16:42:50   Log-Likelihood:               -3270.5
No. Observations:                  300   AIC:                            6549.
Df Residuals:                      296   BIC:                            6564.
Df Model:                            3
Covariance Type:              nonrobust
=================================================================================
                        coef    std err        t     P>|t|     [0.025    0.975]
---------------------------------------------------------------------------------
Segment[moving up]   5.176e+04  1579.756   32.767    0.000   4.87e+04  5.49e+04
Segment[suburb_mix]  5.555e+04  1321.719   42.030    0.000    5.3e+04  5.82e+04
Segment[travelers]   6.261e+04  1477.727   42.369    0.000   5.97e+04  6.55e+04
Segment[urban_hip]   2.027e+04  1869.193   10.843    0.000   1.66e+04  2.39e+04
=================================================================================
Omnibus:                        14.628   Durbin-Watson:                  2.046
Prob(Omnibus):                   0.001   Jarque-Bera (JB):              35.432
Skew:                            0.089   Prob(JB):                    2.02e-08
Kurtosis:                        4.674   Cond. No.                       1.41
=================================================================================
```

With the intercept removed, each coefficient corresponds to the mean income for each segment:

```
In [43]: means = income_segment_lm_adjusted.params
         means

Out[43]: Segment[moving up]     51763.552666
         Segment[suburb_mix]    55552.282925
         Segment[travelers]     62609.655328
         Segment[urban_hip]     20267.737317
         dtype: float64
```

We can plot the mean and confidence intervals from the model, as seen in Fig. 6.1

```
In [44]: ci = income_segment_lm_adjusted.conf_int()
         means.plot(kind='bar', yerr=ci[1]-means, color='0.7')
```

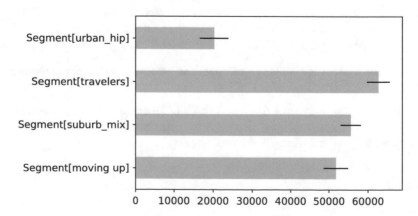

Fig. 6.1 Confidence intervals for income by segment, from an analysis of variance model with `statsmodels.formula.api.ols()`

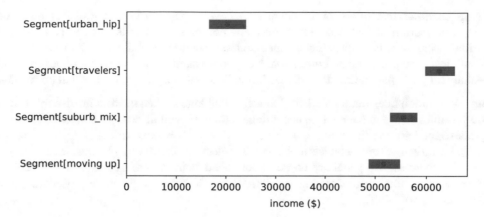

Fig. 6.2 Another representation of confidence intervals for income by segment, from an analysis of variance model with `statsmodels.formula.api.ols()`

Or we can create a more polished figure:

```
In [45]: import matplotlib.pyplot as plt
         plt.figure(figsize=(8,4))
         plt.barh(y=range(4), left=ci[0], width=ci[1]-ci[0],
                 height=0.2, color='0.4')
         plt.xlabel('income ($)')
         plt.yticks(range(len(means)), ci.index)
         plt.plot(means, range(4), 'ro')
         plt.xlim((0, 68000))
```

In Fig. 6.2 we see confidence intervals for the mean income of each segment. It is clear that the average income of Urban hip segment members is substantially lower than the other three groups.

We can turn this confidence interval visualization into a function, so that we can use it later:

```
In [46]: def plot_confidence_intervals(centers, conf_ints, zero_line=False):
             '''Plot centers and confidence intervals'''
             plt.figure(figsize=(8,4))
             sort_index = np.argsort(centers.values)
             centers = centers[sort_index]
             conf_ints = conf_ints.iloc[sort_index]
             plt.barh(y=range(len(centers)), left=conf_ints[0],
                     width=conf_ints[1]-conf_ints[0],
                     height=0.2, color='0.4')
             plt.yticks(range(len(centers)), conf_ints.index)
             plt.plot(centers, range(len(centers)), 'ro')
             if zero_line:
               plt.plot([0,0],[-.5, len(centers) - 0.5], 'gray',
                       linestyle='dashed')
             plt.xlim((-.05, 1.1 * conf_ints.iloc[:,1].max()))
             plt.ylim((-.5, len(centers) - 0.5))
```

6.6 Learning More*

Linear Models T-tests and ANOVA are nothing more than flavors of general linear models, which we cover in more depth in Chap. 7. A few recommended texts to learn more are *Introduction to Mathematical Statistics* by Hogg et al. (2005) and, for a more detailed discussion of inference tests, *Statistical Inference: Vol. 2* by Casella and Berger (2002).

Parametric and Non-parametric Models In this chapter, we covered parametric tests: tests that are based on assumptions about the underlying distribution of that data. There are many non-parametric tests that can be used to analyze data that have non-parametric distributions. Examples include median tests (e.g. Mann Whitney U, Kruskal–Wallis), rank tests (e.g. Wilcoxon signed-rank test, Spearman's rank correlation, etc.), bootstrap methods, permutation testing, and many others. If your work entails analyzing non-parametric datasets, exploring these alternative approaches will be worthwhile.

Variable Selection A common question for statistical models of all kinds, when the data involve more than a few variables, is how to select the variables to use in a model. In upcoming sections we will discuss the dangers of *overfitting* (Sect. 7.5.2), demonstrate progressive modeling in linear regression (Sect. 7.4), and show how variable selection works in random forest models (Sect. 11.1.3). Historically, some analysts used *stepwise* selection, where variables are successively added or removed to see whether a model changes. We generally do not recommend stepwise procedures because they present dangers of overfitting and "hypothesizing after results are known" (HARKing; Kerr 1998). Stepwise procedures are discussed further in Chapman and Feit (2019, pp. 148ff).

6.7 Key Points

This chapter introduced formal statistical tests in Python. Following are some of the important lessons.

To perform statistical tests on differences by group:

- `chisquare()` from the Scipy `stats` module performs hypothesis tests on frequency tables (Sect. 6.2).
- `binom_test()` and `proportion_confint()` from the Statmodels `stats.proportion` module perform hypothesis tests and finds confidence intervals, respectively, on proportion data. They offer options such as Agresti–Coull versions of binomial tests that may be more informative and robust than standard exact binomial tests. Additionally the `binom` module from Scipy `stats` allows actions on binomial distributions, such as the probability mass function `pmf()` (Sect. 6.3).
- `ttest_ind()` module from Scipy `stats` is a common way to test for differences between the means of two groups (or between one group and a fixed value) (Sect. 6.4).
- Analysis of variance (ANOVA) is a more general way to test for differences in mean among several groups that are identified by one or more factors. Using the Statsmodels package, the basic model is fit with `statsmodels.formula.api.ols()` and common summary statistics are reported with `statsmodels.stats.anova.anova_lm()` (Sect. 6.5).
- The `anova_lm()` command is also useful to compare two or more ANOVA or other linear models, provided that they are nested models (Sect. 6.5.3).

Chapter 7
Identifying Drivers of Outcomes: Linear Models

In this chapter we investigate linear models, which are often used in marketing to explore the relationship between an outcome of interest and other variables. A common application in survey analysis is to model satisfaction with a product in relation to specific elements of the product and its delivery; this is called "satisfaction drivers analysis." Linear models are also used to understand how price and advertising are related to sales, and this is called "marketing mix modeling." There are many other situations in which it is helpful to model an outcome, known formally as a *response* or *dependent* variable, as a function of predictor variables, known as *explanatory* or *independent* variables. Once a relationship is estimated, one can use the model to make predictions of the outcome for other values of the predictors. For example, in a course, we might find that final exam scores can be predicted based on the midterm exam score, e.g.:

$$Score_{\text{final}} = 1.1 \cdot Score_{\text{midterm}} + 10 \tag{7.1}$$

In this case, if someone received a 70% on the midterm exam, we would expect them to receive a score of 87% on the final exam.

In this chapter, we illustrate linear modeling with a satisfaction drivers analysis using survey data for customers who have visited an amusement park. In the survey, respondents report their levels of satisfaction with different aspects of their experience, and their overall satisfaction. Marketers frequently use this type of data to figure out what aspects of the experience *drive* overall satisfaction, asking questions such as, "Are people who are more satisfied with the rides also more satisfied with their experience overall?" If the answer to this question is "no," then the company may decide to invest in improving other aspects of the experience.

An important thing to understand is that, despite its name, *driver* does *not* imply causation. A model only represents an association among variables. Consider a survey of automobile purchasers that finds a positive association between satisfaction and price paid. If a brand manager wants customers to be more satisfied, does this imply that she should raise prices? Probably not. It is more likely that price is associated with higher quality, which then leads to higher satisfaction. Results should be interpreted cautiously and considered in the context of domain knowledge.

Linear models are a core tool in statistics, and the `statsmodels` package offers an excellent set of functions for estimating them. As in other chapters, we review the basics and demonstrate how to conduct linear modeling in Python. The chapter does not review everything that one would wish to know in practice. We encourage readers who are unfamiliar with linear modeling to supplement this chapter with a review of linear modeling in a statistics or marketing research textbook, where it might appear under a name such as *regression analysis*, *linear regression*, or *least-squares fitting*.

7.1 Amusement Park Data

In this section, we simulate data for a hypothetical survey of visitors to an amusement park. This dataset comprises a few objective measures:

- whether the respondent visited on a weekend (which will be the variable `weekend` in the dataframe)
- the number of children brought (`num_child`)
- distance traveled to the park (`distance`)

There are also subjective measures of satisfaction: expressed satisfaction overall (`overall`) and satisfaction with the rides, games, waiting time, and cleanliness (`rides`, `games`, `wait`, and `clean`, respectively).

Unlike earlier chapters, in this one we recommend that you *skip* the simulation section and download the data. There is no new Python syntax, and this will allow you to review the models without knowing the outcome in advance. To download and check:

```
In [1]: import pandas as pd
        sat_df = pd.read_csv('http://bit.ly/PMR-ch7')
        sat_df.head()
```

```
Out[1]:    is_weekend  num_child   distance  rides  games   wait  clean
        0        True          0   9.844503   82.0   64.0   82.0   88.0 ...
        1       False          1   2.720221   85.0   83.0  100.0   90.0 ...
        2       False          3   1.878189   88.0   81.0   80.0   91.0 ...
        3       False          0  14.211682   73.0   52.0   68.0   74.0 ...
        4       False          1   9.362776   78.0   93.0   56.0   82.0 ...
```

If you were able to load the data, skip to Sect. 7.2 for now, and return later to review the simulation code.

7.1.1 Simulating the Amusement Park Data

To start the data simulation, we set the random number seed to make the process repeatable and declare a variable for the number of observations:

```
In [2]: import numpy as np
        import pandas as pd
        np.random.seed(8266)
        n_resp = 500 # Number of survey responses
```

Our hypothetical survey includes four questions about a customer's satisfaction with different dimensions of a visit to the amusement park: satisfaction with rides (`rides`), games (`games`), waiting times (`wait`), and cleanliness (`clean`), along with a rating of overall satisfaction (`overall`). In such surveys, respondents often answer similarly on all satisfaction questions; this is known as the *halo effect*.

We simulate a satisfaction halo with a random variable for each customer, `halo`, that does not appear in the final data but is used to influence the other ratings:

```
In [3]: halo = np.random.normal(loc=0, scale=5, size=n_resp)
```

We generate responses for the satisfaction ratings by adding each respondent's halo to the value of another arbitrary variable that is specific to the survey item (satisfaction with rides, cleanliness, and so forth).

We convert the continuous values to integers using `floor()`. We then constrain value to the range 0–100 by replacing any values outside of that range (*clipping* the values). This gives us a final value for each satisfaction item on a 100-point scale. Such near-continuous values might be obtained by measuring where respondents mark levels of satisfaction along a line on paper or by touching a screen. Although scales rating 1–5, 1–7, or 1–11 may be more common in practice, such discrete scales introduce complications that we discuss in 7.6; those would detract from our presentation here. So we assume that the data come from a 100-point scale.

We write a function to generate the data:

```
In [4]: def generate_satisfaction_scores(mean, std, halo,
                                          score_range=(0, 100)):
            """Simulate satisfaction scores of a survey questions from a normal
            distributions.
            """
            # Draw scores from a normal distribution
            scores = np.random.normal(loc=mean, scale=std, size=len(halo))
            # Add the halo
            scores = scores + halo
```

```
                # Floor the scores so that they are all integers and clip to limit range
                scores = np.floor(scores)
                scores = np.clip(scores, score_range[0], score_range[1])

                return scores
```

Creating the n_resp responses can be done in just one command per variable:

```
In [5]: rides = generate_satisfaction_scores(mean=81, std=3, halo=halo)
        games = generate_satisfaction_scores(mean=75, std=7, halo=halo)
        wait = generate_satisfaction_scores(mean=74, std=10, halo=halo)
        clean = generate_satisfaction_scores(mean=86, std=2, halo=halo)
```

Satisfaction surveys often include other questions related to the customer experience. For the amusement park data, we include whether the visit was on a weekend, how far the customer traveled to the park in miles, and the number of children in the party. We generate these data using two functions: np.random.lognormal(mean, sigma, size) to sample a log-normal distribution for distance, and np.random.choice(a, size, replace, p) to sample discrete distributions for weekend and number of children (num_child):

```
In [6]: np.random.seed(82667)
        distance = np.random.lognormal(mean=3, sigma=1, size=n_resp)
        num_child = np.random.choice(a=range(6),
                                     size=n_resp,
                                     replace=True,
                                     p=[0.3, 0.15, 0.25, 0.15, 0.1, 0.05])
        weekend = np.random.choice(a=[True, False],
                                   size=n_resp,
                                   replace=True,
                                   p=[0.5, 0.5])
```

We create the overall satisfaction rating as a function of ratings for the various aspects of the visit (satisfaction with rides, cleanliness, and so forth), distance traveled, and the number of children:

```
In [7]: overall = np.floor(0.7*(halo + 0.5*rides + 0.15*games + 0.3*wait
                    + 0.2*clean + 0.07*distance + 5*(num_child == 0)
                    + 0.3*wait*(num_child > 0)
                    + np.random.normal(loc=0, scale=7, size=n_resp)))
        overall = np.clip(overall, 0, 100)
```

Although this is a lengthy formula, it is relatively simple with five parts:

1. Start with halo to capture the latent satisfaction (also included in rides and the other ratings)
2. Add the satisfaction variables (rides, games, wait, and clean) with a weight for each one
3. Add weighted contributions for other influences such as distance
4. Add random normal variation using random.normal()
5. Use floor() to produce an integer
6. Use np.clip() to restrict values to between 0 and 100, inclusive

When a variable like overall is a *linear combination* of other variables plus random noise, we say that it follows a *linear model*. What does it mean to be a linear combination of variables? It means that each *variable* is added together, with scaling factors, to form the overall output variable. None of the variables are multiplied, squared, etc, which would make it a nonlinear combination.

Although these ratings are not a model of real amusement parks, the structure exemplifies the kind of linear model one might propose. With real data, one would wish to discover the contributions from the various elements, which are the weights associated with the various predictors. In the next section, we examine how to fit such a linear model.

Before proceeding, we combine the data points into a dataframe:

```
In [8]: sat_df = pd.DataFrame({'is_weekend': weekend,
                               'num_child': num_child,
                               'distance': distance,
```

```
                        'rides': rides,
                        'games': games,
                        'wait': wait,
                        'clean': clean,
                        'overall': overall})
        sat_df.is_weekend = sat_df.is_weekend.astype(pd.api.types.
                                                CategoricalDtype())
```

```
In [9]: sat_df.head()

Out[9]:     is_weekend  num_child   distance  rides  games    wait  clean  overall
         0        True          0   9.844503   82.0   64.0    82.0   88.0     88.0
         1       False          1   2.720221   85.0   83.0   100.0   90.0     90.0
         2       False          3   1.878189   88.0   81.0    80.0   91.0     91.0
         3       False          0  14.211682   73.0   52.0    68.0   74.0     74.0
         4       False          1   9.362776   78.0   93.0    56.0   82.0     82.0
```

7.2   Fitting Linear Models with `ols()`

Every modeling effort should begin with an inspection of the data, so we start with a `describe()` of the data:

```
In [10]: sat_df.describe().round(2)

Out[10]:         num_child  distance   rides    games    wait   clean  overall
         count      500.00    500.00  500.00   500.00  500.00  500.00   500.00
         mean         1.75     31.58   80.18    73.96   73.32   85.25    75.34
         std          1.53     35.77    6.02     8.74   10.70    5.73    12.16
         min          0.00      0.64   64.00    44.00   46.00   65.00    42.00
         25%          0.00      9.07   76.00    68.00   66.00   82.00    67.00
         50%          2.00     19.26   80.00    74.00   73.00   85.00    76.00
         75%          3.00     39.01   84.00    80.00   80.00   89.00    85.00
         max          5.00    233.30   99.00   100.00  100.00  100.00   100.00
```

The data comprise eight variables from a survey of satisfaction with a recent visit to an amusement park. The first three variables describe features of the visit: is_weekend is a boolean, `True` or `False`; num_child is the number of children in the party, 0–5; and `distance` is the distance traveled to the park. The remaining five variables are satisfaction ratings for the customers' experience of the rides, games, wait times, cleanliness, and overall experience of the park, on a 100 point scale. Note that is_weekend is excluded from the `describe()` output, as it is categorical (but we could have included it with the `include='all'` command), but is present in the output of `head()`.

7.2.1   Preliminary Data Inspection

Before modeling, there are two important things to check: that each individual variable has a reasonable distribution, and that joint relationships among the variables are appropriate for modeling.

We do an initial check of the variable distributions and relationships in sat_df using `seaborn.PairGrid()` as described in Sect. 4.4.2. Note that we cast the `False` and `True` values in the is_weekend column to 0 and 1, respectively, so that they get treated as numerics.

```
In [11]: import seaborn as sns
         sns.set_context('paper')
         import matplotlib.pyplot as plt
         g = sns.PairGrid(sat_df.replace({False: 0, True: 1}))
         g.map_upper(sns.scatterplot, linewidths=1, edgecolor="w", s=10,
             alpha=0.5)
```

```
g.map_diag(plt.hist)
g.map_lower(sns.kdeplot)
```

The result is Fig. 7.1, where we see from the histograms on the diagonal that all of the satisfaction ratings are close to normally distributed, except for weekend which is binomial, as expected, and distance, which has a highly skewed distribution. For most purposes it is a good idea to transform such a variable to a more normal distribution. As we discussed in Sect. 4.5.4, a common transformation for such data is a logarithmic transform; we take the log() of distance and add that to the dataframe:

```
In [12]: sat_df['log_dist'] = sat_df.distance.apply(np.log)
```

We could then use a histogram to confirm that the new variable log_dist is more normally distributed (see Fig. 7.2):

```
In [13]: sat_df.log_dist.hist()
         plt.xlabel('log distance')
         plt.ylabel('Count')
```

As an alternative to the hist() method from pandas we could have used plt.hist(sat_df.log_dist) or re-created the full scatterplot matrix with seaborn.PairGrid().

To check the relationships among variables, we examine the bivariate scatterplots in the upper triangle and the kernel density estimates in the lower triangle of Fig. 7.1. They show few concerns apart from the need to transform distance. For example, the pairwise scatterplots of our continuous measures are generally elliptical in shape, which is a good indication that they are appropriate to use in a linear model. One question, however, concerns the fact that the variables in the middle right of Fig. 7.1 appear to be positively correlated (e.g., rides vs clean).

Why is this a concern? A common issue with marketing data and especially satisfaction surveys is that variables may be highly correlated with one another. Although we as marketers care about individual elements of customers' experiences such as their amusement park experience with rides and games, when completing a survey, the respondents might not give independent ratings to each of those items. They may instead form an overall *halo* rating and rate individual elements of the experience in light of that overall feeling.

When variables are strongly related in this way, it is difficult to assess their individual effects with statistical models. As we will see in Sect. 8.1, the effect can be so severe that the relationships become uninterpretable without taking some action to handle the high correlations.

Given the positive associations shown in Fig. 7.1, we investigate the correlation structure further using pandas corr() and sns.heatmap() as demonstrated in Sect. 4.5.2:

```
In [14]: sat_df_corr = sat_df.corr()
         sns.heatmap(sat_df_corr, annot=True, fmt=".2f",
                     mask=~np.tri(sat_df_corr.shape[1], k=-1, dtype=bool),
                     cbar=False)
```

The result is the correlation plot shown in Fig. 7.3. We see that the satisfaction items are moderately to strongly associated with one another. However, none of the items appear to be nearly identical, as would be indicated by correlations exceeding $r > 0.8$ for several of them, or $r > 0.9$ for particular pairs. Thus, on an initial inspection, it appears to be acceptable to proceed with modeling the relationships among these variables.

In Chap. 8 we discuss how to assess this question in more detail and what to do when high correlations pose a more significant problem. In Chap. 9 we discuss strategies to find underlying dimensions that appear in highly correlated data.

7.2.2 Recap: Bivariate Association

The goal of a satisfaction drivers analysis is to discover relationships between customers' satisfaction with features of the of the service (or product) and their overall experience. For example, to what extent is satisfaction with the park's rides related to overall experience? Is the relationship strong or weak? One way to assess this is to plot those two variables against each other as we did in Chap. 4:

```
In [15]: sat_df.plot(kind='scatter', x='rides', y='overall')
         plt.xlabel('Satisfaction with rides')
         plt.ylabel('Satisfaction overall')
```

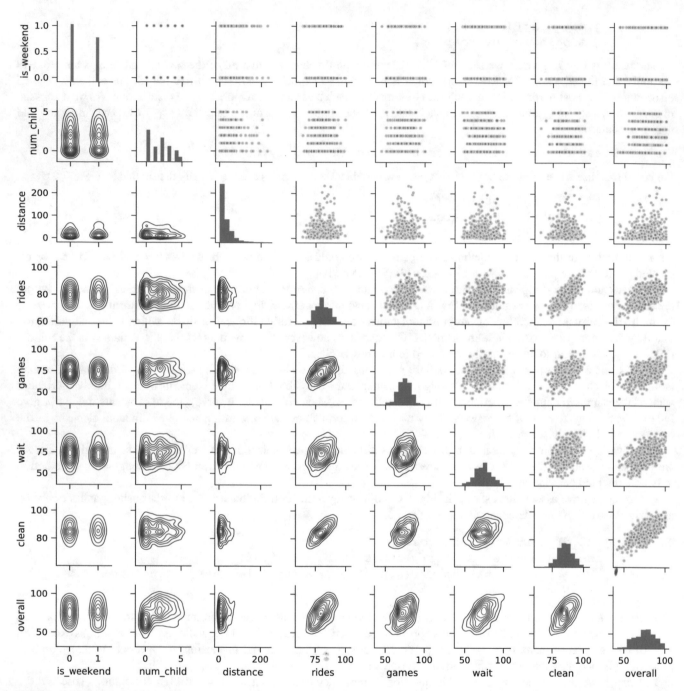

Fig. 7.1 An inspection of data using `seaborn.PairGrid()` before we perform further modeling. This reveals that `distance` has a highly skewed distribution and should be transformed before modeling. Additionally, several variables are positively associated and should be examined further for the strength of association

In Fig. 7.4, we see that the points on the plot show that there is a tendency for people with higher satisfaction with rides to also have higher overall satisfaction. This is also apparent in Fig. 7.1, but a separate plot of those variables allows closer inspection.

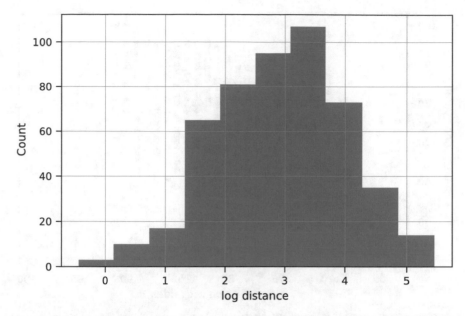

Fig. 7.2 An inspection of the log-transformed distance data demonstrates that distance follows a log-normal distribution

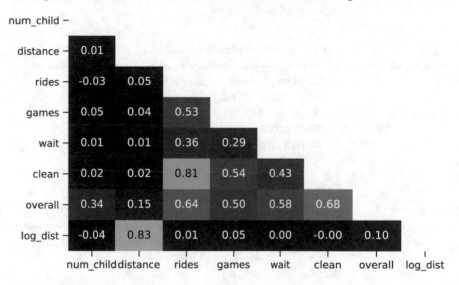

Fig. 7.3 A correlation plot for the amusement park data. Inspection of the item associations is always recommended before linear modeling, in order to check for extremely high correlations between items (such as $r > 0.9$). In the present data, `rides` and `clean` are highly related ($r = 0.81$) but not so strongly that remediation is strictly required

7.2.3 Linear Model with a Single Predictor

A linear model estimates a best fit line through the cloud of points. The function to estimate a linear model is `statsmodels.formula.api(formula, data)`, where `data` is a dataframe containing the data and `formula` is a formula, as we saw in Sect. 6.5 for ANOVA. To estimate a linear model relating overall satisfaction to satisfaction with rides, we would use the formula `overall ~ rides`, can be read as "`overall` varies with `rides`." When we call `ols().fit()`, Python finds a line that best fits the relationship of `sat_df.rides` and `sat_df.overall`:

```
In [16]: import statsmodels.formula.api as smf
         smf.ols('overall ~ rides', data=sat_df).fit().summary()
```

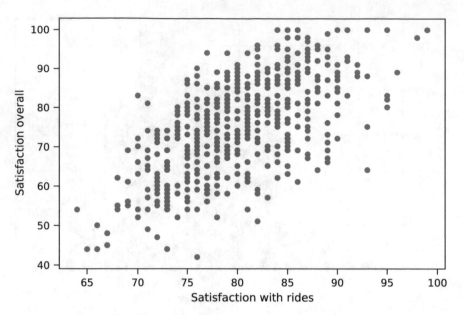

Fig. 7.4 Scatterplot comparing satisfaction with rides to overall satisfaction among recent visitors to an amusement park

Out[16]:

```
                                 OLS Regression Results
===============================================================================
Dep. Variable:                   overall   R-squared:                     0.407
Model:                               OLS   Adj. R-squared:                0.405
Method:                    Least Squares   F-statistic:                   341.3
Date:                   Thu, 30 Jan 2020   Prob (F-statistic):         2.02e-58
Time:                           04:41:55   Log-Likelihood:              -1827.7
No. Observations:                    500   AIC:                           3659.
Df Residuals:                        498   BIC:                           3668.
Df Model:                              1
Covariance Type:               nonrobust
===============================================================================
                 coef    std err          t      P>|t|      [0.025      0.975]
-------------------------------------------------------------------------------
Intercept     -27.9869      5.609     -4.990      0.000     -39.007     -16.967
rides           1.2887      0.070     18.474      0.000       1.152       1.426
===============================================================================
Omnibus:                           5.897   Durbin-Watson:                 1.890
Prob(Omnibus):                     0.052   Jarque-Bera (JB):              5.361
Skew:                             -0.194   Prob(JB):                     0.0685
Kurtosis:                          2.674   Cond. No.                   1.08e+03
===============================================================================
```

To view the details of the model, we use the summary() method, which displays a variety of values including the intercept value and any fitted coefficients as well as many values related to the goodness of the fit.

This summarizes the principal information to review for a linear model. More advanced models are reported similarly, so it is useful to become familiar with this format. In addition to listing the model that was estimated, we get information about coefficients, residuals, and the overall fit.

The most important section is the middle one, which shows the model coefficients in the coef column. The coefficient for rides is 1.2887, so each additional rating point for rides is estimated to result in an increase of 1.2887 points of overall rating. (In case you're wondering, the coefficient for the Intercept shows where the linear model line crosses the y-axis, but this is usually not interpretable in a satisfaction drivers analysis—for instance, there is no such thing as a possible negative rating on our scale—so it is generally ignored by marketing analysts.)

The `std err` column indicates uncertainty in the coefficient estimate, under the assumption that the data are a random sample of a larger population. The "`t value`", p-value ("`Pr>|t|`") and confidence intervals indicate whether the coefficient is significantly different than zero. A traditional estimate of a 95% confidence interval for the coefficient estimate is that it will fall within $\pm 1.96 \times std.error$. In this case, $1.2887 \pm 1.96 \times 0.07 = (1.152, 1.426)$. So we are confident— assuming the model is appropriate and the data are representative—that the true coefficient for `ride` is somewhere in the range 1.152–1.426.

The intercept and coefficient can be used to determine the best estimate for any respondent's report of `overall` based on knowing their value for `rides`. For example, from this model we would expect that a customer who gives a rating of 95 for satisfaction with `rides` would give an `overall` rating of:

```
In [17]: -27.9869 + 1.2887*95
```

```
Out[17]: 94.43959999999998
```

Using coefficients manually is not very efficient. This brings us to our next topic, `ols` objects.

7.2.4   *ols Objects*

`ols()` returns an object that we can save and use for other purposes. Typically, we assign the result of `ols().fit()` to an object that is used in subsequent lines of code. For example, we can assign the result of `ols().fit()` to a new object `m1`:

```
In [18]: m1 = smf.ols('overall ~ rides', data=sat_df).fit()
```

We can then reuse the model by accessing `m1`. We can inspect the `m1` object, for example we can access the coefficients with the `.params` suffix:

```
In [19]: m1.params
```

```
Out[19]: Intercept    -27.986876
         rides          1.288694
         dtype: float64
```

If we want to estimate `overall` based on the model, rather than manually accessing the coefficients for prediction, we can use the `predict()` method of the `ols` object. It takes as an argument structured data which has to be indexed with the same names as those that were in the formula, e.g. 'ride' in this case. This can be in the form of a `DataFrame` or as a `dict`:

```
In [20]: m1.predict({'rides': [95]})
```

```
Out[20]: 0    94.439017
         dtype: float64
```

If we redraw the scatterplot for `overall ~ rides`, we can add the linear fit line using model prediction:

```
In [21]: sat_df.plot(kind='scatter', x='rides', y='overall')
         plt.plot(sat_df.rides, m1.predict(sat_df.rides))
```

The result is shown in Fig. 7.5. This creates a plot similar to the one in Fig. 7.4, except that it includes a line representing the model fit.

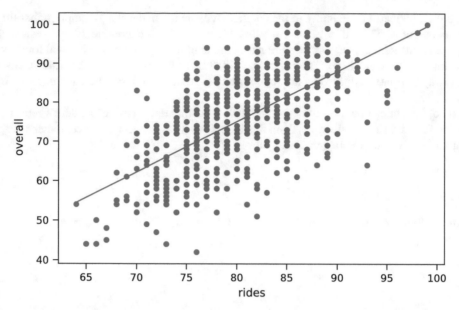

Fig. 7.5 Scatterplot comparing satisfaction with rides to overall satisfaction among recent visitors to an amusement park with a fitted line

As above, the `summary()` method of `ols` objects that summarizes all these features of the fitted model:

```
In [22]: m1.summary() #  # Not shown
```

What about the confidence interval? Once again, Python does not make you compute things by hand. The confidence intervals can be accessed using the `confint()` method:

```
In [23]: m1.conf_int()
```

```
Out[23]:                       0          1
          Intercept  -39.006778  -16.966974
          rides        1.151636    1.425752
```

This confirms our computation by hand in Sect. 7.2.3, that the best estimate for the relationship `overall ~ rides` is 1.1516–1.4258 (with slight differences due to rounding). It is a best practice to report the range of an estimate, not just the single best point.

In the first section of the output, `m1.summary()` provides measures of how well the model fits the data. The first line reports the estimate of *R-squared*, a measure of how much variation in the dependent variable is captured by the model. In this case, the R-squared is 0.407, indicating that about 41% of the variation in overall satisfaction is explained by variation in satisfaction with rides. When a model includes only a single predictor, R-squared is equal to the square of the correlation coefficient r between the predictor and the outcome:

```
In [24]: np.corrcoef(sat_df.rides, sat_df.overall)**2
```

```
Out[24]: array([[1.        , 0.40662807],
           [0.40662807, 1.        ]])
```

Finally, the line labeled `F-statistic` provides a statistical test of whether the model predicts the data better than simply taking the average of the outcome variable and using that as the single prediction for all the observations. In essence, this test tells whether our model is better than a model that predicts overall satisfaction using no predictors at all. For reasons we will not describe in detail, this is the same test reported by the `statsmodels.stats.anova.anova_lm()` function that we saw in Chap. 5; you could find the same value with `anova_lm(m1)`. Check a statistics textbook for a description of the *F-test* in more detail. In the present case, the `F-statistic` shows a p-value $<<.05$, so we reject the null hypothesis that a model without predictors performs as well as model `m1`.

Additionally, we can inspect the residuals. A *residual* is the difference between the model-predicted value of a point and its actual value. In Fig. 7.5, this is the vertical distance between a plotted point (actual value) and the blue line (predicted value).

We can observe the range of the residuals:

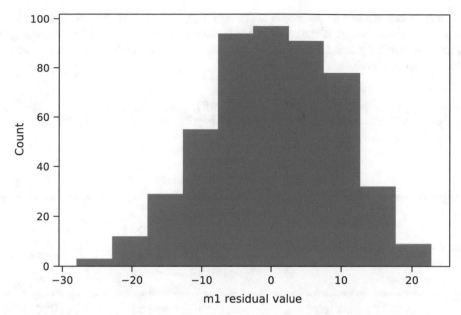

Fig. 7.6 The distribution of residuals from m1. The residuals are symmetrical around 0 with the majority being less than 7

```
In [25]: m1.resid.max(), m1.resid.min()

Out[25]: (22.75746829230569, -27.953838097780633)
```

The range is quite wide, ranging from -27.954 to 22.757, which means our predictions can be rather off for any given data point (more than 27 points on the rating scale). The quartiles of the residuals suggest that they are fairly symmetric around 0, at least in the interquartile range:

```
In [26]: np.percentile(m1.resid, q=range(0,120,25))

Out[26]: array([-27.9538381 ,  -6.56470511,  -0.04165295,   7.18008107,
                 22.75746829])
```

Another way to check for symmetry of the residuals would be with a histogram, which also gives an indication of the spread, as see in Fig. 7.6:

```
In [27]: plt.hist(m1.resid)
         plt.xlabel('m1 residual value')
         plt.ylabel('Count')
```

As we discuss in Sect. 7.2.5, that is a good sign that the model is unbiased (although perhaps imprecise).

We can also look at the standard deviation of the residuals:

```
In [28]: np.std(m1.resid)

Out[28]: 9.360403552873873
```

This value isn't very useful on its own, but can be valuable for comparing models as we'll see in Sect. 7.3.

7.2.5 Checking Model Fit

Because it is easy to fit linear models, too many analysts fit models and report results without considering whether the models are *reasonable*. There are a variety of ways to assess model fit and adequacy that are easy to perform in Python. While we cannot possibly cover this material comprehensively, we would like to give you a few pointers that will help you assess model adequacy.

There are several assumptions when a linear model is fitted to data. The first assumption is that the relationship between the predictors and the outcomes is *linear*. If the relationship is not linear, then the model will make systematic errors. For example, if we generate data where y is a function of x^2 and then fit a linear model $y \sim x$, this will draw a straight line through a cloud of points that is curved.

```
In [29]: x = np.random.normal(size=500)
         y = x**2 + np.random.normal(size=500)
         toy_model = smf.ols('y ~ x', data={'x': x, 'y': y}).fit()
         toy_model.summary()
```

Out[29]:

OLS Regression Results

Dep. Variable:	y	R-squared:	0.004
Model:	OLS	Adj. R-squared:	0.002
Method:	Least Squares	F-statistic:	1.999
Date:	Thu, 30 Jan 2020	Prob (F-statistic):	0.158

...

	coef	std err	t	P>|t|	[0.025	0.975]
Intercept	1.1192	0.085	13.184	0.000	0.952	1.286
x	-0.1129	0.080	-1.414	0.158	-0.270	0.044

...

In the summary, you can see that the fitted coefficient for x is -0.1129 and the t-test indicates that the coefficient is not significantly different from zero. Without model checking, a sloppy analyst might conclude that x is not related to y. However, if we plot x versus y and then draw our fitted line on the plot, we can see more clearly what is going on. Note that in this and subsequent summaries, we remove rows that are not relevant for the discussion at hand.

```
In [30]: plt.scatter(x,y)
         plt.plot(x, toy_model.predict({'x': x}))
         plt.xlabel('x')
         plt.ylabel('y')
         plt.title('x vs y with fit line')
```

The resulting plot is shown in Fig. 7.7. The plot shows that our fitted linear model (illustrated with a blue line) completely misses the curvature in the relationship between x and y.

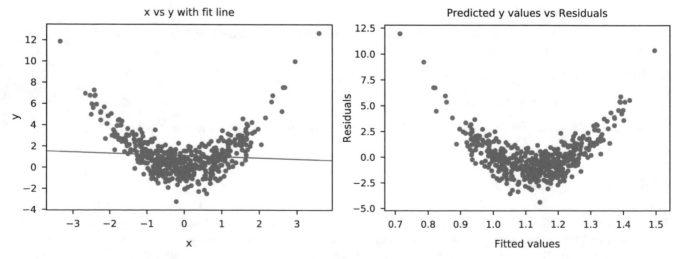

Fig. 7.7 Fitting a linear model when the true relationship is non-linear (as in the data and linear fit line shown in the left hand plot) results in unusual residual patterns (the residuals after removing the linear fit line; as shown in the right hand plot)

Another assumption of a linear model is that prediction errors—the parts of the data that do not exactly fit the model—are normally distributed and look like random noise with no pattern. One way to examine this is to plot the model's *fitted values* (the predictions) versus the *residuals* (the prediction errors).

```
In [31]: plt.scatter(x=toy_model.fittedvalues, y=toy_model.resid)
         plt.xlabel('Fitted values')
         plt.ylabel('Residuals')
         plt.title('Predicted y values vs Residuals')
```

This results in the plot on the right hand side of Fig. 7.7 and you can see from the plot that there is a clear pattern in the residuals: our model under-predicts the value of y near zero and over-predicts far from zero. When you come across this problem in real data, the solution is usually to transform x; you can use the methods described in Sect. 4.5.4 to find a transformation that is suitable. If you begin by inspecting scatterplots as we recommend in Sect. 7.2.1, you will be unlikely to commit such a simple error. Still, it is good to know that later checks can help prevent errors as well.

We can create similar goodness of fit plots for our satisfaction drivers data. A reasonable first-pass set of diagnostic plots can be generated using a function which includes a fitted values versus residuals plot as well as a few others:

```
In [32]: from statsmodels.graphics import gofplots
         from statsmodels.graphics import regressionplots


         def plot_gof_figures(model):
             '''Plot a multipanel figure of goodness of fit plots'''
             sns.residplot(model.fittedvalues, model.resid, lowess=True)
             plt.xlabel('Fitted values')
             plt.ylabel('Residuals')
             plt.title('Residuals vs Fitted')
             plt.show()


             _ = gofplots.qqplot(model.resid, fit=True, line='45')
             plt.title('Normal Q-Q')
             plt.show()


             plt.scatter(model.fittedvalues, np.abs(model.resid)**.5)
             plt.xlabel('Fitted values')
             plt.ylabel('Square root of the standardized residuals')
             plt.title('Scale-Location')
             plt.show()


             regressionplots.plot_leverage_resid2(model)
```

And we can see that applied that to the `toy_model` in Fig. 7.8:

```
In [33]: plot_gof_figures(toy_model)
```

And to our model, `m1`, in Fig. 7.9:

```
In [34]: plot_gof_figures(m1)
```

In Figs. 7.8 and 7.9, the first plot (in the upper left corner) shows the fitted values versus residuals. Unlike in Fig. 7.8, in the upper left panel of Fig. 7.9 there is no obvious pattern between the fitted values for overall satisfaction and the residuals; this is consistent with the idea that the residuals are due to random error, and supports the notion that the model is reasonable and is not ignoring an obvious non-linearity.

The second plot in the lower left of each figure is similar to the first, except that instead of plotting the *raw* residual value, it plots the *square root* of the absolute value of the residual (referred to as the *standardized residual*). Again, there should be no clear pattern; *if there were it might indicate a non-linear relationship*, as we see in 7.8.

A common pattern in residual plots is a *cone* or *funnel*, where the range of errors gets progressively larger for larger fitted values. This is called *heteroskedasticity* and is a violation of linear model assumptions. A linear model tries to maximize fit to the line; when values in one part of the range have a much larger spread than those in another area, they have undue influence on the estimation of the line. Sometimes a transformation of the predictor or outcome variable will resolve heteroskedasticity (see Sect. 4.5.3).

The third panel in the upper right is a *Normal QQ plot*. A QQ plot helps you see whether the residuals follow a normal distribution, another key assumption (see Sect. 3.4.3). It compares the values that residuals would be *expected* to take if they are normally distributed, versus their actual values. When the model is appropriate, these points are similar and fall close to a diagonal line; when the relationship between the variables is non-linear or otherwise does not match the assumption, the points deviate from the diagonal line. In the present case, the QQ plot suggests that the data fits the assumption of the model in Fig. 7.9, but not in Fig. 7.8.

The final plot in the lower right panel of each Figure again helps to identify potential *outliers*, observations that may come from a different distribution than the others. Outliers are a problem because, if they are far from other points, they unduly influence the fitted line. We do not want a small set of observations to have a large effect on the coefficients. The lower right plot shows the *leverage* of each point, a measure of how much influence the point has on the model coefficients. When a point has a high residual and high leverage, it indicates that the point has both a different pattern (residual) and undue influence (leverage). One measure of the leverage of a data point is *Cook's distance*, an estimate of how much predicted (y) values would change if the model were re-estimated with that point eliminated from the data.

In the lower right panel of Fig. 7.9, points are automatically labeled with row numbers if they are potentially problematic outliers based on high standardized residual distance and leverage on the model. We do not recommend routinely removing outliers, yet we do recommend to inspect them and determine whether there is a problem with the data. We inspect several of the identified points in Fig. 7.9 by selecting those rows:

```
In [35]: sat_df.loc[[405, 48, 176]]

Out[35]: is_weekend  num_child   distance   rides   games   wait   clean  \
    405       True           0  11.445116    93.0    77.0   75.0    89.0
```

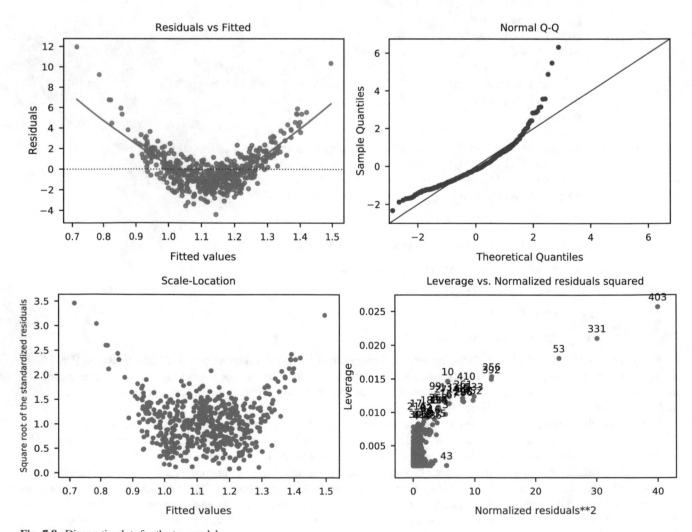

Fig. 7.8 Diagnostic plots for the toy model

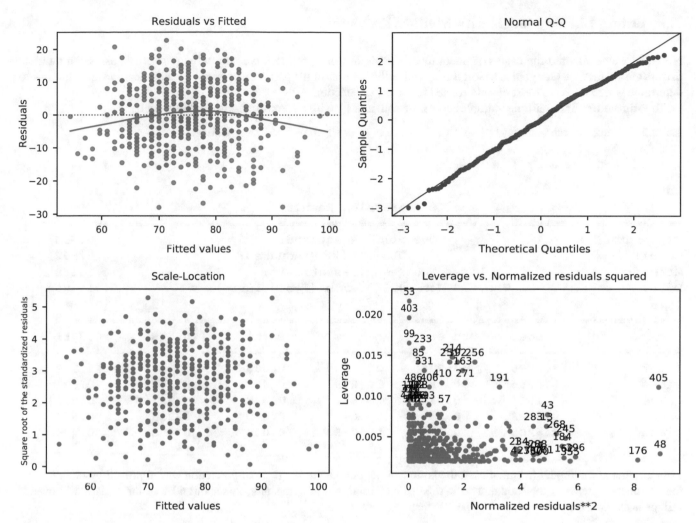

Fig. 7.9 Diagnostic plots for the model relating overall satisfaction to satisfaction with rides

```
48        False       0   8.434066   76.0   61.0   48.0   73.0
176       True        0   18.318936  82.0   61.0   74.0   84.0

      overall   log_dist
405    64.0     2.437563
48     42.0     2.132279
176    51.0     2.907935
```

In this case, none of the data points is obviously invalid (for instance, with values below 1 or greater than 100). We generally do not omit outliers except when they represent obvious errors in the data. In the present case, we would keep all of the observations.

Overall, Fig. 7.9 looks good and suggests that the model relating overall satisfaction to satisfaction with rides is reasonable.

But we've only examined a single variable so far. In the next section, we consider multiple predictors. For brevity, in following sections we omit the checks of model adequacy that were shown in this section, but we encourage you to check and interpret such diagnostic plots for the models.

7.3 Fitting Linear Models with Multiple Predictors

Now that we've covered the basics of linear models using just one predictor, we turn to the problem of assessing multiple drivers of satisfaction. Our goal is to sort through all of the features of the park—rides, games, wait times, and cleanliness—to determine which ones are most closely related to overall satisfaction.

To estimate our first multiple variable model, we call `ols()` with a formula describing the model:

```
In [36]: m2 = smf.ols('overall ~ rides + games + wait + clean',
                    data=sat_df).fit()
         m2.summary()

Out[36]:
                          OLS Regression Results
================================================================================
Dep. Variable:                  overall   R-squared:                     0.595
Model:                              OLS   Adj. R-squared:                0.592
Method:                   Least Squares   F-statistic:                   181.9
Date:                Thu, 30 Jan 2020   Prob (F-statistic):          9.91e-96
...

================================================================================
                 coef     std err          t      P>|t|      [0.025      0.975]
--------------------------------------------------------------------------------
Intercept    -53.6088       5.246    -10.219      0.000     -63.916     -43.302
rides          0.4256       0.099      4.279      0.000       0.230       0.621
games          0.1861       0.048      3.843      0.000       0.091       0.281
wait           0.3842       0.036     10.647      0.000       0.313       0.455
clean          0.6205       0.108      5.725      0.000       0.408       0.834
...
```

Looking first at the model fit statistics at the bottom of the output, we see that our prediction was improved by including all the satisfaction items in the model. The R-squared increased to 0.595, meaning that about 60% of the variation in overall ratings is explained by the ratings for specific features.

```
In [37]: np.std(m2.resid)

Out[37]: 7.732470220113991
```

The residual standard error is now 7.732, whereas it was 9.360 for the simpler model, meaning that the predictions are more accurate.

```
In [38]: np.percentile(m2.resid, q=range(0,101,25))

Out[38]: array([-26.0408112 ,  -4.89848961,   0.88100141,   5.56376647,
        18.2162639 ])
```

Our residuals also appear to be relatively symmetric, again, at least in the interquartile range. As noted above, we recommend also to inspect the model using diagnostic plots (e.g., our `plot_gof_figures()` function) to confirm that there are no patterns in the residuals indicative of non-linearity or outliers, although we omit that step here.

Next we examine the model coefficients. Each coefficient represents the strength of the relationship between satisfaction with that feature and overall satisfaction, conditional on the values of the other predictors. All four features are identified as being statistically significant (p-value, shown as P>|t| <0.05). Rather than just comparing the numbers in the output, it can be helpful to visualize the coefficients. We can import the function we wrote in Sect. 6.5.4, to display confidence intervals, with a dotted line at zero to indicate non-significance (see Sect. 2.4.9 for a refresher on installing packages).

```
In [39]: !pip install python_marketing_research
         from python_marketing_research_functions import chapter6
```

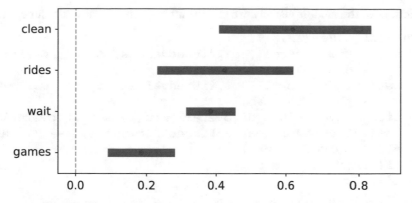

Fig. 7.10 A coefficient plot produced for an initial multivariate `ols()` model of satisfaction in the amusement park data. In the model, satisfaction with cleanliness is most strongly associated with overall satisfaction, and rides and wait times are also associated

We can then pass the coefficients and confidence intervals to that function to generate a plot, show in Fig. 7.10:

```
In [40]: chapter6.plot_confidence_intervals(m2.params[1:],
                                            m2.conf_int().iloc[1:,:],
                                            zero_line=True)
```

In Fig. 7.10 we see that satisfaction with cleanliness is estimated to be the most important feature associated with overall satisfaction, followed by satisfaction with the rides and wait times. Satisfaction with games is estimated to be relatively less important. Note that the confidence intervals for several of the coefficients are overlapping, indicating that those coefficients might not truly differ. For example, while clean satisfaction is clearly more important than game satisfaction to overall satisfaction, the relative importance of wait times versus rides is less clear, despite the fact that the coefficient for rides is higher than the coefficient for wait times. See Sect. 6.3.1 for a discussion of confidence intervals and their interpretation.

A plot of coefficients is often a key output from a satisfaction drivers analysis. Sorting the plot so that the coefficients are in order based on their estimated coefficient (as we have here) may make it easier to quickly identify the features that are most closely related to overall satisfaction if you have a large number of predictors.

7.3.1 Comparing Models

Now that we have two model objects, `m1` and `m2` we might ask which one is better. One way to evaluate models is to compare their R-squared values.

```
In [41]: print(m1.rsquared)
         print(m2.rsquared)

0.4066280681606046
0.5950752098970709
```

Based on the R-squared values we can say that `m2` explains more of the variation in satisfaction than `m1`. However, a model with more predictors usually has a higher R^2, so we could instead compare *adjusted* R-squared values, which control for the number of predictors in the model.

```
In [42]: print(m1.rsquared_adj)
         print(m2.rsquared_adj)

0.4054365582573126
0.5918030903810876
```

The adjusted R-squared still suggests that the `m2` explains more of the variation in overall satisfaction, even accounting for the fact that `m2` uses more predictors.

To compare the predictions of the models visually, we plot the fitted versus actual values for each:

```
In [43]: plt.figure(figsize=(12,8))
         plt.scatter(sat_df.overall, m1.fittedvalues, c='r', marker='x',
                 alpha=0.75, label='m1')
         plt.scatter(sat_df.overall, m2.fittedvalues, c='b', marker='x',
                 alpha=0.75, label='m2')
         satisfaction_range = [sat_df.overall.min(), sat_df.overall.max()]
         plt.plot(satisfaction_range, satisfaction_range, '--k', label = 'x=y')
         plt.xlabel('Observed value')
         plt.ylabel('Predicted value')
         plt.legend()
```

If the model fit the data perfectly, it would fall along a line of $y = x$ in this plot, but, of course, it is nearly impossible to fit customer satisfaction data perfectly. By comparing the red and the blue points in the resulting plot in Fig. 7.11, you can see that the blue cloud of points is more tightly clustered along a diagonal line, which shows that m2 explains more of the variation in the data than m1, although the magnitude of that effect is hard to determine from this figure.

For a more formal test, which is possible because the models here are nested (see Sect. 6.5.3), we can use anova_lm() function to determine whether m2 explains more of the variation than m1:

```
In [44]: from statsmodels.stats import anova as sms_anova
         sms_anova.anova_lm(m1,m2)
```

```
Out [44]:      df_resid            ssr    df_diff          ss_diff           F        Pr(>F)
        0         498.0   43808.577336        0.0              NaN         NaN           NaN
        1         495.0   29895.547852        3.0     13913.029484   76.789021  8.500020e-41
```

The low p-value indicates that the additional predictors in m2 significantly improve the fit of the model. If these two models were the only ones under consideration, we would proceed with m2 rather than m1.

You may have noticed that the coefficient for rides changed from m1 to m2. The value in m1 was $1.2887 \times rides$, while in m2 it is $0.4256 \times rides$. Why is this happening? The reason is because rides is not independent of all the other variables; Fig. 7.1 shows that customers who are more satisfied with the rides tend to be more satisfied with the wait times and games. When those variables are added as predictors in model m2, they now perform some of the work in predicting the overall rating, and the contribution of rides is a smaller share of the total model.

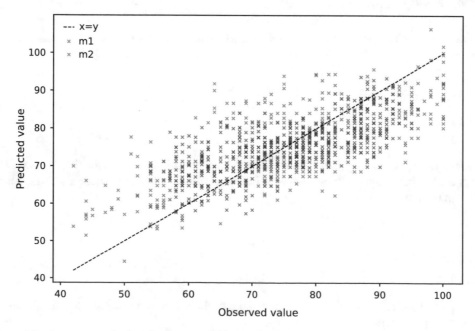

Fig. 7.11 Comparison of fitted versus actual values for linear models m1 and m2

Neither coefficient for `rides` is more correct in itself because a coefficient is not right or wrong but part of a larger model. Which model is preferable? Because model m2 has better overall fit, we would interpret its coefficient for `rides`, but only in the context of the total model. In the sections below, we see that as the structure of a model changes, the coefficients generally change as well (unless the variables are entirely uncorrelated).

7.3.2 Using a Model to Make Predictions

As we saw for the single variable case, we could use the model coefficients to predict the `overall` outcome for different combinations of the explanatory variables. `m2.params` is a pandas `Series`, we access the individual coefficients here using their names. If we wanted to predict the overall rating for a customer who rated the four separate aspects as 100 points each, we could multiply those ratings by the coefficients and add the intercept:

```
In [45]: m2.params.Intercept + m2.params.rides*100 + m2.params.games*100\
             + m2.params.wait*100 + m2.params.clean*100

Out[45]: 108.02382449445317
```

The best estimate is 108.024 using model m2. Note, that's greater than the maximum rating! But the linear model is unconstrained; it has no representation of a maximum rating. This does make intuitive sense though: someone who rates everything at 100 is likely to also give a rating of 100 overall as well.

The prediction equation above is clunky to type, and there are more efficient ways to compute model predictions. We can use `ols.predict(newdata)` where `newdata` is a `DataFrame` with the same column names as the data that was used to estimate the model. For example, if we want to find the predictions for the first 10 customers in our dataset we would pass the first 10 rows of `sat_df` to `predict()`:

```
In [46]: m2.predict(sat_df.head(10))
])

Out[46]: 0    79.303964
         1    92.271882
         2    86.113782
         3    59.175321
         4    69.286346
         5    72.019136
         6    79.708122
         7    75.172110
         8    75.774821
         9    80.446600
         dtype: float64
```

This predicts satisfaction for the first 10 customers. The predictions for observations used to estimate the model are also stored in the model object, and can be accessed with the `fittedvalues` suffix:

```
In [47]: m2.fittedvalues[:10]

Out[47]: 0    79.303964
         1    92.271882
         2    86.113782
         3    59.175321
         4    69.286346
         5    72.019136
         6    79.708122
         7    75.172110
         8    75.774821
         9    80.446600
         dtype: float64
```

The `predict()` method will also accept a `dict` object:

```
In [48]: m2.predict({'rides': 100,
                      'games': 100,
                      'wait': 100,
                      'clean': 100})

Out[48]: 0    108.023824
         dtype: float64
```

7.3.3 Standardizing the Predictors

Thus far, we have interpreted raw coefficients in order to evaluate the contributions of different aspects of a visit (each rated on a 100 point scale) to the overall satisfaction with the amusement park (also rated on a 100 point scale). However, if the variables have different *scales*, such as a survey where `rides` is rated on a 1–10 scale while cleanliness is rated 1–5 scale, then their coefficient values would not be directly comparable. In the present data, this occurs with the `distance` and `log_dist` variables, which are not on a 100 point scale.

When you wish to compare coefficients, it can be helpful to *standardize* data on a common scale before fitting a model (and *after* transforming any variables to a normally distributed scale). The most common standardization converts values to zero-centered *units of standard deviation*. This subtracts a variable's `mean` from each observation and then divides by the standard deviation (`std()`), and is also known as a *Z score*:

```
In [49]: ((sat_df.rides - sat_df.rides.mean())/sat_df.rides.std()).head(10)

Out[49]: 0     0.302715
         1     0.801147
         2     1.299580
         3    -1.192583
         4    -0.361862
         5     0.468859
         6     0.136571
         7    -0.361862
         8    -0.029574
         9    -0.528006
         Name: rides, dtype: float64
```

If we do not want to worry about the scale of our variables, only their relative contributions, we may create a scaled version of `sat_df`:

```
In [50]: sat_df_scaled = sat_df.copy()
         idx = ['clean', 'games', 'rides', 'wait', 'log_dist', 'overall']
         sat_df_scaled[idx] = (sat_df[idx] - sat_df[idx].mean(axis=0))\
           /sat_df[idx].std(axis=0)

In [51]: sat_df_scaled.head()

Out[51]:    is_weekend  num_child   distance      rides      games      wait  \
         0        True          0   9.844503   0.302715  -1.139289  0.811454
         1       False          1   2.720221   0.801147   1.034490  2.494194
         2       False          3   1.878189   1.299580   0.805671  0.624483
         3       False          0  14.211682  -1.192583  -2.512202 -0.497343
         4       False          1   9.362776  -0.361862   2.178584 -1.619169
```

```
          clean     overall    log_dist
0    0.480319  -0.603270   -0.598161
1    0.829134   2.027508   -1.801954
2    1.003542   1.616449   -2.148627
3   -1.961389  -1.672024   -0.254534
4   -0.566127  -1.014329   -0.645118
```

In this code, we first copied `sat_df` to the new dataframe `sat_df_scaled`. Then we standardized each of the numeric columns, except `distance` because we will be using `log_dist` instead. We do not standardize `weekend` because it is a factor variable rather than numeric. We leave `num_child` as is for now because we have not yet analyzed it.

Note that we do not alter the original dataframe `sat_df` when standardizing it. Instead, we copy it to a new dataframe and alter the new one. This process makes it easier to recover from errors; if anything goes wrong with `sat_df_scaled` we can just run these few commands again to recreate it.

The question of standardizing values depends primarily on how you want to use a model's coefficients. If you want to interpret coefficients in terms of the original scales, then you would not standardize data first. However, in satisfaction driver analysis we are usually more concerned with the relative contribution of different predictors and wish to compare them, and standardization assists with this. Additionally, we often transform variables before analysis such that they are no longer on the original scale.

After standardizing, you should check the results. A standardized variable should have a mean of 0 and values within a few units of the mean. Checking the `describe()`:

```
In [52]: sat_df_scaled[idx].describe().round(2)
```

```
Out[52]:        clean    games    rides     wait   log_dist   overall
         count  500.00   500.00   500.00   500.00   500.00    500.00
         mean     0.00     0.00     0.00     0.00    -0.00      0.00
         std      1.00     1.00     1.00     1.00     1.00      1.00
         min     -3.53    -3.43    -2.69    -2.55    -3.16     -2.74
         25%     -0.57    -0.68    -0.69    -0.68    -0.68     -0.69
         50%     -0.04     0.00    -0.03    -0.03     0.03      0.05
         75%      0.65     0.69     0.64     0.62     0.69      0.79
         max      2.57     2.98     3.13     2.49     2.36      2.03
```

We see that `sat_df_scaled` matches expectation.

There is a technical point we should mention when standardizing variables. If the outcome and predictors are all standardized, their means will be zero and thus the intercept will be zero. However, that does *not* imply that the intercept could be removed from the model. The model is estimated to minimize error in the overall fit, which includes error for the intercept. This implies that the intercept should remain in a model after standardization if it would have been there otherwise (as it usually should be; see Sect. 7.5.1).

7.4 Using Factors as Predictors

While m2 above was reasonable, we can continue to improve it. It is typical to try many models before arriving at a final one.

For the next step, we wonder whether satisfaction is different for customers who come on the weekend, travel farther, or have more children. We add these predictors to the model using standardized data:

```
In [53]: m3 = smf.ols('overall ~ rides + games + wait + clean + is_weekend'
                   ' + log_dist + num_child', data=sat_df_scaled).fit()
         m3.summary()
```

```
Out[53]:
                           OLS Regression Results
==============================================================================
Dep. Variable:                overall   R-squared:                       0.715
Model:                            OLS   Adj. R-squared:                  0.711
Method:                 Least Squares   F-statistic:                     176.3
Date:                Thu, 30 Jan 2020   Prob (F-statistic):           1.01e-129
...
==============================================================================
                     coef    std err          t      P>|t|      [0.025      0.975]
------------------------------------------------------------------------------
Intercept         -0.3516      0.042     -8.423      0.000      -0.434      -0.270
is_weekend[T.True] -0.0724     0.049     -1.485      0.138      -0.168       0.023
rides              0.2558      0.042      6.147      0.000       0.174       0.338
games              0.0992      0.029      3.371      0.001       0.041       0.157
wait               0.3363      0.027     12.591      0.000       0.284       0.389
clean              0.2718      0.043      6.310      0.000       0.187       0.356
log_dist           0.1069      0.024      4.423      0.000       0.059       0.154
num_child          0.2190      0.016     13.864      0.000       0.188       0.250
...
```

The model summary shows a substantial improvement in fit (R-squared of 0.715) and the coefficients for `log_dist` and `num_child` are significantly greater than zero, suggesting that people who travel further and have more children have higher overall satisfaction ratings.

Notice that the coefficient for `weekend` is labeled `weekend[T.True]`, which seems a bit unusual. Recall that `weekend` is a boolean variable, or factor, which doesn't fit naturally in our linear model; you cannot multiply `True` by a number. statsmodels handles this by converting the data to a numeric value where 1 is assigned to the value of `True` and 0 to `False`. It labels the output so that we know which direction the coefficient applies to. So, we can interpret the coefficient as meaning that on average those who come on the weekend rate their overall satisfaction 0.07 standard units (standard deviations) lower than those who come on a weekday, although it is not a significant effect.

When your data include factors, you must be careful about the data type. For example, `num_child` is a numeric variable, ranging 0–5, but it doesn't necessarily make sense to treat it as a number, as we did in m3. In doing so, we implicitly assume that satisfaction goes up or down linearly as a function of the number of children, and that the effect is the same for each additional child. (Anyone who has taken a group of children to an amusement park might guess that this is an unreasonable assumption.)

We correct this by converting `num_child` to a factor and re-estimating the model:

```
In [54]: dummy_vals = pd.get_dummies(sat_df_scaled.num_child, prefix='num_child')
         dummy_vals.head()

Out[54]:      num_child_0   num_child_1   num_child_2   num_child_3   num_child_4  \
         0             1             0             0             0             0
         1             0             1             0             0             0
         2             0             0             0             1             0
         3             1             0             0             0             0
         4             0             1             0             0             0


              num_child_5
         0             0
         1             0
         2             0
         3             0
         4             0

In [55]: sat_df_child_factor = sat_df_scaled.join(dummy_vals)
```

```
In [56]: m4 = smf.ols('overall ~ rides + games + wait + clean + log_dist'
                      '+ num_child_0 + num_child_1 + num_child_2 + num_child_3'
                      '+ num_child_4 + num_child_5',
                      data=sat_df_child_factor).fit()
         m4.summary()

Out[56]:
```

```
                           OLS Regression Results
==============================================================================
Dep. Variable:                overall   R-squared:                       0.818
Model:                            OLS   Adj. R-squared:                  0.815
Method:                 Least Squares   F-statistic:                     220.3
Date:                Thu, 30 Jan 2020   Prob (F-statistic):          5.23e-174
...

==============================================================================
                 coef    std err          t      P>|t|      [0.025      0.975]
------------------------------------------------------------------------------
Intercept      0.1059      0.020      5.391      0.000       0.067       0.144
rides          0.2604      0.033      7.803      0.000       0.195       0.326
games          0.0968      0.024      4.097      0.000       0.050       0.143
wait           0.3139      0.022     14.570      0.000       0.272       0.356
clean          0.2710      0.035      7.819      0.000       0.203       0.339
log_dist       0.1001      0.019      5.154      0.000       0.062       0.138
num_child_0   -0.7978      0.035    -22.574      0.000      -0.867      -0.728
num_child_1    0.2097      0.047      4.456      0.000       0.117       0.302
num_child_2    0.2549      0.039      6.492      0.000       0.178       0.332
num_child_3    0.2108      0.046      4.563      0.000       0.120       0.302
num_child_4    0.1315      0.053      2.471      0.014       0.027       0.236
num_child_5    0.0968      0.077      1.253      0.211      -0.055       0.249
...
```

We now see that there are 6 fitted coefficients for num_child: one for parties with 0 children, one for parties with 1 child, etc. Note that the coefficient for num_child_0 is negative, indicating that parties without children rate lower. Comparing the coefficients for num_child_1 and num_child_0, parties with 1 child rate their overall satisfaction on average 1.0075 standard deviations higher than parties without children (the difference between 0.2097 and −0.7978).

Using pandas.get_dummies(), we have created a new variable num_child_1 that is equal to 1 for those cases where num_child represents one child (a factor level of "1"), and is 0 otherwise. Similarly, num_child_2 is 1 for cases with two children, and 0 otherwise, and so forth. The coefficient for num_child_2 is 0.2549, meaning that people with two children rate their overall satisfaction on average over a full standard deviation (0.2549 - (-0.7978) = 1.0527) higher than those with no children.

A striking thing about m4 is that the increase in overall satisfaction is about the same regardless of how many children there are in the party—about 1 standard deviation higher for any number of children. This suggests that we don't actually need to estimate a different increase for each number of children. In fact, if the increase is the same for 1 child as for 3 children, attempting to fit a model that scales increasingly per child would result in a less accurate estimate.

Instead, we declare a new variable called has_child that is TRUE when the party has children in it and FALSE when the party does not have children. We then estimate the model using that new factor variable. We also drop weekend from the model because it doesn't seem to be a significant predictor:

```
In [57]: sat_df_scaled['has_child'] = sat_df_scaled.num_child.apply(lambda x:
                                                                    x > 0)
         m5 = smf.ols('overall ~ rides + games + wait + clean + log_dist'
                      '+ has_child', data=sat_df_scaled).fit()
         m5.summary()
```

```
Out[57]:
===============================================================================
Dep. Variable:                  overall   R-squared:                      0.817
Model:                              OLS   Adj. R-squared:                 0.814
Method:                   Least Squares   F-statistic:                    365.9
Date:               Thu, 30 Jan 2020     Prob (F-statistic):          5.25e-178
...

===============================================================================
                   coef     std err          t     P>|t|     [0.025    0.975]
-------------------------------------------------------------------------------
Intercept        -0.6919      0.035    -19.929     0.000     -0.760    -0.624
has_child[T.True] 1.0028      0.042     23.956     0.000      0.921     1.085
rides             0.2645      0.033      7.950     0.000      0.199     0.330
games             0.0970      0.024      4.125     0.000      0.051     0.143
wait              0.3184      0.021     14.872     0.000      0.276     0.361
clean             0.2654      0.035      7.691     0.000      0.198     0.333
log_dist          0.1005      0.019      5.197     0.000      0.062     0.138
...
```

Is this still a good model? The change in R-squared between model m4 and m5 is negligible, suggesting that our simplification did not deteriorate the model fit.

Model m5 estimates overall satisfaction to be about 1 standard deviation higher for parties with children. However, one might now wonder how children influence other aspects of the ratings. For instance, is the relationship between satisfaction and waiting times different for parties with and without children? One might guess from experience that wait time would be more important to parties with children. To explore this question, we need to incorporate *interactions* into the model.

7.5   Interaction Terms

We can include an interaction of two terms by using the : operator between variables in a formula. For instance, to estimate overall as a function of rides plus the interaction of wait and has_child, we could write the formula as overall ~ rides + wait:has_child. There are other ways to specify interaction terms (see Sect. 7.5.1) but we prefer to specify them explicitly in this way.

We create a new model with interactions between the satisfaction ratings and two variables that describe the visit: no_child and is_weekend:

```
In [58]: m6 = smf.ols('overall ~ rides + games + wait + clean + log_dist'
                      '+ has_child + rides:has_child + games:has_child'
                      '+ wait:has_child + clean:has_child + rides:is_weekend'
                      '+ games:is_weekend + wait:is_weekend + clean:is_weekend',
                      data=sat_df_scaled).fit() \
         m6.summary()

Out[58]:
                         OLS Regression Results
===============================================================================
Dep. Variable:                  overall   R-squared:                      0.825
Model:                              OLS   Adj. R-squared:                 0.820
Method:                   Least Squares   F-statistic:                    163.3
Date:               Thu, 30 Jan 2020     Prob (F-statistic):          2.59e-173
...

===============================================================================
                   coef     std err          t     P>|t|     [0.025    0.975]
-------------------------------------------------------------------------------
Intercept        -0.6893      0.035    -19.895     0.000     -0.757    -0.621
has_child[T.True] 0.9985      0.042     23.996     0.000      0.917     1.080
```

rides	0.2116	0.067	3.138	0.002	0.079	0.344
rides:has_child[T.True]	0.0641	0.070	0.916	0.360	-0.073	0.202
rides:is_weekend[T.True]	-0.0010	0.066	-0.015	0.988	-0.131	0.129
games	0.1001	0.047	2.141	0.033	0.008	0.192
games:has_child[T.True]	-0.0452	0.051	-0.888	0.375	-0.145	0.055
games:is_weekend[T.True]	0.0746	0.048	1.564	0.119	-0.019	0.168
wait	0.1917	0.043	4.468	0.000	0.107	0.276
wait:has_child[T.True]	0.1943	0.047	4.179	0.000	0.103	0.286
wait:is_weekend[T.True]	-0.0304	0.043	-0.708	0.479	-0.115	0.054
clean	0.3332	0.072	4.611	0.000	0.191	0.475
clean:has_child[T.True]	-0.0781	0.076	-1.030	0.303	-0.227	0.071
clean:is_weekend[T.True]	-0.0081	0.069	-0.118	0.906	-0.143	0.127
log_dist	0.1054	0.019	5.459	0.000	0.067	0.143

...

The model object m6 now includes eight interaction terms between ratings for features of the park and has_child and weekend. Only one of these interactions is significant: the wait:has_child interaction. This suggests we could drop the non-significant interactions to create a new model m7:

```
In [59]: m7 = smf.ols('overall ~ rides + games + wait + clean + log_dist'
                      '+ has_child + wait:has_child',
                 data=sat_df_scaled).fit()
         m7.summary()
```

Out[59]:

```
                       OLS Regression Results
==========================================================================
Dep. Variable:              overall   R-squared:                   0.823
Model:                          OLS   Adj. R-squared:              0.820
Method:               Least Squares   F-statistic:                 326.8
Date:              Thu, 30 Jan 2020   Prob (F-statistic):       1.83e-180
...
```

	coef	std err	t	P>|t|	[0.025	0.975]
Intercept	-0.7002	0.034	-20.471	0.000	-0.767	-0.633
has_child[T.True]	1.0092	0.041	24.497	0.000	0.928	1.090
rides	0.2597	0.033	7.931	0.000	0.195	0.324
games	0.1002	0.023	4.329	0.000	0.055	0.146
wait	0.1961	0.036	5.458	0.000	0.126	0.267
wait:has_child[T.True]	0.1739	0.041	4.202	0.000	0.093	0.255
clean	0.2710	0.034	7.978	0.000	0.204	0.338
log_dist	0.1057	0.019	5.547	0.000	0.068	0.143

...

In these results, we see that attending the park with children is a predictor of higher satisfaction, and waiting time is more important predictor among those with children (wait:has_child[T.True]) than those without children. We don't know the reason for this, but perhaps children go on more rides and their parents are therefore more influenced by wait times.

What do we do with these results as marketers? We identify several possible marketing interventions. If we want to increase satisfaction overall, we could perhaps do so by trying to increase the number of visitors with children. Alternatively, if we want to appeal to visitors without children, we might engage in further research to understand why their ratings are lower. If we are allocating budget to personnel, the importance of cleanliness suggests continuing to allocate resources there (as opposed, say, to games). We might also want to learn more about the association between children and waiting time, and whether there are things we could do to make waiting less frequent or more enjoyable.

There are many more such questions one could pose from results like these; a crucial step in analysis is to think carefully about the implications and where one might be able to make a product or market intervention. When considering actions to

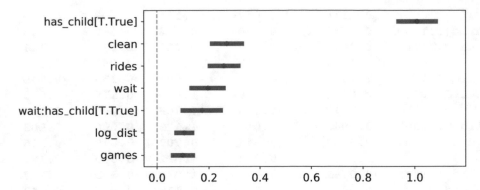

Fig. 7.12 Satisfaction drivers for visitors to an amusement park (simulated). The model reveals that the variable most strongly (and positively) associated with satisfaction is visiting the park with children. Satisfaction with waiting time is a stronger predictor of overall satisfaction among visitors with children than those without, as shown in the `wait:has_child[T.True]` interaction. Of the individual park features, satisfaction with cleanliness is most associated with overall satisfaction

take, it is especially important to remember that the model assesses association, not causation. Possible changes in outcome should be viewed as hypotheses suggested by the model, to be confirmed separately.

To share these results with others, it is helpful to create a new satisfaction drivers plot using `plot_confidence_intervals()`:

```
In [60]: chapter6.plot_confidence_intervals(m7.params[1:], m7.conf_int().iloc[1:],
                                 zero_line=True)
```

The result is Fig. 7.12 summarizing the relative contribution of each element on overall satisfaction.

When including interaction terms in a model, there are two important points. First, it is especially important to consider standardizing the predictors when modeling interactions in order to have an interpretable and comparable scale for coefficients. Second, one should always include main effects (such as `x + y`) when including an interaction effect (`x:y`). If you don't estimate the main effects, you won't know whether a purported interaction is in fact due to an interaction, or is instead due to one of the individual variables' unestimated main effects.

7.5.1   Language Brief: Advanced Formula Syntax*

This section is optional for those who wish to construct more complex formulas with interaction effects. As in the examples above, we generally write formulas using only + (for main effects) and : (specific interactions), but the following may help create more compact formulas when you have many variables or interactions.

As we've seen, you can include an interaction between `x` and `z` by including `x:z` in the formula. If you want to include two variables along with their interaction, you can use `x*z`, which is the equivalent to writing `x + z + x:z`.

The intercept can be removed from a model by including `-1` in the formula. This is ill-advised in general linear models with continuous predictors, because it forces the line to go through the origin (0, 0), which alters the other coefficients. However, it can be helpful in some kinds of models, such as those with purely categorical predictors.

Table 7.1 summarizes the common options for formula syntax and their interpretation in terms of a linear equation (where β is a model coefficient with β_0 for the intercept, β_1 for the first predictor, and so forth; ε is the error term).

7.5.2   Caution! Overfitting

Now that we've seen the complete process of creating a model, from initial data inspection to the potential implications, we have a caution about linear models. As you become more comfortable with linear models, you may want to put more and more predictors into your equation. Be careful about that.

A typical satisfaction drivers survey might include dozens of different features. As you add predictors to a model, estimates of the coefficients become less precise due to both the number of effects and associations among the variables. This shows

Table 7.1 Syntax for including interactions in model formulas

R formula syntax	Linear model	Description
`y ~ x`	$y_i = \beta_0 + \beta_1 x_i + \varepsilon_i$	y is a linear function of x
`y ~ x - 1`	$y_i = \beta_1 x_i + \beta_2 z_i + \varepsilon_i$	Omit the intercept
`y ~ x + z`	$y_i = \beta_0 + \beta_1 x_i + \beta_2 z_i + \varepsilon_i$	y is a linear combination of x and z
`y ~ x:z`	$y_i = \beta_0 + \beta_1 x_i z_i + \varepsilon_i$	Include the interaction between x and z
`y ~ x*z`	$y_i = \beta_0 + \beta_1 x_i + \beta_2 z_i + \beta_3 x_i z_i \varepsilon_i$	Include x, z and the interaction between them
`y ~ (u + v + w)**3`	$y_i = \beta_0 + \beta_1 u_i + \beta_2 v_i + \beta_3 w_i + \beta_4 u_i v_i +$ $\beta_5 u_i w_i + \beta_6 v_i w_i + \beta_7 u_i v_i w_i + \varepsilon_i$	Include u, v, and w, and all interactions among them up to three-way (`u:v:w`)
`y ~ (u+v+w)**3 - u:v`	$y_i = \beta_0 + \beta_1 u_i + \beta_2 v_i + +\beta_3 w_i + \beta_5 u_i w_i +$ $\beta_6 v_i w_i + \beta_7 u_i v_i w_i + \varepsilon_i$	Include these variables and all interactions up to three-way, but remove the `u:v` interaction

up in the `ols()` output as larger standard errors of the coefficients, indicating lower confidence in the estimates. This is one reason we like to plot confidence intervals for coefficients, as in Fig. 7.12

Despite the potentially low confidence in estimates, as you add variables to a model, the value of R^2 will become higher and higher. On a first impression, that might seem as if the model is getting better and better. However, if the estimates of the coefficients are imprecise, then the utility of the model will be poor; it could lead to making the wrong inferences about relationships in your data.

This process of adding too many variables and ending up with a less precise or inappropriate model is called *overfitting*. One way to avoid it is to keep a close eye on the standard errors for the coefficients; small standard errors are an indicator that there are sufficient data to estimate the model. Another approach is to select a subset of the data to *hold out* and not use to estimate the model. After fitting the model, use `predict()` on the hold out data and see how well it performs. Overfitted models will perform poorly when predicting outcomes for holdout data. Other approaches include using variable importance measures, such as those obtained from random forest models (Sect. 11.1.3), stepwise selection procedures with caution (Sect. 6.6), or Bayesian information criteria. See Chapter 19 in Kuhn and Johnson (2013) for more.

We recommend to keep models as parsimonious as possible. Although it is tempting to create large, impressive, omnibus models, it is usually more valuable in marketing practice to identify a few interventions with clear and confident interpretations.

7.5.3 Recommended Procedure for Linear Model Fitting

We followed a lengthy process to arrive at the final model `m7`, and it is helpful to recount the general steps we recommend in creating such a linear model.

1. Inspect the dataset to make sure it is clean and has the structure you expect, following the outline in Sect. 3.3.2.
2. Check the distributions of the variables to make sure they are not highly skewed (Sect. 7.2.1). If one is skewed, consider transforming it (Sect. 4.5.4).
3. Examine the bivariate scatterplots and correlation matrix (Sect. 7.2.1) to see whether there are any extremely correlated variables (such as $r > 0.9$, or several with $r > 0.8$). If so, omit some variables or consider transforming them if needed; see Sect. 8.1 for further discussion.
4. If you wish to estimate coefficients on a consistent scale, standardize the data (Sect. 7.3.3).
5. After fitting a model, check the residual quantiles in the output. The residuals show how well the model accounts for the individual observations (Sect. 7.2.4).
6. Check the standard model plots using diagnostic goodness of fit plots, which will help you judge whether a linear model is appropriate or whether there is nonlinearity, and will identify potential outliers in the data (Sect. 7.2.4).
7. Try several models and compare them for overall interpretability and model fit by inspecting the residuals' spread and overall R^2 (Sect. 7.3.1). If the models are nested, you could also use ANOVA for comparison (Sect. 6.5.3).
8. Report the confidence intervals of the estimates with your interpretation and recommendations (Sect. 7.3).

7.6 Learning More*

Applications In this chapter we've given an overview of linear modeling in Python using the `statsmodels` module and its application to satisfaction drivers analysis. The same modeling approach could be applied to many other marketing applications, such as advertising response (or *marketing mix*) modeling (Bowman and Gatignon 2010), customer retention (or *churn*) modeling, and pricing analysis.

Models We covered traditional random normal linear models in this chapter, which relate continuous or near-continuous outcomes to predictors. Other models apply in cases where the variables are different in structure, such as binary outcomes or counts. However, the process of estimating those is similar to the steps here. Such models include Poisson and binomial regression model for outcomes that are counts, hazard regression for event occurrence (also known as timing regression or survival modeling), and logistic regression for binary outcomes (see Sect. 8.2). Those models are covered within `statsmodels` with the *generalized linear model* (GLM) framework, an elegant way of representing many families of models, and such models can be estimated with the `statsmodels.GLM()` function. To learn more about generalized models, consult an introduction to GLM such as Dobson (2018).

Outcome Variables In our synthetic satisfaction drivers data, hypothetical customers rated satisfaction on a 100-point scale, making it reasonable for us to analyze the data as if the ratings were continuous. However, many survey studies collect ratings on a 5- or 7- point scale, which may be questionable to fit with a linear model. Although many analysts use `ols()` for outcomes on 5- or 7-point scales, an alternative is a *cut-point model*, such as an ordered logit or probit model. Such a model will fit the data better and won't make nonsensical predictions like a rating of 6.32 on a 5-point scale (as `ols()` might). These models can be fit with the `statsmodels.api.Logit()` and `statsmodels.api.Probit()` functions.

Individual-Level Results In this chapter, we used models in which an effect has uniform influence. For example, we assumed that the effect of satisfaction with cleanliness is a single influence that is the same for every respondent (or, more precisely, whose *average* influence is the same, apart from random individual variation). You might instead consider a model in which the effect varies for different people, with both a group-level and an individual-level effect, known as a *hierarchical* model. We examine ways to estimate individual-level effects using hierarchical models in Chap. 8.3.5.

Correlated Measures Finally, many datasets have variables that are highly correlated (known as *collinearity*), and this can affect the stability and trustworthiness of linear modeling. In Sect. 8.1 we introduce additional ways to check for collinearity and strategies to mitigate it. One approach is to reduce the number of dimensions under consideration by extracting underlying patterns from the correlated variables; we review such *principal component* and *factor analytic* procedures in Chap. 9.

7.7 Key Points

There are many applications for linear models in marketing: satisfaction drivers analysis, advertising response modeling, customer churn modeling, and so forth. Although these use different kinds of data, they are all implemented in similar ways in the Python `statsmodels` module. The following points are some of the important considerations for such analyses. We also summarized the basic process of linear modeling in Sect. 7.5.3.

- Linear models relate continuous scale *outcome* variables to *predictors* by finding a straight line that best fits the points. A basic linear model function in Python is `statsmodels.api.ols(formula, data)`. `ols()` produces an object that can be used with `summary()`, `predict()`, plotting, and other functions to inspect the model fit and estimates of the coefficients.
- Before modeling, it is important to check the data quality and the distribution of values on each variable. For distributions, approximately normal distributions are generally preferred, and data such as counts and revenue often need to be transformed. Also check that variables do not have excessive correlation (Sect. 7.2.1).
- To interpret coefficients on a standardized scale, such that they are comparable to one another, you will either need predictors that are on identical scales or that have been standardized to be on a uniform scale. The most common standardization is conversion to units of standard deviation, performed by subtracting each column mean from each element and dividing by the column standard deviation (Sect. 7.3.3).
- A linear model assumes that the relationship between predictors and an outcome is linear and that errors in fit are symmetric with similar variability across their range (a property known as *homoskedasticity*). Results may be misleading

when these assumptions do not match the data. Diagnostic goodness of fit plots of a model can help you assess whether these assumptions are reasonable for your data (Sect. 7.2.5.)

- The `summary()` function for `ols` objects provides output that analysts review most frequently, reporting model coefficients along with their standard errors and p-values for hypothesis tests assessing whether the coefficients differ from zero (Sect. 7.2.4)

- Factor variables may be included in a model simply by converting the factor to dummy-coded 0/1 values using `pandas.get_dummies()`. You must check the direction shown in the output to ensure you interpret these correctly (Sect. 7.4).

- An interaction is a predictor that is the product of two other predictors, and thus assesses the degree to which the predictors reinforce (or cancel) one another. You can model an interaction between `x` and `y` by including `x:y` in a model formula (Sect. 7.5).

- Model building is the process of adding and removing predictors from a model to find a set of predictors that fits the data well. We can compare the fit of different models using the R-squared value or, if models are nested (see Sect. 6.5) by using the more formal ANOVA test (`statsmodels.stats.anova.anova_lm()`) (Sect. 7.3.1).

- We recommend to interpret coefficients in terms of their estimated ranges, such as confidence intervals in the case of `ols()` (Sect. 7.2.4).

Chapter 8
Additional Linear Modeling Topics

As we noted in Chap. 7, the range of applications and methods in linear modeling and regression is vast. In this chapter, we discuss three additional topics in linear modeling that often arise in marketing:

- Handling highly correlated observations, which pose a problem known as *collinearity*, as mentioned in Sect. 7.2.1. In Sect. 8.1 we examine the problem in detail, along with ways to detect and remediate collinearity in a dataset.
- Fitting models for yes/no, or *binary* outcomes, such as purchasing a product. In Sect. 8.2 we introduce *logistic regression* models to model binary outcomes and their influences.
- Finding a model for the preferences and responses of *individuals*, not only for the sample as a whole. In marketing, we often wish to understand individual consumers and the diversity of behavior and product interest among people. In Sect. 8.3 we consider *hierarchical linear models* (HLM) for consumer preference in ratings-based conjoint analysis data.

These topics are not especially closely related to one another; unlike other chapters in this book, they may be read independently within this chapter. Still, each section builds on models presented earlier in the book and will extend your knowledge of issues and applications for linear modeling. More importantly, each is a foundational part of a complete toolbox for marketing analysis.

8.1 Handling Highly Correlated Variables

We have mentioned several times (as in Sect. 7.2.1) that highly correlated explanatory variables cause problems with linear models. In this section, we examine why that is the case and strategies to address the problem.

We consider a question that might arise with the retail sales data in Chap. 4, which simulated summaries of 12 month online and in-store transactions by customer (see Sect. 4.1). The question is this: which variables are most predictive of online spending? If we wished to increase online spending by customers, which factors might we consider?

8.1.1 An Initial Linear Model of Online Spend

Either create the simulated retail sales data (Sect. 4.1), load it from a local copy (see Sect. 6.1 for an example of how), or load it from the book's website:

```
In [1]: import pandas as pd
        cust_df = pd.read_csv('http://bit.ly/PMR-ch8pt1')
        cust_df.head() # Not shown
        cust_df.describe(include='all') # Not shown
```

Now we use `ols()` from the `statsmodels` library to model spend as a function of all other variables. We omit customers with zero online spend; having exactly zero spend is probably related to different factors than positive spend, and we are interested here in the associations for those who spend anything. We omit the customer ID column, which is uninformative, by selecting columns `'age':` in the `.loc` argument:

© Springer Nature Switzerland AG 2020
J. S. Schwarz et al., *Python for Marketing Research and Analytics*, https://doi.org/10.1007/978-3-030-49720-0_8

```
In [2]: import statsmodels.formula.api as smf
        spend_m1 = smf.ols('online_spend ~ age + credit_score + email'
                           '+ distance_to_store + online_visits'
                           '+ online_trans + store_trans + store_spend '
                           '+ sat_service + sat_selection',
                           data=cust_df.loc[cust_df.online_spend > 0,
                                            'age':]).fit()
spend_m1.summary()

Out[2]:
...
Dep. Variable:              online_spend   R-squared:                   0.983
Model:                               OLS   Adj. R-squared:              0.983
...

                  coef     std err          t       P>|t|      [0.025     0.975]
----------------------------------------------------------------------------------
Intercept       6.7189      33.538      0.200       0.841     -59.210     72.648
...
online_visits  -0.0723       0.204     -0.354       0.723      -0.473      0.329
online_trans   20.6107       0.667     30.880       0.000      19.299     21.923
store_trans     0.1350       3.212      0.042       0.966      -6.179      6.449
store_spend     0.0018       0.079      0.023       0.982      -0.153      0.157
sat_service     5.6388       3.016      1.870       0.062      -0.290     11.568
...
```

We have omitted much of the summary to show a few key points. First, online spend is closely related to the number of online transactions (coefficient = 20.6) but not the number of online visits. That is puzzling. Second, the model accounts for almost all the available variance, $R^2 = 0.98$. These results should cause concern. Because online transactions are dependent on visits, shouldn't those two variables show a similar pattern? How could we be so lucky as to fit a model that nearly perfectly predicts online spending (insofar as it is assessed by R^2)? And notice that the standard error on store_trans is quite large, showing that its estimate is very uncertain.

If we turn to data visualization using seaborn.PairGrid() (Sect. 7.2.1), we see some problems:

```
In [3]: import seaborn as sns
        import matplotlib.pyplot as plt
        sns.set_context('paper')

        g = sns.PairGrid(cust_df.loc[:, 'age':].fillna(-1), height=1.1)
        g.map_upper(plt.scatter, linewidths=1, edgecolor="w", s=5, alpha=0.5)
        g.map_diag(plt.hist)
        g.map_lower(sns.kdeplot)
```

The result in Fig. 8.1 shows variables with extreme skew and pairs of variables that are very highly correlated.

Our first step to remediate the situation is to transform the data using a Box-Cox transformation. Building on the transformation routines we saw in Sect. 4.5.5, we write a short function that uses boxcox() from the scipy.stats library to select the transformation *lambda* automatically (Pedregosa et al. 2011). At the same time, we standardize the data with scale() from the sklearn.preprocessing library (Sect. 7.3.3):

```
In [4]: import scipy.stats as ss
        import sklearn.preprocessing as pp
        def autotransform(x):
            x_bc, lmbd = ss.boxcox(1 + x)
            return pp.scale(x_bc)
```

We select the complete cases from our dataframe, again dropping the customer ID column (using .loc['age':]) because it is not a predictor. Then we take only the rows with positive online spend. We create a vector to index all the columns except email (which is not numeric), and then apply() the autoTransform() function to each numeric column:

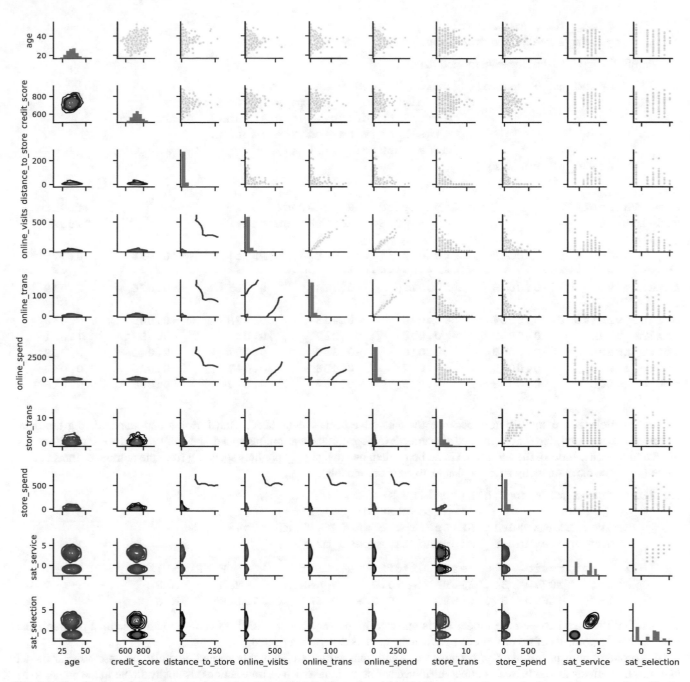

Fig. 8.1 Visualization of the customer data using `PairGrid()`. Several variables have extreme skew and other pairs are nearly perfectly correlated; both situations pose problems for linear modeling

```
In [5]: idx_complete = (cust_df.isna().sum(axis=1) == 0)
        cust_df_bc = cust_df.loc[(idx_complete) &
                            (cust_df.online_spend > 0), 'age':].copy()
        col_idx = cust_df_bc.columns != 'email'
        cust_df_bc.iloc[:, col_idx] = \
          cust_df_bc.iloc[:,col_idx].apply(autotransform)
```

The result is a dataframe with standardized, more normally distributed values, which we can check with `describe()` and `PairPlot()`:

```
In [6]: g = sns.PairGrid(cust_df_bc, height=1.1,)
        g.map_upper(plt.scatter, linewidths=1, edgecolor="w", s=5, alpha=0.5)
```

```
        g.map_diag(plt.hist)
        g.map_lower(sns.kdeplot)# Not shown
```

We refit the model using the transformed data:

```
In [7]: spend_m2 = smf.ols('online_spend ~ age + credit_score + email'
                           '+ distance_to_store + online_visits'
                           '+ online_trans + store_trans + store_spend '
                           '+ sat_service + sat_selection',
                           data=cust_df_bc).fit()
        spend_m2.summary()
```

```
Out[7]:
Dep. Variable:              online_spend   R-squared:                    0.992
Model:                               OLS   Adj. R-squared:               0.992
...
                   coef      std err          t        P>|t|       [0.025      0.975]
-------------------------------------------------------------------------------------
Intercept       -0.0035       0.011       -0.313       0.755       -0.026       0.019
...
online_visits    0.0067       0.016        0.415       0.678       -0.025       0.038
online_trans     0.9892       0.016       61.297       0.000        0.957       1.021
store_trans     -0.0068       0.018       -0.385       0.701       -0.041       0.028
store_spend      0.0079       0.017        0.458       0.647       -0.026       0.042
sat_service      0.0048       0.005        0.884       0.377       -0.006       0.016
...
```

The coefficients are smaller now because the data have been standardized. Transforming and standardizing the data, although a good idea, have not changed the unbelievable estimate that online spend is highly related to transactions yet unrelated to visits. Indeed, the full model is no better than one that simply predicts spending from the number of transactions alone (see Sect. 6.5.3 on using anova_lm() to compare models):

```
In [8]: spend_m3 = smf.ols('online_spend ~ online_trans',
                           data=cust_df_bc).fit()
        from statsmodels.stats import anova as sms_anova
        sms_anova.anova_lm(spend_m2, spend_m3)
```

```
Out[8]:    df_resid       ssr   df_diff   ss_diff          F    Pr(>F)
        0     407.0  3.303249       0.0       NaN        NaN       NaN
        1     416.0  3.330058      -9.0  -0.02681   0.372126       NaN
```

The small difference between the model fits is reflected in the very low F statistics (leading to an undefined p-value), and thus the null hypothesis of no difference between the models cannot be rejected.

The problem here is *collinearity*: because visits and transactions are so highly related, and also because a linear model assumes that effects are additive, an effect attributed to one variable (such as transactions) is not available in the model to be attributed jointly to another that is highly correlated (visits). This will cause the standard errors of the predictors to increase, which means that the coefficient estimates will be highly uncertain or *unstable*. As a practical consequence, this may cause coefficient estimates to differ dramatically from sample to sample due to minor variations in the data even when underlying relationships are the same.

8.1.2 Remediating Collinearity

The degree of collinearity in data can be assessed as the *variance inflation factor* (VIF). This estimates how much the standard error (variance) of a coefficient in a linear model is increased because of shared variance with other variables, compared to the situation if the variables were uncorrelated or simple single predictor regression were performed.

We can assess VIF in the spend_m2 model using variance_inflation_factor() from the statsmodels library. The variance_inflation_factor() function takes as an argument the exog attribute, which contains the data used to train the model. It also requires an index value, `exog_idx`, which indicates which term to assess. The zeroeth index corresponds to the intercept. We can first see the VIF for the first coefficient:

```
In [9]: from statsmodels.stats.outliers_influence \
        import variance_inflation_factor

        variance_inflation_factor(spend_m2.model.exog, 1)
```

`1.0505934508885986`

But we want to look at this for all coefficients. And it would be helpful to see the coefficient name for each VIF as well. We can use a `for` loop and `print` statement to do this. Better yet, let's put this in a function so we can reuse it easily later. Note that we use `{:.3f}` in the string to specify that this should be displayed as a float with three decimal places of precision; additional digits will be truncated (see Sect. 2.4.5 for a refresher on `format()` syntax):

```
In [10]: def print_variance_inflation_factors(model):
            for i, param in enumerate(model.params.index):
               print('VIF: {:.3f}, Parameter: {}'.format(
                  variance_inflation_factor(model.model.exog, i), param))

         print_variance_inflation_factors(spend_m2)
```

```
VIF: 6.504, Parameter: Intercept
VIF: 1.051, Parameter: email[T.yes]
VIF: 1.095, Parameter: age
VIF: 1.112, Parameter: credit_score
VIF: 1.375, Parameter: distance_to_store
VIF: 13.354, Parameter: online_visits
VIF: 13.413, Parameter: online_trans
VIF: 15.977, Parameter: store_trans
VIF: 15.254, Parameter: store_spend
VIF: 1.524, Parameter: sat_service
VIF: 1.519, Parameter: sat_selection
```

A common rule of thumb is that VIF > 5.0 indicates a need to mitigate collinearity. In `spend_m2`, the VIF suggests that collinearity should be addressed for the `online...` and `store...` variables. Note that we generally ignore the intercept term, as the VIF of the intercept is not easily interpretable.

There are three general strategies for mitigating collinearity:

- Omit variables that are highly correlated.
- Eliminate correlation by extracting principal components or factors for sets of highly-correlated predictors (see Chap. 9).
- Use a method that is robust to collinearity, i.e., something other than traditional linear modeling. There are too many options to consider this possibility exhaustively, but one method to consider would be a random forest approach, which only uses a subset of variables at a time (see Sect. 11.1.2).

Another option for the present data would be to construct a new measure of interest that combines the collinear variables (such as spend per transaction). For purposes here, we explore the first two options above and create models `spend_m4` and `spend_m5`.

We omit highly correlated variables for model `spend_m4` by excluding `online_trans` and `store_trans`:

```
In [10]: spend_m4 = smf.ols('online_spend ~ age + credit_score + email'
                  '+ distance_to_store + online_visits'
                  '+ store_spend + sat_service + sat_selection',
                  data=cust_df_bc).fit()
         spend_m4.summary()
```

```
Out[10]: <class 'statsmodels.iolib.summary.Summary'>
Dep. Variable:          online_spend  R-squared:              0.919
Model:                          OLS  Adj. R-squared:         0.917
...
```

	coef	std err	t	P>|t|	[0.025	0.975]
Intercept	-0.0637	0.036	-1.781	0.076	-0.134	0.007
...						
online_visits	0.9534	0.014	66.818	0.000	0.925	0.981
store_spend	0.0047	0.016	0.291	0.771	-0.027	0.036
sat_service	-0.0076	0.017	-0.440	0.660	-0.042	0.026
...						

```
In [11]: print_variance_inflation_factors(spend_m4)

VIF: 6.450, Parameter: Intercept
VIF: 1.040, Parameter: email[T.yes]
VIF: 1.082, Parameter: age
VIF: 1.104, Parameter: credit_score
VIF: 1.299, Parameter: distance_to_store
VIF: 1.028, Parameter: online_visits
VIF: 1.313, Parameter: store_spend
VIF: 1.518, Parameter: sat_service
VIF: 1.518, Parameter: sat_selection
```

The VIF is now acceptable and we see that the number of online visits is still the best predictor of online spend.

Another approach is to use the principal components of the correlated data. We discuss Principal Components Analysis in details in Chap. 9, so see Sect. 9.2 for more information, but principal components analysis breaks down a multidimensional dataset into components that are uncorrelated (orthogonal). Thus, PCA provides a way to extract composite variables that are by definition free of collinearity with other variables that are included in the same PCA.

We use PCA to extract the first component for the online variables, and then do this again for the store variables, and add those two initial components to the dataframe:

```
In [12]: from sklearn import decomposition

         # Create a combined online variable using PCA
         online_pca = decomposition.PCA().\
           fit_transform(cust_df_bc[['online_visits','online_trans']])
         cust_df_bc['online'] = online_pca[:,0]

         # Create a combined store variable using PCA
         store_pca = decomposition.PCA().\
           fit_transform(cust_df_bc[['store_spend',
                                     'store_trans']])
         cust_df_bc['store'] = store_pca[:,0]

In [13]: spend_m5 = smf.ols('online_spend ~ age + credit_score + email'
                            '+ distance_to_store + online + store'
                            '+ sat_service + sat_selection',
                            data=cust_df_bc).fit()
         spend_m5.summary()

Out[13]:
```

Dep. Variable:		online_spend	R-squared:			0.974
Model:		OLS	Adj. R-squared:			0.973
	coef	std err	t	P>|t|	[0.025	0.975]
Intercept	-0.0267	0.020	-1.306	0.192	-0.067	0.013
...						
online	0.7028	0.006	120.640	0.000	0.691	0.714
store	0.0013	0.007	0.188	0.851	-0.012	0.014
sat_service	-0.0010	0.010	-0.100	0.920	-0.020	0.018
...						

```
In [13]: print_variance_inflation_factors(spend_m5)
VIF: 6.474, Parameter: Intercept
VIF: 1.045, Parameter: email[T.yes]
VIF: 1.082, Parameter: age
VIF: 1.102, Parameter: credit_score
VIF: 1.337, Parameter: distance_to_store
VIF: 1.032, Parameter: online
VIF: 1.350, Parameter: store
VIF: 1.518, Parameter: sat_service
VIF: 1.519, Parameter: sat_selection
```

VIF poses no problem in this model, and we see that online spend is still associated primarily with online activity (as captured in the first component of the PCA model, `online`). One caution when interpreting results that use principal components as explanatory variables is that the components have arbitrary numerical direction; `online` could have a negative coefficient here, but that would not necessarily imply that online activity results in lower sales.

Although this result—that online sales relate primarily to online activity—may at first appear to be uninteresting, it is better to have an obvious result than an incorrect result. This result might prompt us to collect other data, such as attitudes about our website or online shopping, to build a more complete understanding of factors associated with online spending.

8.2 Linear Models for Binary Outcomes: Logistic Regression

Marketers often observe yes/no outcomes: did a customer purchase a product? Did she take a test drive? Did she sign up for a credit card, or renew her subscription, or respond to a promotion? All of these kinds of outcomes are *binary* because they have only two possible observed states: *yes* or *no*. We often want to build a model to predict these binary outcomes.

At first it is tempting to fit such a model with a typical linear regression model as we saw in Chap. 7, predicting the outcome (1=yes, 0=no) as a linear combination of the features. That is not incorrect to do, but a more flexible and useful way to fit such outcomes is with a *logistic* model (also called a *logit* model for reasons we'll discuss below).

8.2.1 Basics of the Logistic Regression Model

The core feature of a logistic model is this: it relates the *probability* of an outcome to an *exponential function* of a predictor variable. We'll illustrate that and show the formula in a moment, but before examining that, let's consider why those are desirable properties and are improvements on a basic linear model.

By modeling the *probability* of an outcome, a logistic model accomplishes two things. First, it more directly models what we're interested in, which is a probability or proportion, such as the likelihood of a given customer to purchase a product, or the expected proportion of a segment who will respond to a promotion. Second, it limits the model to the appropriate range for a proportion, which is [0, 1]. A basic linear model as generated with `ols()` does not have such a limit and could estimate a nonsensical probability such as 1.05 or −0.04.

We ask indulgence to consider the formula here because it is instrumental in understanding how the model works. The equation for the logistic function is:

$$logistic : p(y) = \frac{e^{v_x}}{e^{v_x} + 1} \qquad (8.1)$$

In this equation, the outcome of interest is y and we compute its likelihood $p(y)$ as a function of v_x. When y is a decision to purchase or test a product, we typically estimate v_x as a function of the features (x) of the product, such as price. v_x can take any real value, so we are able to treat it as a continuous function in a linear model. In that case, v_x is composed from one or more coefficients of the model and indicates the importance of the corresponding features of the product.

This formula gives a value between [0, 1]. The likelihood of y is less than 50% when v_x is negative, is 50% when $v_x = 0$, and is above 50% when v_x is positive. We compute this first by hand, but we can also use the Scipy `expit()` function:

```
In [14]: import numpy as np
         np.exp(0) / ( np.exp(0) + 1 )
```

```
Out[14]: 0.5
```

```
In [15]: from scipy.special import expit
         expit(0)
```

```
Out[15]: 0.5
```

```
In [16]: expit(-np.inf) # infinitely low = likelihood 0
```

```
Out[16]: 0.0
```

```
In [17]: expit(2) # moderate probability = 88% chance of outcome
```

```
Out[17]: 0.8807970779778824
```

```
In [18]: expit(-0.2) # weak likelihood
```

```
Out[18]: 0.4501660026875221
```

Such a model is known as a *logit* model, which determines the value of v_x from the logarithm of the relative probability of occurrence of y:

$$logit : v_x = log(\frac{p(y)}{1 - p(y)}) \tag{8.2}$$

`scipy` includes a built-in function `logit()` for the logit function:

```
In [19]: np.log(0.88/(1-0.88)) # moderate high likelihood
```

```
Out[19]: 1.9924301646902063
```

```
In [20]: from scipy.special import logit
         logit(0.88) # equivalent to hand computation
```

```
Out[20]: 1.9924301646902063
```

In practice, the expressions *logit model* and *logistic regression* are used interchangeably.

8.2.2 Data for Logistic Regression of Season Passes

We considered an amusement park example in Chap. 7. Suppose that we now have data on the sales of season tickets to the park. The data consist of a table of season ticket *pass sales* (with values of *yes* or *no*), on the basis of two factors: the *channel* used to extend the offer (email, postal mail, or in-person at the park) and whether it was *promoted* in a bundle offering the season ticket with another feature such as free parking, or not. The marketing question is this: are customers more likely to purchase the season pass when it is offered in the bundle (with free parking), or not?

In this section, we see how to simulate such data, and how to create a full dataframe from tabulated data. If you wish to load the data from the website instead of working through the data creation, you can retrieve it with:

```
In [21]: pass_df = pd.read_csv('http://bit.ly/PMR-ch8pt2')
         pass_df.Pass = pass_df.Pass.astype(
           pd.api.types.CategoricalDtype(categories=['YesPass','NoPass'],
                                         ordered=True))
         pass_df.Promo = pass_df.Promo.astype(
           pd.api.types.CategoricalDtype(categories=['NoBundle','Bundle'],
                                         ordered=True))
         pass_df.head()
```

```
Out[21]:     Channel   Promo      Pass
          0    Mail   Bundle   YesPass
          1    Mail   Bundle   YesPass
          2    Mail   Bundle   YesPass
          3    Mail   Bundle   YesPass
          4    Mail   Bundle   YesPass

In [22]: pass_df.describe()

Out[22]:         Channel   Promo      Pass
         count     3156    3156      3156
         unique       3       2         2
         top       Mail   Bundle   YesPass
         freq      1328    1674      1589
```

Note that the `astype()` commands above are required for reasons we describe in Sect. 7.1. Be sure to run it after loading the CSV and check that the `head()` and `describe()` match outputs the above.

We encourage you to read the rest of this simulation section. But if you loaded the data and prefer to skip ahead to analysis, you could continue with Sect. 8.2.4.

8.2.3 Sales Table Data

Suppose that we have been given sales data as shown in Table 8.1.

There are several ways to analyze tabular data as shown in Table 8.1, including chi-square analysis (Sect. 6.2), but a versatile approach when the dataset is not too large is to convert it to long form and recreate a dataframe of individual observations. This lets us use a full range of approaches such as linear modeling with minimal hassle.

To generate the data in such a format, we first define a `list` for each data type:

```
In [23]: channels = ['Mail', 'Park', 'Email']
         passes = ['NoPass','YesPass']
         promos = ['NoBundle', 'Bundle']
```

We then then create a `list` with the counts for each combination of types:

```
In [24]: pass_counts = [278, 449, 359, 242, 49, 223, 284, 639, 485, 83, 27, 38]
```

And use a set of nested for loops the generate the data:

```
In [25]: i = 0
         pass_array = []
         for c in channels:
           for p in passes:
             for b in promos:
               pass_array.append(np.repeat([[c, b, p]], pass_counts[i],
                                           axis=0))
               i += 1
```

We then concatenate the array into a matrix and create a dataframe:

Table 8.1 Counts of sales of season tickets broken out by promotion status (bundled or not bundled with a promotion), and channel by which a customer was reached (mail, at the park, by email)

	Bundle	NoBundle		Bundle	NoBundle
Bought season pass (count)			*Did not buy season pass (count)*		
Mail	242	359	Mail	449	278
Park	639	284	Park	223	49
Email	38	27	Email	83	485

```
In [26]: pass_df = pd.DataFrame(np.concatenate(pass_array),
                                 columns=['Channel', 'Promo', 'Pass'])
         pass_df.head()

Out[26]:    Channel     Promo      Pass
         0     Mail  NoBundle   NoPass
         1     Mail  NoBundle   NoPass
         2     Mail  NoBundle   NoPass
         3     Mail  NoBundle   NoPass
         4     Mail  NoBundle   NoPass
```

It's important to check that the counts match, which we can do using the `groupby()` method:

```
In [27]: pass_df.groupby(['Pass', 'Promo', 'Channel']).Pass.count()\
           .unstack(level=2).T

Out[27]: Pass        NoPass              YesPass
         Promo    Bundle NoBundle   Bundle NoBundle
         Channel
         Email        83      485       38       27
         Mail        449      278      242      359
         Park        223       49      639      284
```

The counts match Table 8.1.

We can use `groupby()` on these data to create cross-tabs other than those in Table 8.1. For example, to see purchases of a pass (`Pass`) by promotion bundle (`Promo`):

```
In [28]: pass_df.groupby(['Pass', 'Promo']).Pass.count().unstack(level=1)

Out[28]: Promo    Bundle  NoBundle
         Pass
         NoPass      755       812
         YesPass     919       670
```

Statistical modeling is a detail-oriented process, and before building a model from the data, there is one minor detail to attend to: the factors in `pass_df` are alphabetized—which is how pandas handles factor names by default—but that is counterintuitive. We might think that `NoBundle` should have a lower implicit value (such as "bundle=0") than `Bundle` (which might be "bundle=1"). However, in the table we just saw, `NoBundle` appears in the second column because it has a higher value thanks to alphabetic ordering.

In a regression model, that would mean that a positive effect of `Bundle` would have a *negative* value (think about it). Rather than having to remember such convoluted logic ("we see a negative effect for *no bundle*, which really means a *positive* effect for bundle after we reverse the signs …"), it is easier just to set the order straight by setting each columns as ordered categorical data (as we did above for the CSV):

```
In [29]: pass_df.Pass = pass_df.Pass.astype(
             pd.api.types.CategoricalDtype(categories=['YesPass','NoPass'],
                                           ordered=True))
         pass_df.Promo = pass_df.Promo.astype(
             pd.api.types.CategoricalDtype(categories=['NoBundle','Bundle'],
                                           ordered=True))
```

Somewhat unexpectedly, `statsmodels` orders dependent and independent variables differently, so these two factors appear to have the opposite order, *Bundle > NoBundle* but *NoPromo > Promo*. However this ordering makes the model itself most intuitive. We could confirm this by replacing *YesPass* with 1, *NoPass* with 0, *Bundle* with 1, and *NoBundle* with 0, and then running the model, which would produce the same model that we get with the factors ordered as indicated. See the statsmodels glm documentation for more information on this.

Why not just replace those values with 0s and 1s? That would be fine for the initial model, but as we add other factors, it would become difficult to keep track of what each numerical value means, particularly when we have more than two factors that aren't inherently ordered (e.g. Mail vs Park vs Email). In general, it's best to maintain categorical variables as factors.

With the data ordered sensibly, we proceed with modeling.

8.2.4 Fitting a Logistic Regression Model

A logistic regression model in Python is fit as a *generalized linear model* (GLM) using a process similar to linear regression that we saw in Chap. 7 using the `statsmodels` library, but with the difference that a GLM can handle dependent variables that are not normally distributed. Thus, generalized linear models can be used to model data counts (such as number of purchases) or time intervals (such as time spent on a website) or binary variables (e.g., did/didn't purchase). The common feature of all GLM models is that they relate normally distributed predictors to a non-normal outcome using a function known as a *link*. This means that they are able to fit models for many different distributions using a single, consistent framework.

In the present case, we model a binary outcome, and the appropriate distribution is a *binomial* distribution (see Sect. 6.3). `glm()` takes an argument `family=` that specifies the distribution for the outcome variable. For a binary outcome, set `family=statsmodels.api.families.Binomial()`. The default link function for a binomial model is the logit function that we saw in Sect. 8.2.1, so we do not have to specify that. (But, as an example, if we wished to use a probit link function instead, we could specify `family=statsmodels.api.families.Binomial(link=sm_probit_ Link)`, and similarly for other link functions.)

Our marketing question was, "does the promotion bundle have an effect on season pass sales?" and we model this initially with a logistic regression of `Pass` on `Promo`, using `glm(..., family=statsmodels.api.families. Binomial())` and syntax otherwise identical to `ols()`:

```
In [30]:
        import statsmodels.api as sm
        import statsmodels.formula.api as smf

        pass_m1 = smf.glm('Pass ~ Promo', data=pass_df,
                    family=sm.families.Binomial()).fit()
        pass_m1.summary()
```

```
Out[30]:
                    coef      std err        z        P>|z|      [0.025      0.975]
-------------------------------------------------------------------------------
Intercept          -0.1922     0.052      -3.683      0.000      -0.295      -0.090
Promo[T.Bundle]     0.3888     0.072       5.425      0.000       0.248       0.529
```

The initial model appears to confirm that the bundle is effective. There is a positive coefficient for the bundle condition, and the effect is statistically significant.

What does a coefficient of 0.3888 mean? We can use it to calculate the association of pass sales, as associated with the promotion bundle factor, by examining the ratio of success (using our `expit()` function defined above) to non-success $(1 - success)$. A manual way to do this is to use `expit()` directly:

```
In [31]: # ratio of outcome % to alternative %
        expit(0.3888) / (1-expit(0.3888))
```

```
Out[31]: 1.4752094799309121
```

This shows that the effect of `Bundle` is an estimated *odds ratio* of 1.475, meaning that the odds that customers are purchase the pass when it is offered in the bundle are 1.475 times higher than when it is not. An easier and equivalent way to calculate this is to exponentiate the coefficient:

```
In [32]: np.exp(0.3888) # identical
```

```
Out[32]: 1.4752094799309121
```

It's worth a brief digression to discuss the relationship between *odds* and *likelihood* or *probability*. The bundle increases the odds by 1.475 times, but how does that relate to the likelihood of purchase in each condition?

We can find the actual odds in each condition by exponentiating the model output in each condition, which is -0.1922 without the bundle and 0.3888 minus 0.1922 with the bundle:

```
In [32]: print('Odds of pass:no pass, bundle: {:.3f} : 1'
            .format(np.exp(0.3888 - 0.1922)))
        print('Odds of pass:no pass, without bundle: {:.3f} : 1'
            .format(np.exp(-0.1922)))
```

```
Odds of pass:no pass, bundle: 1.217 : 1
Odds of pass:no pass, without bundle: 0.825 : 1
```

So, among individuals who received the bundle, for every 1.217 people who bought a pass, there was 1 who did not. Among those who did not receive the bundle, for every 0.825 people who bought a pass, there was 1 who did not.

If you're more used to thinking of things in terms of probabilities, we can easily convert these. We can take the odds and divide them by the odds plus one to get the probability. For example, if there are 2:1 odds for some event, there is a $\frac{2}{2+1} = \frac{2}{3}$ (or 66.67%) probability of that event occurring. The probability of a customer buying with the bundle is:

```
In [33]: np.exp(0.3888 - 0.1922)/(1 + np.exp(0.3888 - 0.1922))

0.54899229916247
```

We can calculate the likelihood of buying a pass in each condition:

```
In [34]: prob_pass_with_bundle = (np.exp(0.3888 - 0.1922)/
                                  (1 + np.exp(0.3888 - 0.1922)))
         print('Probability of pass, bundle: {:.3f}'
            .format(prob_pass_with_bundle))
         prob_pass_without_bundle = np.exp(-0.1922)/(1 + np.exp(-0.1922))
         print('Probability of pass, no bundle: {:.3f}'
            .format(prob_pass_without_bundle))
         print('Odds ratio: {:.3f}'
            .format((prob_pass_with_bundle/(1-prob_pass_with_bundle))
                  /(prob_pass_without_bundle/(1-prob_pass_without_bundle))))
         print('Odds ratio: {:.3f}'.format(np.exp(0.3888)))
```

```
Probability of pass, bundle: 0.549
Probability of pass, no bundle: 0.452
Odds ratio: 1.475
Odds ratio: 1.475
```

We can find the odds ratios from the model by extracting the coefficients from the `params` attribute on the model object and using `exp()`:

```
In [33]: np.exp(pass_m1.params)
```

```
Out[33]: Intercept        0.825123
         Promo[T.Bundle]  1.475196
         dtype: float64
```

We can obtain a confidence interval for the odds ratio using `exp(model.confint())`:

```
In [34]: np.exp(pass_m1.conf_int())
```

```
Out[34]:                        0          1
         Intercept        0.744890   0.913998
         Promo[T.Bundle]  1.281868   1.697681
```

The odds ratio for the promotion bundle is estimated to be between 1.28 and 1.70, a significant positive effect. This demonstrates that the promotion is highly effective, right? Not necessarily, because the effects are estimated *under the assumption that the model is the one we want to interpret*. But is the model `Pass ~ Promo` really the one we should interpret?

8.2.5 Reconsidering the Model

If we explore the data further, we notice something interesting. Consider a breakdown of season pass purchases by channel:

```
In [35]: pass_df.groupby(['Pass']).Channel.value_counts().unstack()
```

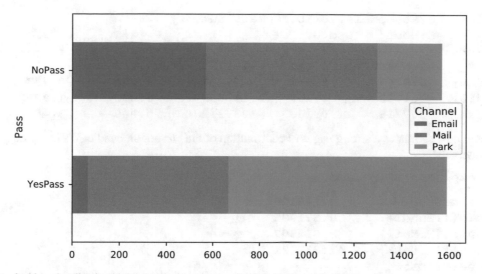

Fig. 8.2 A simple stacked bar visualization highlights the importance of the Park channel for selling passes

```
Out[35]: Channel  Email  Mail  Park
         Pass
         YesPass     65   601   923
         NoPass     568   727   272
```

The channel that was most successful in selling season tickets was at the park, regardless of whether the promotion was offered.

This is even more striking with a figure (Fig. 8.2):

```
In [36]: pass_df.groupby(['Pass']).Channel.value_counts().unstack()\
           .plot(kind='barh', stacked=True)
```

It's clear that passes are sold most effectively at the park, but what effect does the bundle have? And how does it vary by channel? We can use a multipanel figure of bar charts to compare the effect of bundles on pass sales:

```
In [37]: channels = ['Mail', 'Park', 'Email']
         plt.figure(figsize=(15,8))
         for i,c in enumerate(channels):
           ax = plt.subplot(1,3,i+1)
           pass_df.loc[pass_df.Channel == c].groupby('Promo')\
             .Pass.value_counts(normalize=True).unstack().plot(kind='bar',
                                                      ax=ax,
                                                      stacked=True)
           plt.title(c)
           plt.ylim((0,1.3))
```

The result is shown in Fig. 8.3, where we see that the three channels have somewhat different effects. Sales of season passes are very successful at the park, and very unsuccessful by email. This implies that our model `Pass ~ Promo` may be inadequate and needs to account for the effect of `Channel`.

We model a main effect of channel by adding + `Channel` to the model formula:

```
In [38]: pass_m2 = smf.glm('Pass ~ Promo + Channel',
                           data=pass_df,
                           family=sm.families.Binomial()).fit()
         pass_m2.summary()
```

```
Out[38]: <class 'statsmodels.iolib.summary.Summary'>
                   coef     std err          z      P>|z|       [0.025      0.975]
         --------------------------------------------------------------------------
         Intercept        -2.0786     0.132    -15.785      0.000      -2.337      -1.821
         Promo[T.Bundle]  -0.5602     0.090     -6.203      0.000      -0.737      -0.383
         Channel[T.Mail]   2.1762     0.147     14.853      0.000       1.889       2.463
         Channel[T.Park]   3.7218     0.160     23.312      0.000       3.409       4.035
```

The resulting model now estimates a strong *negative* contribution of the promotion bundle. We compute the odds ratios and their confidence intervals:

```
In [39]: np.exp(pass_m2.params)
```

```
Out[39]: Intercept          0.125105
         Promo[T.Bundle]    0.571085
         Channel[T.Mail]    8.812507
         Channel[T.Park]   41.337121
         dtype: float64
```

```
In [40]: np.exp(pass_m2.conf_int())
```

```
Out[40]:                          0          1
         Intercept         0.096648   0.161943
         Promo[T.Bundle]   0.478438   0.681672
         Channel[T.Mail]   6.612766  11.743993
         Channel[T.Park]  30.230619  56.524069
```

In this model, promotion is associated with a 32–53% lower odds of purchasing a season pass (between $1 - 0.478$ and $1 - 0.682$). On the other hand, offers in person at the park are associated with season ticket sales 30–56x higher in this model.

But is this the appropriate model? Should we also consider an interaction effect, where Promo might have a different effect by Channel? Our data exploration suggests a possible interaction effect, especially because of the dramatically different pattern for the influence of Bundle in the Email channel in Fig. 8.3.

We add an interaction term using the : operator, as noted in Sect. 7.5:

```
In [41]: pass_m3 = smf.glm('Pass ~ Promo + Channel + Promo:Channel',
                           data=pass_df,
                           family=sm.families.Binomial()).fit()
         pass_m3.summary()
```

```
Out[41]:
                                         coef    std err       z     P>|z|   [0.025   0.975]
         --------------------------------------------------------------------------------------
         Intercept                     -2.8883     0.198   -14.607    0.000   -3.276   -2.501
         Promo[T.Bundle]                2.1071     0.278     7.571    0.000    1.562    2.653
         Channel[T.Mail]                3.1440     0.213    14.742    0.000    2.726    3.562
         Channel[T.Park]                4.6455     0.251    18.504    0.000    4.153    5.138
         Promo[T.Bundle]:Channel[T.Mail]  -2.9808   0.300    -9.925    0.000   -3.570   -2.392
         Promo[T.Bundle]:Channel[T.Park]  -2.8115   0.328    -8.577    0.000   -3.454   -2.169
```

The interaction of promotion with channel is statistically significant, and is strongly negative for the mail and in-park channels, as opposed to the baseline (omitted) email channel in these simulated data.

In the odds ratios, we see that the promotion is only 2–11% as effective through the mail and in-park channels as it is in email:

```
In [42]: np.exp(pass_m3.conf_int())
```

```
Out[42]:
         ...                                            0          1
         Promo[T.Bundle]:Channel[T.Mail]         0.028170   0.091430
         Promo[T.Bundle]:Channel[T.Park]         0.031621   0.114288
```

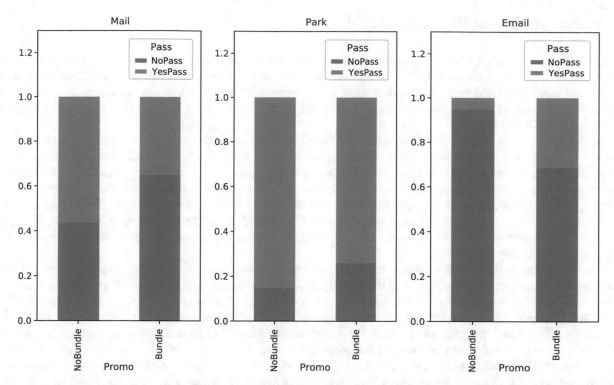

Fig. 8.3 A multipanel figure of bar plots of sales of season passes by channel and promotion in simulated amusement park data. Season passes ("YesPass," plotted as orange areas) are sold most frequently at the park and least frequently by email. The promotion bundle ("Bundle," the second column within each channel) is associated with higher sales through the email channel, but lower sales in regular mail and at the park, thus showing an interaction effect

We now have a much better answer to our question. Is the promotion bundle effective? It depends on channel. There is good reason to continue the promotion campaign by email, but its success there does not necessarily imply success at the park or through a regular mail campaign. In case you're wondering how the statistical model is advantageous to simply interpreting Fig. 8.3, one answer is that the model estimates confidence intervals and statistical significance for the effect.

8.2.6 Additional Discussion

Before moving to the topic of hierarchical models, we have a few observations for the current section:

- Although we performed logistic regression here with categorical predictors (factor variables) due to the structure of the amusement park sales data, we could also use continuous predictors in `glm()`. Just add those to the right hand side of the model formula as we did with `ols()` in Chap. 7.
- We saw that the estimated effect of promotion in these data was positive when we estimated one model, yet negative when we estimated another, and this shows that it is crucial to explore data thoroughly before modeling or interpreting a model. For most marketing data, no model is ever definitive. However, though careful data exploration and consideration of multiple models, we may increase our confidence in our models and the inferences drawn from them.
- The data here are an example of *Simpson's paradox*, which is when the estimate of an aggregate effect is misleading and markedly different than the effect seen in underlying categories. A famous example occurred in graduate admissions at the University of California at Berkeley, where an apparent bias in admissions was explained (at least partially) by the fact that different departments had different overall admissions rates and numbers of applicants (Bickel et al. 1975).

Logistic regression is a powerful method and one that is a particularly good fit for many marketing problems that have binary outcomes. To learn more, see Sect. 8.4.

8.3   An Introduction to Hierarchical Models

In Chap. 7 we saw how to estimate a linear model for data for a sample of respondents. What if we want to estimate the values in the model for *each* respondent? As marketers, it is very useful to determine individual-level effects such as which customers are more interested in a product or service, who among them wants which features, and who is most or least price sensitive. We may use such information to see the diversity of preference or for purposes such as customer targeting or segmentation (see Chap. 10).

To estimate both a population-level effect and an individual-level effect, we can use a *hierarchical* linear model (HLM). The model is hierarchical because it proposes that individual effects follow a distribution across the population. There are various algorithms to fit such models, but the general approach is that the algorithm fits the overall model to all the data, and then attempts to determine the best fit for each individual within that overall estimate (and repeats as necessary).

In general, a dataset for HLM at an individual level needs multiple observations per individual. Such observations may come from responses over time (as in transactions or a customer relationship management system) or from multiple responses at one time (as in a survey with repeated measures). We consider the case of conjoint analysis, where a respondent rates multiple items on a survey at one time.

How is this different from simply adding the individual, store, or other grouping variable as a factor variable in the model? The key difference is that a factor variable would add a single term that adjusts the model up or down according to the individual. In HLM, however, we can estimate *every* coefficient—or any that we wish—for each individual.

There are other uses for hierarchical models besides customer-level estimation. For example, one might wish to estimate differences by a factor such as geographic region, store, salesperson, product, or promotion campaign. Each of these might provide many responses that could be grouped and allow estimation of a group-level effect within an overall hierarchy. We can't cover every application of HLM here—hierarchical models are the subject of entire books (e.g., Gelman and Hill 2006)—yet we hope this discussion will help you to understand when and how they may be useful, and how to begin with them in Python.

8.3.1   Some HLM Concepts

A few words of jargon are required. Hierarchical models distinguish two types of effects. One type is *fixed* effects, which are effects that are the same for every respondent. In a standard linear model (Chap. 7) all effects are fixed effects. For instance, in Sect. 8.1.2, we saw that online spend was highly associated with online transactions. This estimate is a fixed effect that predicts the same pattern of association for everyone in the sample.

An HLM also estimates *random* effects, which are additional adjustments to the model coefficients estimated for each individual (or group). These are known as "random" because they are estimated as random variables that follow a distribution around the fixed estimates. However, for the estimate of each individual, they are *best* estimates according to the model, not random guesses in that sense.

Such models are also known as *multilevel* models, where individuals and the full sample are at different levels. They are a subset of models known as *mixed effect* models, where *mixed* reflects the fact that the total effect for each respondent has (at least) two effects that are combined: the overall fixed effect plus the individual-level random effect.

A final variation on mixed effects models is a *nested* model, where a factor of interest might occur only within subgroups of the total sample. For example, if we consider sales in response to different promotions that each occur at different stores, we might model both the effect of store (as a random effect, such that there are different sales intercepts for different stores) and the effect of promotion within store as a nested effect. We do not examine a nested model here.

8.3.2   Ratings-Based Conjoint Analysis for the Amusement Park

For a hierarchical model, we return to the fictional amusement park from Sect. 7.1. The park is considering designs for a new roller coaster and hopes to find out which roller coaster features appeal to its customers. They are considering coasters with various possible levels of maximum *speed* (40, 50, 60 or 70 mph), *height* (200, 300, or 400 feet), *construction* type (wood or steel), and *theme* (dragon or eagle). The stakeholders wish to know which combination of features would be most popular according to customers' stated preference.

One way to examine this is a survey that asks customers to rate different roller coasters. For example:

On a 10 point scale, where 10 is the best and 1 is the worst, how would you rate a roller coaster that is made of **wood**, is **400 feet** high, has a maximum speed of **50 mph**, with a **dragon theme**?

In a real survey, it would be important to illustrate such a question with photographs or videos for more realism; we omit those here.

Customers' ratings might be analyzed with a linear model where the ratings are predicted from the various features of the roller coasters. This would tell us the contribution of each feature to the total rating.

Additionally, we wish to understand these preferences at an individual level, such that we can see the distribution of preference or identify individuals for potential marketing actions. To do this, we use a hierarchical linear model (HLM) that estimates both the overall fixed effect and the individual level random effect.

In the following section we simulate consumers' ratings for such a survey. The code is brief and illustrative of the data, but if you wish to skip the simulation, you can load the data from the book's website:

```
In [43]: import pandas as pd
         conjoint_df = pd.read_csv('http://bit.ly/PMR-ch8pt3')
         conjoint_df.speed = conjoint_df.speed.astype('category')
         conjoint_df.height = conjoint_df.height.astype('category')
         conjoint_df.head() # Not shown
         conjoint_df.describe(include='all') # Not shown
```

Given these data, you may skip to Sect. 8.3.4.

8.3.3 Simulating Ratings-Based Conjoint Data

In this section we simulate responses for a hypothetical conjoint analysis survey with 200 respondents who each rate the same set of 16 roller coaster profiles. If you have worked through the data simulation in previous chapters, this code should be relatively simple in structure, although a few functions are new.

We set the structure: 200 respondents who rate 16 designs, each with 4 roller coaster attributes and then we generate the features for the 16 questions:

```
In [44]: import pandas as pd
         import numpy as np
         np.random.seed(12814)
         response_id = range(200) # respondent ids
         n_questions = 16 # number of conjoint ratings per respondent
         speed_options = ['40', '50', '60', '70']
         speed = np.random.choice(speed_options,
                                  size=n_questions,
                                  replace=True)
         height_options = ['200', '300', '400']
         height = np.random.choice(height_options,
                                   size=n_questions,
                                   replace=True)
         const_options = ['Steel', 'Wood']
         const= np.random.choice(const_options,
                                 size=n_questions,
                                 replace=True)
         theme_options = ['Dragon', 'Eagle']
         theme = np.random.choice(theme_options,
                                  size=n_questions,
                                  replace=True)
```

In this example we assume that all respondents rate the same set of 16 coaster designs. Depending on your study's goal, you might instead want to have a different, random set for each respondent. A single set of designs is convenient for printed surveys, while an online study could easily have a different set for every respondent.

Next we create a model matrix for the combinations of features to rate. First we combine the vectors we just generated:

```
In [45]: profiles_df = pd.DataFrame([speed, height, const, theme],
                              index=['speed', 'height',
                                       'const', 'theme']).T
         profiles_df
Out[45]:     speed height  const    theme
         0      70    200  Steel   Dragon
         1      40    400   Wood   Dragon
         ...
         15     70    200  Steel    Eagle
```

Here .T serves to transpose the dataframe so that each row represents a coaster design with a column for each feature.

Now we want to represent users' preference for each attribute, but first we need to transform profiles_df into a binary format that will enable us to multiply it by each user's preference vector. We will encode each profile such that an attribute will be 1 if it is present in that profile and 0 otherwise. These are often referred to as "dummy" or "indicator" variables. We will use the same pandas function that we used in Sect. 7.4 to encode the number of children as factors:

```
In [46]: profile_dummies = pd.get_dummies(profiles_df)
         profile_dummies.drop(
             ['speed_40', 'height_200', 'const_Steel', 'theme_Dragon'],
             axis=1, inplace=True)
         profiles_model = pd.concat(
             [pd.Series(np.ones(16, dtype=int), name='Intercept'),
              profile_dummies],
             axis=1)
         profiles_model
Out[46]:         Intercept  speed_50  speed_60  speed_70  height_300  height_400  \
         0           1          0         0         1          0           0
         1           1          0         0         0          0           1
         ...
         15          1          0         0         1          0           0

                 const_Wood  theme_Eagle
         0           0            0
         1           1            0
         ...
         15          0            1
```

We dropped several columns, which will serve as our baseline condition. We also added in a column of ones to represent the intercept.

To model the user preferences, we draw multivariate random normal values for respondents' preferences using numpy.random.multivariate_normal(). Each row of that matrix represents the preference of a single user for each attribute. Estimating those later is the key feature that distinguishes a hierarchical model from a standard linear model. Again, note that speed_40, height_200, const_Steel and theme_Dragon are treated as baseline conditions and so a weight is not generated for those attributes, but they are of de facto weight 1.0:

```
In [47]: weights = np.random.multivariate_normal(
             mean=[-3, 0.5, 1, 3, 2, 1, -0.2, -0.5],
             cov=np.diag([0.2, 0.1, 0.1, 0.1, 0.2, 0.3, 1, 1]),
             size=len(response_id)
         )
```

Given the designs to be rated and individuals' preferences, we compile the simulated individual ratings. For each respondent, we multiply the preference weights by the design matrix to get the total preference (utility) for each design, adding some random noise with numpy.random.normal(). We convert the utility to a 10-point rating scale using pandas.cut(), and add the respondent's result to the overall dataframe:

```
In [48]: conjoint_df = pd.DataFrame()
         for i in response_id:
             utility = (profiles_model * weights[i]).sum(axis=1) + \
                 np.random.normal(size=16)
             ratings = pd.cut(utility, 10, labels=range(1,11))
             conjoint_resp = profiles_df.copy()
             conjoint_resp['rating'] = pd.to_numeric(ratings)
             conjoint_resp['resp_id'] = i
             conjoint_df = conjoint_df.append(conjoint_resp,
                                              ignore_index=True)
         conjoint_df.head()
```

```
Out[48]:    speed  height  const   theme  rating  resp_id
        0     70    200   Steel  Dragon     9       0
        1     40    400   Wood   Dragon     6       0
        2     70    300   Steel  Eagle      8       0
        3     40    400   Wood   Dragon     7       0
        4     50    200   Steel  Eagle      1       0
```

Building a dataframe using `append()` repeatedly instead of preallocating a whole matrix is not efficient, but it is easy to understand and it is fast enough for this dataset. For large datasets, it would be better to preallocate the dataframe for the size needed and fill in the rows or use a more memory efficient data structure such as a list of dictionaries and then convert to a dataframe at the end (which wouldn't require a reallocation of the entire dataframe on each iteration, as this approach does). With a bit of matrix manipulation, one might instead create the whole dataframe at once; but a simple, readable method like the one here may be more effective overall if it's easier and more reliable to code.

8.3.4 An Initial Linear Model

We begin as always with a quick `describe()` of our conjoint data to check it (create or load the data as described in Sect. 8.3.2 if needed):

```
In [49]: conjoint_df.describe(include='all')
```

```
Out[49]:           speed  height   const    theme      rating     resp_id
         count      3200    3200     3200     3200  3200.000000  3200.000000
         unique        4       3        2        2         NaN          NaN
         top          70     200    Steel   Dragon         NaN          NaN
                    ...
         min         NaN     NaN      NaN      NaN     1.000000     0.000000
         25%         NaN     NaN      NaN      NaN     3.000000    49.750000
         50%         NaN     NaN      NaN      NaN     5.000000    99.500000
         75%         NaN     NaN      NaN      NaN     8.000000   149.250000
         max         NaN     NaN      NaN      NaN    10.000000   199.000000
```

Ratings of the designs range from 1 (strongly disprefer) to 10 (strongly prefer).

Our goal is to determine how the four features relate to the ratings. At an aggregate level, we might use `groupby()` to find the average rating for levels of each attribute. For example, the averages by `height` are:

```
In [50]: conjoint_df.groupby('height').rating.mean()
```

```
Out[50]: height
         200    4.758571
         300    6.958000
         400    4.775000
```

The average rating for designs with 300 foot height is 6.96 points on the 10-point scale, compared to 4.76 and 4.78 for heights of 200 and 400 feet. So, respondents prefer the middle of our height range.

We could examine each individual feature in that way, but a more comprehensive linear model considers all of the effects in combination. To start, we'll estimate a regular linear model without a hierarchical component using `ols()` (Chap. 7):

```
In [51]: import statsmodels.formula.api as smf
         ride_lm = smf.ols('rating ~ speed + height + const + theme',
                           data=conjoint_df).fit()
         ride_lm.summary()
```

Out[51]:

```
==========================================================================
Dep. Variable:                    rating   R-squared:                 0.470
Model:                               OLS   Adj. R-squared:            0.469
Method:                    Least Squares   F-statistic:               404.5
Date:                   Tue, 11 Dec 2018   Prob (F-statistic):         0.00
Time:                           23:26:03   Log-Likelihood:          -6831.1
...
                  coef    std err        t      P>|t|     [0.025     0.975]
--------------------------------------------------------------------------
Intercept       2.6953      0.113   23.888      0.000      2.474      2.917
speed[T.50]     0.8809      0.111    7.922      0.000      0.663      1.099
speed[T.60]     1.6578      0.107   15.538      0.000      1.449      1.867
speed[T.70]     4.5877      0.122   37.628      0.000      4.349      4.827
height[T.300]   2.9201      0.090   32.493      0.000      2.744      3.096
height[T.400]   1.4614      0.115   12.699      0.000      1.236      1.687
const[T.Wood]  -0.0327      0.085   -0.384      0.701     -0.200      0.134
theme[T.Eagle] -0.6686      0.097   -6.913      0.000     -0.858     -0.479
```

In this abbreviated output, the coefficients indicate the association with preference (the `rating`). The highest rated roller coaster on average would have a top speed of 70 mph, a height of 300ft, steel construction, and the dragon theme (steel and dragon because wood and eagle have negative values). We estimate an overall rating for this most-desired coaster; it would be the `intercept + speed_70 + height_300` (steel and dragon are included in the intercept), or 2.69+4.59+2.92 = 10.20 points on our 10-point rating scale.

But wait! That's not possible; our scale is capped at 10 points. This shows that simply interpreting the "average" result can be misleading. The coefficients are estimated on the basis of designs that mostly combine both desirable and undesirable attributes, and are not as reliable at the extremes of preference. Additionally, it could happen that few people prefer that exact combination even though the individual features are each best on average.

Consider that the coefficient for `const[T.Wood]` is near zero. Are people indifferent between wood and steel coasters, or do they have strong preferences that cancel out when averaged? If people are strongly but almost equally divided, that's important for us to know as marketers; it might suggest that we construct different rides that appeal to two different groups. On the other hand, if they are truly indifferent, we could choose between steel and wood on the basis of cost and other factors.

To understand our respondents better, we turn next to a hierarchical model that will estimate both the overall average preference level and individual preferences within the group.

8.3.5 *Hierarchical Linear Model with* `mixedlm`

The linear model `ride_lm` has only fixed effects that are estimated at the sample level. In a hierarchical linear model, we add one or more individual-level effects to those.

The simplest HLM allows individuals to vary only in terms of the constant intercept. For example, we might expect that individuals vary in their usage of a rating scale such that some will rate our roller coaster designs higher or lower than the average respondent. This would be an individual-level random effect for the intercept term.

To estimate an HLM with fixed effects plus a per-respondent intercept, we change the code for running an `ols()` model from above in three ways. First, instead of `ols()`, we use a hierarchical estimation function, `mixedlm()` from `statsmodels`.

Second, we specify the grouping variable, for which a random effect will be estimated for each unique group. In our conjoint data, the group is the set of responses for a single respondent, which is identified in the dataframe by respondent number, `resp_id`. To do this, we pass that column to the `groups` argument.

Third, we must specify the term(s) for which to estimate random effects, which we do with a formula to the `re_formula` argument. For the intercept, we do not have to add a specification, but to be explicit we include one: `re_formula='~1'`.

Otherwise, the `mixedlm()` function is treated very similarly to the `ols()` function:

```
In [52]: ride_hlm_1 = smf.mixedlm('rating ~ speed + height + const + theme',
                                   data=conjoint_df,
                                   groups=conjoint_df['resp_id'],
                                   re_formula='~ 1')
         ride_hlm_1_f = ride_hlm_1.fit(maxiter=200, method='nm')
         ride_hlm_1_f.summary()
```

Out [52]:

Model:	MixedLM	Dependent Variable:	rating
No. Observations:	3200	Method:	REML
No. Groups:	200	Scale:	3.8833
Min. group size:	16	Likelihood:	-6802.8210
Max. group size:	16	Converged:	Yes

...

	Coef.	Std.Err.	z	P>|z|	[0.025	0.975]
Intercept	2.695	0.116	23.328	0.000	2.469	2.922
speed[T.50]	0.881	0.107	8.235	0.000	0.671	1.091
speed[T.60]	1.658	0.103	16.151	0.000	1.457	1.859
speed[T.70]	4.588	0.117	39.112	0.000	4.358	4.818
height[T.300]	2.920	0.086	33.774	0.000	2.751	3.090
height[T.400]	1.461	0.111	13.200	0.000	1.244	1.678
const[T.Wood]	-0.033	0.082	-0.400	0.689	-0.193	0.128
theme[T.Eagle]	-0.669	0.093	-7.186	0.000	-0.851	-0.486
Group Var	0.313	0.029				

In this output, we see that the fixed effects are nearly identical to those estimated by `ols()` above. But now we have also estimated a unique intercept term adjustment for each respondent. The summary shows 3200 total observations (survey questions) grouped into 200 respondents for which a random effect was estimated (such as the effect for (`Group Var`)). We specified the optimization method to be the Nelder-Mead method using the `method='nm'` argument to the fit method.

The `fe_params` parameter contains just the fixed (population level) effects:

```
In [53]: ride_hlm_1_f.fe_params
```

```
Out [53]: Intercept          2.695285
          speed[T.50]        0.880890
          speed[T.60]        1.657826
          speed[T.70]        4.587728
          height[T.300]      2.920103
          height[T.400]      1.461405
          const[T.Wood]     -0.032737
          theme[T.Eagle]    -0.668577
          dtype: float64
```

The 200 per-respondent random effect estimates for intercept, which `ride_hlm_1_f.summary()` does not display because there could be many of them, are accessed via the `random_effects` attribute (and we additionally cast them into a dataframe to format the output and use `head()` to shorten it):

```
In [54]: re_params = pd.DataFrame(ride_hlm_1_f.random_effects).T
         re_params.head()
```

```
Out[54]:     Group
        0    0.028169
        1   -0.922545
        2   -0.957757
        3    0.239439
        4    0.309862
```

The complete effect for each respondent comprises the overall fixed effects that apply to everyone, plus the individually-varying random effects (in this case, just the intercept). We can generate those by combining the fixed effects with the random effects. We convert the fixed effects parameters to a dataframe and then pass an array to `iloc` to generate repeats of it. We then add the random effects to the intercept column:

```
In [55]: ride_hlm_1_f_coef = \
            ride_hlm_1_f.fe_params.to_frame().T\
              .iloc[()].T.iloc[np.zeros(len(re_params))]
         ride_hlm_1_f_coef.index = range(len(re_params))
         ride_hlm_1_f_coef.Intercept += re_params.Group

         ride_hlm_1_f_coef.head()
```

```
Out[55]:     Intercept   const[T.Wood]   height[T.300]   height[T.400]  \
        0    2.723451      -0.032737       2.920103        1.461405
        1    1.772844      -0.032737       2.920103        1.461405
             ...

             speed[T.50]   speed[T.60]   speed[T.70]   theme[T.Eagle]
        0    0.88089       1.657826      4.587728      -0.668577
        1    0.88089       1.657826      4.587728      -0.668577
             ...
```

In `ride_hlm_1_f_coef`, each respondent has the overall sample-level value of the effect on all coefficients except for intercept, and the final intercept coefficient is the same as the fixed effect plus the random effect. For example, for respondent 1, the intercept is 2.69(fixef) − 0.92(ranef) = 1.77(coef).

8.3.6 The Complete Hierarchical Linear Model

The most common hierarchical model in marketing practice is to estimate a random effect parameter for every coefficient of interest for every respondent. This is easy to do with the `mixedlm()` syntax; simply add all the variables of interest to the predictors in the random effects specification (`re_formula`).

For the conjoint data, we write the random effects part of the formula as (`~speed + height + const + theme`). Before estimating that model, we should note that this is a much more complex model than the intercept model above. Whereas the random intercept-only HLM estimated 8 fixed parameters and 200 random effects, the full model will estimate 8 fixed effects plus 8 ∗ 200 random effects. And it will do this for a total dataframe of 3200 observations.

This fact has two implications. First, the estimation can be rather slow, taking several minutes for the present model at the time of writing. Second, there are so many parameters that even 3200 observations is not a lot, and one can expect some difficulty finding a stable *converged* model.

With those facts in mind, we estimate the full model as follows (this will take some time, perhaps several minutes):

```
In [56]: ride_hlm_2 = smf.mixedlm('rating ~ speed + height + const + theme',
                          data=conjoint_df,
                          groups=conjoint_df['resp_id'],
                          re_formula='~ speed + height + const + theme')
         ride_hlm_2_f = ride_hlm_2.fit(maxiter=1000, method='nm')
```

Compared to model `ride_hlm_1` above, this model has two changes. First, we added all four roller coaster factors to be estimated for random effects. Second, we added an argument to `fit()`, method: `maxiter=1000` which increases the number of iterations to attempt convergence to 1000. We again set `method='nm'`, which specifies the optimization method as Nelder-Mead, which is among the most robust optimizers in Scipy. Any optimizer from `scipy.optimizer` can be specified. The default is BFGS (named after the mathematicians CG Broyden, R Fletcher, D Goldfarb, and D Shanno) and it works well if the initial parameters are close to the minimum. These parameters allow the model to converge better, although still not completely as we see in the resulting warnings when it finishes:

```
/usr/local/lib/python3.6/dist-packages/statsmodels/base/model.py:496:
ConvergenceWarning: Maximum Likelihood optimization failed to converge.
Check mle_retvals
  "Check mle_retvals", ConvergenceWarning)
```

Despite the warnings, we proceed with data analysis here because it is quite slow to run the model to convergence and the exact results are for illustration, not for an important business decision. For a model of importance, we recommend to run to convergence whenever possible.

If you run into warnings, we suggest four potential remedies. First, increase the `maxiter` argument by a factor of 2, 5, or 10 to see if convergence results (and repeat that if necessary). Second, do a web search for the warnings you receive and consider the suggestions offered on discussion forums. Third, consider using a different optimization function (see `mixedlm` documentation; Perktold et al. 2019). Fourth, consider collecting more data, or evaluate your data for internal consistency. Again, we skip these steps now primarily for convenience.

Fixed effects are present on the `fe_params` attribute:

```
In [57]: ride_hlm_2_f.fe_params

Out[57]: Intercept        2.695285
         speed[T.50]      0.880890
         speed[T.60]      1.657826
         speed[T.70]      4.587728
         height[T.300]    2.920103
         height[T.400]    1.461405
         const[T.Wood]   -0.032737
         theme[T.Eagle]  -0.668577
         dtype: float64
```

This part of the `ride_hlm_2` model is identical to the model estimated for `ride_hlm_1` above, so the coefficients are identical.

The random effects now include an estimate for each parameter for each respondent:

```
In [58]: ride_hlm_2_f_re_df = pd.DataFrame(ride_hlm_2_f.random_effects).T
         ride_hlm_2_f_re_df.rename({'Group': 'Intercept'},
                                    axis=1, inplace=True)
         ride_hlm_2_f_re_df.head()

Out[58]:        Intercept   speed[T.50]   speed[T.60]   speed[T.70]   height[T.300]   \
         0       0.740959    -0.088424     0.055348      0.233541      -0.124533
         1      -0.724949    -0.049684    -0.233311     -0.080976      -0.260567
                   ...

                height[T.400]   const[T.Wood]   theme[T.Eagle]
         0         0.770034       -0.020209       -2.451112
         1        -0.071083       -1.738253        0.261211
                   ...
```

Notice that the random intercepts are no longer identical to those estimated in model `ride_hlm_1`, because we added seven explanatory variables and the predicted outcome rating points are distributed differently across the predictors.

We obtain the total coefficients per respondent by adding the random effects to the fixed effects:

```
In [59]: hlm_2_f_coef = ride_hlm_2_f_re_df + ride_hlm_2_f.fe_params
         hlm_2_f_coef.head()
```

```
Out[59]:        Intercept   speed[T.50]   speed[T.60]   speed[T.70]   height[T.300]   \
           0    3.436244    0.792466      1.713173      4.821269      2.795570
           1    1.970336    0.831206      1.424515      4.506752      2.659536
           2    1.707103    0.878848      1.322931      4.541597      2.624884
           ...

                height[T.400]   const[T.Wood]   theme[T.Eagle]
           0      2.231439       -0.052947       -3.119690
           1      1.390322       -1.770990       -0.407366
           2      1.822914       -1.627908       -0.131214
           ...
```

8.3.7 Interpreting HLM

How can we use these random effects? One option is to find which preferences go together. We can do this by looking at the correlation of parameter random effects across respondents. A clustermap of the correlations is a great first step for exploration.

```
In [60]:  import matplotlib.pyplot as plt
          import seaborn as sns

          cg = sns.clustermap(ride_hlm_2_f_re_df.iloc[:,1:].corr(), vmax=0.5,
                              vmin=-0.5,cmap=plt.cm.bwr, center=0)
          plt.setp(cg.ax_heatmap.yaxis.get_majorticklabels(), rotation=0)
          plt.setp(cg.ax_heatmap.xaxis.get_majorticklabels(), rotation=45)
```

A clustermap can be used to show the correlation between parameters (i.e. preferences) across users. Unlike a standard correlation matrix, the clustermap attempts to organize the parameters into sets that are correlated. In Fig. 8.4, we can see a few distinct sets of preferences. In the upper left we see that preference for a rollercoaster with a height of 300 is positively correlated with preference for speed of 60.

There is another related set of preferences in the middle cluster: a rollercoaster with speed of 50 and eagle theme (or a speed of 50 and height of 400 and NOT the eagle theme).

Individual-level estimates effectively form new data for each respondent or customer, and thus may be used for all the kinds of analyses that are described elsewhere in this book. For example, we might plot the distribution of preference to learn how many customers prefer a particular feature such as wooden coasters or tall coasters (Chaps. 3 and 5). We might look at the association of preference with other data (Chap. 7). Or we might cluster the data to find customer segments (Chap. 10).

8.3.8 Conclusion for HLM

This concludes our discussion of hierarchical models. In this section, we hope to have convinced you that, when you have multiple observations for an individual or other grouping factor of interest, you should consider a hierarchical model that estimates both sample-level and individual- or group-level effects. These models are relatively straightforward to estimate using the mixedlm() from the statsmodels library.

Besides *customer*-level models, which are most common in marketing, other factors for which one might wish to estimate a hierarchical model include *store*, *country*, *geographic region*, *advertising campaign*, *advertising creative*, *channel*, *bundle*, and *brand*.

If this section has inspired you to consider adding hierarchical modeling to your toolbox, see "Learning More" (Sect. 8.4) for pointers to other resources.

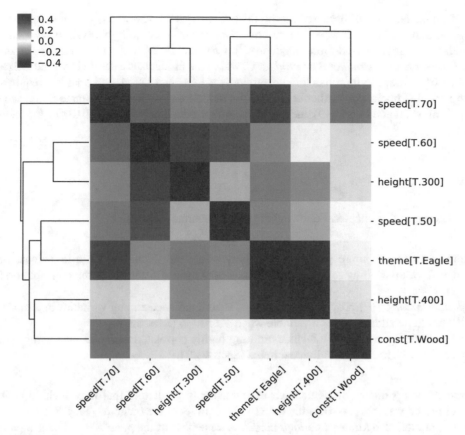

Fig. 8.4 A clustermap visualization of random effects from the HLM model show a few distinct preference clusters

8.4 Learning More*

The topics in this chapter are drawn from the vast range of topics related to linear modeling, and the best general recommendation is to learn about those topics broadly, as in Harrell (2015) on strategies and issues for effective regression modeling and Dobson (2018) on generalized linear models. The following notes provide further guidance on specific topics.

Collinearity The best way to learn more about collinearity and how to detect and address it is to become more fluent in linear modeling in general. Good texts for learning broadly about regression modeling are Harrell (2015), and Fox and Weisberg (2011).

Logistic Regression Logistic regression models are especially common in health sciences (modeling improvement after treatment, for instance), and much of that literature is approachable for marketers with modest translation. Hosmer et al. (2013) is a standard text on such models and demonstrates the importance of model building and assessment. Binary outcomes are also often the subject of models in the machine learning community. We consider machine learning models in the context of classification in Chap. 11. A general text on those methods is Kuhn and Johnson (2013).

Hierarchical Models The best overall didactic text on hierarchical models is Gelman and Hill (2006), which provides outstanding conceptual explanation and a breadth of models with detailed code in R. The one, comparatively minor limitation of Gelman and Hill is that its level of detail and discussion can make it difficult to determine what to do when confronted with an immediate modeling need. Another didactic text is Gałecki and Burzykowski (2013).

Bayesian Hierarchical Models We did not introduce hierarchical Bayes models and their importance, but if hierarchical models are important to your research, we would encourage you to learn more. To learn more about such models, there are technical introductions at varying levels of mathematical sophistication from Kruschke (2016), Gelman et al. (2013), and Rossi et al. (2005). Gelman and Hill (2006) discusses hierarchical models from both Bayesian and non-Bayesian perspectives, with examples in R (despite our love of Python, for most practitioners R remains a more complete option for Bayesian modeling, although PyMC3 (Salvatier et al. 2016) is a great resource for those with a solid foundation in Bayesian statistics).

Conjoint Analysis In this chapter we discussed metric (also known as ratings-based) conjoint analysis. Such surveys are easy to construct, field, and analyze. However, in practice, *choice-based* conjoint analysis (CBC) and its near neighbor *discrete choice modeling* (DCM) are used more frequently. In CBC and DCM, users make choices among options, such as whether they prefer *Product A* over *Product B* or *Product C*, where the products are defined by randomized features, brands, and prices. At the time of writing, Python has limited support for CBC and DCM, and analysis requires custom code that goes beyond the scope of this book. For further details on the models and options to estimate them, see Chapter 13 in this book's related R text (Chapman and Feit 2019), the more general introduction in Orme (2010), or the technical discussion in Rossi et al. (2005).

8.5 Key Points

We covered a lot of material in this chapter. Following are some important lessons.

Collinearity
- Collinearity occurs when two or more variables are highly associated. Including them in a linear model can result in confusing, nonsensical, or misleading results, because the model cannot differentiate the contribution from each of them (Sect. 8.1).
- The *variance inflation factor* (VIF) provides a measure of shared variance among variables in a model. A rule of thumb is that collinearity should be addressed for a variable when $VIF > 5$ (Sect. 8.1.2).
- Common approaches to fixing collinearity include omitting highly-correlated variables, and using principal components or factor scores (see Chap. 9) instead of individual items (Sect. 8.1.2).

Logistic Regression
- *Logistic regression* relates a binary outcome such as purchase to predictors that may include continuous and factor variables, by modeling the variables' association with the probability of the outcome (Sect. 8.2.1).
- A logistic regression model, also known as a *logit model*, is a member of the *generalized* linear models family, and is fit using `glm( , family=statsmodels.api.families.Binomial())` (Sect. 8.2.4).
- Coefficients in a logit model can be interpreted in terms of *odds ratios*, the degree to which they are associated with the increased or decreased likelihood of an outcome. This is done simply by exponentiating the coefficients with `exp()` (Sect. 8.2.4).
- A statistically significant result does not always mean that the model is appropriate. It is important to explore data thoroughly and to construct models on the basis of careful consideration (Sect. 8.2.5).

Hierarchical Linear Models
- In common marketing discussion, a *hierarchical model* estimates both group level effects and individual differences in effects. Such models are popular in marketing because they provide insight into differences among customers (*heterogeneity*) and distribution of preference. Hierarchical linear models (HLMs) estimate the importance of effects for individuals as well as for an overall population (Sect. 8.3).
- Effects that are associated with all observations are known as *fixed* effects, and those that differ across various grouping levels are known as *random* effects (Sect. 8.3.1).
- These models are also known as *mixed effect* models, because the total effect for each person is composed of the effect for the overall population (the fixed effect) plus the per-individual (random) effect. We estimated an HLM using `mixedlm()` from the `statsmodels` package (Sect. 8.3.5).
- The difference between estimating hierarchical effects, as opposed to including the grouping variable as a factor in a standard linear model, is that a hierarchical model estimates *every* specified effect for each individual or group, not only a single adjustment term.
- The formula for a mixed effect model is the same as for other linear models, but a grouping term is specified in the `group` argument. To estimate an individual-level model, the grouping term is typically the respondent identifier. The variables for which to estimate the random effects are specified in the `re_formula` argument, for example `'~1'` for intercept only or `'~speed + height'` to estimate several variables.
- Hierarchical models can be used to group observations at other levels than the individual level. For example, we might wish to group by store, advertising campaign, salesperson, or some other factor, if we want to estimate effects that are specific to such a grouping (Sect. 8.3.8).
- A common marketing application of HLM is conjoint analysis, to estimate both overall preference and individual differences in preference. In this chapter, we demonstrated ratings-based, or *metric* conjoint analysis (Sect. 8.3.2).

Part III
Advanced Data Analysis

Chapter 9
Reducing Data Complexity

Marketing datasets often have many variables—many *dimensions*—and it is advantageous to reduce these to smaller sets of variables to consider. For instance, we might have many questions (e.g. 9) on a consumer survey that reflect a smaller number (such as 3) of underlying concepts such as *customer satisfaction* with a service, *category leadership* for a brand, or *luxury* for a product. If we can reduce the data to its underlying dimensions, we can more clearly identify the underlying relationships among concepts.

In this chapter we consider three common methods to reduce data complexity by reducing the number of dimensions in the data. *Principal component analysis* (PCA) attempts to find uncorrelated linear dimensions that capture maximal variance in the data. *Exploratory factor analysis* (EFA) also attempts to capture variance with a small number of dimensions while seeking to make the dimensions interpretable in terms of the original variables. *Multidimensional scaling* (MDS) maps similarities among observations in terms of a low-dimension space such as a two-dimensional plot. MDS can work with metric data and with non-metric data such as categorical or ordinal data.

In marketing, PCA is often associated with *perceptual maps*, which are visualizations of respondents' associations among brands or products. In this chapter we demonstrate perceptual maps for brands using principal component analysis. We then look at ways to draw similar perceptual inferences from factor analysis and multidimensional scaling.

9.1 Consumer Brand Rating Data

We investigate dimensionality using a simulated dataset that is typical of consumer *brand perception* surveys. These data reflect consumer ratings of *brands* with regard to *perceptual adjectives* as expressed on survey items with the following form:

On a scale from 1 to 10 — where 1 is *least* and 10 is *most* — how [ADJECTIVE] is [BRAND A]?

In these data, an observation is one respondent's rating of a brand on one of the adjectives. Two such items might be:

1. How *trendy* is *Intelligentsia Coffee*?
2. How much of a *category leader* is *Blue Bottle Coffee*?

Such ratings are collected for all the combinations of adjectives and brands of interest.

The data here comprise simulated ratings of 10 brands ("a" to "j") on 9 adjectives ("performance," "leader," "latest," "fun," and so forth), for N = 100 simulated respondents. The dataset is provided on this book's web site. We start by loading and checking the data:

```
In [1]: import pandas as pd
        brand_ratings = pd.read_csv('http://bit.ly/PMR-ch9')
        brand_ratings.head()
```

```
Out[1]:    perform  leader  latest  fun  serious  bargain  value  trendy  \
      0        2       4       8    8      2        9        7      4
      1        1       1       4    7      1        1        1      2
      2        2       3       5    9      2        9        5      1
      3        1       6      10    8      3        4        5      2
      4        1       1       5    8      1        9        9      1
```

© Springer Nature Switzerland AG 2020
J. S. Schwarz et al., *Python for Marketing Research and Analytics*, https://doi.org/10.1007/978-3-030-49720-0_9

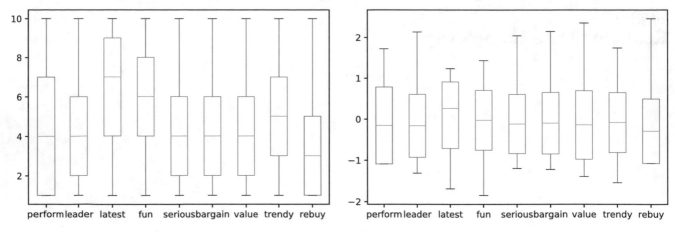

Fig. 9.1 Boxplots for the unscaled (left) and scaled (right) data offer a quick way to check the distribution of the dataset

```
        rebuy brand
   0        6     a
   1        2     a
   2        6     a
   3        1     a
   4        1     a
In [2]: brand_ratings.tail()# Not shown
```

Each of the 100 simulated respondents has provided ratings for each of the 10 brands, so there are 1000 total rows. We inspect the describe() to check the data quality and structure:

```
In [3]: brand_ratings.describe().round(2)
```

Out[3]:		perform	leader	latest	fun	serious	bargain	\
	count	1000.00	1000.00	1000.00	1000.00	1000.00	1000.00	
	mean	4.49	4.42	6.20	6.07	4.32	4.26	
	std	3.20	2.61	3.08	2.74	2.78	2.67	
	min	1.00	1.00	1.00	1.00	1.00	1.00	
	25%	1.00	2.00	4.00	4.00	2.00	2.00	
	50%	4.00	4.00	7.00	6.00	4.00	4.00	
	75%	7.00	6.00	9.00	8.00	6.00	6.00	
	max	10.00	10.00	10.00	10.00	10.00	10.00	

		value	trendy	rebuy
	count	1000.00	1000.00	1000.00
	mean	4.34	5.22	3.73
	std	2.40	2.74	2.54
	min	1.00	1.00	1.00
	25%	2.00	3.00	1.00
	50%	4.00	5.00	3.00
	75%	6.00	7.00	5.00
	max	10.00	10.00	10.00

We see in describe() that the ranges of the ratings for each adjective are 1–10. The data appear to be clean and formatted appropriately.

We can also use a boxplot for another view of the distribution of each variable, as displayed in the left panel of Fig. 9.1:

```
In [4]: brand_ratings.plot.box()
```

Table 9.1 Adjectives in the `brand_ratings` data and examples of survey text that might be used to collect rating data

Perceptual adjective (column name)	Example survey text:
Perform	*Brand* has strong performance
Leader	*Brand* is a leader in the field
Latest	*Brand* has the latest products
Fun	*Brand* is fun
Serious	*Brand* is serious
Bargain	*Brand* products are a bargain
Value	*Brand* products are a good value
Trendy	*Brand* is trendy
Rebuy	I would buy from *Brand* again

There are nine perceptual adjectives in this dataset. Table 9.1 lists the adjectives and the kind of survey text that they might reflect.

9.1.1 Rescaling the Data

It is often good practice to rescale raw data. This makes data more comparable across individuals and samples. A common procedure is to *center* each variable by subtracting its mean from every observation, and then *rescaling* those centered values as units of standard deviation. This is commonly called *standardizing*, *normalizing*, or *Z-scoring* the data (Sect. 7.3.3). Note that we use `np.arange()` here rather than `range()` because we want the output to be a NumPy array rather than a list so we can do vectorized operations on it.

In Python, data could be standardized with a mathematical expression using `mean()` and `sd()`:

```
In [5]: import numpy as np
        x = np.arange(1000)
        x_sc = (x - x.mean())/x.std()
        print('mean: {}\nmedian: {}\nmax: {}\nmin: {}'.format(x_sc.mean(),
                                                    np.median(x_sc),
                                                    x_sc.max(),
                                                    x_sc.min()))


mean: 0.0
median: 0.0
max: 1.7303196219213355
min: -1.7303196219213355
```

As we saw in Sect. 7.3.3, a simpler way is to use `sklearn.preprocessing.scale()` to rescale all variables at once. We never want to alter raw data, so we assign the raw values first to a new dataframe `brand_ratings_sc` and alter that:

```
In [6]: from sklearn.preprocessing import scale
        brand_ratings_sc = brand_ratings.copy()
        brand_ratings_sc.iloc[:, :-1] = scale(brand_ratings_sc.iloc[:, :-1])
        brand_ratings_sc.plot.box()
        brand_ratings_sc.describe().round(2)
```

```
Out[6]:         perform   leader   latest      fun   serious   bargain  \
        count   1000.00  1000.00  1000.00  1000.00   1000.00   1000.00
        mean      -0.00     0.00    -0.00     0.00     -0.00     -0.00
        std        1.00     1.00     1.00     1.00      1.00      1.00
        min       -1.09    -1.31    -1.69    -1.85     -1.20     -1.22
        25%       -1.09    -0.93    -0.71    -0.75     -0.84     -0.85
        50%       -0.15    -0.16     0.26    -0.02     -0.12     -0.10
```

75%	0.78	0.61	0.91	0.70	0.60	0.65
max	1.72	2.14	1.24	1.43	2.04	2.15

	value	trendy	rebuy
count	1000.00	1000.00	1000.00
mean	-0.00	-0.00	0.00
std	1.00	1.00	1.00
min	-1.39	-1.54	-1.07
25%	-0.97	-0.81	-1.07
50%	-0.14	-0.08	-0.29
75%	0.69	0.65	0.50
max	2.36	1.74	2.47

In this code we name the new dataframe with extension "_sc" to remind ourselves that observations have been scaled. We operate on columns 1–9 because the tenth column is a string variable for brand. (This is accomplished by selecting those columns using .iloc[:, :-1], which excludes the last column of the dataframe.) We see that the mean of each adjective is correctly 0.00 across all brands because the data are rescaled. Observations on the adjectives have a spread (difference between min and max) of roughly 3 standard deviation units. This means the distributions are *platykurtic*, flatter than a standard normal distribution, because we would expect a range of more than 4 standard deviation units for a sample of this size. (Platykurtosis is a common property of survey data, due to floor and ceiling effects.)

For our initial exploration, we will use the unscaled data. It is generally a good idea to start with the unscaled data, as it's more interpretable. However differences in scale between the variables can complicate an analysis. In practice, we generally run our full analysis on unscaled and then scaled data and evaluate both. Generally, scaled data are "safer" to work with, as any effects from differences in scale between variables are eliminated. In this chapter we will start our exploration with the unscaled data and then move to the scaled data when we start the dimensionality reduction analyses.

9.1.2   Correlation Between Attributes

We can generate the correlation matrix using corr() and visualize it using Seaborn for initial inspection of bivariate relationships among the variables:

```
In [7]: import matplotlib.pyplot as plt
        import seaborn as sns

        sns.clustermap(brand_ratings.corr(), annot=True, fmt=".2f",
                       cmap=plt.cm.bwr)
```

Using clustermap() rather than heatmap(), reorders the rows and columns according to variables' similarity in a hierarchical cluster solution such that adjectives close to each other (such as rebuy, bargain, value) are plotted adjacent to each other (see Sect. 10.3.2 for more on hierarchical clustering). The annot=True argument adds the value in each grid cell and the fmt="0.2f" specifies the formatting as floats with two decimal places. The result is shown in Fig. 9.2, where we see that the ratings seem to group into three clusters of similar variables, a hypothesis we examine in detail in this chapter.

9.1.3   Aggregate Mean Ratings by Brand

Perhaps the simplest business question in these data is: "What is the average (mean) position of the brand on each adjective?" We can use groupby() (see Sects. 3.2.1 and 5.2) to find the mean of each variable by brand:

```
In [8]: brand_means = brand_ratings.groupby('brand').mean().round(3)
        brand_means
```

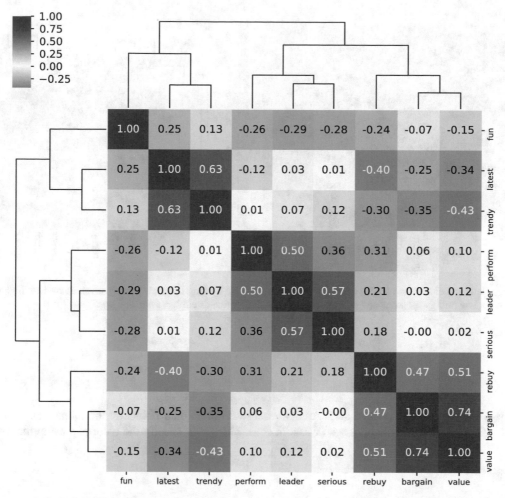

Fig. 9.2 Correlation plot for the simulated consumer brand ratings. This visualization of the basic data appears to show three general clusters that comprise *fun/latest/trendy*, *rebuy/bargain/value*, and *perform/leader/serious* respectively

```
Out[8]:        perform  leader  latest   fun  serious  bargain  value \
        brand
        a          1.65    3.04    7.46  7.87     1.77     4.83   4.78
        b          7.47    7.21    8.43  3.40     7.61     4.37   4.70
        c          6.57    7.45    5.88  3.75     7.72     2.64   3.28
        d          2.31    2.87    7.28  6.58     2.40     1.91   2.10
        e          2.68    4.92    7.60  6.88     4.44     5.73   5.34
        f          4.30    5.12    2.31  5.47     5.96     6.59   6.79
        g          7.43    3.98    2.24  4.65     2.84     6.65   7.35
        h          4.44    3.64    7.74  8.03     3.93     2.29   2.46
        i          5.56    3.58    7.29  7.20     3.91     3.58   2.41
        j          2.47    2.36    5.72  6.85     2.65     4.00   4.16


               trendy  rebuy
        brand
        a          3.78   2.21
        b          7.25   4.33
        c          5.29   3.39
        d          7.24   2.47
        e          5.60   3.82
        f          2.99   7.18
```

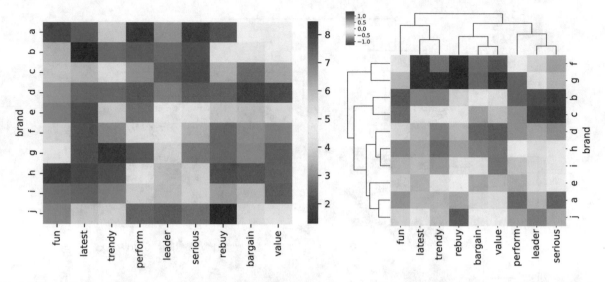

Fig. 9.3 A heatmap (left) and clustermap (right) of the mean of each adjective by brand. Brands *f* and *g* are similar—with high ratings (in green) for *rebuy* and *value* but low ratings for *latest* and *fun*. Other groups of similar brands are *b/c*, *i/h/d*, and *a/j*

```
g          1.72      7.19
h          7.59      2.19
i          6.84      3.21
j          3.90      1.28
```

A *heatmap* is a useful way to examine such results because it colors data points by the intensities of their values. We use `heatmap()` from the `seaborn` package (Waskom et al. 2018). We specify the colormap using the `cm` module from matplotlib.

```
In [9]: from matplotlib import cm

        sns.heatmap(brand_means[['fun', 'latest', 'trendy', 'perform',
                                 'leader', 'serious', 'rebuy', 'bargain',
                                 'value']], cmap=cm.BrBG)
```

The resulting heatmap is shown in the left panel of Fig. 9.3. In this chart's brown-to-blue-green (`"BrBG"`) palette a brown color indicates a low value and dark green indicates a high value; lighter colors are for values in the middle of the range. The brands are clearly perceived differently with some brands rated high on performance and leadership (brands *b* and *c*) and others rated high for value and intention to rebuy (brands *f* and *g*). We order the columns to match the correlation plot above, but the rows are in alphabetical order, i.e. arbitrary order.

We can use `clustermap()`, which sorts the columns and rows in order to emphasize similarities and patterns in the data, which can be seen in the right panel of Fig. 9.3:

```
In [10]: sns.clustermap(brand_means, cmap=cm.BrBG)
```

It does this using a form of hierarchical clustering (see Sect. 10.3.2). We should use some caution interpreting those clusters, but it can be a helpful way to visualize groupings in the data, and is a good preliminary analysis to a more formal cluster analysis. See Chap. 10 for an introduction to clustering.

Looking at Figs. 9.2 and 9.3 we could guess at the groupings and relationships of adjectives and brands. For example, there is similarity in the color pattern across columns for the *bargain/value/rebuy*; a brand that is high on one tends to be high on another. But it is better to formalize such insight, and the remainder of this chapter discusses how to do so.

9.2 Principal Component Analysis and Perceptual Maps

Principal Component Analysis (PCA) recomputes a set of variables in terms of linear equations, known as *components*, that capture linear relationships in the data (Jolliffe 2002). The first component captures as much of the variance as possible from all variables as a single linear function. The second component captures as much variance as possible that remains after the first component. This continues until there are as many components as there are variables. We can use this process to reduce data complexity by then retaining and analyzing only a subset of those components—such as the first one or two components—that explain a large proportion of the variation in the data.

By extracting components, one can derive a reduced set of variables that captures as much of the variance as desired, yet where each of the measures is independent of the others, which can help us better interpret high-dimensional data.

9.2.1 PCA Example

We explore PCA first with a simple dataset to see and develop intuition about what is happening. We create highly correlated data by copying a random vector `xvar` to a new vector `yvar` while replacing half of the data points. Then we repeat that procedure to create `zvar` from `yvar`:

```
In [11]: np.random.seed(98286)
         xvar = np.random.randint(low=0, high=10, size=100)
         yvar = xvar.copy()
         yvar[:50] = np.random.randint(low=0, high=10, size=50)
         zvar = yvar.copy()
         zvar[25:75] = np.random.randint(low=0, high=10, size=50)
         myvars = np.array([xvar, yvar, zvar])
```

`yvar` will be correlated with `xvar` because 50 of the observations are identical while 50 are newly sampled random values. Similarly, `zvar` keeps 50 values from `yvar` (and thus also inherits some from `xvar`, but fewer). We compile those three vectors into a matrix. Note that we use these data only to have a simple demonstration; this procedure is not a good way to generate formally correlated variables. If you want to generate correlated data, see `np.random.multivariate_normal()`.

We check one of the three possible bivariate plots along with the correlation matrix. If we simply plotted the raw data, there would be many overlapping values because the responses are discrete (integers 1–10). To separate and visualize multiple points with the same values, we use `swarmplot()`, which adjusts points so you can see how many points there are at the same value (similar to jittering, see Sect. 4.6.1):

```
In [11]: sns.swarmplot(x=xvar, y=yvar, color='k')
```

The bivariate plot in Fig. 9.4 shows a clear linear trend for `yvar` vs. `xvar` on the diagonal.

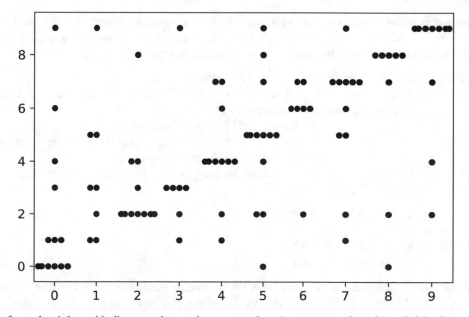

Fig. 9.4 Scatterplot of correlated data with discrete values, using `swarmplot()` to separate the values slightly for greater visual impact of overlapping points

```
In [12]: np.corrcoef(myvars)

Out[12]: array([[1.        , 0.5755755 , 0.23837089],
                [0.5755755 , 1.        , 0.48224687],
                [0.23837089, 0.48224687, 1.        ]])
```

In the correlation matrix, xvar correlates highly with yvar and less so with zvar, as expected, and yvar has strong correlation with zvar (using the rules of thumb from Sect. 4.5).

Using intuition, what would we expect the components to be from these data? First, there is shared variance across all three variables because they are positively correlated. So we expect to see one component that picks up that association of all three variables. After that, we expect to see a component that shows that xvar and zvar are more differentiated from one another than either is from yvar. That implies that yvar has a unique position in the dataset as the only variable to correlate highly with both of the others, so we expect one of the components to reflect this uniqueness of yvar.

Let's check the intuition. We use PCA() from the sklearn.decomposition library to perform PCA:

```
In [13]: from sklearn import decomposition
         my_pca = decomposition.PCA().fit(myvars.T)
```

We create a helper function to print some relevant statistics from the PCA:

```
In [14]: def pca_summary(pca, round_dig=3):
             '''Print a summary of the PCA fit'''
             return pd.DataFrame(
                 [pca.explained_variance_,
                  pca.explained_variance_ratio_,
                  np.cumsum(pca.explained_variance_ratio_)],
                 columns=['pc{}'.format(i) for i in
                             range(1, 1+len(pca.explained_variance_))],
                 index=['variance', 'proportion of variance explained',
                        'cumulative proportion']
                 ).round(round_dig)
         pca_summary(my_pca)
```

```
Out[14]:                                   pc1     pc2     pc3
         variance                          16.473   7.050   3.042
         proportion of variance explained   0.620   0.265   0.114
         cumulative proportion              0.620   0.886   1.000
```

There are three components because we have three variables. The first component accounts for 62% of the explainable linear variance, while the second accounts for 27%, leaving 11% for the third component. How are those components related to the variables? We check the rotation matrix, using another helper function to format the output:

```
In [15]: def pca_components(pca, variable_names):
             '''Return loading of variables on specific components in the PCA'''
             return pd.DataFrame(pca.components_,
                                 index=['pc{}'.format(i+1)
                                         for i in range(len(pca.components_))],
                                 columns=variable_names).T
         my_pca_components = pca_components(my_pca, ['xvar', 'yvar', 'zvar'])
         my_pca_components.round(3)
```

```
Out[15]:          pc1     pc2     pc3
         xvar   -0.544   0.637   0.545
         yvar   -0.622   0.129  -0.772
         zvar   -0.563  -0.760   0.326
```

Interpreting PCA rotation loadings is difficult because of the multivariate nature—factor analysis is a better procedure for interpretation, as we will see later in this chapter—but we examine the loadings here for illustration and comparison to our expectations. In component 1 (PC1) we see loading on all three variables as expected from their overall shared variance (the negative direction is not important; the key is that they are all in the same direction).

In component 2, we see that xvar and zvar are differentiated from one another as expected, with loadings in opposite directions. Finally, in component 3, we see residual variance that differentiates yvar from the other two variables and is consistent with our intuition about yvar being unique.

In addition to the loading matrix, we can use the PCA to compute scores for each of the principal components that express the underlying data in terms of its loadings on those components using the transform() method on the PCA object. The columns ([:, 0], [:, 1], and so forth) may be used to obtain the values of the components for each observation. We can use a small number of those columns in place of the original data to obtain a set of observations that captures much of the variation in the data.

A less obvious feature of PCA, but implicit in the definition, is that extracted PCA components are *uncorrelated* with one another, because otherwise there would be more linear variance that could have been captured. We see this in the transformed values returned for observations in a PCA model, where the correlations (off-diagonal values) are effectively zero (approximately 10^{-16} as shown in scientific notation):

```
In [16]: myvars_transformed = my_pca.transform(myvars.T)
         np.corrcoef(myvars_transformed.T)

Out[16]: array([[1.00000000e+00, 1.36938301e-16, 3.98753086e-16],
                [1.36938301e-16, 1.00000000e+00, 7.27332599e-17],
                [3.98753086e-16, 7.27332599e-17, 1.00000000e+00]])
```

9.2.2 Visualizing PCA

A good way to examine the results of PCA is to map the first few components, which allows us to visualize the data in a lower-dimensional space. A common visualization is a *biplot*, a two-dimensional plot of data points with respect to the first two PCA components, overlaid with a projection of the variables on the components. We can produce a biplot by first plotting the data points in a scatter plot:

```
In [17]: import matplotlib.pyplot as plt
         plt.scatter(x=myvars_transformed[:,0],
                     y=myvars_transformed[:,1],
                     color='k')
         plt.xlabel('PC1')
         plt.ylabel('PC2')
```

The result is Fig. 9.5. To that we add the vectors representing the loading of each variable, shown in Fig. 9.6.

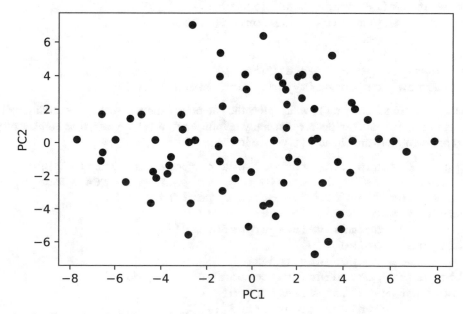

Fig. 9.5 A scatterplot showing data points plotted on the first two components

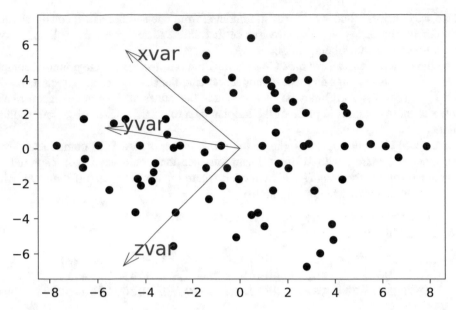

Fig. 9.6 A simple *biplot()* of a principal component analysis solution for the simple, constructed example, showing data points plotted on the first two components

```
In [18]: def plot_arrow_component(pca_components, variable, scale=1):
             '''Plot an arrow of component dimensions in PCA space'''
             plt.arrow(x=0, y=0,
                       dx=pca_components.loc[variable]['pc1'] * scale,
                       dy=pca_components.loc[variable]['pc2'] * scale,
                       color='r',
                       head_width=.5, overhang=1)
             plt.text(x=pca_components.loc[variable]['pc1'] * scale,
                      y=pca_components.loc[variable]['pc2'] * scale,
                      s=variable,
                      color='r',
                      fontsize=16)

         plt.scatter(x=myvars_transformed[:,0],
                     y=myvars_transformed[:,1],
                     color='k')

         for v in my_pca_components.index:
           plot_arrow_component(my_pca_components, v, 8)
```

Finally, we produce a function `biplot()`, which plots the datapoints and the vectors and additionally labels each data point with its index, as in Fig. 9.7. Such plots are especially helpful when there are a smaller number of points (as we will see below for brands) or when there are clusters (as we see in Chap. 10).

```
In [19]: def biplot(values_transformed, pca_components, label=[]):
             '''Create a biplot, a scatterplot of points in PCA space with arrows
             representing the loadings of each variable.
             Points can optionally be labelled'''
             scale = 1.2* np.max(values_transformed[:,1])
             plt.figure(figsize=(10, 10))
             for v in pca_components.index:
               plot_arrow_component(pca_components, v, scale)
             plt.scatter(x=values_transformed[:,0],
                         y=values_transformed[:,1],
```

```
                          color='gray', s=4)
        if len(label) == values_transformed.shape[0]:
          for i, txt in enumerate(label):
            plt.text(s=txt,
                     x=values_transformed[i,0]+.01*scale,
                     y=values_transformed[i,1]+.01*scale,
                     fontsize=14)
      plt.xlabel('PC1')
      plt.ylabel('PC2')

In [20]: biplot(myvars_transformed, my_pca_components,
             label=range(myvars.shape[1]))
```

In Fig. 9.7, there are arrows that show the best fit of each of the variables on the principal components—a projection of the variables onto the 2-dimensional space of the first two PCA components, which explain a large part of the variation in the data. These are useful to inspect because the *direction* and *angle* of the arrows reflect the relationship of the variables; a closer angle indicates higher positive association, while the relative direction indicates positive or negative association of the variables.

In the present case, we see in the variable projections (arrows) that yvar is closely aligned with the first component (X axis). In the relationships among the variables themselves, we see that xvar and zvar are more associated with yvar, relative to the principal components, than either is with the other. Thus, this visually matches our interpretation of the correlation matrix and loadings above.

By plotting against principal components, a biplot benefits from the fact that components are uncorrelated; this helps to disperse data on the chart because the x- and y-axes are independent. When there are several components that account for substantial variance, it is also useful to plot components beyond the first and second.

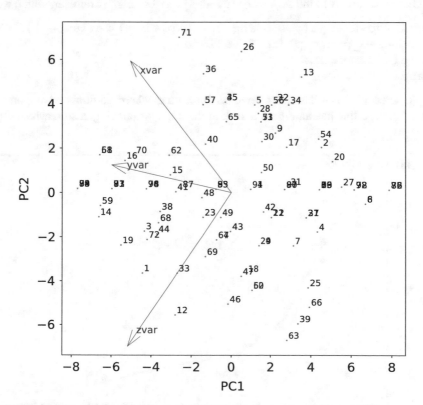

Fig. 9.7 A *biplot()* with point labels, generated from our biplot() function

9.2.3 PCA for Brand Ratings

Let's look at the principal components for the brand rating data (refer to Sect. 9.1 above if you need to load the data). We find the components with `PCA.fit()`, selecting just the rating columns, for which we will make two new variables, `brand_rating_names` for the rating names and `brand_rating_sc_vals` for the values (as we will be using these several more times):

```
In [21]: brand_rating_names = brand_ratings_sc.columns[:-1]
         brand_ratings_sc_vals = brand_ratings_sc[brand_rating_names]
         brand_pca = decomposition.PCA().fit(brand_ratings_sc_vals)
```

We can use our `pca_summary()` function defined in the previous section to see the variance covered by each component:

```
In [22]: pca_summary(brand_pca)
```

```
Out[22]:                                   pc1     pc2     pc3     pc4     pc5    \
         variance                        2.982   2.099   1.080   0.728   0.638
         proportion of variance explained 0.331   0.233   0.120   0.081   0.071
         cumulative proportion           0.331   0.564   0.684   0.765   0.836

                                          pc6     pc7     pc8     pc9
         variance                        0.535   0.390   0.312   0.243
         proportion of variance explained 0.059   0.043   0.035   0.027
         cumulative proportion           0.895   0.938   0.973   1.000
```

An important plot when analyzing a PCA is a *scree plot*, which shows the successive proportion of additional variance that each component adds. This corresponds to the `PCA.explained_variance_` parameter, which we can plot:

```
In [23]: plt.plot(1+np.arange(len(brand_pca.explained_variance_)),
                   brand_pca.explained_variance_, 'o-')
         plt.xlabel('Component')
         plt.ylabel('Variance')
```

The result is Fig. 9.8. A scree plot is often interpreted as indicating where additional components are not worth the complexity; this occurs where the line has an *elbow*, a kink in the angle of bending, a somewhat subjective determination.

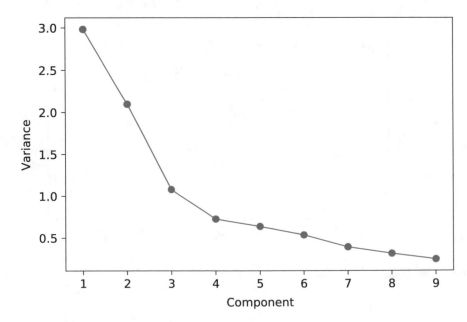

Fig. 9.8 A scree plot of a PCA solution shows the successive variance accounted by each component. For the brand rating data, the proportion largely levels out after the third component

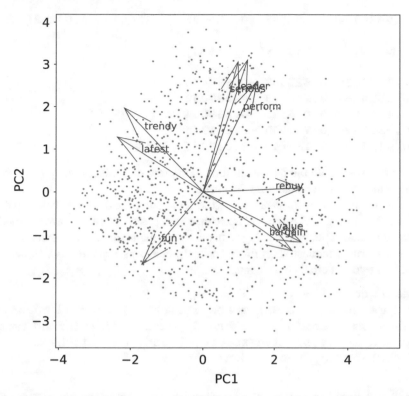

Fig. 9.9 A biplot of an initial attempt at principal component analysis for consumer brand ratings. Although we see adjective groupings on the variable loading arrows in red, and gain some insight into the areas where ratings cluster (as dense areas of observation points), the chart would be more useful if the data were first aggregated by brand

In Fig. 9.8, the elbow occurs at either component 3 or 4, depending on interpretation; and this suggests that the first two or three components explain most of the variation in the observed brand ratings.

We can use several of our helper functions from the previous section to plot a biplot of the first two principal components reveals how the rating adjectives are associated:

```
In [24]: brand_ratings_sc_trans = brand_pca.transform(brand_ratings_sc_vals)
         brand_pca_components = pca_components(brand_pca, brand_rating_names)
         biplot(brand_ratings_sc_trans, brand_pca_components)
```

We see the result in Fig. 9.9, where adjectives map in four regions: category leadership ("serious," "leader," and "perform" in the upper right), value ("rebuy," "value," and "bargain"), trendiness ("trendy" and "latest"), and finally "fun" on its own.

But there is a problem: the plot of individual respondents' ratings is too dense and it does not tell us about the brand positions! A better solution is to construct a biplot that shows the *aggregated* ratings by brand.

9.2.4 Perceptual Map of the Brands

First we compile the mean scaled rating of each adjective by brand as we found above using groupby() (see Sect. 9.1).

```
In [25]: brand_means_sc = brand_ratings_sc.groupby('brand').mean()
         brand_means_sc.head()

Out[25]:        perform    leader     latest       fun    serious   bargain  \
         brand
         a     -0.886362 -0.528168  0.411179  0.656974 -0.919400  0.214203
         b      0.931336  1.071294  0.726470 -0.972701  1.183733  0.041640
         c      0.650249  1.163350 -0.102388 -0.845098  1.223346 -0.607347
         d     -0.680231 -0.593373  0.352671  0.186665 -0.692521 -0.881197
```

```
e        -0.564673   0.192933   0.456685   0.296039   0.042135   0.551826


            value      trendy      rebuy
brand
a         0.184785  -0.525407  -0.596465
b         0.151415   0.740679   0.237092
c        -0.440898   0.025541  -0.132504
d        -0.933102   0.737030  -0.494236
e         0.418373   0.138649   0.036566
```

Prior to creating the biplot, we rescale the data; even though the raw data were already rescaled, the aggregated means have a somewhat different scale than the standardized data itself.

Note, that we manually scaled the data using mean() and std(). Since the data were held in a dataframe with a relevant index, this simplified the process. Using sklearn.preprocessing.scale would have returned a NumPy matrix, from which we could have created a dataframe, but by doing it manually we maintained those labels.

A biplot of the PCA-transformed mean ratings gives an interpretable *perceptual map*, showing where the brands are placed with respect to the first two principal components:

```
In [26]: brand_means_sc = (
            ((brand_means_sc - brand_means_sc.mean()) / brand_means_sc.std()))
         brand_means_sc_transformed = brand_pca.transform(brand_means_sc)
         biplot(brand_means_sc_transformed, brand_pca_components,
            label=brand_means.index)
```

The result is Fig. 9.10.

What does the map tell us? First we interpret the adjective clusters and relationships and see four areas with well-differentiated sets of adjectives and brands that are positioned in proximity. Brands *f* and *g* are high on "value," for instance, while *a* and *j* are relatively high on "fun," which is opposite in direction from leadership adjectives ("leader" and "serious").

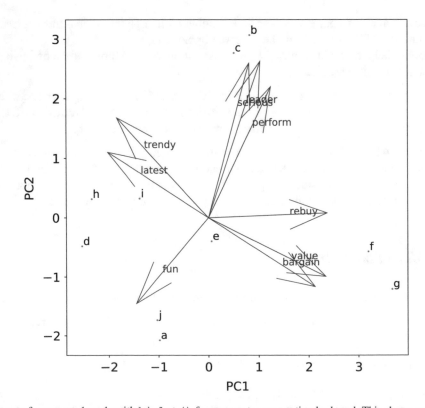

Fig. 9.10 A perceptual map of consumer brands with biplot() for aggregate mean rating by brand. This shows components almost identical to those in Fig. 9.9 but the mean brand positions are clear

With such a map, one might form questions and then refer to the underlying data to answer them. For instance, suppose that you are the brand manager for brand *e*. What does the map tell you? For one thing, your brand is in the center and thus appears not to be well-differentiated on any of the dimensions. That could be good or bad, depending on your strategic goals. If your goal is to be a safe brand that appeals to many consumers, then a relatively undifferentiated position like *e* could be desirable. On the other hand, if you wish your brand to have a strong, differentiated perception, this finding would be unwanted (but important to know).

What should you do about the position of your brand *e*? Again, it depends on the strategic goals. If you wish to increase differentiation, one possibility would be to take action to shift your brand in some direction on the map. Suppose you wanted to move in the direction of brand *c*. You could look at the specific differences from *c* in the data:

```
In [27]: brand_means_sc.loc['c'] - brand_means_sc.loc['e']

Out[27]: perform     1.775362
         leader      1.440484
         latest     -0.774450
         fun        -1.886670
         serious     1.544750
         bargain    -1.811159
         value      -1.131735
         trendy     -0.151604
         rebuy      -0.212361
         dtype: float64
```

This shows you that *e* is relatively stronger than *c* on "bargain" and "fun", which suggests dialing down messaging or other attributes that reinforce those (assuming, of course, that you truly want to move in the direction of *c*). Similarly, *c* is stronger on "perform" and "serious," so those could be aspects of the product or message for *e* to strengthen.

Another option would be *not* to follow another brand but to aim for differentiated space where no brand is positioned. In Fig. 9.10, there is a large gap between the group *b* and *c* on the bottom of the chart, versus *f* and *g* on the upper right. This area might be described as the "value leader" area or similar.

How do we find out how to position there? Let's assume that the gap reflects approximately the average of those four brands (see Sect. 9.2.5 for some of the risks with this assumption). We can find that average as the mean of the brands' rows, and then take the difference of *e* from that average:

```
In [28]: brand_means_sc.loc[['b','c','f','g']].mean(axis=0) - brand_means_sc.loc['e']

Out[28]: perform     1.717172
         leader      0.580749
         latest     -1.299004
         fun        -1.544598
         serious     0.750005
         bargain    -0.391245
         value       0.104383
         trendy     -0.629646
         rebuy       0.840802
         dtype: float64
```

This suggests that brand *e* could target the gap by increasing its emphasis on performance while reducing emphasis on "latest" and "fun."

To summarize, when you wish to compare several brands across many dimensions, it can be helpful to focus on just the first two or three principal components that explain variation in the data. You can select how many components to focus on using a scree plot, which shows how much variation in the data is explained by each principal component. A perceptual map plots the brands on the first two principal components, revealing how the observations related to the underlying dimensions (the components).

PCA may be performed using survey ratings of the brands (as we have done here) or with objective data such as price and physical measurements, or with a combination of the two. In any case, when you are confronted with multidimensional data on brands or products, PCA visualization is a useful tool for understanding how they differ from one another in the market.

9.2.5 Cautions with Perceptual Maps

There are three important caveats in interpreting perceptual maps. First, you must choose the level and type of aggregation carefully. We demonstrated the maps using mean rating by brand, but depending on the data and question at hand, it might be more suitable to use median (for ordinal data) or even modal response (for categorical data). You should check that the dimensions are similar for the full data and aggregated data before interpreting aggregate maps. You can do this by examining the variable positions and relationships in biplots of both aggregated data (such as means) and raw data (or a random subset of it), as we did above.

Second, the relationships are strictly relative to the product category and the brands and adjectives that are tested. In a different product category, or with different brands, adjectives such as "fun" and "leader" could have a very different relationship. Sometimes simply adding or dropping a brand can change the resulting map significantly because the positions are relative. In other words, if a new brand enters the market (or one's analysis), the other positions may change substantially. One must also be confident that all of the key perceptions (adjectives, in this example) have been assessed. One way to assess sensitivity here is to run PCA and biplot on a few different samples from your data, such as 80% of your observations, and perhaps dropping an adjective each time. If the maps are similar across those samples, you may feel more confident in their stability.

Third, it is frequently misunderstood that the positions of brands in such a map depend on their relative positioning in terms of the principal components, which are constructed composites of all dimensions. This means that *the strength of a brand on a single adjective cannot be read directly from the chart*. For instance, in Fig. 9.10, it might appear that brands *b* and *c* are weaker than *d*, *h*, and *i* on "latest" but are similar to one another. In fact, *b* is the single strongest brand on "latest" while *c* is weak on that adjective. Overall, *b* and *c* are quite similar to one another in terms of their scores on the two components that aggregate all of the variables (adjectives), but they are not necessarily similar on any single variable. When we use PCA to focus on the first one or two dimensions in the data, we are looking at the largest-magnitude similarities, and that may obscure smaller differences that do not show up strongly in the first one or two dimensions.

This last point is a common area of confusion with analysts and stakeholders who want to read adjective positions directly from a biplot. We recommend to explain that positions are not absolute but are *relative*. We often explain positions with language such as, "compared to its position on other attributes, brand X is *relatively* differentiated by perceptions of strength (or weakness) on such-and-such attribute."

Despite these caveats, perceptual maps can be a valuable tool. We use them primarily to form hypotheses and to provide material to inform strategic analyses of brand and product positioning. If they are used in that way—rather than as absolute assessments of position—they can contribute to engaging discussions about position and potential strategy.

Although we illustrated PCA with brand position, the same kind of analysis could be performed for product ratings, position of consumer segments, ratings of political candidates, evaluations of advertisements, or any other area where you have metric data on multiple dimensions that is aggregated for a modest number of discrete entities of interest.

9.3 Exploratory Factor Analysis

Exploratory factor analysis (EFA) is a family of techniques to assess the relationship of *constructs* (concepts) in surveys and psychological assessments. Factors are regarded as *latent variables* that cannot be observed directly, but are imperfectly assessed through their relationship to other variables.

In psychometrics, canonical examples of factors occur in psychological and educational testing. For example, "intelligence," "knowledge of mathematics," and "anxiety" are all abstract concepts (constructs) that are not directly observable in themselves. Instead, they are observed empirically through multiple behaviors, each one of which is an imperfect indicator of the presumed underlying latent variable. These observed values are known as *manifest variables* and include indicators such as test scores, survey responses, and other empirical behaviors. Exploratory factor analysis attempts to find the degree to which latent, composite *factors* account for the observed variance of those manifest variables.

In marketing, we often observe a large number of variables that we believe should be related to a smaller set of underlying constructs. For example, we cannot directly observe *customer satisfaction* but we might observe responses on a survey that asks about different aspects of a customer's experience, jointly representing different facets of the underlying construct *satisfaction*. Similarly, we cannot directly observe *purchase intent*, *price sensitivity*, or *category involvement* but we can observe multiple behaviors that are related to them.

In this section, we use EFA to examine respondents' attitudes about brands, using the brand rating data from above (Sect. 9.1) and to uncover the latent dimensions in the data. Then we assess the brands in terms of those estimated latent factors.

9.3.1 Basic EFA Concepts

The result of EFA is similar to PCA: a matrix of factors (similar to PCA components) and their relationship to the original variables (*loadings* of the factors on the variables). Unlike PCA, EFA attempts to find solutions that are maximally *interpretable* in terms of the manifest variables. In general, it attempts to find solutions in which a small number of loadings for each factor are very high, while other loadings for that factor are low. When this is possible, that factor can be interpreted in terms of that small set of variables.

To accomplish this, EFA uses *rotations* that start with an uncorrelated (*orthogonal*) mathematical solution and then mathematically alter the solution to explain an identical amount of variance but with different loadings on the original variables. There are many such rotations available, and they typically share the goals of maximizing the loadings on a few variables while making factors as distinct as possible from one another.

Instead of reviewing that mathematically (see Mulaik 2009), let's consider a loose analogy. One might think about EFA in terms of a pizza topped with large items such as tomato slices and mushrooms that will be cut into a certain number of slices. The pizza could be rotated and cut in an infinite number of ways that are all mathematically equivalent insofar as they divide up the same underlying structure.

However, some rotations are more useful than others because they fall in-between the large items rather than dividing them. When this occurs, one might have a "tomato slice," a "mushroom slice," a "half-and-half tomato and mushroom slice," and so forth. By rotating and cutting differently, one makes the underlying substance more interpretable relative to one's goals (such as having differentiated pizza slices). No rotation is inherently better or worse, but some are more useful than others. Similarly, the manifest variables in EFA can be sliced in many ways according to one's goals for interpreting the latent factors. For example, in our dataset, a rotation that associates "value" and "bargain" together might be more interpretable than one that placed them apart, as we can imagine that they both represent a similar underlying concept. We will see how this works in Sect. 9.3.3.

Because EFA produces results that are interpretable in terms of the original variables, an analyst may be able to interpret and act on the results in ways that would be difficult with PCA. For instance, EFA can be used to refine a survey by keeping items with high loading on factors of interest while cutting items that do not load highly. EFA is also useful to investigate whether a survey's items actually go together in a way that is consistent with expectations.

For example, if we have a 10-item survey that is supposed to assess the single construct *customer satisfaction*, it is important to know whether those items in fact go together in a way that can be interpreted as a single factor, or whether they instead reflect multiple dimensions that we might not have considered. Before interpreting multiple items as assessing a single concept, one might wish to test that it is appropriate to do so. In this chapter, we use EFA to investigate such structure.

EFA serves as a data reduction technique in three broad senses:

1. In the technical sense of dimensional reduction, we can use *factor scores* instead of a larger set of items. For instance, if we are assessing satisfaction, we could use a single satisfaction score instead of several separate items. (In Sect. 8.1.2 we review how this is also useful when observations are correlated.)
2. We can reduce uncertainty. If we believe *satisfaction* is imperfectly manifest in several measures, the combination of those will have less noise than the set of individual items.
3. We might also reduce data collection by focusing on items that are known to have high contribution to factors of interest. If we discover that some items are not important for a factor of interest, we can discard them from data collection efforts.

In this chapter we use the brand rating data to ask the following questions: How many latent factors are there? How do the survey items map to the factors? How are the brands positioned on the factors? What are the respondents' factor scores?

9.3.2 Finding an EFA Solution

The first step in exploratory factor analysis is to determine the number of factors to estimate. There are various ways to do this, and two traditional methods are to use a scree plot (Sect. 9.2.3), and to retain factors where the *eigenvalue* (a metric for proportion of variance explained) is greater than 1.0. An eigenvalue of 1.0 corresponds to the amount of variance that might be attributed to a single independent variable; a factor that captures less variance than such an item may be considered relatively uninteresting.

As we saw in Sect. 9.2, a scree plot of the brand rating data suggests two or three components. We can also examine the eigenvalues using numpy.linalg.eig() on a correlation matrix:

```
In [29]: np.linalg.eig(np.corrcoef(brand_ratings_sc_vals.T))[0]

Out[29]: array([2.97929556, 2.09655168, 1.07925487, 0.72721099, 0.63754592,
                0.53484323, 0.39010444, 0.24314689, 0.31204642])
```

The first three eigenvalues are greater than 1.0, although barely so for the third value. This again suggests three or possibly two factors.

The final choice of a model depends on whether it is useful. For EFA, a best practice is to check a few factor solutions, including the ones suggested by the scree and eigenvalue results. Thus, we test a 3-factor solution and a 2-factor solution to see which one is more useful.

sklearn has a factor analysis module sklearn.decomposition.FactorAnalysis(). However, it is a bit limited in functionality, so we will use the factor_analyzer package (Biggs 2017), which we can install using pip if necessary:

```
In [30]: !pip install factor_analyzer
```

We can then instantiate a FactorAnalyzer() object and analyze the scaled brand ratings:

```
In [31]: import factor_analyzer

         fa = factor_analyzer.FactorAnalyzer(n_factors=2, rotation='varimax')
         fa.fit(brand_ratings_sc_vals)
         pd.DataFrame(fa.loadings_, index=brand_rating_names).round(2)

Out[31]:            0      1
         perform  0.09   0.60
         leader  -0.02   0.81
         latest  -0.59  -0.04
         fun     -0.19  -0.39
         serious -0.07   0.68
         bargain  0.69   0.05
         value    0.78   0.11
         trendy  -0.65   0.10
         rebuy    0.60   0.33
```

In the 2-factor solution, factor 0 loads strongly on "bargain" and "value," and therefore might be interpreted as a "value" factor while factor 1 loads on "leader" and "serious" and thus might be regarded as a "category leader" factor.

This is not a bad interpretation, but let's compare it to a 3-factor solution:

```
In [32]: fa = factor_analyzer.FactorAnalyzer(n_factors=3, rotation='varimax')
         fa.fit(brand_ratings_sc_vals)
         pd.DataFrame(fa.loadings_, index=brand_rating_names).round(2)

Out[32]:            0      1      2
         perform  0.07   0.60  -0.06
         leader   0.06   0.80   0.10
         latest  -0.16  -0.08   0.98
         fun     -0.07  -0.41   0.21
         serious -0.01   0.68   0.08
         bargain  0.84  -0.00  -0.11
         value    0.85   0.08  -0.21
         trendy  -0.35   0.08   0.59
         rebuy    0.50   0.32  -0.30
```

The 3-factor solution retains the "value" and "leader" factors (factors 0 and 1 in the output) and adds a clear "latest" factor (factor 2) that loads strongly on "latest" and "trendy." This adds an easily interpretable concept to our understanding of the data. It also aligns with the bulk of suggestions from the scree and eigen tests, and fits well with the perceptual maps we saw in Sect. 9.2.4, where those adjectives were in a differentiated space. So we regard the 3-factor model as superior to the 2-factor model because the factors are more interpretable. Solutions may be formally compared using confirmatory factor analysis (CFA), which we do not cover in this book (see Chapman and Feit 2019, Chap. 10).

9.3.3 EFA Rotations

As we described earlier, a factor analysis solution can be rotated to have new loadings that account for the same proportion of variance. Although a full consideration of rotations is out of scope for this book, there is one issue worth considering in any EFA: do you wish to allow the factors to be *correlated* with one another or not?

You might think that one should let the data decide. However, the question of whether to allow correlated factors is less a question about the *data* than it is about your *concept* of the underlying latent factors. Do you think the factors should be conceptually independent, or does it make more sense to consider them to be related? (To return to the pizza analogy, we could choose to slice our pizza such that mushrooms tend to appear alongside tomatoes, or we could cut it such that the two tend to be separated.) An EFA rotation can be obtained under either assumption.

The default in general is to find factors that have zero correlation (using a *varimax* rotation). In case you're wondering how this differs from PCA, it differs mathematically because EFA finds latent variables that may be observed with error (see Mulaik 2009) whereas PCA simply recomputes transformations of the observed data. In other words, EFA focuses on the underlying latent dimensions, whereas PCA focuses on transforming the dimensionality of the data.

Returning to our present data, we might judge that *value* and *leader* are reasonably expected to be related; in many categories, the leader can command a price premium, and thus we might expect those two latent constructs to be negatively correlated rather than independent of one another. This suggests that we could allow correlated factors in our solution. This is known as an *oblique* rotation ("oblique" because the dimensional axes are not perpendicular but are skewed by the correlation between factors).

A common oblique rotation is the "oblimin" rotation. We add that to our 3-factor model with `rotation="oblimin"`:

```
In [33]: fa = factor_analyzer.FactorAnalyzer(n_factors=3, rotation='oblimin')
         fa.fit(brand_ratings_sc_vals)
         fa_loadings_df = pd.DataFrame(fa.loadings_,
                               index=brand_rating_names)
         fa_loadings_df.round(2)

Out[33]:              0     1     2
         perform   0.01  0.60 -0.09
         leader    0.02  0.81  0.07
         latest    0.03 -0.00  1.01
         fun       0.00 -0.39  0.24
         serious  -0.05  0.68  0.03
         bargain   0.88 -0.05  0.07
         value     0.86  0.03 -0.04
         trendy   -0.26  0.14  0.54
         rebuy     0.45  0.28 -0.22
```

When we compare this oblimin result to the default varimax rotation above, we see the loadings are slightly different for the relationships of the factors to the adjectives. However, the loadings are similar enough in this case that there is no substantial change in how we would interpret the factors. There are still factors for "value," "leader," and "latest."

We can check the factor correlation matrix showing the relationships between the estimated latent factors:

```
In [34]: np.corrcoef(fa.transform(brand_ratings_sc_vals).T)

Out[34]: array([[ 1.        ,  0.12904599, -0.41410012],
                [ 0.12904599,  1.        , -0.04888392],
                [-0.41410012, -0.04888392,  1.        ]])
```

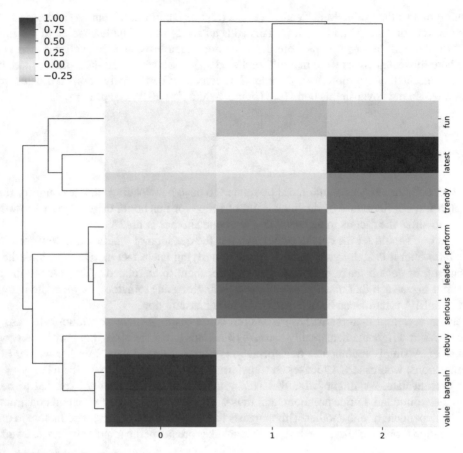

Fig. 9.11 A clustermap of item-factor loadings

Factor 1 (value) is negatively correlated with Factor 3 (latest), $r = -0.41$, and is essentially uncorrelated with Factor 2 (leader), $r = 0.13$.

The negative correlation between factors 1 and 3 is consistent with our theory that brands that are value brands are less likely to be trendy, and thus we think this is a more interpretable result. However, in other cases a correlated rotation may or may not be a better solution than an orthogonal one; that is largely an issue to be decided on the basis of domain knowledge and interpretive utility rather than statistics.

In the output above, the item-to-factor loadings are displayed. In the returned model object, those are present as the `loadings` parameter. We can then visualize item-factor relationships with a clustermap of `loadings`:

```
In [35]: sns.clustermap(fa_loadings_df, cmap=cm.BrBG, center=0)
```

The result is Fig. 9.11, which shows a distinct separation of items into three factors, which are roughly interpretable as *value*, *leader*, and *latest*. Note that the item `rebuy`, which reflects stated intention to repurchase, loads on both Factor1 (*value*) and Factor2 (*leader*). This suggests that in our simulated data, consumers say they would rebuy a brand for either reason, because it is a good value or because it is a leader.

Overall, the result of the EFA for this dataset is that instead of using nine distinct variables, we might instead represent the data with three underlying latent factors. We have seen that each factor maps to 2–4 of the manifest variables. However, this only tells us about the relationships of the rating variables among themselves in our data; in the next section, we use the estimated factor scores to learn about the *brands*.

9.3.4 Using Factor Scores for Brands

In addition to estimating the factor structure, EFA will also estimate latent factor *scores* for each observation. In the present case, this gives us the best estimates of each respondent's latent ratings for the "value," "leader," and "latest" factors. We can then use the factor scores to determine brands' positions on the factors. Interpreting factors eliminates the separate dimensions associated with the manifest variables, allowing us to concentrate on a smaller, more reliable set of dimensions that map to theoretical constructs instead of individual items.

Factor scores are calculated from the `FactorAnalyzer()` object using the `transform()` method, which we can store as a separate dataframe:

```
In [36]: fa = factor_analyzer.FactorAnalyzer(n_factors=3, rotation='oblimin')
         brand_ratings_fa_trans = fa.fit_transform(brand_ratings_sc_vals)
         brand_rating_fa_scores = pd.DataFrame(brand_ratings_fa_trans)
         brand_rating_fa_scores['brand'] = brand_ratings_sc.brand
         brand_rating_fa_scores.head()

Out[36]:            0          1          2  brand
         0   1.388590  -0.491354   0.531693      a
         1  -1.188916  -1.352280  -0.658905      a
         2   1.038597  -0.801256  -0.372207      a
         3   0.037803  -0.318029   1.190962      a
         4   1.688281  -1.525753  -0.453958      a
```

The result is an estimated score for each respondent on each factor and brand. If we wish to investigate individual-level correlates of the factors, such as their relationship to demographics or purchase behavior, we could use these estimates of factor scores. This can be very helpful in analyses such as regression and segmentation because it reduces the model complexity (number of dimensions) and uses more reliable estimates (factor scores that reflect several manifest variables). Instead of nine items, we have three factors.

To find the overall position for a brand, we aggregate the individual scores by brand as usual using `groupby()`:

```
In [37]: brand_rating_fa_mean = brand_rating_fa_scores.groupby('brand').mean()
         brand_rating_fa_mean.columns = ['Value', 'Leader', 'Latest']
         brand_rating_fa_mean.round(3)

Out[37]:         Value   Leader   Latest
         brand
         a        0.147  -0.863    0.388
         b        0.067   1.205    0.710
         c       -0.492   1.120   -0.077
         d       -0.921  -0.625    0.368
         e        0.416  -0.035    0.437
         f        1.048   0.406   -1.265
         g        1.236   0.086   -1.326
         h       -0.804  -0.271    0.528
         i       -0.555  -0.169    0.388
         j       -0.142  -0.854   -0.150
```

Finally, a clustermap graphs the scores by brand:

```
In [38]: sns.clustermap(brand_rating_fa_mean, cmap=cm.BrBG, center=0)
```

The result is Fig. 9.12. When we compare this to the chart of brand by adjective in Fig. 9.3, we see that the chart of factor scores is significantly simpler than the full adjective matrix. The brand similarities are evident again in the factor scores, for instance that f and g are similar, as are b and c, and so forth.

We conclude that EFA is a valuable way to examine the underlying structure and relationship of variables. When items are related to underlying constructs, EFA reduces data complexity by aggregating variables to create simpler, more interpretable latent variables.

In this exposition, we have only explored a small number of the possibilities for factor analysis; to learn more, see Sect. 9.5.

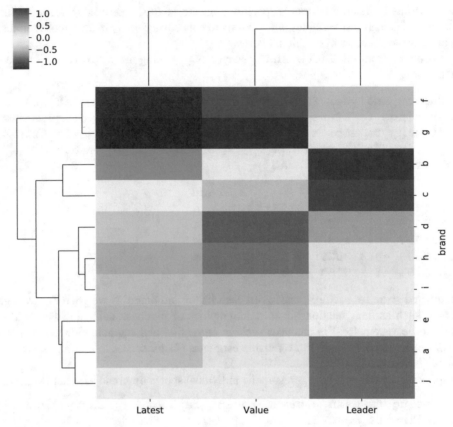

Fig. 9.12   A heatmap of the latent factor scores for consumer brand ratings, by brand

9.4   Multidimensional Scaling

Multidimensional scaling (MDS) is a family of procedures that can also be used to find lower-dimensional representations of data. Instead of extracting underlying components or latent factors, MDS works instead with a *distance matrix* (also known as a *similarity matrix*). MDS attempts to find a lower-dimensional map that best preserves all the observed similarities between items.

The `sklearn.manifold.MDS` module works with vectors directly: it calculates pairwise Euclidean distances and then looks for lower-dimensional representations:

```
In [39]: from sklearn import manifold

         np.random.seed(889783)
         brand_mds = manifold.MDS().fit_transform(brand_means)
         brand_mds

Out[39]: array([[ 0.59217926,  5.19146726],
                [-2.74412002, -6.30675543],
                [-0.51645595, -5.64921129],
                [-4.33444294,  3.51765049],
                [ 0.69182752,  0.80286252],
                [ 6.14100233, -2.84581818],
                [ 8.40903503, -0.33459353],
                [-4.67731306,  1.14429619],
                [-3.16204417,  0.12390567],
                [-0.399668  ,  4.35619632]])
```

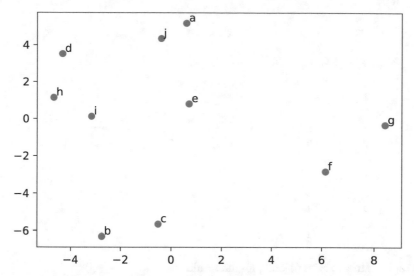

Fig. 9.13 A metric multidimensional scaling chart for mean brand rating, using `sklearn.manifold.MDS()`. The brand positions are quite similar to those seen in the `biplot()` in Fig. 9.10

The result of `MDS.fit_transform()` is a list of X and Y dimensions indicating 2-dimensional estimated plot coordinates for entities (in this case, brands). We see the plot locations for brands *a* and *b* in the output above. Given those coordinates, we can simply `scatter()` the values and label them:

```
In [40]: plt.scatter(x=brand_mds[:,0],
                      y=brand_mds[:,1],
                      color='grey')
         for i,p in enumerate(brand_mds):
           plt.annotate(s=brand_means.index[i], xy=p+.1)
```

In this code, plot (`plt.annotate()`) adds the text brand annotation to each point (as before in our `biplot()` code. The result is Fig. 9.13. The relative brand positions are grouped nearly identically to what we saw in the perceptual map in Fig. 9.10.

9.4.1 Non-metric MDS

For *non-metric* data such as rankings or categorical variables, you simply pass the `metric=False` argument to the sklearn.manifold.MDS() instantiation.

For purposes of illustration, let's convert the mean ratings to rankings instead of raw values; this will be non-metric, ordinal data. We apply `argsort()` to the columns using `apply()` which codes each resulting column as its rank rather than overall rating:

```
In [41]: brand_ranks = brand_means.apply(lambda col: col.argsort().argsort())
         brand_ranks
```

```
Out[41]:        perform  leader  latest  fun  serious  bargain  value  \
         brand
         a             0       2       6    8        0        6      6
         b             9       8       9    0        8        5      5
         c             7       9       3    1        9        2      3
         d             1       1       4    4        1        0      0
         e             3       6       7    6        6        7      7
         f             4       7       1    3        7        8      8
         g             8       5       0    2        3        9      9
         h             5       4       8    9        5        1      2
```

| i | 6 | 3 | 5 | 7 | 4 | 3 | 1 |
| j | 2 | 0 | 2 | 5 | 2 | 4 | 4 |

	trendy	rebuy
brand		
a	2	2
b	8	7
c	4	5
d	7	3
e	5	6
f	1	8
g	0	9
h	9	1
i	6	4
j	3	0

We then pass that brand rank matrix to MDS() and plot the result:

```
In [42]: brand_mds_nonmetric = manifold.MDS(metric=False).fit_transform(brand_ranks)

In [43]: plt.scatter(x=brand_mds_nonmetric[:,0],
                     y=brand_mds_nonmetric[:,1],
                     color='grey')
         for i,p in enumerate(brand_mds_nonmetric):
            plt.annotate(s=brand_means.index[i], xy=p+.01)
```

The resulting chart is shown in Fig. 9.14. Compared to Fig. 9.13, we see that brand positions in the non-metric solution are considerably different, but most of the nearest neighbors of brands are largely consistent with the exception of brands *b* and *c*, which are separated quite a bit more than in the metric solution. (This occurs because the rank-order procedure loses some of the information that is present in the original metric data solution, resulting in a slightly different map.)

We generally recommend principal component analysis as a more informative procedure than multidimensional scaling for typical metric or near-metric (e.g., survey Likert scale) data. However, PCA will not work with non-metric data. In those cases, multidimensional scaling is a valuable alternative.

MDS may be of particular interest when handling text data such as consumers' feedback, comments, and online product reviews, where text frequencies can be converted to distance scores. For example, if you are interested in similarities between brands in online reviews, you could count how many times various pairs of brands occur together in consumers' postings.

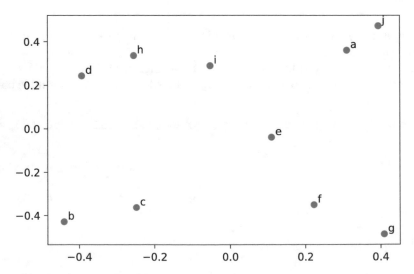

Fig. 9.14 A non-metric multidimensional scaling chart for mean brand ratings expressed as ordinal ranks. The brand groupings are similar to but more diffuse than those in Fig. 9.13

The co-occurrence matrix of counts—brand A mentioned with brand B, with brand C, and so forth—could be used as a measure of similarity between the two brands and serve as the distance metric in MDS (see Netzer et al. 2012).

9.4.2 Visualization Using Low-Dimensional Embeddings

Visualizing high-dimensional data is difficult, as we are effectively limited to two dimensions. PCA can be used to reduce dimensionality to two dimensions, but the resulting scatterplots are often very difficult to interpret. There are several non-linear dimensionality reduction tools that are explicitly tailored to visualization, representing high-dimensional structure in two dimensions.

t-SNE

t-SNE, t-distributed Stochastic Neighbor Embedding (McInnes et al. 2008), is a nonlinear dimensionality technique that is primarily used for visualizing high-dimensional systems, such as the high-level representations learned by a neural network architecture. It is sensitive to the specific parameters, and is stochastic, so each time it is run the representation will be different. But it does an excellent job at highlighting high-dimensional structure in the data.

A t-SNE method is included in `sklearn` in the `manifold` library:

```
In [44]: brand_tsne = manifold.TSNE().fit_transform(brand_ratings_sc_vals)
         brand_tsne_df = pd.DataFrame(brand_tsne, columns=['x', 'y'])
         brand_tsne_df['brand'] = brand_ratings_sc.brand
```

We get each response transformed into the t-SNE fitted space. If we overlay the brand on a scatterplot of all the points, we can see the relative position of the different brands in the t-SNE space in the upper-left panel of Fig. 9.15:

```
In [45]: sns.pairplot(brand_tsne_df, x_vars=['x'], y_vars=['y'],
                      hue='brand', size=10,
                      palette=sns.color_palette('Paired', n_colors=10))
```

UMAP

We can also use a similar technique, Uniform Manifold Approximation and Projection (McInnes et al. 2018), or UMAP, another dimensionality reduction technique for visualizing high-dimensional structure in two dimensions. The mechanics of training a UMAP model and visualizing the transformed data are similar to t-SNE:

```
In [46]: import umap

         brand_embedding = umap.UMAP().fit_transform(brand_ratings_sc_vals)
         brand_umap_df = pd.DataFrame(brand_embedding, columns=['x', 'y'])
         brand_umap_df['brand'] = brand_ratings_sc.brand

In [47]: sns.pairplot(brand_umap_df, x_vars=['x'], y_vars=['y'],
                      hue='brand', size=10,
                      palette=sns.color_palette('Paired', n_colors=10))
```

The UMAP-transformed data can be seen in the upper-right panel of Fig. 9.15.

The results between the models are similar. UMAP is faster and tends to "collapse" the clusters more. Unlike t-SNE, the trained model can also be saved and applied to new (but similar) data, which can be useful.

Comparing the t-SNE and UMAP representations to the PCA, EFA and MDS in Fig. 9.15, the additional structure provided by the non-linear dimensionality reduction algorithms is clear.

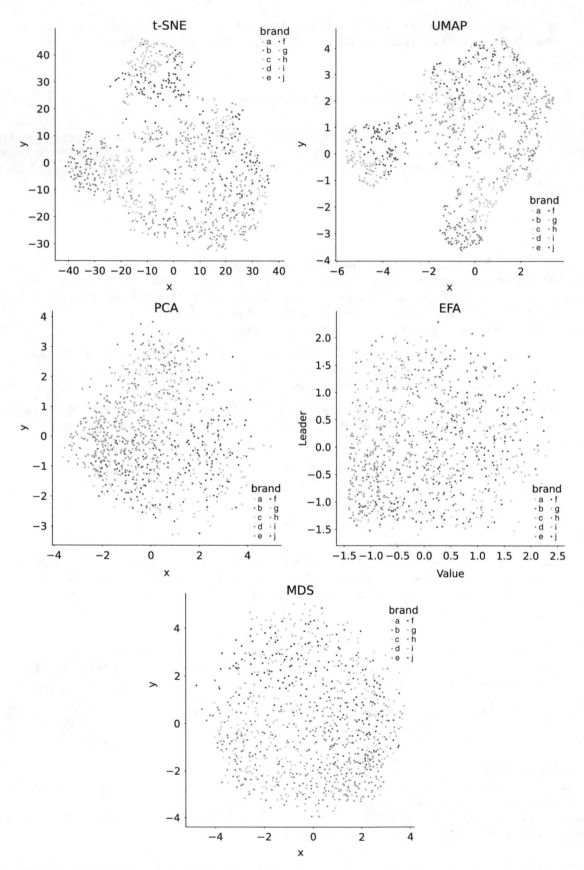

Fig. 9.15 t-SNE (upper-left), UMAP (upper-right), PCA (lower-left), EFA (lower-right), and MDS (bottom) representations of the brand ratings. The similarities between brands *b* and *c* as well as brands *f* and *g* are very evident, but the structure is far more apparent in the t-SNE and UMAP representations than in the others

9.5 Learning More*

Principal Component Analysis There is a large literature describing many procedures, options, and applications for each of the analyses in this chapter. With perceptual mapping, a valuable resource is Gower et al. (2010) which describes common problems and best practices for perceptual maps. Jolliffe (2002) provides a comprehensive text on the mathematics and applications of principal component analysis.

Factor Analysis A good conceptual overview of exploratory factor analysis with procedural notes is Fabrigar and Wegener, *Exploratory Factor Analysis* (Fabrigar and Wegener 2011). A modestly more technical volume that covers exploratory and confirmatory models together, with a social science (psychology) point of view, is Thompson, *Exploratory and Confirmatory Factor Analysis* (Thompson 2004). For examination of the mathematical bases and procedures of factor analysis, a standard text is Mulaik, *Foundations of Factor Analysis* (Mulaik 2009).

A companion to *exploratory* factor analysis is *confirmatory* factor analysis. Whereas EFA infers factor structure from a dataset, CFA tests a proposed model to see whether it corresponds well to observed data. A common use of EFA is to select items that load highly on underlying dimensions of interest. CFA allows you to confirm that the relationships between items and factors are maintained in new datasets. An introduction to CFA is given in this book's companion text, Chapman and Feit (2019), Chap. 10.

Multidimensional Scaling There are many uses and options for multidimensional scaling beyond those considered in this chapter. A readable introduction to the methods and applications is Borg, Groenen, and Mair, *Applied Multidimensional Scaling* (Borg et al. 2018). The statistical foundations and methods are detailed in Borg and Groenen, *Modern Multidimensional Scaling* (Borg and Groenen 2005).

Visualization Visualizing high-dimensional data is always a challenge. Embedding algorithms, such as t-SNE and UMAP, enable visualization through non-linear transforms of the data that maximize local structure and topography, often generating more interpretable visualizations than a PCA. See McInnes et al. (2008) and McInnes et al. (2018) for more information.

9.6 Key Points

Investigation of data complexity has several benefits. It allows inspection of the underlying dimensional relationships among variables, investigation of how observations such as brands or people vary on those dimensions, and estimation of a smaller number of more reliable dimensional scores. The following key points will assist you to investigate the underlying dimensions of your data.

Principal Component Analysis

- Principal component analysis (PCA) finds *linear functions* that explain maximal variance in observed data. A key concept is that such components are *orthogonal* (uncorrelated). A basic Python module is `sklearn.decomposition.PCA` (Sect. 9.2.1).
- A common use for PCA is a *biplot* of aggregate scores for brands or people to visualize relationships. When this is done for attitudinal data such as brand ratings it is called a *perceptual map*. This is created by aggregating the statistic of interest by entity and charting a biplot (Sect. 9.2.2).
- Because PCA components often load on many variables, the results must be inspected cautiously and in terms of relative position. It is particularly difficult to read the status of individual items from a PCA biplot (Sect. 9.2.5).

Exploratory Factor Analysis

- Exploratory factor analysis (EFA) models *latent variables* (factors) that are not observed directly but appear indirectly as observed *manifest variables*. A valuable library is `factor_analysis` (Sect. 9.3.1).
- A fundamental decision in EFA is the *number of factors* to extract. Common criteria involve inspection of a *scree* plot and extraction of factors such that all *eigenvalues* are greater than 1.0. The final determination depends on one's theory and the utility of results (Sect. 9.3.2).
- EFA uses *rotation* to adjust an initial solution to one that is mathematically equivalent but more interpretable according to one's aims. Another key decision in EFA is whether one believes the underlying latent variables should be uncorrelated (calling for an *orthogonal* rotation such as `varimax`) or correlated (calling for an *oblique* rotation such as `oblimin`) (Sect. 9.3.3).

- After performing EFA, you can extract *factor scores* that are the best estimates for each observation (respondent) on each factor. These can be extracted from the `FactorAnalysis()` object using the `get_scores()` method (Sect. 9.3.4).

Multidimensional Scaling

- Multidimensional scaling (MDS) is similar to principal component analysis but is able to work with both *metric* and *non-metric* data. MDS scaling can be performed using `sklearn.manifold.MDS()` for (Sect. 9.4).
- One advantage of MDS is that the dimensionality is constrained: you can limit it to two dimensions, in which case 100% of the variance will be represented in those dimensions
- Another advantage of MDS is that the relationship between variables is preserved, so if there is clear structure in the data, it is less likely to be lost
- However, the MDS model itself is generally less useful for subsequent analysis, unlike for the PCA or EFA

Low-Dimensional Embedding Visualization

- Like MDS, t-SNE and UMAP represent two algorithms for projecting high-dimensional structure into two dimensions (or an arbitrary number), which can be a way to understand a single observation's position within the environment of all other observations as well as visualizing overall structure within the system (Sect. 9.4.2)
- Unlike MDS, t-SNE and UMAP do not maintain relationships between observations, but rather make apparent topography present in higher dimensions. This means that clusters stand out more clearly in these representations than in the others discussed in the chapter

Chapter 10
Segmentation: Unsupervised Clustering Methods for Exploring Subpopulations

In this chapter, we tackle a canonical marketing research problem: finding, assessing, and predicting customer segments. In previous chapters we've seen how to assess relationships in data (Chap. 4), compare groups (Chap. 5), and assess models (Chap. 7). In a real segmentation project, one would use those methods to ensure that data have appropriate multivariate structure, and then begin segmentation analysis.

Segmentation is not a well-defined process and analysts vary in their definitions of segmentation as well as their approaches and philosophies. This chapter demonstrates our approach using basic models in Python. As always, this should be supplemented by readings we suggest at the end of the chapter.

We start with a warning: we have definite opinions about segmentation and what we believe are common misunderstandings and poor practices. We hope you'll be convinced by our views—but even if not, the methods here will be useful to you.

10.1 Segmentation Philosophy

The general goal of market segmentation is to find groups of customers that differ in important ways that are associated with product interest, market participation, or response to marketing efforts. By understanding the differences among groups, a marketer can make better strategic choices about opportunities, product definition, and positioning, and can engage in more effective promotion.

10.1.1 The Difficulty of Segmentation

The definition of segmentation above is a textbook description and does not reflect what is most difficult in a segmentation project: finding actionable business outcomes. It is not particularly difficult to find *groups* within consumer data; indeed, in this chapter we see several ways to do this, all of which "succeed" according to one statistical criterion or another. Rather, the difficulty is to ensure that the outcome is *meaningful* for a particular business need.

It is outside the range of this book to address the question of business need in general. However, we suggest that you ask a few questions along the following lines. If you were to find segments, what would you do about them? Would anyone in your organization use them? Why and how? Are the differences between segments large enough to be meaningful for your business? Among various solutions you might find, are there organizational efforts or politics that would make one solution more or less influential than another?

There is no magic bullet to find the "right" answer. For segmentation this means that there is no all-purpose method or algorithm that is a priori preferable to others. This does not mean that the choice of a method is irrelevant or arbitrary; rather, one cannot necessarily determine in advance which approach will work best for a novel problem. As a form of optimization, segmentation is likely to require an iterative approach that successively tests and improves its answer to a business need.

Segmentation is like slicing a pie, and any pie might be sliced in an infinite number of ways. Your task as an analyst is to consider the infinity of possible data that might be gathered, the infinity of possible groupings of that data, and the infinity of possible business questions that might be addressed. Your goal is to find a solution within those infinities that represents real differences in the data and that informs and influences business decisions.

© Springer Nature Switzerland AG 2020

J. S. Schwarz et al., *Python for Marketing Research and Analytics*, https://doi.org/10.1007/978-3-030-49720-0_10

Statistical methods are only part of the answer. It often happens that a "stronger" statistical solution poses complexity that makes it impossible to implement in a business context while a slightly "weaker" solution illuminates the data with a clear story and fits the business context so well that it can have broad influence.

To maximize chances of finding such a model, we recommend that an analyst expects—and prepares management to understand—two things. First, a segmentation project is not a matter of "running a segmentation study" or "doing segmentation analysis on the data." Rather, and second, it is likely to take multiple rounds of data collection and analysis to determine the important data that should be collected in the first place, to refine and test the solutions, and to conduct rounds of interpretation with business stakeholders to ensure that the results are actionable.

10.1.2   Segmentation as Clustering and Classification

In this chapter and the next, we demonstrate several methods in Python that will get you started with segmentation analysis. We explore two distinct yet related areas of statistics: *clustering* or *cluster analysis* (in this chapter) and *classification* (in Chap. 11). These are the primary branches of what is sometimes called *statistical learning* or *machine learning*, i.e., learning from data through statistical model fitting.

A key distinction in statistical learning is whether the method is *supervised* or *unsupervised*. In *supervised learning*, a model is presented with observations whose outcome status (dependent variable) is known, with a goal to predict that outcome status from the independent variables of novel observations. For example, we might use data from previous direct marketing campaigns—with a known outcome of whether each target responded or not, plus other predictor variables—to fit a model that predicts likelihood of response in a new campaign. We refer to this process as *classification*, which we discuss in the next chapter, Chap. 11.

In *unsupervised learning* we do not know the outcome groupings but are attempting to discover them from structure in the data. For instance, we might explore a direct marketing campaign and ask, "Are there groups that differ in how and when they respond to offers? If so, what are the characteristics of those groups?" We use the term *clustering* for this approach.

Clustering and classification are both useful in segmentation projects. Stakeholders often view segmentation as discovering groups in the data in order to derive new insight about customers. This obviously suggests clustering approaches because the possible customer groups are unknown. Still, classification approaches are also useful in such projects for at least two reasons: there may be outcome variables of interest that are known (such as observed in-market response) that one wishes to predict from segment membership, and if you use clustering to discover groups you will probably want to predict (i.e., classify) future responses into those groups. Thus, we view clustering and classification as complementary approaches.

A topic we do not address is how to determine what data to use for clustering, the observed *basis variables* that go into the model. That is primarily a choice based on business need, strategy, and data availability. Still, you can use the methods here to evaluate different sets of basis variables. If you have a large number of measures available and need to determine which ones are most important, the *variable importance* assessment method we review in Sect. 11.1.3 might assist. Aside from that, we assume in this chapter that the basis variables have been determined (and we use the customer relationship data from Chap. 5).

There are hundreds of books, thousands of articles, and many Python packages for clustering and classification methods, all of which propose hundreds of approaches with—as we noted above—no single "best" method. This chapter cannot cover clustering or classification in a comprehensive way, but we can give an introduction that will get you started, teach you the basics, accelerate your learning, and help you avoid some traps. As you will see, in most cases the process of fitting such models in Python is extremely similar from model to model.

10.2   Segmentation Data

We use the segmentation data (object `seg_df`) from Chap. 5. If you saved that data in Sect. 5.1.2, you can reload it (see Sect. 2.6.2 for a review of importing data):

```
In [1]: from google.colab import files

        f = files.upload()
Saving segment_dataframe_Python_intro_Ch5.csv to segment_dataframe_Python_intro_Ch5.csv
```

```
In [2]: import pandas as pd

        seg_df = pd.read_csv('segment_dataframe_Python_intro_Ch5.csv',
                             index_col=0)
```

Otherwise, you could download the dataset from the book website:

```
In [3]: import pandas as pd
        seg_df = pd.read_csv('http://bit.ly/PMR-ch5')
```

As you may recall from Chap. 5, these are simulated data with four identified segments of customers for a subscription product, and contain a few variables that are similar to data from typical consumer surveys. Each observation has the simulated respondent's age, gender, household income, number of kids, home ownership, subscription status, and assigned segment membership. In Chap. 5, we saw how to simulate this data and how to examine group differences within it. Other data sources that are often used for segmentation are customer relationship management (CRM) records, attitudinal surveys, product purchase and usage, and most generally, any dataset with observations about customers.

We check the data after loading:

```
In [4]: seg_df.head()

Out[4]:      Segment       age  gender          income  kids  own_home  \
        0   travelers  60.794945    male    57014.537526     0      True
        1   travelers  61.764535  female    43796.941252     0     False
        2   travelers  47.493356    male    51095.344683     0      True
        3   travelers  60.963694    male    56457.722237     0      True
        4   travelers  60.594199  female   103020.070798     0      True


           subscribe
        0      False
        1      False
        2      False
        3       True
        4      False
```

We use the subscription segment data for two purposes: to examine clustering methods that find intrinsic groupings (unsupervised learning, in this chapter), and to show how classification methods learn to predict group membership from known cases (supervised learning, in Chap. 11).

10.3 Clustering

We examine three clustering procedures that are illustrative of the hundreds of available methods. You'll see that the general procedure for finding and evaluating clusters in Python is similar across the methods.

To begin, we review two *distance-based* clustering methods, *hierarchical* and *k-means*. Distance-based methods attempt to find groups that minimize the distance between members within the group, while maximizing the distance of members from other groups. Hierarchical clusters does this by modeling the data in a tree structure, while k-means uses group centroids (central points).

Then we examine a *model-based* clustering method, a *Gaussian mixture model*. Model-based methods view the data as a mixture of groups sampled from different distributions, but whose original distribution and group membership has been "lost" (i.e., is unknown). The Gaussian mixture model method attempts to model the data such that the observed variance can be best represented by a small number of Gaussian (normal) variables with specific distribution characteristics such as different means and standard deviations.

10.3.1 The Steps of Clustering

Clustering analysis requires two stages: finding a proposed cluster solution and evaluating that solution for one's business needs. For each method we go through the following steps:

- Transform the data if needed for a particular clustering method; for instance, some methods require all numeric data (e.g., k-means)
- Scale the data if there are large differences in the magnitudes between columns. Distance-based methods are sensitive to those and can be dominated by a single dimension if it is much larger than the others (e.g., income in our data).
- Check for outliers in the data, which can dominate the clustering. Consider removing outlier data points. Note that we skip this step in our analysis.
- Apply the clustering method and save its result to an object. For most methods this requires specifying the number (K) of groups desired.
- For some methods, further parse the object to obtain a solution with K groups (e.g., `fcluster()` for extracting clusters from a linkage matrix).
- Examine the solution in the model object with regards to the underlying data, and consider whether it answers a business question.

As we've already argued, the most difficult part of that process is the last step: establishing whether a proposed statistical solution answers a business need. Ultimately, a cluster solution is largely just a vector of purported group assignments for each observation, such as "1, 1, 4, 3, 2, 3, 2, 2, 4, 1, 4 ...." It is up to you to figure out whether that tells a meaningful story for your data.

Transforming and Scaling the Data

The original dataset `seg_df` contains "known" segment assignments that have been provided for the data from some other source (as might occur from some human coding process). Because our task here is to discover segments, we create a copy `seg_sub` that omits those assignments, so we don't accidentally include the known values when exploring segmentation methods. (Later, in the chapter on classification, we will use the correct assignments because they are needed to train the classification models.)

While some clustering models can make use of categorical variables, the approaches we describe in this chapter use numerical data. In this dataset, all categorical variables are binary. `subscribe` and `own_home` are already explicitly binary, coded as booleans. Python functions that expect numeric values generally treat booleans as numeric values, 0 or 1 for `False` or `True`, respectively. We will convert `gender` to a boolean variable `is_female` and drop the `gender` column when we drop the `Segment` columns:

```
In [5]: seg_df['is_female'] = seg.gender == 'female'
        seg_sub = seg.drop(['Segment', 'gender'], axis=1)
        seg_sub.head()
```

Additionally, distance-based clustering approaches are sensitive to the scale of the variables. A change of 10 is relatively insignificant in income, but quite significant in the number of children! However, the distance metric would treat those equally. To address this we can scale the data as we have in past chapters:

```
In [6]: from sklearn import preprocessing

        seg_sc = pd.DataFrame(preprocessing.scale(seg_sub),
                        columns=seg_sub.columns)
        seg_sc.head()
```

```
Out[6]:        age    income       kids   own_home   subscribe  is_female
        0  1.551729  0.328689  -0.902199   1.120553   -0.363422  -0.960769
        1  1.627442 -0.356010  -0.902199  -0.892416   -0.363422   1.040833
        2  0.513037  0.022062  -0.902199   1.120553   -0.363422  -0.960769
        3  1.564906  0.299844  -0.902199   1.120553    2.751623  -0.960769
        4  1.536053  2.711871  -0.902199   1.120553   -0.363422   1.040833
```

The scaled data look appropriate. We have created two new dataframes. One, `seg_sub`, has all the columns that we need for this analysis and no more. The other, `seg_sc`, has the same columns, but scaled such that columns are directly comparable.

A Quick Check Function

We recommend that you think hard about how you would know whether a solution—assignments of observations to groups—that is proposed by a clustering method is useful for your business problem. Just because some grouping is proposed by an algorithm does not mean that it will help your business. One way we often approach this is to write a simple function that summarizes the data and allows quick inspection of the high-level differences between groups.

A segment inspection function may be complex depending on the business need and might include plotting in addition to data summarization. Pandas provides the `pivot_table()` function that allows us to aggregate by any arbitrary index:

```
In [7]: pd.pivot_table(seg_sub, index=seg_df.Segment)
```

```
Out[7]:                  age          income   is_female       kids   own_home  \
        Segment
        moving up    36.216087   51763.552666      0.700   1.857143   0.357143
        suburb_mix   39.284730   55552.282925      0.530   1.950000   0.480000
        travelers    57.746500   62609.655328      0.325   0.000000   0.662500
        urban_hip    23.873716   20267.737317      0.320   1.140000   0.140000


                     subscribe
        Segment
        moving up     0.214286
        suburb_mix    0.070000
        travelers     0.025000
        urban_hip     0.220000
```

The `pivot_table()` function calculates the mean by default, but any suitable function or list of functions can be passed to the `aggfunc` argument:

```
In [8]: import numpy as np

        # Output not shown
        pd.pivot_table(seg_sub, index=seg_df.Segment,
                       aggfunc=[np.mean, np.std]).unstack()
In [9]: pd.pivot_table(seg_sub, index=seg_df.Segment,
                       aggfunc=lambda x: np.percentile(x, 95))
```

However, for purposes here we use a simple function that reports the mean by group. We use `mean` here instead of a more robust metric such as `median` because we have several binary variables and `mean()` easily shows the mixture proportion for them (i.e., 0.5 means a 50% mix of 0 and 1).

We create our own function to simplify calling it:

```
In [10]: def check_clusters(data, labels):
             return pd.pivot_table(data,
                                   index=labels)

         # Output not shown
         check_clusters(seg_sub, seg_df.Segment)
```

While making this a function isn't really necessary in this case, there are several reasons to do so. Writing our own function allows us to minimize typing by providing a short command. By providing a consistent and simple interface, it reduces risk of error. And it is extensible; as an analysis proceeds, we might decide to add to the function, expanding it to report variance metrics or to plot results, without needing to change how we invoke it (something we will do in this chapter, see Sect. 10.3.4).

With a summary function of this kind we are easily able to answer the following questions related to the business value of a proposed solution:

- Are there obvious differences in group means?
- Does the differentiation point to some underlying story to tell?
- Do we see immediately odd results such as a mean equal to the value of one data level?

This simple function will help us to inspect cluster solutions efficiently. It is not intended to be a substitute for detailed analysis—and it takes shortcuts such as treating categorical variables as numbers, which is inadvisable except for analysts who understand what they're doing—yet it provides a quick first check of whether there is something interesting (or uninteresting) occurring in a solution.

10.3.2 Hierarchical Clustering

Pairwise Distances

The primary information in hierarchical clustering is the *distance* between observations. There are many ways to compute distance, and we start by examining the best-known method, the *Euclidean distance*. For two observations (vectors) X and Y, the Euclidean distance d is:

$$d = \sqrt{\sum (A - B)^2} \tag{10.1}$$

For single pairs of observations, such as $A = \{1, 2, 3\}$ and $B = \{2, 3, 2\}$ we can compute the distance easily in Python using numpy:

```
In [11]: # Vector of differences
         np.array([1, 2, 3]) - np.array([2, 3, 2])

Out[11]: array([-1, -1,  1])

In [12]: # Sum of the squared distances
         np.sum((np.array([1, 2, 3]) - np.array([2, 3, 2]))**2)

Out[12]: 3

In [13]: # Root sum of the squared distances
         np.sqrt(np.sum((np.array([1, 2, 3]) - np.array([2, 3, 2]))**2))

Out[13]: 1.7320508075688772
```

When there are many pairs, this can be done with the `pdist()` function from the scipy `distance` module. Let's check it first for the simple X, Y example:

```
In [14]: from scipy.spatial import distance

         distance.pdist([np.array([1, 2, 3]), np.array([2, 3, 2])])

Out[14]: array([1.73205081])
```

A limitation is that Euclidean distance is only defined when observations are numeric. In our data `seg_df` it is impossible to compute the distance between `male` and `female`. This is why we transformed the gender column into a boolean column. If we did not care about the factor variables, then we could compute Euclidean distance using only the numeric columns.

The `scipy.spatial.distance` module also includes the `squareform` function which computes a distance matrix. We can observe how it works on the first three rows of the `seg_sc` dataframe:

```
In [15]: distance.squareform(distance.pdist(seg_sc.iloc[:3]))

Out[15]: array([[0.        , 2.92113022, 1.08300539],
                [2.92113022, 0.        , 3.07299428],
                [1.08300539, 3.07299428, 0.        ]])
```

To find the distance between the second and third variable, we can look at the second row, third column or the third row, second column and see that the distance is 3.07. The distance matrix is symmetric and, as expected, the distance of an observation from itself is 0. Notice that the square-form distance matrix has a lot of redundant information, which we can remove to make it more memory efficient. This can be important when dealing with datasets with a large number of columns.

To get a more compact form, we use `pdist()` which returns a *condensed*, *vector-form* distance matrix:

```
In [16]: distance.pdist(seg_sc.iloc[:3])

Out[16]: array([2.92113022, 1.08300539, 3.07299428])
```

The condensed distance matrix is more memory efficient, but is harder for a human to inspect.

If we inspect the pairwise distances in our dataset, the importance of scaling the data becomes clear.

```
In [17]: import matplotlib.pyplot as plt
         plt.style.use('seaborn-white')

         plt.figure(figsize=(5,10))
         plt.subplot(2,1,1)
         plt.hist(distance.pdist(seg_sub))
         plt.title('Pairwise distances from unscaled data')
         plt.xlabel('Distance')
         plt.ylabel('Count')
         plt.subplot(2,1,2)
         plt.hist(distance.pdist(seg_sc))
         plt.title('Pairwise distances from scaled data')
         plt.xlabel('Distance')
         plt.ylabel('Count')
```

As we can see in the left panel of Fig. 10.1, the unscaled data produces a highly skewed distribution of distances, which is dominated by differences in income between customers (rows in the data). Contrast that with the distribution of distances from the scaled data in the right panel.

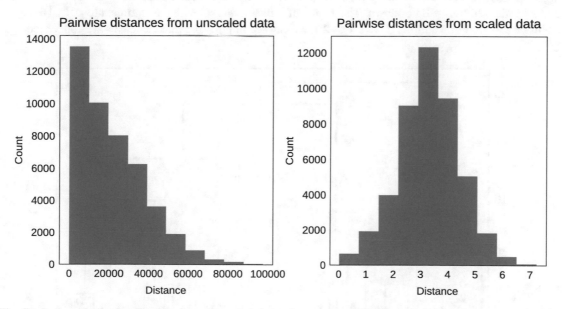

Fig. 10.1 The distribution of pairwise distances from the unscaled data is very skewed (left panel), in contrast to the approximately normal distribution from the scaled data (right panel)

Hierarchical Clustering in Python

Hierarchical clustering is a popular method that groups observations according to their similarity. The linkage() function from the scipy hierarchy module generates hierarchical clustering. The clusters are generated using a distance-based algorithm that operates on a *dissimilarity* matrix, an N-by-N matrix that reports a metric for the *distance* between each pair of observations.

The hierarchical clustering method begins with each observation in its own cluster. It then successively joins neighboring observations or clusters one at a time according to their distances from one another, and continues this until all observations are linked. This process of repeatedly joining observations and groups is known as an *agglomerative* method. Because it is both very popular and exemplary of other methods, we present hierarchical clustering in more detail than the other clustering algorithms.

We pass our data into the linkage() function, which calculates distances and runs the clustering algorithm, producing a linkage matrix:

```
In [18]: from scipy.cluster import hierarchy

         linkages = hierarchy.linkage(seg_sc, method='ward')
```

We use the *Ward* linkage method, which forms groups that minimize the total within-cluster variance.

Passing the linkage matrix to the dendrogram() function will plot a tree representing the linkage matrix:

```
In [19]: hierarchy.dendrogram(linkages)
         plt.show()
```

The resulting tree for all $N = 300$ observations of seg_sub is shown in Fig. 10.2.

A hierarchical dendrogram is interpreted primarily by height and where observations are joined. The height represents the dissimilarity between elements that are joined. At the lowest level of the tree in Fig. 10.2 we see that elements are combined into small groups of 2–10 that are relatively similar, and then those groups are successively combined with less similar groups moving up the tree. The horizontal ordering of branches is not important; branches could exchange places with no change in interpretation.

Figure 10.2 is difficult to read. There are two ways in which we can make it simpler to read.

One is with the truncate_mode and p arguments to dendrogram(). If truncate_mode is set to 'lastp' or to 'level', a condensed tree will be shown. The degree of truncation is set with the argument to p. In lastp mode, only p branches will be shown. For example, if we set p=20, we can see in Fig. 10.3 that the leaves are condensed.

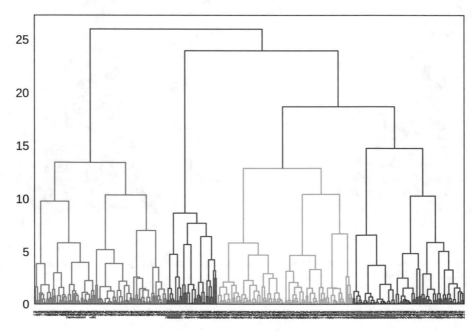

Fig. 10.2 Complete dendrogram for the scaled segmentation data, using linkage() and dendrogram() from the scipy hierarchy module

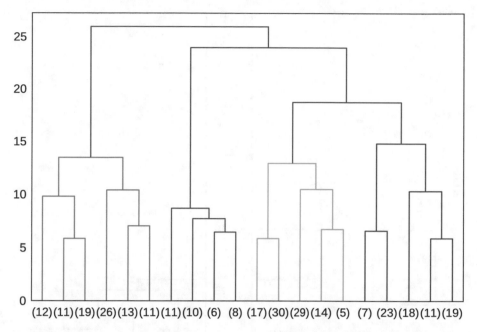

Fig. 10.3 A truncated tree, showing only 20 branches, each of which represents multiple leaves (the number of leaves are shown in parentheses)

```
In [20]: hierarchy.dendrogram(linkages, orientation='top',
                              truncate_mode='lastp', p=20)
         plt.show()
```

The number of leaves that each branch represents are indicated in parentheses. If an individual leaf is present, its label will not have parentheses.

It is also helpful to zoom in on one section of the chart. We can do so using the `xlim()` function:

```
In [21]: plt.subplot(1,2,1)
         hierarchy.dendrogram(linkages, leaf_rotation=0)
         plt.xlim((0,200))
         plt.subplot(1,2,2)
         hierarchy.dendrogram(linkages, leaf_rotation=0)
         plt.xlim((2800, 3000))
         plt.show()
```

The result is shown in Fig. 10.4, where we are now able to read the observation labels (which defaults to the row names—usually the row numbers—of observations in the dataframe). Each node at the bottom represents one customer, and the tree show how each has been grouped progressively with other customers. Here we can see the far left and right edges of the tree and the observations present in those parts of the tree.

We can check the similarity of observations by selecting a few rows listed in Fig. 10.4. Observations 17 and 51 are represented as being quite similar because they are linked at a very low height, as are observations 163 and 88. On the other hand, observations 17 and 163 are only joined at the highest level of the tree and thus should be relatively dissimilar. We can check those directly:

```
In [22]: # Similar
         seg_sub.loc[[17, 51]]
```

```
Out[22]:         age          income  kids  own_home  subscribe  is_female
         17  73.266707  70157.058678     0     False      False       True
         51  71.172291  75554.353842     0     False      False       True
```

```
In [23]: # Similar
         seg_sub.loc[[163, 88]]
```

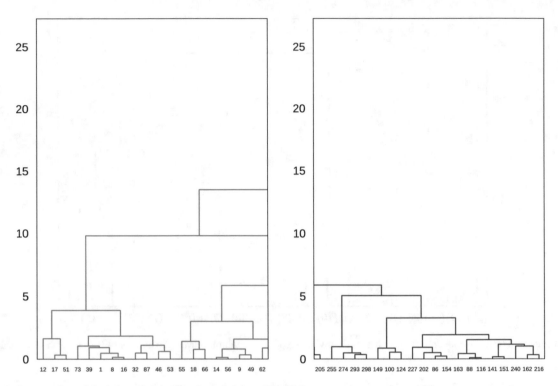

Fig. 10.4 A close up view of the left- and right-most branches from Fig. 10.2

```
Out[23]:           age          income  kids  own_home  subscribe  is_female
          163  39.653607   48996.400976     2      True      False      False
           88  40.106702   41744.977842     2      True      False      False

In [24]: # Dissimilar
         seg_sub.loc[[17,163]]

Out[24]:           age          income  kids  own_home  subscribe  is_female
           17  73.266707   70157.058678     0     False      False       True
          163  39.653607   48996.400976     2      True      False      False
```

The first two pairs—observations that are neighbors in the dendrogram—are similar on all variables (age, gender, income, etc.). The third pair—observations taken from widely separated branches—differ substantially.

We can check one of the goodness-of-fit metrics for a hierarchical cluster solution. One method is the *cophenetic correlation* coefficient (CPCC), which assesses how well the dendrogram matches the distance metric (Sokal and Rohlf 1962). We use `cophenet()` to compare the distances from the linkages with the `pdist()` metrics:

```
In [25]: hierarchy.cophenet(linkages, distance.pdist(seg_sc))[0]

Out[25]: 0.5985290160084774
```

CPCC is interpreted similarly to Pearson's r. In this case, CPCC is about 0.6, indicating a moderately strong fit, meaning that the hierarchical tree represents the distances between customers well.

10.3.3 Hierarchical Clustering Continued: Groups from `fcluster`

How do we get specific segment assignments? A dendrogram can be cut into clusters at any height desired, resulting in different numbers of groups. For instance, if Fig. 10.2 is cut at a height of 25 there are $K = 2$ groups (draw a horizontal line at 25 and count how many branches it intersects; each cluster below is a group), while cutting at height of 9 defines $K = 11$ groups.

Because a dendrogram might be cut at any point, an analyst must specify the number of groups desired. We can see the clusters based on where the dendrogram would be cut by passing the `color_thresh` argument, which will color only the branches below that threshold. In Fig. 10.2, the default value selected 4 clusters, but we can manually set it to a different value:

```
In [26]:  # Not shown
          hierarchy.dendrogram(linkages, color_threshold=9)
          plt.show()
```

We obtain the assignment vector for observations using `fcluster()`. We specify a criterion type as `'maxclust'` and a threshold of 4 (t=4), which tells `fcluster()` that we expect 4 clusters. There are other clustering criteria that you can read about in the `fcluster()` documentation.

```
In [27]:  labels = hierarchy.fcluster(linkages, t=4, criterion='maxclust')
          list(zip(*np.unique(labels, return_counts=True)))

Out[27]:  [(1, 92), (2, 35), (3, 95), (4, 78)]
```

`fcluster()` returned the cluster label for each observation. We use `np.unique(return_counts=True)` to get the observation count for each cluster. We use `list(zip(...))` just as a formatting trick. Here we use the "`*`" operator to unpack the tuple of values returned by `np.unique()` and pass them to the `zip()` function. What does "unpacking" mean in this context? Since the values are returned in a tuple, they cannot be directly passed as arguments. We could have assigned the output to a variable, say `unique_label_counts` and then used the command `zip(unique_label_counts[0], unique_label_counts[1])` to achieve the same effect.

We see that groups 1, 3, and 4 are similar in size while group 2 is less than half the size of the others. Note that the class labels (1, 2, 3, 4) are in arbitrary order and are not meaningful in themselves.

We use our custom summary function `check_clusters()`, defined above, to inspect the variables in `seg_sub` with reference to the four clusters:

```
In [28]:  check_clusters(seg_sub, labels)
```

```
Out[28]:          age          income  is_female        kids  own_home  subscribe
       1  54.474706  63219.658293   0.250000    0.152174  0.521739        0.0
       2  34.523881  41685.199147   0.542857    1.514286  0.314286        1.0
       3  38.204641  51578.802282   1.000000    1.873684  0.463158        0.0
       4  31.122503  38790.506683   0.089744    1.756410  0.384615        0.0
```

We see that group 2 contains all of the subscribers. Group 1 is the oldest and has the highest income and home ownership. Group 3 contains only women and has an intermediate level of income, age, and home ownership. Group 4 is predominately male and younger, with the lowest income.

For comparison, we can run the same analysis with the unscaled data and see what we find:

```
In [29]:  linkages_unscaled = hierarchy.linkage(seg_sub, method='ward')
          hierarchy.dendrogram(linkages_unscaled)
          plt.show()
```

We see in Fig. 10.5 that 3 clusters are more appropriate than 4. Also, note that the distances (indicated on the y-axis) are much larger the before: these clusters are dominated by income.

Using our `check_clusters()` function, we see a slightly different pattern:

```
In [30]:  labels_unscaled = hierarchy.fcluster(linkages_unscaled, t=3,
                                          criterion='maxclust')
          check_clusters(seg_sub, labels_unscaled)
```

```
Out[30]:          age          income  is_female        kids  own_home  subscribe
       1  26.238778  20026.508497   0.320755    1.113208  0.150943   0.207547
       2  48.102952  74464.263260   0.394737    1.052632  0.500000   0.052632
       3  42.283774  49591.504755   0.567251    1.421053  0.508772   0.116959
```

The three clusters are clearly very segregated by income, with group 1 being low, group 2 being high, and group 3 being intermediate. But we see potentially interesting patterns beyond that. Group 1 is low in income, young, two-thirds male, with

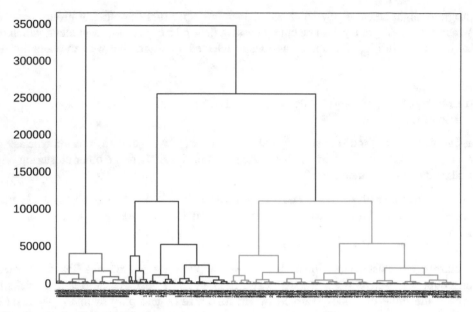

Fig. 10.5 Complete dendrogram for the unscaled segmentation data

few kids and low home-ownership, but a high subscription rate. Group 2 has the lowest subscription rate, but the highest income. Group 3 has a similar home-ownership rate as group 2, but twice the subscription rate, the most women, and more children.

It is interesting that, in this case, despite being defined by income, the clusters are well-differentiated in the other dimensions as well. We would argue that these clusters are probably more actionable from a business perspective. This goes to show that clustering is more about *interpretability* than about *accuracy*. In this case, the unscaled data outperformed the scaled data because *income is a good proxy for other demographics in our dataset*, something that will not surprise marketing researchers.

However, if the variable with the longest range had not been informative, the unscaled data would have likely done a better job revealing structure within the dataset.

We can visualize cluster membership based on values to get a better understanding. We create a helper function to produce a scatterplot of two of the columns and then color each point based on cluster membership. We can then investigate, for example, cluster membership based on age and income:

```
In [31]: def cluster_plot_raw(x, y, labels):
             for l in np.unique(labels):
                 idx = labels == l
                 plt.scatter(x[idx],
                             y[idx],
                             label=l)
             plt.legend()
             plt.xlabel(x.name)
             plt.ylabel(y.name)
```

```
In [32]: cluster_plot_raw(seg_sub.age, seg_sub.income, labels_unscaled)
```

This visualization (Fig. 10.6) confirms what we suspected: income dominates the clustering. Whether this is interesting or uninteresting depends on your objective. Overall, this demonstrates why you should expect to try several methods and iterate in order to find something useful.

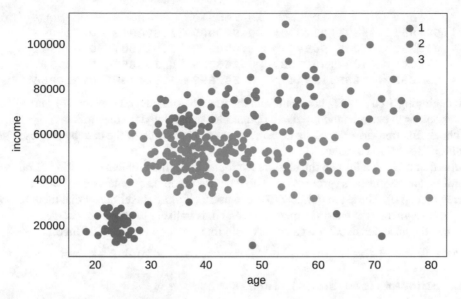

Fig. 10.6 Plotting the 3-segment hierarchical solution from the unscaled segmentation data by age and income, with color representing segment membership. We see that the clustering appears to be defined primarily by income

10.3.4 Mean-Based Clustering: k_means ()

K-means clustering attempts to find groups that are most compact, in terms of the mean sum-of-squares deviation of each observation from the multivariate center (*centroid*) of its assigned group. Like hierarchical clustering, k-means is a very popular approach.

How does the basic algorithm work? It starts with an initial set of means, which may be random or nonrandom. The number of means is a parameter that must be specified. The algorithm then alternates between two steps:

- **Assign:** Each observation is assigned to the cluster represented by the nearest mean, nearness being defined by the least squared Euclidean distance
- **Update:** Calculate the centroid of each cluster, which collectively become the new means

This alteration repeats until the assignment of observations is stable.

Because it explicitly computes a mean deviation, k-means clustering relies on Euclidean distance. Thus it is only appropriate for numeric data or data that can be reasonably coerced to numeric, unlike hierarchical clustering which can utilize different distance metrics and thus be applied to categorical data as well.

We will extend our check_clusters () function by adding a line to determine cluster sizes:

```
In [33]: def check_clusters(data, labels):
             print(list(zip(*np.unique(labels, return_counts=True))))

             return pd.pivot_table(data,
                                   index=labels)
```

We can run the k_means () function from the cluster module of sci-kit learn. K-means requires specification of the number of clusters to find. We ask for four clusters with n_clusters=4. We will first run this on our scaled data:

```
In [34]: import numpy as np
         from sklearn import cluster

         np.random.seed(536)
         centroids, labels, inertia = cluster.k_means(seg_sc, n_clusters=4)
         check_clusters(seg_sub, labels)

[(0, 73), (1, 101), (2, 91), (3, 35)]
```

```
Out[34]:              age           income   is_female        kids   own_home   subscribe
        0      31.672851     39921.012710    0.000000    1.821918   0.315068         0.0
        1      37.043120     49285.905471    1.000000    1.811881   0.405941         0.0
        2      55.112042     64282.900228    0.263736    0.142857   0.637363         0.0
        3      34.523881     41685.199147    0.542857    1.514286   0.314286         1.0
```

Note that the line beginning [(0, 73), is output from the function check_clusters() and will appear in the output block in a Colab notebook or in between the input and output blocks in a Jupyter notebook.

We also ran our check function check_clusters() to do a quick check of the data by proposed group, where cluster assignments are found in the labels vector.

These clusters superficially look a lot like the clusters we found in the hierarchical clustering of our scaled data. We have a group containing all of our subscribers (group 4). We now have a group that contains only women (group 1) and a group that contains only men (group 0). These are unlikely to prove useful. Telling stakeholders that there are two really important groups uncovered by our segmentation analysis, men and women, is unlikely to receive accolades!

What about if we use the unscaled data? We can check with four groups and also with three:

```
In [35]: centroids, k_labels_unscaled4, inertia = cluster.k_means(seg_sub,
                                                            n_clusters=4)
        check_clusters(seg_sub, k_labels_unscaled4)

[(0, 96), (1, 55), (2, 42), (3, 107)]

Out[35]:              age           income   is_female        kids   own_home   subscribe
        0      42.346106     60157.505981    0.541667    1.625000   0.447917    0.093750
        1      27.809087     20457.938690    0.327273    1.072727   0.163636    0.200000
        2      52.117381     81545.927332    0.309524    0.476190   0.571429    0.023810
        3      41.993915     45566.356272    0.570093    1.373832   0.532710    0.130841

In [36]: centroids, k_labels_unscaled3, inertia = cluster.k_means(seg_sub,
                                                            n_clusters=3)
        check_clusters(seg_sub, k_labels_unscaled3)

[(0, 64), (1, 65), (2, 171)]

Out[36]:              age           income   is_female        kids   own_home   subscribe
        0      29.635597     22520.530838    0.343750    1.109375   0.171875    0.187500
        1      49.494653     76393.497749    0.384615    0.923077   0.507692    0.046154
        2      41.889908     51426.578619    0.567251    1.467836   0.520468    0.116959
```

These groups, again, look rather like the hierarchical clusters we found with the unscaled data. Similar to those, they look potentially interesting. In each grouping, we have a young, lower-income group that is predominately male, with low home-ownership and a high subscription rate. We also have an older, higher-income group with a low subscription rate. In the four-segment model, both of those groups are better differentiated.

In the four-segment model, the intermediate group is split in two. This could be of interest or not. One might, for example, try to understand what is underlying the substantial difference in subscription rates between these otherwise undifferentiated groups.

Note that in clustering models, the group labels are in arbitrary order, so don't worry if your solution shows the same pattern with different labels.

We can visually check the differences in income between the groups using a boxplot:

```
In [37]: import matplotlib.pyplot as plt
        seg_sub.boxplot(column='income', by=k_labels_unscaled4)
        plt.xlabel('Cluster')
        plt.ylabel('Income')
        plt.suptitle('') # Remove cluster id subtitle
```

The result is Fig. 10.7, which shows substantial differences in income by segment.

We may also visualize the clusters by plotting them against a dimensional plot. We write a function to perform dimensional reduction with principal components and then plot the observations with cluster membership identified (see Chap. 9 to review principal component analysis and plotting):

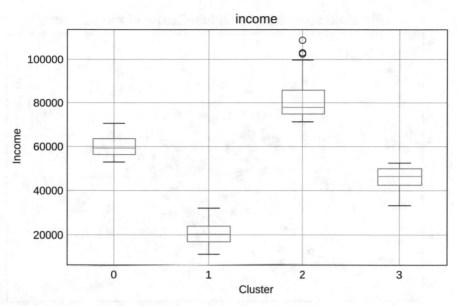

Fig. 10.7 Boxplot of income by cluster as found with k_means()

```
In [38]: from sklearn import decomposition
         from matplotlib import cm

         def cluster_plot(data_df, labels):
           p = decomposition.PCA(random_state=132, svd_solver='full')
           scaled_transformed = p.fit_transform(preprocessing.scale(data_df))
           for l in np.unique(labels):
             idx = np.where(labels == l)[0]
             plt.scatter(scaled_transformed[idx, 0],
                     scaled_transformed[idx, 1],
                  label=l)
           plt.legend()
           plt.title('First two components explain {}% of the variance'
                  .format(round(100*p.explained_variance_ratio_[:2].sum())))
           plt.xlabel('First principal component')
           plt.ylabel('Second principal component')


         cluster_plot(seg_sub, k_labels_unscaled4)
```

This produces Fig. 10.8, which plots cluster assignment by color against the first two principal components of the predictors (see Sect. 9.2.2). Groups 1 and 2 are largely overlapping (in this dimensional reduction) while groups 0 and 3 are more differentiated. This is consistent with what we observed using the output from check_clusters().

Overall, this is an interesting cluster solution for our segmentation data. The groups here are clearly differentiated on key variables such as age and income. With this information, an analyst might cross-reference the group membership with key variables (as we did using our check_clusters()) function and then look at the relative differentiation of the groups (as in Fig. 10.8).

This may suggest a business strategy. In the present case, for instance, we see that group 3 is modestly well-differentiated, and has the highest average income. That may make it a good target for a potential campaign. Or we might focus on group 0 as our segment with the highest subscription rate and understand how to grow our market there. Many other strategies are possible, too; the key point is that the analysis provides interesting options to consider.

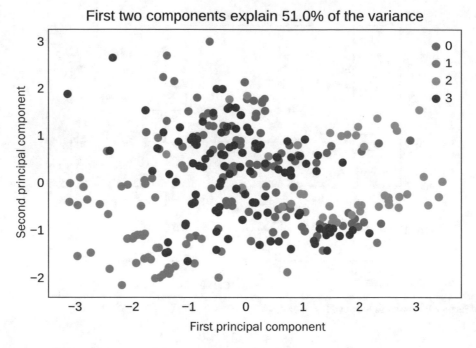

Fig. 10.8 Cluster plot created for the four group solution from k_means(). This shows the observations on a multidimensional scaling plot with group membership identified by the color

10.3.5   Model-Based Clustering: `GaussianMixture()`

The key idea for model-based clustering is that observations come from groups with different statistical distributions (such as different means and variances). The algorithms try to find the best set of such underlying distributions to explain the observed data. We use the `mixture` module from scikit-learn to demonstrate this.

Such models are also known as "mixture models" because it is assumed that the data reflect a mixture of observations drawn from different groups called components, although we don't know which component each observation was drawn from. `GaussianMixture()` models assume the observations are drawn from a mixture of normal (also known as *Gaussian*) distributions. We are trying to estimate the underlying component parameters and the mixture proportions.

How does this work? The most common approach is called the *expectation maximization (EM) algorithm*, which is analogous to that used for k-means, but rather than iteratively estimating centroids and using distances from those centroids to it estimates the probability of each point belonging to each Gaussian component (which is defined by its mean and variance). So, starting with random parameters for each model, the algorithm repeats these steps:

- **Assign:** Each observation is assigned to the component that it is most likely to belong to
- **Update:** The parameters for each component are updated given the points assigned to it

As you might guess, because `GaussianMixture()` models data with normal distributions, it uses only numeric data. The model is estimated with the `fit()` method on the `GaussianMixture()` and labels are generated with the `predict()` method:

```
In [39]: from sklearn import mixture

         gmm4 = mixture.GaussianMixture(n_components=4,
                                        covariance_type='full',
                                        random_state=323).fit(seg_sub)
         gmm4_labels = gmm4.predict(seg_sub)
         gmm4.bic(seg_sub)

Out[39]: 7892.76042330893
```

`GaussianMixture()` requires as input the number of model components and the covariance structure within each component. Above, we fit the model with four components, i.e. four groups or clusters, which each have a full covariance

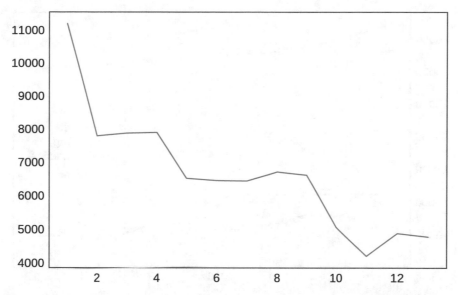

Fig. 10.9 BIC values of `GaussianMixture()` models as a function of the number of components. Model fit does not improve beyond five components until we get to ten components, which is likely too many to interpret effectively

structure. Note that since this is a probability model, we have available metrics on the model goodness of fit, such as the Bayesian Information Criterion (BIC) (Raftery 1995). This gives us an objective function on which to optimize the model, for instance, by optimizing the number of components. Additionally, since the cluster assignments are probabilistic, we can inspect the model confidence for each individual point.

First, let's determine what the best number of clusters is. We can do so by fitting models with different numbers of components and comparing the BIC values:

```
In [40]: gmm_n_test = [mixture.GaussianMixture(n_components=n,
                                    covariance_type='full',
                                    random_state=323)
                       .fit(seg_sub) for n in range(1,14)]
         plt.plot(range(1, 14), [g.bic(seg_sub) for g in gmm_n_test])
```

Lower BIC values mean a better model fit. We can see in Fig. 10.9 that four components is not optimal, but beyond five components the BIC values do not continue to drop until we get to ten components. Note that BIC values for good fits would be expected to be *negative*, suggesting that these model fits are not very robust.

Another feature we must choose for the Gaussian mixture models is the covariance type. We can vary both the covariance type and the number of components to improve our model further. Note that here we are using *dictionary comprehension* as well as *list comprehension*. Dictionary comprehension is analogous to list comprehension, but generates a `dict` object rather than a `list`. See Sect. 2.4.10 for a refresher on list comprehension.

```
In [41]: gmm_n_v_test = {v: [mixture.GaussianMixture(n_components=n,
                                      covariance_type=v,
                                      random_state=323)
                             .fit(seg_sub) for n in range(1,14)]
                         for v in ['full', 'tied', 'diag', 'spherical']}
         gmm_n_v_test_bic = {v: [g.bic(seg_sub) for g in m]
                             for v, m in gmm_n_v_test.items()}
         pd.DataFrame(gmm_n_v_test_bic).plot()
```

We can see in Fig. 10.10 that the full covariance that we tried initially does a reasonable job, but diagonal covariance gives the best fit, and six components is an appropriate number.

Let's next inspect the clusters we find with six components:

```
In [42]: gmm5 = mixture.GaussianMixture(n_components=5,
                             covariance_type='diag',
```

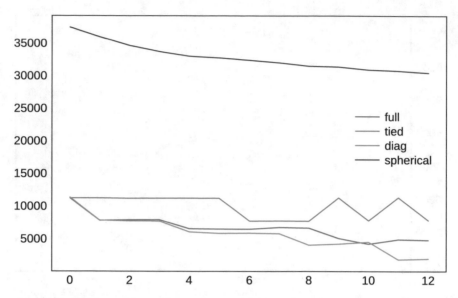

Fig. 10.10 BIC values of `GaussianMixture()` models as a function of the number of components and covariance type. Diagonal and full covariance provide the best fits

```
                                              random_state=323).fit(seg_sub)
        gmm5_labels = gmm5.predict(seg_sub)

In [43]: check_clusters(seg_sub, gmm5_labels)

[(0, 129), (1, 32), (2, 21), (3, 4), (4, 114)]


Out[43]:          age         income   is_female       kids  own_home  subscribe
        0   37.366073   52743.873543   0.581395   2.248062  0.465116     0.0000
        1   23.630276   20251.707688   0.375000   1.593750  0.000000     0.3125
        2   36.492245   51554.737478   0.619048   1.857143  0.333333     1.0000
        3   52.523755   44005.211404   0.000000   0.500000  1.000000     1.0000
        4   50.212110   56931.154434   0.385965   0.000000  0.543860     0.0000
```

These clusters do not look to be very actionable. Nearly all observations fall in either group 0 or group 4, which include all non-subscribers. Those two groups are differentiated on a few measures, most notably children: individuals in group 4 have no children whereas those in group 0 have, on average, 2.24 children. Again, the idea that individuals with and without children might be important segments very well may be accurate and business-relevant, but it wouldn't really take a sophisticated clustering analysis to find that!

10.3.6   Recap of Clustering

We've covered three methods to identify potential groups of observations in a dataset. In the next section we examine the problem of how to predict (classify) observations into groups after those groups have been defined. Before we move to that problem, there are two points that are crucial for success in segmentation projects:

- Different methods are likely to yield different solutions, and in general there is no absolute "right" answer. We recommend trying multiple clustering methods with different potential numbers of clusters.
- The results of segmentation are primarily about business value, and solutions should be evaluated in terms of both model fit (e.g., using BIC) *and* business utility. Although model fit is an important criterion and should not be overlooked, it is ultimately necessary that an answer can be communicated to and used by stakeholders.

10.4 Learning More*

We covered the basics of clustering . There are many places to learn more about those methods and related statistical models. A recommended introduction to the field of statistical learning is James et al., *An Introduction to Statistical Learning* (ISL) (James et al. 2013). A more advanced treatment of the topics in ISL is Hastie et al., *The Elements of Statistical Learning* (Hastie et al. 2016).

For cluster analysis, a readable text is Everitt et al., *Cluster Analysis* (Everitt et al. 2011). An introduction to latent class analysis is Collins and Lanza, *Latent Class and Latent Transition Analysis* (Collins and Lanza 2010).

Python has support for a vast number of clustering algorithms that we cannot cover here, but a few are worth mentioning. Exploring the scikit-learn `cluster` module (scikit-learn developers 2019a) and reading the associated references is a great place to learn more.

Marketing segmentation has developed approaches and nuances that differ from the typical description in statistics texts. For instance, in addition to the static, cross-sectional models considered in this chapter (where segmentation examines data at just one point in time), one might wish to consider dynamic models that take into account customer lifestyle changes over time. An overview of diverse approaches in marketing is Wedel and Kamakura, *Market Segmentation: Conceptual and Methodological Foundations* (Wedel and Kamakura 2000).

There are various ways to model changes in class membership over time. One approach is latent transition analysis (LTA), described in Collins and Lanza (2010). At the time of writing, LTA was not supported by a specific package in Python. Another approach is a finite state model such as Markov chain model (cf. Ross 2019). An alternative when change over time is metric (i.e., is conceptualized as change in a *dimension* rather than change between *groups*) is to use longitudinal structural equation modeling or latent growth curve models.

10.5 Key Points

We addressed segmentation through the lens of clustering. We examined several varieties of clustering methods and compared them. Once segments or groups are identified, classification methods can help to predict group membership status for new observations.

- The most crucial question in a segmentation project is the business aspect: will the results be useful for the purpose at hand? Will they inspire new strategies for marketing to customers? It is important to try multiple methods and evaluate the utility of their results (cf. Sect. 10.1.1).
- Distance-based clustering methods attempt to group similar observations. We examined `scipy.cluster.hierarchy()` for hierarchical clustering (Sect. 10.3.2) and `sklearn.cluster.k_means()` for k-means grouping (Sect. 10.3.4). Distance-based measures rely on having a way to express metric distance, which is a challenge for categorical data.
- Model-based clustering methods attempt to model an underlying distribution that the data express. We examined `sklearn.mixture.GaussianMixture` for model-based clustering of data assumed to be a mix of normal distributions (Sect. 10.3.5).
- Model-based methods enable calculation of Bayesian Information Criterion (BIC), which allows us to identify models with the best statistical fit (Sect. 10.3.5). We recommend that the ultimate decision to use a model's solution be made on the grounds of both statistics (i.e., excellent fit) and the business applicability of the solution (i.e., actionable implications).

Chapter 11
Classification: Assigning Observations to Known Categories

In Chap. 10, we learned about using clustering methods to identify structure within a dataset. We learned about how the most challenging part of clustering is not applying a model, but interpreting the output in a meaningful and useful way. In this chapter, we will explore *supervised learning* methods. Unlike with clustering, generally, the value of a supervised model output is inherent in the framing of the question. This makes interpretation easier, but it requires an outcome variable to have a strong relationship with its indicator variables, and it benefits from data that are well structured and clean. With statistical modeling, people often say "garbage in, garbage out," meaning that even a very sophisticated model will not be able to produce reliable results if the data are not high quality or there is no actual relationship between input and output variables.

11.1 Classification

Whereas clustering is the process of *discovering* group membership, classification is the *prediction* of membership. In this section we look at two examples of classification: predicting segment membership, and predicting who is likely to subscribe to a service.

Classification uses observations whose status is *known* to derive predictors, and then applies those predictors to new observations. When working with a single dataset it is typically split into a *training* set that is used to develop the classification model, and a *test* set that is used to determine performance. It is crucial not to assess performance on the same observations that were used to develop the model.

A classification project typically includes the following steps at a minimum:

- A dataset is collected in which group membership for each observation is known or assigned (e.g., assigned by behavioral observation, expert rating, or clustering procedures)
- The dataset is split into a training set and a test set. A common pattern is to select 50–80% of the observations for the training set (70% seems to be particularly common), and to assign the remaining observations to the test set.
- A prediction model is built, with a goal to predict membership in the training data as well as possible.
- The resulting model is then assessed for performance using the test data. Performance is assessed to see that it exceeds chance (base rate). Additionally one might assess whether the method performs better than a reasonable alternative (and simpler or better-known) model.

Classification is an even more complex area than clustering, with hundreds of methods, thousands of academic papers each year, and enormous interest with technology and data analytics firms. Our goal is not to cover all of that but to demonstrate the common patterns, in Python generally and scikit-learn specifically, using two of the best-known and most useful classification methods, the naive Bayes and random forest classifiers.

11.1.1 Naive Bayes Classification: `GaussianNB()`

A simple yet powerful classification method is the *Naive Bayes* (NB) classifier. Naive Bayes uses training data to learn the probability of class membership as a function of each predictor variable considered independently (hence "naive"). When applied to new data, class membership is assigned to the category considered to be most likely according to the joint

© Springer Nature Switzerland AG 2020
J. S. Schwarz et al., *Python for Marketing Research and Analytics*, https://doi.org/10.1007/978-3-030-49720-0_11

probabilities assigned by the combination of predictors. We use the `naive_bayes` library from scikit-learn (Pedregosa et al. 2011).

We will use the same data as in Chap. 10:

```
In [0]: import pandas as pd
        seg_df = pd.read_csv('http://bit.ly/PMR-ch5')
        seg_df['is_female'] = seg_df.gender == 'female'
        seg_sub = seg_df.drop(['Segment', 'gender'], axis=1)
        seg_sub.head()
```

The first step in training a classifier is to split the data into *training* and *test* data, which will allow one to check whether the model works on the test data (or is instead overfitted to the training data). We select 70% of the data to use for training and keep the unselected cases as holdout (test) data. Classification requires known segment assignments in order to learn how to assign new values, which we will store in `seg_labels`. The convention is that the independent variables are assigned to X, e.g. `X_train` and `X_test`, and the dependent variable (or *label*) to y, e.g. `y_train` and `y_test`.

```
In [1]: import numpy as np


        seg_labels = seg_df.Segment
        np.random.seed(537)
        rand_idx = np.random.rand(seg_labels.shape[0])
        train_idx = rand_idx <= 0.7
        test_idx = rand_idx > 0.7


        X_train = seg_sub.iloc[train_idx]
        X_test = seg_sub.iloc[test_idx]


        y_train = seg_labels.iloc[train_idx]
        y_test = seg_labels.iloc[test_idx]
```

Why do we hold out a subset of the data in `X_test` and `y_test`? We do so to assess *overfitting* of the model. The model might learn the training data incredibly well and be able to assign labels within the training dataset with 100% accuracy, but we want the model to be *generalizable*, to be effective for data it has not observed. By training the model on one subset of the data and then evaluating its performance on another subset, we can estimate its performance on unknown data.

We then use the training data to train a naive Bayes classifier to predict Segment membership from all other variables in the training data. This is a very simple command:

```
In [2]: from sklearn import naive_bayes


        nb = naive_bayes.GaussianNB()


        nb.fit(X_train, y_train)


        list(zip(nb.classes_, nb.class_prior_))
Out[2]: [('moving up', 0.27102803738317754),
         ('suburb_mix', 0.32242990654205606),
         ('travelers', 0.2523364485981308),
         ('urban_hip', 0.1542056074766355)]
```

Looking at the `class_prior_` values offers some insight into how the model works. First, the a priori likelihood of segment membership—i.e., the estimated odds of membership before any other information is added—is 27.1% for the Moving up segment, 32.2% for the Suburb mix segment, and so forth. The model uses probabilities conditional on each predictor.

The NB classifier starts with the observed probabilities of gender, age, etc., *conditional on segment* found in the training data. It then uses Bayes' Rules to compute the *probability of segment*, conditional on gender, age, etc. This can then be used to estimate segment membership (i.e., assign a label or make a prediction) in new observations such as the test data. You have likely seen a description of how Bayes' Rule works, and we will not repeat it here. For details, refer to a general text on Bayesian methods such as Kruschke (2016).

What does this look like in practice? We can generate predictions for the whole input dataset, including both training and test data, and look at the true and predicted labels for a few users:

```
In [3]: predictions = nb.predict(seg_sub)
        seg_sub_pred = seg_sub.copy()
        seg_sub_pred['prediction'] = predictions
        seg_sub_pred['true_segment'] = seg_df['Segment']
        seg_sub_pred.sample(5)

Out[3]:            age        income   kids  own_home   subscribe   is_female  \
        183   32.806946   60752.625106     5     False       False        True
        194   43.302666   71789.130948     1     False       False       False
        201   34.294615   62236.114534     5     False       False       False
        99    31.673893   75433.895743     3      True       False       False
        10    79.650722   32013.086824     0      True       False       False

             prediction   true_segment
        183   moving_up     moving_up
        194   suburb_mix    moving_up
        201   moving_up     moving_up
        99    suburb_mix    suburb_mix
        10    travelers     travelers
```

What do we see here? First, comparing the `prediction` and `true_segment` columns, the model appears to be performing well: only a single row does not match. The model has used those other fields, age, income, kids, etc., to generate a reasonable prediction.

We see it performed fairly well on these few users, but how well did the model perform overall? Using the test data, we can check the accuracy of the model using the `score()` method:

```
In [4]: nb.score(X_test, y_test)

Out[4]: 0.8488372093023255
```

This returns an accuracy score, the agreement between predicted and actual segment membership, which in this case is about 85%.

However, when the base rate of an outcome is high, then a high level of raw agreement is not meaningful on its own. For example, if 98% of consumers do not purchase a product, then a prediction accuracy of 95% (off by 3%) is worse than simply predicting 100% non-purchase (off by 2%). Instead of raw agreement, one should assess performance of the model in terms of predictive power. A common metric used is the F_1 *score*, which is the harmonic mean of precision and recall (which we introduce in detail below).

In this case, we see that NB was able to recover the segments in the test data imperfectly but substantially better than chance, the F_1 score is also about 85%:

```
In [5]: from sklearn import metrics

        y_pred = nb.predict(X_test)

        metrics.f1_score(y_true=y_test, y_pred=y_pred, average='weighted')

Out[5]: 0.8532809445929236
```

The `average` parameter specifies how the performance for the four different segments (called *classes* in `sklearn`) should be combined, in this case `weighted`. This means that the F_1 score will be calculated for each class and the average calculated, weighted by the class proportions in the population.

We compare performance for each category using what is known in machine learning as a *confusion matrix*:

```
In [6]: import seaborn as sns
        import matplotlib.pyplot as plt
```

```
def confusion_matrix(y_true, y_pred, model):
  conf_mat = metrics.confusion_matrix(y_true, y_pred)

  sns.heatmap(conf_mat.T,
              xticklabels=model.classes_, yticklabels=model.classes_,
              annot=True, fmt='d')
  plt.xlabel('true label')
  plt.ylabel('predicted label')
```

In [7]: confusion_matrix(y_test, y_pred, nb)

The output can be seen in Fig. 11.1

Correct predictions are indicated on the diagonal. The NB prediction (shown in the rows) was correct for the vast majority of observations in each segment, except moving_up. When we examine individual categories, we see that NB was correct for every proposed member of the Urban hip segment (17 correct out of 17 proposed), and for over 96% of the Traveler proposals (26 correct out of the proposed 27). However, it incorrectly classified 10 of the actual 31 Suburb mix respondents into other segments, and similarly failed to identify 9 of the true Moving up segment.

This demonstrates the asymmetry of prediction: the model needs to correctly identify both true positives *and* true negatives. There is tension between those requirements, which correspond to two important statistical concepts in machine learning.

The first is *precision*, which is the proportion of the sample identified with a particular label that truly has that label, i.e. the proportion of all labeled positives that are true positives:

$$precision = \frac{true\ positives}{true\ positives + false\ positives} \qquad (11.1)$$

Precision can be read from the rows of the confusion matrix. In this case, the NB model demonstrated a precision of 100% for the Urban hip segment (17/17), 96% for the travelers segment (26/27), 87.5% for the Suburban mix segment (21/24), and only 50% for the Moving up segment (9/18).

The second important concept is *recall* or *sensitivity*, also called the *true positive rate*. It is the proportion of all positives that were correctly identified:

$$recall = \frac{true\ positives}{true\ positives + false\ negatives} \qquad (11.2)$$

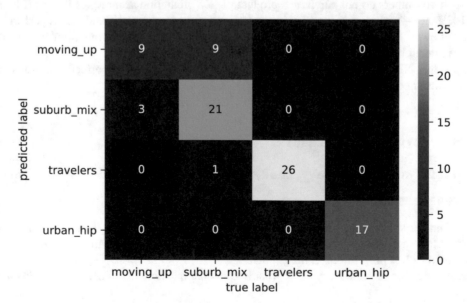

Fig. 11.1 A confusion matrix exposes class-specific performance of the model. The NB model performed well on identifying travelers and urban_hip, slightly less well on suburb_mix, and rather poorly on moving_up

Recall can be read from the columns of the confusion matrix. Here the NB model demonstrated a recall of 100% for the Urban hip (17/17) and Travelers (26/26) segments, but only 68% for the Suburban mix segment (21/31), and 75% for the Moving up segment (9/12).

If we return to our F_1 score from earlier, the formula for that is:

$$F_1 = 2 \cdot \frac{precision \cdot recall}{precision + recall} \tag{11.3}$$

We can write a function to calculate these values:

```
In [8]: def return_precision_recall(y_true, y_pred, model):
            conf_mat = metrics.confusion_matrix(y_true, y_pred)

            precision = pd.Series(metrics.precision_score(y_test,
                                                          y_pred,
                                                          average=None),
                                  index=model.classes_)
            recall = pd.Series(metrics.recall_score(y_test,
                                                    y_pred,
                                                    average=None),
                               index=model.classes_)
            f1 = pd.Series(2 * (precision * recall)/(precision + recall),
                           index=model.classes_)

            return pd.DataFrame([precision, recall, f1], index=['precision',
                                                                'recall', 'f1'])

In [9]: return_precision_recall(y_test, y_pred, nb)

Out[9]:            moving up   suburb_mix   travelers   urban_hip
        precision      0.50     0.875000    0.962963         1.0
        recall         0.75     0.677419    1.000000         1.0
        f1             0.60     0.763636    0.981132         1.0
```

There is likely to be a different business gain for identifying true positives and true negatives, versus the costs of false positives and false negatives. If you have estimates of these costs, you can use the confusion matrix to compute a custom metric for evaluating your classification results.

To better understand the model performance, we can visualize the decision boundaries in the PCA space, as show in Fig. 11.2:

```
In [10]: from sklearn import clone, decomposition

         def plot_decision_pca(model, X, y):
             width, height = 500, 500

             # Transform the X values using a PCA
             p = decomposition.PCA(random_state=132, svd_solver='full')
             X_transformed = p.fit_transform(X.iloc[:,:2])

             # Pull the first two dimensions
             x0 = X_transformed[:, 0]
             x1 = X_transformed[:, 1]

             # Get evenly spaced values between the min and max values
             x0_g = np.linspace(x0.min(), x0.max(), width)
             x1_g = np.linspace(x1.min(), x1.max(), height)

             # Create a "grid" of those evenly spaced values from each vector
```

```
        xx, yy = np.meshgrid(x0_g, x1_g)

        # Stack together all of the sampled values
        X_grid_transformed = np.vstack([xx.ravel(), yy.ravel()]).T

        # Do the inverse transform to get the non-PCA transformed values
        X_grid = p.inverse_transform(X_grid_transformed)

        # Fit a clone of the model using use inverse transformed columns
        # From the first two PCA dimensions.
        # Predict values on the sampled values
        model_c = clone(model)
        model_c.fit(p.inverse_transform(np.vstack([x0, x1]).T), y)
        X_grid_labels = model_c.predict(X_grid)

        # Create a class mapper to map from class string to an integer
        class_mapper = {class_:i for i,class_ in enumerate(model.classes_)}

        plt.figure(figsize=(6,6))
        # Plot the predicted values
        a = plt.scatter(x0, x1,
                        c=[class_mapper[label] for label in y],
                        cmap=plt.cm.rainbow, edgecolor='k', vmin=0, vmax=3)
        plt.contourf(xx, yy,
                     np.reshape([class_mapper[label]
                                 for label in X_grid_labels],
                                (width, height)),
                     cmap=a.cmap, alpha=0.5, levels=3)
        cb = plt.colorbar(ticks=[0.5, 1.2, 2, 2.8])
        _ = cb.ax.set_yticklabels(model.classes_)
        plt.title('Decision boundaries with true values overlaid')
        plt.xlabel('First principal component')
        plt.ylabel('Second principal component')

In [11]: plot_decision_pca(nb, X_test, y_test)
```

The code to generate Fig. 11.2 is somewhat complex. Briefly, what it does is sample evenly in a grid from within the first two components of the PCA space, assessing the model prediction at each point. It then overlays the true values for the test set, and we can see where they disagree from the model prediction.

Looking at decision boundary plots can offer insight into the model's performance, or lack thereof. In this case, we can see that the Suburban mix and Moving up segments are interspersed, which is consistent with what we saw in the confusion matrix. The question of how to deal with that becomes a business decision. We might, for example, decide that we don't need to distinguish between these two segments and collapse them. Or we might try to collect another type of data for which these two segments do differ, perhaps education level or car ownership.

As we did for clustering, we check the predicted segments' summary values using the summary function we wrote in Chap. 10. However, because we now have labeled test data, we can also compare that to the summary values using the true membership:

```
In [12]: !pip install python_marketing_research
         from python_marketing_research_functions import chapter10
         chapter10.check_clusters(seg_sub, nb.predict(seg_sub))

[('moving up', 75), ('suburb_mix', 91), ('travelers', 84), ('urban_hip', 50)]


Out[12]:                    age          income  is_female      kids  own_home  \
         moving up    34.550570   49054.980474   0.760000  1.906667  0.400000
```

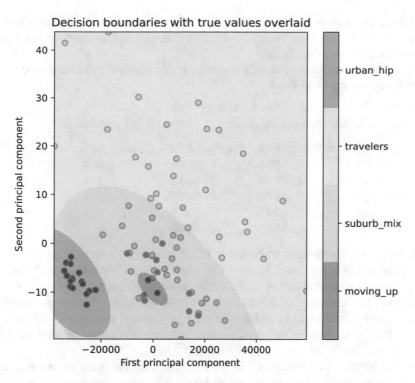

Fig. 11.2 Mapping the decision boundaries in PCA space exposes why the model discriminates poorly between the Suburban mix and Moving up segments: they are interspersed in the first two principal components

suburb_mix	40.251478	57644.538964	0.461538	1.978022	0.461538
travelers	57.489784	62650.866954	0.345238	0.023810	0.642857
urban_hip	23.873716	20267.737317	0.320000	1.140000	0.140000

	subscribe
moving up	0.213333
suburb_mix	0.054945
travelers	0.035714
urban_hip	0.220000

```
In [13]: chapter10.check_clusters(seg_sub, seg_labels)
```

[('moving up', 70), ('suburb_mix', 100), ('travelers', 80), ('urban_hip', 50)]

Out[13]:		age	income	is_female	kids	own_home \
	Segment					
	moving up	36.216087	51763.552666	0.700	1.857143	0.357143
	suburb_mix	39.284730	55552.282925	0.530	1.950000	0.480000
	travelers	57.746500	62609.655328	0.325	0.000000	0.662500
	urban_hip	23.873716	20267.737317	0.320	1.140000	0.140000

	subscribe
Segment	
moving up	0.214286
suburb_mix	0.070000
travelers	0.025000
urban_hip	0.220000

The summary of demographics for the proposed segments (the first summary above) is very similar to the values in the true segments (the second summary). Thus, although NB assigned some observations to the wrong segments, its overall model of the segment descriptive values—at least at the mean values—is similar for the proposed and true segments. By making such a comparison using the test data, we gain confidence that although assignment is not perfect on a case by case basis, the overall group definitions are quite similar.

For naive Bayes models, we can estimate not only the most likely segment but also the odds of membership in each segment, using the `predict_proba()` method:

```
In [14]: pd.DataFrame(nb.predict_proba(seg_sub),
                      columns=nb.classes_).sample(5).round(4)

Out[14]:      moving_up   suburb_mix   travelers   urban_hip
        26      0.0000       0.0065      0.9935        0.0
       188      0.7116       0.2851      0.0033        0.0
       263      0.0000       0.0000      0.0000        1.0
       129      0.5240       0.4759      0.0001        0.0
       192      0.5957       0.4043      0.0000        0.0
```

This tells us that Respondent 188 is estimated to be about 71% likely to be a member of Moving up, yet 29% likely to be in Suburban mix. Respondent 26 is estimated nearly 100% likely to be in Travelers. This kind of individual-level detail can suggest which individuals to target according to the difficulty of targeting and the degree of certainty. For high-cost campaigns, we might target only those most certain to be in a segment; whereas for low-cost campaigns, we might target people for second-best segment membership in addition to primary segment assignment. Because we are able to predict membership for new cases that have not been assigned, we can score new customers or others in a database, as long as we have the relevant predictor data used in the classification model.

We conclude that the naive Bayes model works well for the data analyzed here, with performance much better than chance, overall 85% accuracy in segment assignment, and demographics that are similar between the proposed and actual segments. It also provides interpretable individual-level estimation of membership likelihood.

Of course there are times when naive Bayes may not perform well, and it's always a good idea to try multiple methods. For an alternative, we next examine random forest models.

11.1.2 Random Forest Classification: `RandomForestClassifier()`

A random forest (RF) classifier does not attempt to fit a single model to data but instead builds an *ensemble* of models that jointly classify the data (Breiman 2001; Liaw and Wiener 2002). RF does this by fitting a large number of classification trees. In order to find an assortment of models, each tree is optimized to fit only *some* of the observations (in our case, customers) using only *some* of the predictors. The ensemble of all trees is the *forest*.

When a new case is predicted, it is predicted by every tree and the final decision is awarded to the *consensus* value that receives the most votes. In this way, a random forest avoids dependencies on precise model specification while remaining resilient in the face of difficult data conditions, such as data that are collinear or wide (more columns than rows). Random forest models perform well across a wide variety of datasets and problems (Fernández-Delgado et al. 2014).

In Python, a random forest may be created with code very similar to that for naive Bayes models. We use the same `X_train` training data as in Sect. 11.1.1, and call `RandomForestClassifier()` from the scikit-learn `ensemble` package to fit the classifier:

```
In [15]: from sklearn import ensemble

         np.random.seed(23432)
         rf = ensemble.RandomForestClassifier(n_estimators=50)

         rf.fit(X_train, y_train)
```

There are two things to note about the call to `RandomForestClassifier()`. First, random forests are random to some extent, as the name says. They select variables and subsets of data probabilistically. Thus, we use `set.seed()` before modeling, so that we get the same model if we re-run the code later. Second, we used the argument `n_estimators=50` to specify the number of trees to create in the forest.

Note that it's common to use many more trees for a RF model, as there is little risk of overfitting. Many people will start with 1000 trees, for example. In practice, this often does not improve the accuracy of the model relative to a model

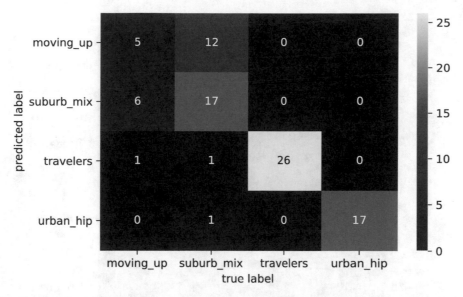

Fig. 11.3 Like the NB model, the RF model performed well on identifying travelers and urban_hip, but less well on suburb_mix, and moving_up

with fewer trees. However, it often improves the precision of the model, providing higher resolution values for the predicted class probabilities and variable importance (see Sect. 11.1.3). To determine the optimal number of trees, it's common to use hyperparameter tuning (see Sect. 11.2).

We can again check the F$_1$ score of the model:

```
In [16]: rf.score(X_test, y_test)

Out[16]: 0.7558139534883721

In [17]: y_pred = rf.predict(X_test)

         metrics.f1_score(y_test, y_pred, average='micro')

Out[17]: 0.7582299105153958
```

We see that the RF model performed a bit less well than the NB model, but is still a reasonably strong fit.

We can inspect the confusion matrix in Fig. 11.3 to better understand the class-level performance:

```
In [18]: confusion_matrix(y_test, y_pred, rf)
```

And look at class-specific precision and recall:

```
In [19]: return_precision_recall(y_test, y_pred, rf)

Out[19]:          moving up   suburb_mix   travelers   urban_hip
         precision  0.294118     0.739130    0.928571    0.944444
         recall     0.416667     0.548387    1.000000    1.000000
         f1         0.344828     0.629630    0.962963    0.971429
```

Overall, the RF model performed similarly to—albeit slightly worse than—the NB model. It showed poor discrimination of the Suburban mix and Moving up segments.

Inspecting the decision boundary visualization in Fig. 11.4 (code omitted) also gives us insight into the difference between the NB and RF models. Whereas the decision boundaries were smooth and convex for the NB model, the RF model gives jagged and discontinuous boundaries. This reflects the fact that the NB model boundaries are defined by gaussian estimates of feature distributions, whereas the RF model makes no assumptions about the underlying distribution of the features, but can find different association patterns in different parts of the space.

What does a random forest look like? Figure 11.5 shows one trees from among those we fit above. The complete forest comprises 50 such trees that differ in structure and the predictors used. When an observation is classified, it is assigned to the group that is predicted by the greatest number of trees within the ensemble. This ensemble of trees are what enable the "jagged" decision boundaries that are common in RF models. The tree in Fig. 11.5 is produced with this code:

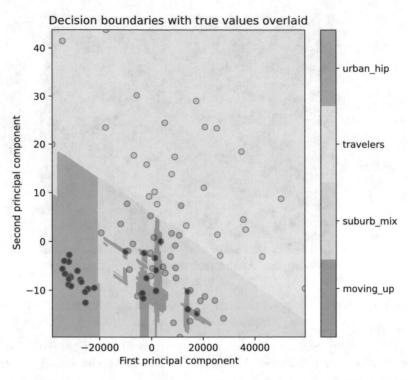

Fig. 11.4 The decision boundaries of the RF model are much more "jagged" and discontinuous than the NB model. This is because the RF model consists of decision trees that can learn disconnected boundaries, whereas the boundaries in the NB model are defined by smooth gaussians

```
In [20]:  import graphviz
          from sklearn import tree
          from IPython.display import Image


          tree_0 = rf.estimators_[0]
          dot_data = tree.export_graphviz(tree_0, out_file=None,
                                          feature_names=X_train.columns,
                                          class_names=rf.classes_)
          tree_graph = graphviz.Source(dot_data, format='png')
          tree_graph.render('tmp', view=True)
          Image('tmp.png', width=1000, height=1000)
```

Inspecting the decision space in PCA space can help us understand areas of model weakness, but it does not offer much insight into what is driving model decisions based on actual features. We can also inspect the decision boundaries for pairs of features, such as age and income. We can write a similar function to do this:

```
In [21]:  def pairwise_decision_boundary(model, X_train, y_train,
                                         X_test, y_test,
                                         first_column, second_column,
                                         jitter=False):
              width, height = 1000, 1000
              # Create a class mapper to map from class string to an integer
              class_mapper = {c:i for i,c in enumerate(model.classes_)}

              x0 = X_train[first_column]
              x1 = X_train[second_column]
              # Get evenly spaced values between the min and max values
              x0_g = np.linspace(x0.min(), x0.max(), width)
              x1_g = np.linspace(x1.min(), x1.max(), height)
```

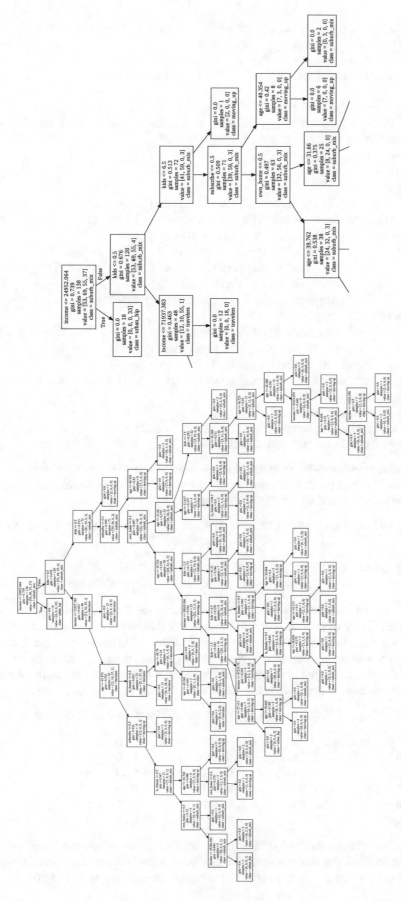

Fig. 11.5 One example among the 50 trees in the ensemble found by RandomForestClassifier() for segment prediction in seg_sub. The trees differ substantially in structure and variable usage. No single tree is expected to be a particularly good predictor in itself, yet the ensemble of all trees may predict well in aggregate by voting on the assignment of observations to outcome groups. The overall structure of the tree can be seen in the zoomed out view (upper panel) and the details of individual notes in a subset of the tree (lower panel)

```
# Create a "grid" of those evenly spaced values from each vector
xx, yy = np.meshgrid(x0_g, x1_g)
# Stack together all of the sampled values
X_grid = np.vstack([[xx.ravel(), yy.ravel()]]).T

model_c = clone(model)
model_c.fit(X_train.loc[:,[first_column, second_column]], y_train)
X_grid_labels = model_c.predict(X_grid)
# Plot the predicted values
j_x0, j_x1 = 0, 0
if jitter:
    j_x0 = (np.random.random(X_test.shape[0])-0.5)/10.
    j_x1 = (np.random.random(X_test.shape[0])-0.5)/10.
a = plt.scatter(X_test[first_column] + j_x0,
                X_test[second_column] + j_x1,
                c=[class_mapper[l] for l in y_test],
                cmap=plt.cm.rainbow,
                edgecolor='k', vmin=0, vmax=3)
plt.contourf(xx, yy,
             np.reshape([class_mapper[l] for l in X_grid_labels],
                        (width, height)),
             cmap=a.cmap, alpha=0.5, levels=3)
plt.title('Decision boundaries with true values overlaid')
plt.xlabel(first_column)
plt.ylabel(second_column)
cb = plt.colorbar(ticks=[0.5, 1.2, 2, 2.8])
cb.ax.set_yticklabels(model.classes_)
```

We can then look at the decision boundaries between age & income and between subscription status & number of children, shown in Fig. 11.6. We have an optional jitter argument for when we are looking at discrete or boolean values, such as subscription state (otherwise the points would all overlay each other).

```
In [22]: pairwise_decision_boundary(rf, X_train, y_train, X_test, y_test,
                                    'age', 'income')

In [23]: pairwise_decision_boundary(rf, X_train, y_train, X_test, y_test,
                                    'age', 'kids', jitter=True)
```

In Fig. 11.6, we see a few things of interest. From the left panel, we can see that the model has learned that individuals above about 50 years old are very likely to be Travelers and those below that age and below about $32,000 in income are likely to be from the Urban hip segment. Individuals who make more than Urban hip but are younger than Travelers belong to either Suburban mix or Moving up, without a really clear pattern, although Suburban mix tends to be a bit older or wealthier.

In the right panel of Fig. 11.6, we can see that in the model the number of kids only differentiates the Travelers segment.

It is possible to inspect the distribution of predictions for individual cases, again using the `predict_proba()` method:

```
In [24]: pd.DataFrame(rf.predict_proba(X_test), columns=rf.classes_).sample(5)
```

Out[24]:	moving up	suburb_mix	travelers	urban_hip
76	0.00	0.00	0.00	1.0
19	0.02	0.06	0.92	0.0
39	0.24	0.76	0.00	0.0
73	0.00	0.00	0.00	1.0
56	0.10	0.76	0.14	0.0

These values reflect the number of trees the "voted" that a particular observation belonged in a particular class. As for the NB model, we can then understand the model's overall confidence in each assignment. For example, the model has assigned 100% probability that samples 73 and 76 are in the Urban hip segment. Samples 39 and 56 each have a 76% chance

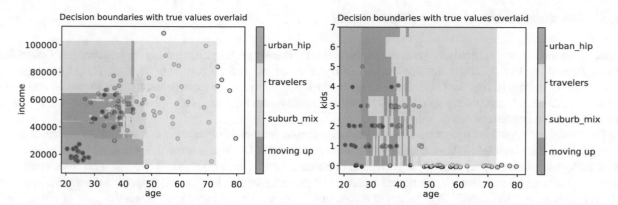

Fig. 11.6 Our `pairwise_decision_boundary()` function visualizes an estimation of the boundaries between classes that the model has learned. In the left panel, we see that the model associates high age with the Travelers group and low age and low income with the Urban hip group. The Suburb mix and Moving up groups are less well differentiated, but the Moving up tend to be either younger or have lower income than the Suburb mix group. In the right panel, we see that having few children and high age is associated with Travelers, but that the number of kids is not very predictive between the other groups

of being in the Suburban mix segment, but sample 39 is next most likely to be in Moving up, whereas for sample 56 its second-most-likely class is Traveler.

The proposed and actual segments are quite similar in the mean values of the variables in our summary function:

```
In [25]: chapter10.check_clusters(seg_sub, rf.predict(seg_sub))

[('moving up', 75), ('suburb_mix', 92), ('travelers', 82), ('urban_hip', 51)]
```

```
Out[25]:              age          income    is_female        kids   own_home  \
         moving up    35.983633    51603.477437  0.640000   1.933333   0.386667
         suburb_mix   39.465911    56134.885424  0.554348   1.923913   0.467391
         travelers    57.522142    62472.064488  0.341463   0.000000   0.658537
         urban_hip    24.128490    20459.935615  0.333333   1.176471   0.137255

                      subscribe
         moving up    0.253333
         suburb_mix   0.032609
         travelers    0.024390
         urban_hip    0.215686
```

```
In [26]: chapter10.check_clusters(seg_sub, seg_labels)

[('moving up', 70), ('suburb_mix', 100), ('travelers', 80), ('urban_hip', 50)]
```

```
Out[26]:              age          income    is_female        kids   own_home  \
         Segment
         moving up    36.216087    51763.552666     0.700   1.857143   0.357143
         suburb_mix   39.284730    55552.282925     0.530   1.950000   0.480000
         travelers    57.746500    62609.655328     0.325   0.000000   0.662500
         urban_hip    23.873716    20267.737317     0.320   1.140000   0.140000

                      subscribe
         Segment
         moving up    0.214286
         suburb_mix   0.070000
         travelers    0.025000
         urban_hip    0.220000
```

11.1.3   Random Forest Variable Importance

Random forest models are particularly good for one common marketing problem: estimating the importance of classification variables. Remember that RF fits many trees, where each tree is optimized for a portion of the data. It uses the remainder of the data—known as "out of bag" or OOB data—to assess the tree's performance more generally. Because each tree uses only a subset of variables, RF models are able to handle very *wide* data where there are more—even many, many more—predictor variables than there are observations.

An RF model assesses the importance of a variable in a simple yet powerful way: for one variable at a time, it randomly permutes (alters) the variable's values, computes the model accuracy in OOB data using the permuted values, and compares that to the accuracy with the real data. If the variable is important, then its performance will degrade when its observed values are randomly permuted. If, however, the model remains just as accurate as it is with real data, then the variable in question is not very important (Breiman 2001). As noted before, it is common to use more trees when the goal of the model is to determine variable importance, as the overall model will have more coverage of the variable space and variable importance values will have higher precision.

We can view the calculated importance of each feature in the `feature_importances_` parameter on the RF model:

```
In [27]: pd.Series(rf.feature_importances_,
                    index=seg_sub.columns).sort_values(ascending=False)

Out[27]: age          0.437028
         income       0.313560
         kids         0.150136
         is_female    0.035421
         own_home     0.032164
         subscribe    0.031691
         dtype: float64
```

Age and income are the most useful variables, which is consistent with the decision boundaries visualizations. Understanding variable importance can enable a deeper understanding of the features that define differences between classes, enabling more intelligent business decisions.

Variable or feature selection is often the first step for developing more advanced machine learning models, such as deep neural networks. Random forests unique properties make them invaluable tools in the process of feature engineering. In this case, we would expect to observe a similar degree of fit by removing the gender, home ownership, and subscription variables, which have minimal predictive power. Eliminating uninformative features is extremely important in other classifier models, many of which are very sensitive to the presence of noise from uninformative features.

11.2   Prediction: Identifying Potential Customers*

We now turn to another use for classification: to predict potential customers. An important business question—especially in high-churn categories such as mobile subscriptions—is how to reach new customers. If we have data on past prospects that includes potential predictors such as demographics, and an outcome such as purchase, we can develop a model to identify customers for whom the outcome is most likely among new prospects. In this section, we use a random forest model and attempt to predict subscription status from our dataset `seg_sub`.

As usual with classification problems, we split the data into a training sample and a test sample:

```
In [28]: subscribe_label = seg_sub.subscribe

         seg_sub_nosub = seg_sub.drop('subscribe', axis=1)

         np.random.seed(7885)
         rand_idx = np.random.rand(subscribe_label.shape[0])
         train_idx = rand_idx <= 0.65
         test_idx = rand_idx > 0.65

         X_train = seg_sub_nosub.iloc[train_idx]
         X_test = seg_sub_nosub.iloc[test_idx]
```

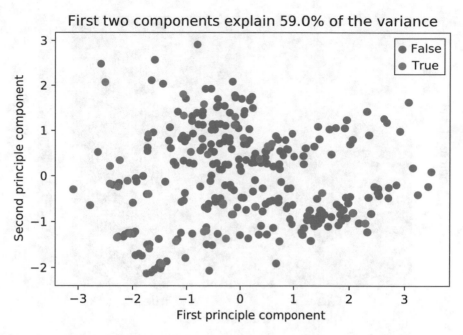

Fig. 11.7 Cluster plot for the subscribers and non-subscribers. The two groups show little differentiation on the principal components, which suggests that classifying respondents into the groups and predicting subscribers could be difficult

```
          y_train = subscribe_label.iloc[train_idx]
          y_test = subscribe_label.iloc[test_idx]
```

Next, we wonder how difficult it will be to identify potential subscribers. Are subscribers in the training set well-differentiated from non-subscribers? We use `cluster_plot()` from Chap. 10 to check the differentiation:

```
In [29]: chapter10.cluster_plot(seg_sub_nosub, subscribe_label)
```

The result in Fig. 11.7 shows that the subscribers and non-subscribers are not well differentiated when plotted against principal components (which reflect about 59% of the variance in the data). This suggests that the problem will be difficult!

We fit an initial RF model to predict `subscribe`:

```
In [30]: rf_sub = ensemble.RandomForestClassifier(n_estimators=100,
                                       random_state=86,
                                       class_weight=\
                                         'balanced_subsample')


          rf_sub.fit(X_train, y_train)

          y_pred = rf_sub.predict(X_test)
In [31]: rf_sub.score(X_test, y_test)
Out[31]: 0.9072164948453608
```

An accuracy of 90% looks good. But lets check the confusion matrix:

```
In [32]: confusion_matrix(y_test, y_pred, rf_sub)
```

The results in Fig. 11.8 are not encouraging. Although the error rate might initially sound good at 90.3% overall, we have a recall of only 10%.

This is expected given the interspersion of the classes in the cluster plot. But it is also exacerbated by the *class imbalance* problem in machine learning. When one category dominates the data, it is very difficult to learn to predict other groups. This frequently arises with small-proportion problems, such as predicting the comparatively rare individuals who will purchase a product, who have a medical condition, who are security threats, and so forth.

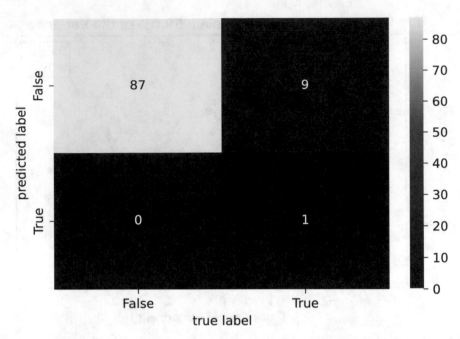

Fig. 11.8 The random forest model did not perform well a predicting the subscription state, achieving a recall of only 10% (1/10)

A general solution is to balance the classes by sampling more from the small group. In RF models, this can be accomplished by telling the classifier to use a balanced group when it samples data to fit each tree, which we did with the `class_weight='balanced_subsample'`. However it was not sufficient to overcome the poor predictive power of the variables themselves.

We used default values for all the model parameters. An important concept in machine learning is *hyperparameter tuning*, where we explore the model parameter space to identify the parameters that lead to the best fit. We can perform a *grid search*, where we sample many combinations of parameters to find an optimum.

This requires a scoring function. The F_1 score is useful because it balances precision and recall. We can run the grid search easily:

```
In [33]: from sklearn import model_selection

         rf_sub_cv = ensemble.RandomForestClassifier(random_state=34,
                                           class_weight=\
                                             'balanced_subsample')
         parameters = {'n_estimators': [10, 100, 500],
                       'max_depth': [5, 10, 30],
                       'min_samples_split': [2,5],
                       'min_samples_leaf': [1,2,5]}
         clf = model_selection.GridSearchCV(rf_sub_cv, parameters,
                                     cv=5, scoring='f1_weighted')
         clf.fit(X_train, y_train)
```

We can inspect the best scoring parameters using the `best_params_` parameter:

```
In [34]: clf.best_params_

Out[34]: {'max_depth': 10,
          'min_samples_leaf': 1,
          'min_samples_split': 2,
          'n_estimators': 100}
```

Looking at the confusion matrix in Fig. 11.9, we see that this model did not perform any better:

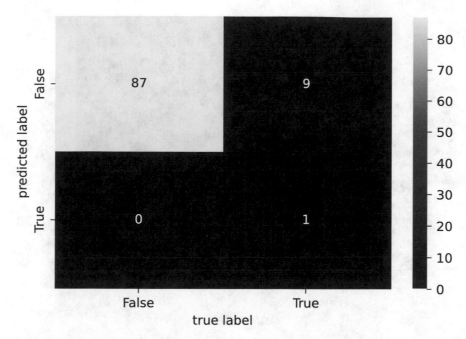

Fig. 11.9 The hyperparameter tuned model did not perform any better

```
In [35]: y_pred_be = clf.best_estimator_.predict(X_test)

         confusion_matrix(y_test, y_pred_be, clf.best_estimator_)
```

What if we try a different scoring function? Let's imagine we want to optimize for recall, that is we want to find as many potential positives as possible, accepting that many will be false positives. We can use recall as the scoring function:

```
In [36]: rf_sub_cv = ensemble.RandomForestClassifier(random_state=34,
                                                     class_weight=\
                                                     'balanced_subsample')

         parameters = {'n_estimators': [10, 100, 500],
                       'max_depth': [5, 10, 30],
                       'min_samples_split': [2,5],
                       'min_samples_leaf': [1,2,5]}
         clf = model_selection.GridSearchCV(rf_sub_cv, parameters,
                                            cv=5, scoring='recall')
         clf.fit(X_train, y_train)

In [37]: clf.best_params_

Out[37]: {'max_depth': 5,
          'min_samples_leaf': 2,
          'min_samples_split': 2,
          'n_estimators': 10}

In [38]: y_pred_be = clf.best_estimator_.predict(X_test)

         confusion_matrix(y_test, y_pred_be, clf.best_estimator_)
```

The confusion matrix in Fig. 11.10 is still not great, but it is at least different! Our precision went from 100% (1/1) to 15% (2/13), but our recall went from 10% (1/10) to 20% (2/10).

Another knob we can turn is the sample weighting. We used a balanced subsample weighting, which accounts for some of the imbalance in the frequency of each class, but we can further oversample the rarer class with the `class_weight` parameter. This will push the model toward recall. One risk with this approach is overfitting: the model becomes so tuned to oversampled rare class that it is not generalizable.

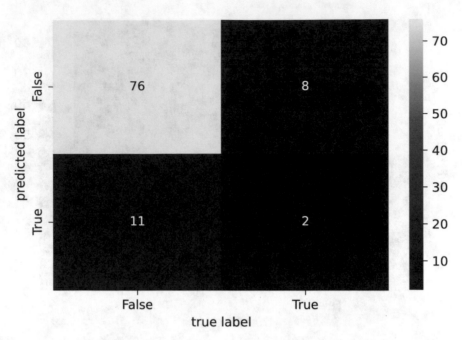

Fig. 11.10 Optimizing the hyperparameter tuning for recall improved the recall at the expense of precision

```
In [39]:rf_sub = ensemble.RandomForestClassifier(n_estimators=10,
                                                  random_state=86,
                                                  max_depth=5,
                                                  min_samples_leaf=2,
                                                  min_samples_split=2,
                                                  class_weight=\
                                                    {False: 1, True:50})


        rf_sub.fit(X_train, y_train)

        y_pred = rf_sub.predict(X_test)
        confusion_matrix(y_test, y_pred, rf_sub)
```

We can see in Fig. 11.11 that this had a large effect. We have boosted our recall to 70% (7/10), but at a substantial cost to precision: only 17.5% (7/40) of the observations that the model labeled as True are true positives; 33 were false positives.

Despite the fact that the variables here have poor predictive power, we can clearly see that optimizing our hyperparameter tuning for a different score led to a differently tuned model with different tradeoffs. This is an important concept in machine learning. An analyst should consider the business outcome carefully and tune a model appropriately. This often differs from a generic or abstract "accuracy" metric.

It's also worth nothing that machine learning is not magic, it is statistics. If there is no strong signal in the data, you cannot build a good prediction. What should one do in that circumstance? The most obvious option would be to find other features that might be more predictive.

11.3 Learning More*

We covered the basics of classification in this chapter. Many of the resources we recommended in Sect. 10.4 for clustering are also relevant for understanding classification. A recommended introduction to the field of statistical learning is James et al., *An Introduction to Statistical Learning* (ISL) (James et al. 2013). A more advanced treatment of the topics in ISL is Hastie et al., *The Elements of Statistical Learning* (Hastie et al. 2016).

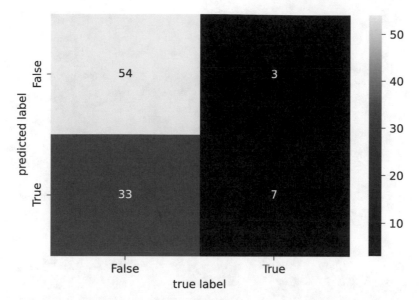

Fig. 11.11 Changing the sample weighting is another means to adjust precision/recall. Here by oversampling the `True` class, we improved the recall at the expense of precision

For classification and especially prediction, in addition to ISL noted above, an applied, practitioner-friendly text is Kuhn and Johnson's *Applied Predictive Modeling*. Scikit-learn has many supervised learning modules (scikit-learn developers 2019b), many of which include classification methods. Overall these packages represent many of the most common methods in machine learning.

11.4 Key Points

In this chapter, we examined the basic structure of classification methods that may be used to predict group membership for new observations. In addition, we saw how classifier visualization techniques may be used to understand model performance. Following are key points to keep in mind when working on classification and prediction models.

- With classification models, data should be split into training and test groups, and models validated on the test (holdout) data (Sect. 11.1).
- We examined naive Bayes models (`sklearn.naive_bayes.GaussianNB()`, Sect. 11.1.1) and random forest models (`sklearn.ensemble.RandomForest Classifier()`, Sect. 11.1.2). These—and many other classification methods—have quite similar syntax, making it easy to try and compare models.
- Precision, or the proportion of all predicted positives that are truly positive, and recall, the proportion of all true positives that were correctly labeled as positive are important concepts in tuning classifiers, are at odds with each other: improving one tends to worsen the other.
- We learned how to explore decision boundary visualizations to better understand the limitations of the model and of the underlying variables.
- A useful feature of random forest models is their ability to determine variable importance for prediction, even when there are a large number of variables (Sect. 11.1.3).
- A common problem in classification is class imbalance, where one group dominates the observations and makes it difficult to predict the other group. We saw how to correct this for random forest models with the `class_weight` argument, resulting in a more successful predictive model (Sect. 11.2).
- We saw how to run a grid search using `sklearn.model_selection. GridSearchCV()` for hyperparameter tuning of the model, enabling us to find an optimal model under different scoring metrics. We also saw that hyperparameter tuning cannot overcome uninformative variables!

Chapter 12
Conclusion

Congratulations! By working through this book, you have established a solid foundation in Python programming, data analytics, and marketing research. We would like to share a few final thoughts that summarize some of the most important points.

1. Before you begin to report any analytics or build statistical models, always explore and visualize your data. It is easy to overlook bad data points … especially if you don't even look (Sects. 3.3.2 and 3.6).
2. Analyses and model building are interactive processes. Start with a simple model and build on it progressively, assessing at each stage whether a more complex model is an improvement (Sects. 7.3 and 7.4).
3. Real data often contain highly correlated observations, because behaviors and attitudes often go together. However, high correlation may make a statistical model unstable. Consider reducing data to key dimensions before modeling, and assess models for collinearity (Sects. 8.1 and 9.2).
4. It is important to understand and to report the uncertainty in any statistic that you estimate from sampled data. Report confidence intervals whenever possible. This can often be done with a minimum of statistical jargon by using graphics (Sects. 6.5.4 and 7.3).
5. Statistical significance is a necessary condition for a model to be interesting, yet it does not imply that a model is appropriate, useful, or even the best-fitting. When possible, compare alternative models and evaluate a model in terms of its usefulness to answer important questions (Sects. 7.4, 10.3.1 and 11.2).
6. Hierarchical models that estimate differences by individual, sample, or group are often very useful in marketing, and are not as complex as they might seem at first. Once you know how to estimate basic linear models, it is relatively easy to start considering hierarchical models (Sect. 8.3.5).
7. Don't assume that a dataset, especially from a consumer survey, will reflect underlying concepts in the way you expect. Analysts must expect to be surprised by how people behave and how they interpret our questions. Methods such as factor analysis make it possible to assess latent variables and determine whether a model fits your data (Sect. 9.3).
8. Machine learning does not provide magic answers to questions about segmentation (e.g., clustering, Chap. 10) or prediction (e.g., classification, Chap. 11). It is essential to consider multiple methods, different models, and—more than anything else—the question of whether a result will be *useful* for your business purpose. Python provides rich and powerful tools, but you must use them with skepticism and attention to confirming results.

Perhaps our most important point is this: there is always more to learn, and the best way to learn is through a combination of practice and teaching others. Python makes it easy to share your code with notebooks; use this to get feedback and to share your work with your colleagues and—when possible—the broader community. This vibrant, growing community is the most important reason for Python's success. With your help, it will only become stronger.

© Springer Nature Switzerland AG 2020
J. S. Schwarz et al., *Python for Marketing Research and Analytics*, https://doi.org/10.1007/978-3-030-49720-0_12

References

Agresti A (2012) *An Introduction to Categorical Data Analysis*, 3rd edn. Wiley-Interscience

Agresti A, Coull BA (1998) Approximate is better than "exact" for interval estimation of binomial proportions. *The American Statistician* 52(2):119–126

Anaconda, Inc (2019) *Anaconda Software Distribution*. URL https://www.anaconda.com

Bickel P, Hammel E, O'Connell J (1975) Sex bias in graduate admissions: data from Berkeley. *Science* 187(4175):398–404

Biggs J (2017) factor_analyzer package. URL https://factor-analyzer.readthedocs.io/en/latest/factor_analyzer.html#module-factor_analyzer.factor_analyzer

Borg I, Groenen PJ (2005) *Modern Multidimensional Scaling: Theory and Applications*. Springer

Borg I, Groenen PJ, Mair P (2018) *Applied Multidimensional Scaling and Unfolding*, 2nd edn. Springer

Bowman D, Gatignon H (2010) *Market Response and Marketing Mix Models*. Foundations and Trends in Marketing, Now Publishers, Inc.

Breiman L (2001) Random forests. *Machine Learning* 45(1):5–32

Bush BM (1996) The perils of floating point. URL http://www.lahey.com/float.htm

Casella G, Berger RL (2002) *Statistical Inference*, vol 2. Duxbury Pacific Grove, CA

Chambers J, Hastie T, Pregibon D (1990) Statistical models in S. *Compstat*

Chapman C, Feit E (2019) *R for Marketing Research and Analytics*, 2nd edn. Springer

Cohen J (1988) *Statistical Power Analysis for the Behavioral Sciences*, 2nd edn. Lawrence Erlbaum Associates

Cohen J (1994) The earth is round (p < .05). *American Psychologist* 49(12):997

Cohen J, Cohen P, West SG, Aiken LS (2003) *Applied Multiple Regression/Correlation Analysis for the Behavioral Sciences*, 3rd edn. Lawrence Erlbaum

Collins LM, Lanza ST (2010) *Latent Class and Latent Transition Analysis: With Applications in the Social, Behavioral, and Health Sciences*. John Wiley & Sons

Dobson AJ (2018) *An Introduction to Generalized Linear Models*, 4th edn. Chapman & Hall

Everitt BS, Landau S, Leese M, Stahl D (2011) *Cluster Analysis*, 5th edn. Wiley Series in Probability and Statistics, John Wiley & Sons

Fabrigar LR, Wegener DT (2011) *Exploratory Factor Analysis*. Oxford University Press

Fernández-Delgado M, Cernadas E, Barro S, Amorim D (2014) Do we need hundreds of classifiers to solve real world classification problems? *Journal of Machine Learning Research* 15:3133–3181

Foundation PS (2020) *Extending Python with C or C++*. URL https://docs.python.org/3.7/extending/extending.html

Fox J, Weisberg S (2011) *An R Companion to Applied Regression*, 2nd edn. Sage, Thousand Oaks, CA

Gałecki A, Burzykowski T (2013) *Linear Mixed-Effects Models Using R: A Step-by-Step Approach*. Springer

Gelman A, Hill J (2006) *Data Analysis Using Regression and Multilevel/Hierarchical Models*. Cambridge University Press

Gelman A, Carlin JB, Stern HS, Dunson DB, Vehtari A, Rubin DB (2013) *Bayesian Data Analysis*, 3rd edn. Chapman & Hall

Gower J, Groenen PJ, Van de Velden M, Vines K (2010) Perceptual maps: the good, the bad and the ugly. Tech. Rep. ERIM Report Series Reference No. ERS-2010-011-MKT, Erasmus Research Institute of Management

Harrell FE (2015) *Regression Modeling Strategies: With Applications to Linear Models, Logistic Regression, and Survival Analysis*, 2nd edn. Springer

Hastie T, Tibshirani R, Friedman J (2016) *The Elements of Statistical Learning: Data Mining, Inference, and Prediction*, 2nd edn. Springer

Hogg R, McKean J, Craig A (2005) *Introduction to Mathematical Statistics*. Pearson Education International, Pearson Education, URL https://books.google.com/books?id=vIEZAQAAIAAJ

Hosmer Jr DW, Lemeshow S, Sturdivant RX (2013) *Applied Logistic Regression*. John Wiley & Sons

Hubbard R, Armstrong JS (2006) Why we don't really know what statistical significance means: Implications for educators. *Journal of Marketing Education* 28(2):114–120

Hunter JD (2007) Matplotlib: A 2d graphics environment. *Computing In Science & Engineering* 9(3):90–95, https://doi.org/10.1109/MCSE.2007.55

James G, Witten D, Hastie T, Tibshirani R (2013) *An Introduction to Statistical Learning: With Applications in R*. Springer

Jolliffe IT (2002) *Principal Component Analysis*, 2nd edn. Springer

Kerr NL (1998) Harking: Hypothesizing after the results are known. *Personality and Social Psychology Review* 2(3):196–217

Kluyver T, Ragan-Kelley B, Pérez F, Granger B, Bussonnier M, Frederic J, Kelley K, Hamrick J, Grout J, Corlay S, Ivanov P, Avila D, Abdalla S, Willing C (2016) Jupyter notebooks – a publishing format for reproducible computational workflows. In: Loizides F, Schmidt B (eds) Positioning and Power in Academic Publishing: Players, Agents and Agendas, IOS Press, pp 87–90

© Springer Nature Switzerland AG 2020

J. S. Schwarz et al., *Python for Marketing Research and Analytics*, https://doi.org/10.1007/978-3-030-49720-0

Knuth D (1997) *The Art of Computer Programming*, vol 2: Seminumerical Algorithms, 3rd edn. Addison-Wesley

Kruschke JK (2010) What to believe: Bayesian methods for data analysis. *Trends in Cognitive Sciences* 14(7):293–300

Kruschke JK (2016) *Doing Bayesian Data Analysis: A Tutorial Introduction with R, JAGS, and Stan*, 2nd edn. Academic Press, Cambridge

Kuhn M, Johnson K (2013) *Applied Predictive Modeling*. Springer

Lauwens B, Downey A (2019) *Think Julia: How to Think Like a Computer Scientist*. O'Reilly Media, URL https://books.google.com/books?id=UlSQDwAAQBAJ

Liaw A, Wiener M (2002) Classification and regression by randomforest. *R News* 2(3):18–22, URL http://CRAN.R-project.org/doc/Rnews/

McInnes L, Healy J, Saul N, Grossberger L (2008) Using t-sne. *The Journal of Machine Learning Research* 9:2579

McInnes L, Healy J, Saul N, Grossberger L (2018) Umap: Uniform manifold approximation and projection. *The Journal of Open Source Software* 3(29):861

McKinney W (2010) Data structures for statistical computing in Python . In: van der Walt S, Millman J (eds) Proceedings of the 9th Python in Science Conference, pp 51 – 56

McKinney W (2018) *Python for Data Analysis: Data Wrangling with Pandas, NumPy, and IPython*, 2nd edn. O'Reilly Media, URL https://github.com/wesm/pydata-book

Met Office (2010–2015) *Cartopy: a cartographic Python library with a Matplotlib interface*. Exeter, Devon, URL http://scitools.org.uk/cartopy

Mulaik SA (2009) *Foundations of Factor Analysis*, 2nd edn. Statistics in the Social and Behavioral Sciences, Chapman & Hall/CRC

Netzer O, Feldman R, Goldenberg J, Fresko M (2012) Mine your own business: Market-structure surveillance through text mining. *Marketing Science* 31(3):521–543

Oliphant T (2006–2020) *A Guide to NumPy*. URL http://www.numpy.org/, [Online; accessed <today>]

Orme BK (2010) *Getting Started with Conjoint Analysis: Strategies for Product Design and Pricing Research*, 2nd edn. Research Publishers

Pedregosa F, Varoquaux G, Gramfort A, Michel V, Thirion B, Grisel O, Blondel M, Prettenhofer P, Weiss R, Dubourg V, Vanderplas J, Passos A, Cournapeau D, Brucher M, Perrot M, Duchesnay E (2011) Scikit-learn: Machine Learning in Python. *Journal of Machine Learning Research* 12:2825–2830

Perktold J, Seabold S, Taylor J, The statsmodels-developers (2019) *statsmodels.regression.mixed_linear_model.MixedLM*. URL https://www.statsmodels.org/dev/generated/statsmodels.regression.mixed_linear_model.MixedLM.html

Peterson B (2008–2019) *Python 2.7 Release Schedule*. URL https://www.python.org/dev/peps/pep-0373/

Raftery AE (1995) Bayesian model selection in social research. *Sociological Methodology* 25:111–164

Rao V (2009) *Handbook of Pricing Research in Marketing*. Elgar Original Reference Series, Edward Elgar, URL https://books.google.com/books?id=22FU4b0NL2UC

Robinson D (2017) The incredible growth of Python. URL https://stackoverflow.blog/2017/09/06/incredible-growth-python

Ross SM (2019) *Introduction to Probability Models*, 12th edn. Academic Press

Rossi PE, Allenby GM, McCulloch RE (2005) *Bayesian Statistics and Marketing*. John Wiley & Sons

RStudio (2019) *RStudio: Integrated Development Environment for R*. RStudio, Boston, MA, URL http://www.rstudio.org/, version 1.2.5033

Salvatier J, Wiecki TV, Fonnesbeck C (2016) Probabilistic programming in Python using PyMC3. *PeerJ Computer Science* 2:e55, https://doi.org/10.7717/peerj-cs.55

scikit-learn developers (2019a) *scikit-learn clustering documentation*. URL https://scikit-learn.org/stable/modules/clustering.html

scikit-learn developers (2019b) *scikit-learn supervised learning documentation*. URL https://scikit-learn.org/stable/supervised_learning.html

Seabold S, Perktold J (2010) Statsmodels: Econometric and statistical modeling with Python. In: 9th Python in Science Conference

Sokal RR, Rohlf FJ (1962) The comparison of dendrograms by objective methods. *Taxon* 11(2):33–40

Thompson B (2004) *Exploratory and Confirmatory Factor Analysis: Understanding Concepts and Applications*. American Psychological Association

Waskom M, Botvinnik O, O'Kane D, Hobson P, Ostblom J, Lukauskas S, Gemperline DC, Augspurger T, Halchenko Y, Cole JB, Warmenhoven J, de Ruiter J, Pye C, Hoyer S, Vanderplas J, Villalba S, Kunter G, Quintero E, Bachant P, Martin M, Meyer K, Miles A, Ram Y, Brunner T, Yarkoni T, Williams ML, Evans C, Fitzgerald C, Brian, Qalieh A (2018) mwaskom/seaborn: v0.9.0 (July 2018). https://doi.org/10.5281/zenodo.1313201

Wedel M, Kamakura WA (2000) *Market Segmentation: Conceptual and Methodological Foundations*, 2nd edn. International Series in Quantitative Marketing, Kluwer Academic

Wong DM (2013) *The Wall Street Journal Guide to Information Graphics: The Dos and Don'ts of Presenting Data, Facts, and Figures*. WW Norton & Company

Index

© Springer Nature Switzerland AG 2020
J. S. Schwarz et al., *Python for Marketing Research and Analytics*, https://doi.org/10.1007/978-3-030-49720-0

Printed in the United States
by Baker & Taylor Publisher Services